THE LISTENING THREADS

THE LISTENING THREADS

THE FORMAL COSMOLOGY
OF
EMANUEL SWEDENBORG

by

Norman Newton

Swedenborg Scientific Association
Bryn Athyn, Pennsylvania
2000

Library of Congress Cataloging-in-Publication Data

Newton, Norman 1929–
    The listening threads : the formal cosmology of Emanuel Swedenborg / by Norman Newton.
       p. cm.
    Includes bibliographical references (p.) and index.
    ISBN 0-915221-70-5 (alk. paper)
     1. Swedenborg, Emanuel, 1688-1772. Principia. 2. Cosmology. I. Title.

    B4468.S83 P7536 2000
    289'.4'092--dc21   99-059854

ISBN: 0-915221-70-5

Formatted in New Century Schoolbook by Kirsten Gyllenhaal
Figures 3 to 6 computer-generated by Daryl Baker

Printed in the United States of America

For
Beryl

The Listening Threads

The Formal Cosmology of Emanuel Swedenborg

by
Norman Newton

For the mechanical world of nature is not unlike a spider's web and natural philosophy may be compared to the spider herself.

—Emanuel Swedenborg: *Principia*, Part I, Chapter I

The spider at the center is the symbol of creation and of the gradual materialisation of the initial rhythm towards the periphery.

—Marius Schneider: *El Origen Musical de los Animales-Simbolos*, p. 334

In the same way as a spider in the centre of the web holds in its feet all the beginnings of the threads, in order to feel by close contact if an insect strikes the web, and where, so does the ruling part of the soul, situated in the middle of the heart, check on the beginnings of the senses in order to perceive their messages from close proximity.

—Chalcidius, quoted in Sambursky's *The Physics of the Stoics*, p. 124

And all the time, in Caverns shut, the golden looms erected
First spun, then wove the Atmospheres; there the Spider & Worm
Plied the wing'd shuttles, piping shrill thro' all the list'ning
     threads...

—William Blake: *The Four Zoas*: II: 145–147

TABLE OF CONTENTS

Figures xi

Foreword xiii

Preface xvii

PART ONE

Chapter

1   The Principles of Natural Things 3

2   Some Definitions 27

3   The Primary Point and the First Element 61

4   The Point of Zeno and the First Element 93

5   The Magnetic Element 119

6   The Ether and the Solar Vortex 153

7   Earth, Air, Water and Fire 183

PART TWO

Chapter

1   Towards the Doctrine of Correspondences 221

2   An Ancient Rhetoric 257

3   Moses and Orpheus 287

4   The Cosmic Egg 317

CONCLUSION

The Logic of Correspondences 357

Appendices 381

Bibliography 401

Index 409

FIGURES

1 Swedenborg's "finite" 37

2 Motion on inclined planes 74

3 Time-space analogy of movement 82–83

4 Appearances of space 85–86

5 Proto-spirals as conceptual forms 88

6 Conceptualization of space 103

7 Halley's map of magnetic declination 134

8 Swedenborg's map of magnetism 135

9 Maps of terrestrial magnetism 136

10 Maps of magnetic dip 137–138

11 North magnetic pole 140–143

12 Declination and dip at London 144

13 Magnetic field of magnetized sphere 148

14 Swedenborg's ether particles 166

15 Diagrams of atomic nuclei 168

16 Formation of the solar system 176–177

FOREWORD

When I started my research into Swedenborg about forty-five years ago, I soon got in contact with some New Church people in Stockholm. Understandably enough they wanted to know why I had become interested in Swedenborg, since so little had been written of him by Swedish scholars after Martin Lamm's fundamental study in 1915. I answered that this very silence seemed a good reason for a new study from a literary point of view of the most internationally influential of Swedish writers. My interlocutor then replied that Swedenborg comes to us in many different ways.

I remember that statement for several reasons. As a young graduate student I found it slightly ridiculous, much to my shame now. It was a matter of course to me that Science with a capital "S" demanded a completely objective attitude of its practioners. It is true that Emanuel Swedenborg's mission of founding a New Church, which still has many followers, gives him a unique position in the history of world literature, but this fact seemed rather embarrasing to me. Most Swedes do not know much more about Swedenborg than that he pretended to converse with angels and spirits, and that there are people who still believe him to be a prophet of the Lord. Surely this must be madness, and why should anyone spend time and energy on studying such writings, however world-famous they might have become?

By pure chance I had already read Kant's *Träume eines Geistersehers* as a high school student, so I may have known a little more than that about Swedenborg. But now when I took a closer look at him, I was immediately fascinated by his erudition and his enormous ambitions. At the same time I realized that his followers had made invaluable efforts to keep his writings available in a great number of languages, achievements which deserved to be respected rather than ridiculed. I also became quickly aware of the terrifying fact that there was a huge international literature to assimilate. Consequently it would be necessary to decide soon on a manageable aspect of his literary achievement, if one were not to risk drowning in the abundant sources. So I focussed on *De Cultu et Amore Dei*, the most "literary" of his many texts, and one which would let me deal with Swedenborg's scientific production and keep a distance from the theological issues.

On the whole I followed this plan for my dissertation, and in some later studies I have also restricted myself to this early period. No doubt Swedenborg's theosophy was decisively influenced by his scientific experiences, and I have certainly found it exciting to investigate his intellectual milieu as an erudite European of the Enlightenment era. That is not to say that his later writings would be of less interest from a scholarly point of view. On the contrary, those are the ones that have exerted a major influence, and most of them definitely deserve their own monographs. But at least for me it has been easier to feel empathy for a scientist intensively attempting to realize a research program than for a prophet in possession of the ultimate truth.

However, over the years my idea of scholarly objectivity has become less rigid than it was in my graduate years, although I have never committed myself to any variant of the deconstructionist creed. I still believe that all scholars must aim at the highest possible objectivity, and I am still prepared to spell Science and Scholarship with capital letters. But I have learnt how strongly our interpretations of texts, or for that matter of reality at large, are influenced by our own attitudes and experiences. It is evident that a reader with some knowledge of a field can profit much more from a deepened study than can a completely ignorant one. On the other hand there is always a risk that a degree of "preunderstanding" may close one's eyes to new aspects. To be objective then demands not only a critical mind but also an open one.

As could be expected, Swedenborg literature illustrates this exceedingly well. Quite a few New Church writers have displayed an apologetic and panegyric attitude, which is easy to understand but nevertheless problematic. And many nonconfessional readers have too easily yielded to the opposite temptation of looking for absurd and obscure passages in Swedenborg's writings to make fun of. Uncritically acquired knowledge on one side, narrow minds and lack of empathy on the other: neither the zealots nor the adversaries can do this remarkable author justice.

Fortunately enough such extremes can be counterbalanced by many examples of sound scholarship, and Emanuel Swedenborg is still able both to attract inquisitive secular readers and to inspire faithful followers. In my opinion Norman Newton's book represents qualified Swedenborgian research in an independent and reassuring manner. The author has chosen to analyze a very difficult problem, complex mainly from the inner side of the texts, and so he may not have much to offer those who want to learn something new of Swedenborg's possible sources. Nevertheless, I am confident that many scholars who are not members of the New Church will find his book as instructive in other respects as I have done. On the following pages the reader will meet the impressive result of an experiment in close reading of extraordinarily complicated texts. Personally I am grateful for still another way in which Swedenborg has now come to me.

Inge Jonsson
Stockholm

PREFACE

Any attempt to discuss the cosmology of Emanuel Swedenborg in modern language, or at the very least to introduce it to the modern reader who knows little or nothing about Swedenborg, must simply face up to one chilling fact. Modern natural philosophy is overwhelmingly atheistic or agnostic in tendency. Individual scientists and natural philosophers may be religious men, perhaps even Christians, but unless they are willing to risk a loss of academic reputation, they are more or less forced to put their beliefs aside when they are discussing their disciplines. When a natural philosophy has even vestigial religious content, as, say, the cosmology of Teilhard de Chardin does, it may be taken up by religious apologists, but it will not be treated as part of mainstream thought. There will always be something suspect about it.

From a specifically Christian viewpoint, atheistic or agnostic systems are more like each other than they appear to be to their warring adherents. Christianity claims to be a universal religion and is certainly no longer a religion of the West. It cannot pick and choose among such systems from motives determined by cultural, social, political or economic biases. Nor can it ignore or condemn scientific discoveries made by materialists, since science proper, if not natural philosophy, is neutral on the question of ultimate causes. It ought to be, at any rate.

So I hope that the reader will not be disconcerted if I refer more than once to Marxist science and formal logic, though not to its atheistic philosophy. Marx and Engels will be with us a long time yet, despite the collapse of Communist regimes. It happens, as some notes in the text will indicate, that of the atheistic complexes with which modern Christian thought must deal—systems which have brought immeasurable suffering to mankind but which must also be treated dispassionately, as philosophies—Marxist logic sometimes throws a greater light on the cosmology of Swedenborg than Western thought does. This is because of its dialectical method. It inherited this from the Christian philosophy of Hegel which, like many of the earlier philosophies which influenced Swedenborg, follows the old program of "reconciling Plato and Aristotle." Swedenborgian and Marxist thought both insist, though from completely opposed positions, on the reality of the material world and the close relationship of its deep structure to the patterns of dialectical logic. The latter idea is not unknown in the West but it tends there to take on an idealist or positivist form. An idealist reading of the Swedenborgian physical universe, though it is common enough (a positivist reading is not), leads to confusion. My attitude will be simply to treat Marxist logic as a perversely materialist interpretation of the splendid logic of Hegel, always keeping in mind that Swedenborg, unlike Hegel, was not an idealist. It is not in a philosophical but a theological work (*Divine Providence*, No. 46) that Swedenborg refers to idealists as visionaries, but this attitude is also reflected in his philosophy.

In comparing the natural philosophy of Swedenborg to those of others, I concentrate mainly—some may think narrowly—on a certain stream of thought which runs from Saint Augustine and such medieval Augustinians as Ramon Lull (as his name is usually anglicised) to Hegel and his disciples and followers. Others have dealt with the affinities of Swedenborg's philosophical thought with the systems of Descartes, Leibniz, Wolff and Kant, often to the extent of exaggerating their importance. In my view, the most significant new element of Swedenborg's thought is his transformation of logical categories into dynamic cosmological ones, always in a completely Christian context. It is this which brings him into relation with the stream referred to above. Perhaps in concentrating on this essential element I have missed some of the more obvious links between his thought and the common thought of the time, but these are more than adequately covered in books listed in the bibliography.

Hegel has to be taken into account because, beside Swedenborg and to some extent Ramon Lull, only he developed an efficacious philosophy of nature. All three were Christians and of the three Hegel, because of the pervasive influence of Marxism, is the best known. Some may be surprised that I call the nature-logic of Hegel "efficacious." This is not the usual response and I was not always of this opinion; yet I found, when I worked through it carefully, granting Hegel his idealist postulates, which are beyond the reach of logical refutation, that it was an enormously impressive construction. Its flaws, due to his limited scientific knowledge, are flaws of application and not inherent in the system.

It is not surprising that Engels in his *Dialectics of Nature* could not leave it alone, though it led him to a very strange form of materialism. For in this book he says, after condemning Hegel's idealism, "If we turn the thing round, then everything becomes simple, and the dialectical laws that look so extremely mysterious in idealist philosophy at once become simple and clear as noonday."[1] They become simple and clear to Engels because he is an atheist and a materialist, and it is easiest for him to look at the Hegelian system from such a viewpoint. He has entered the house by the back door and he has decided that the layout of the house appears highly rational when viewed from the kitchen, while it is a mere jumble of unrelated rooms and passageways when seen from the parlour. In actuality, the layout of the house is rational seen from whatever viewpoint. To turn around a well-made logical system is only to change the arrangement of its components.

This is not a rigorous book. Its logical arguments will be extremely simple on the whole. The scientific references are largely quite basic and the mathematical arguments are easy. An adequate mathematical representation of Swedenborg's ideas, which he had to express largely in words, would be very complicated. Taken one by one, or in small groups, his formal concepts are simple and may be found in basic mathematics and symbolic logic. Because of this a nonscientist such as I am can understand them. However, the ensemble, logically constructed though it is, has no analogy in any modern system known to me, and it has depths which I do not begin to examine.

The reader who has a sense of basic concepts of calculus and Euclidean geometry should therefore have no difficulty with any

---

[1] Engels, Frederick: *Dialectics of Nature*, pp. 26–27.

part of the discussion. In formal logic I refer to nothing more difficult than the books of Eli de Gortari, which are well known in Mexican universities (I have not found English-language texts which are as enlightening). The difficulty of a first approach to Swedenborg's formal thought does not lie in the mathematical and logical complexity of the "surface layer" of his thought, but in its newness. One has to be willing to think, at least provisionally, in a new way.

When I refer to books which are, in the broad sense, "modern," I choose those which, in my opinion, best illuminate the thought of Swedenborg or develop ideas similar to his. In some cases they are now considered to be out of date, in other cases they are advanced and still controversial, but such considerations are irrelevant in a study of this kind.

There is a lot of repetition in this book. Old subjects are always being brought up again, to be looked at in a new light. Swedenborg himself does this sort of thing. This is because we are dealing with objects and ideas which can only be grasped by moving around them as we move around a great building of novel design, examining it from this side and that. If the reader finds he is beginning to lose his bearings in following a particular argument he should keep going. The elements of the argument will probably come up again in another context.

My aim is a quite narrow one, to trace a link between his *Principia* and his early theory of correspondences. This link turns out in the end to have a bearing on the history of religions. In discussing the *Principia* I spend much more time on Swedenborg's theory of the primary point than on his theories of the more complex forms of matter. There are three reasons for this.

First, this theory is at once the most difficult part of the *Principia* and its most essential part. Unless it is understood in at least general outlines, Swedenborg's natural philosophy makes little sense. Second, it is the most interesting from the philosophical viewpoint. Third, Swedenborg's theories about sensually apparent forms of matter—water, air and various solid substances—and his theories about the origins of the solar system are obviously, from the scientific point of view, out of date, even when they anticipate modern discoveries. It is true that he comes up again and again with ideas far ahead of his time. But it may be shown that these apparently prophetic insights are derived from his theory of the primary point. When he applies his theory to the available physical data he encounters the limitations of his time, in which, with some exceptions (astronomy, mechanics, Newtonian physics), the modern sciences were in a very rudimentary stage.

Swedenborgian thought has produced much of great value, of which most readers will be unaware. *The New Philosophy*, a quarterly published by the Swedenborg Scientific Association from about the end of the last century, has included many contributions dealing with the subjects I discuss herein. If I acknowledged all my debts to its contributors this book would be awash in a sea of footnotes. There are perhaps too many of these already, but my excuse is that Swedenborgian thought continually leads us into controversial areas. In the case of Swedenborgian authors, I have limited my notes to those references where I directly paraphrase or quote the words of such contributors, or take issue with them, or where these writers further develop issues specifically touched on in the text. I hope that the very many whom I have not mentioned, and who will recognise their thoughts therein, will accept my silent tribute to their work.[2]

I am particularly grateful, though, to the Rev. Erik Sandstrom, Sr. (formerly, now retired, Dean of the Theological School of the

---

[2] Some of these have been professional scholars and mathematicians who have made acknowledged contributions to their fields. Among these I might refer to Gregory L. Baker and his book *Religion and Science*. Baker is a physicist who has contributed to the fields of magnetic resonance, chaotic dynamics and stochastic processes. He does not much discuss the preillumination philosophy of Swedenborg, being more concerned with the philosophical implications of the theological works. In these latter many ideas from the philosophical works do appear, but in a transmuted and generalised form, as "examples from nature," which the reader need not assent to. In this theological context, Baker offers an illuminating discussion of fractals and chaos theory.

The most extended study of the *Principia* known to me is *Lectures on the Philosophy of Swedenborg's Principia*, by Bishop George de Charms of the General Church of the New Jerusalem. Here the focus is on those teachings of the *Principia* that are most clearly reflected in the theological works. This is a beautiful book, though I feel it somewhat underplays Swedenborg's link with traditional Christian thought. In many respects it represents a point of view quite different from my own, which is closer to that of Dingle (see bibliography). *(continued)*

General Church of the New Jerusalem), who received me into the church many years ago in London. He was the first to encourage me to write this book and he has been untiring in shepherding it through to print. Dr. Erland Brock, the present editor of *The New Philosophy,* and Professor Donald Fitzpatrick were of the greatest help in this project ever since they became associated with it. Dr. William Woofenden, a kindly but always very alert editor, aided me in clarifying my argument. Dr. Gregory Baker, professor of physics at Bryn Athyn College of the New Church, answered my queries in patient detail, which enabled me to correct some rather naive ideas before I set to work. I add that this does not mean that he has identified himself with my interpretation of the *Principia*: his own reading of this book is set out in various articles and his book, *Religion and Science.* I cannot thank Kirsten Gyllenhaal enough for so efficiently keeping track of my many revisions and additions, mailed to Bryn Athyn at various times and in no particular order from the far coasts of British Columbia.

How can I thank my wife, Beryl, for lovingly bearing with me through the strains which always accompany projects of this magnitude? Or my daughter, Elizabeth, who always gave me just the right books for Father's Days, birthdays and Christmases, and always managed to find something encouraging to say? The answer is that words are inadequate but, in this framework of acknowledgments, they are all that I have.

All translations from French or Spanish sources are my own, unless otherwise acknowledged.

Norman Newton
Vancouver

(continued)

Regrettably the analysis of Swedenborgian logic is not a prime concern among Swedenborgian scholars. The *Treatise on Opposites*, published in 1832 by the Rev. John Clowes, Anglican rector of St. John's Church, Manchester, is an early promise of labours not undertaken. Clowes seems to have been very aware, though he does not press the point in the portion of this book (very difficult to obtain) that I have seen, of the Augustinian and patristic affinities of Swedenborgian philosophy.

PART ONE

1

The Principles
of Natural Things

The *Principia* or *The Principles of Natural Things* was published (in Latin) in 1734. Little attention was paid to it. The *Acta Eruditorum* of Leipzig referred to Swedenborg's "rare insight into natural philosophy" but expressed much more interest in the technological works which accompanied it, such as those which revealed hitherto unknown techniques of smelting iron and copper—

> He discloses, with the utmost faithfulness, secrets which smelters have long and jealously concealed, even in many cases from dearly loved children...

The general attitude towards the *Principia* was then, as it was to the end of the nineteenth century, that Swedenborg was mistaken in assuming that nature has intrinsic mathematical form. A reviewer of an earlier publication in which some of the theories of the *Principia* were sketched out, the *Miscellaneous Observations*, had written—

> An exact physicist or mathematician will not readily say that mathematical bodies are actually made up of points, lines and planes, as these are described by mathematicians; and in all fairness we are led to

wonder how the author has come to be of this extraordinary and
incomprehensible opinion...[1]

The belief that matter is deeply and really geometrical is very
old and controversial and much has been written for and against it.
Only in the eighteenth and nineteenth centuries could Swedenborg's opinion have seemed extraordinary and incomprehensible.
In the seventeenth century and earlier it would have been recognized as a respectably Pythagorean, Platonic or Augustinian point
of view, entirely compatible with Christianity. In our time the
triumph of relativity theory has made such a viewpoint, though
rarely expressed in Christian terms, respectable once again.

The *Principia* remains in obscurity. Only New Church publishing houses and the Swedenborg Scientific Association concern themselves with Swedenborg's scientific works, and of course they appear
to be a partisan group, whose objectivity is in question. Yet his
name and a brief biography may be found in any encyclopedia.

Swedenborg was born in 1688, the son of Jesper Swedberg, a
bishop and court-preacher to the king of Sweden, Charles XI. He
was of distinguished family. His mother was a descendant of the
great Gustavus Vasa, king of Sweden from 1523 to 1560, and the
ancestors of his father were wealthy miners. The family name
Swedberg was changed to Swedenborg in 1719, when the family
was ennobled, as was customary with the families of bishops.
Swedenborg was a servant of the court for much of his life, and
when he was accused by the clergy of heresy—a charge which came
to nothing—it was the king who spoke in his defence.

He was educated as a member of the elite, studying with distinction (he is called "a youth of the best talent" in university records)
at Upsala University. He chose the faculty of philosophy, which
included science and mathematics, with particular emphasis in the
last discipline on the methods of Descartes. As instruction was
given in Latin, he acquired an early facility in that language; he
also studied Greek and Hebrew.

He gave an account of his life in a letter he wrote to an English
enquirer, Thomas Hartley, in August of 1769. It should be noted

that he gives his year of birth as 1689, rather than 1688, because of the correspondential significance of that number.

> I was born in Stockholm on the 29th of January in the year 1689, of my father, Jesper Swedberg by name, who was Bishop of West Gothland, and was celebrated in his day. He was also inscribed as a member of the Society for the Propagation of the Faith, having been elected by that Society; for he had been appointed by King Charles XII presiding Bishop over the Swedish Church in Pennsylvania, and also over the Church in London. In the year 1710 I journeyed abroad, first to England and then to Holland, France, and Germany, and from there I returned home in the year 1714.
>
> In 1716 and later, I frequently talked with Charles XII, king of Sweden, who greatly favored me, and in the same year he honored me with the office of Assessor in the College of Mines, an office which I then filled until the year 1747, in which year I resigned, retaining however half the salary of that office to the end of my life. I gave in my resignation solely to the end that I might the better devote myself to the new function enjoined on me by the Lord. A higher rank of dignity was then offered me, but this I absolutely refused, lest pride should thereby invade my mind.
>
> In the year 1719, I was ennobled by Queen Ulrica Eleonora and named Swedenborg, and from that time on, in the Assemblies which take place every three years, I have been numbered among the Nobles of the order of knighthood.[2]

The "new function enjoined on me by the Lord" is again referred to in Swedenborg's statement, later in the letter, "that I have been called to a sacred office by the Lord Himself, who, in the year 1743, most graciously manifested Himself in Person before me, His servant, and then opened my sight into the spiritual world and granted me to speak with spirits and angels..." I shall have little to say, specifically, about Swedenborg's spiritual experiences and his theology in this book. In the minds of those who believe in his Divine commission, his entire scientific career was a preparation, in the intent and act of Divine Providence, for his theological work. I suppose it will become apparent to the reader that I also hold this to be true. Yet I am concerned here simply with the value of his natural philosophy—or with a part of it, because the subject is vast.

When he wrote the letter quoted above Swedenborg was no longer concerned with his scientific and philosophical fame. We should never guess from his letter that he was responsible for a remarkable series of theories, discoveries and inventions—an early form of the nebular hypothesis of planetary formation, pioneering studies in anatomy, and a variety of inventions or anticipations of inventions, from an ear-trumpet and an airtight stove to a flying machine, the last being an ornithopter/glider with auxiliary human power, by all accounts aerodynamically sound, if primitive. He developed a system of octal or base-8 calculation, similar to that used in a form of computer mathematics of our day, apparently with the hope of replacing the decimal system, which he regarded as cumbersome and irrational. Some point out that he was also a musical amateur and a poet—a scientific poet, it might be added, in the line of such poets, infrequently read nowadays, as Michael Drayton, Sir John Davies, Erasmus Darwin, du Bartas and Lefèvre de la Boderie. What is rarely if ever discussed, however, outside New Church and other Swedenborgian publications, is the mode of thought which made it possible for one man to contribute to so many disciplines.

The myth of the universal genius is always with us. We have, for example, Leonardo da Vinci, to whom Swedenborg is sometimes compared, though many others in da Vinci's time were as versatile as he was. Both da Vinci and Swedenborg had remarkable innate gifts. Yet the eighteenth century was not the period of the Renaissance. The Renaissance visual artist and architect was in the forefront of mathematical and technological thought. He knew at least as much mathematics and physics as the pure scholar of his time and sometimes more; we need only recall what modern geometry owes to Renaissance studies in perspective. He was also a skilled anatomist. Similarly, the Renaissance musician or composer or instrument builder—one man might be all three—was often a master of musical acoustics as then understood. The Renaissance poet could be a profound and innovative classical scholar and an expert in symbolic systems. Da Vinci had the intuition of genius, but he was a scientist and mathematician as well.

The eighteenth century, though, prefigured our age of special-
ization. One had, of course, the gentleman amateur, who collected
rock specimens, wrote a little verse and music, and designed his
own garden pavilions. A philosopher might write Latin poems or
play the flute. But true generalization was becoming difficult. With
a few exceptions which prove the rule, the eighteenth-century
artist, though he may have been a master of his techniques, rarely
made significant contributions to the sciences which formed the
basis of technique. He was often fascinated by them—Mozart and
others were interested in musical automata and chance music—
but on the whole he applied the scientific discoveries of others.
Jean-Philippe Rameau, an exception, contributed in a most valuable way to musical acoustics; but he was in type a seventeenth-
century figure, though he lived and flourished in the eighteenth.
On the whole the eighteenth-century visual artist contributed little
to geometry, the composer little to acoustical theory, the poet little
to logic and rhetoric.

In other words, the idea of the "Renaissance man," as one with
an *intuitive* grasp of many fields of knowledge, is deceptive. The
real Renaissance man was an artist-scientist, and though the memory lingered into the eighteenth century the category was dead.
Swedenborg's versatility was unusual for the time and it indicates
much more than a combination of native genius and uncentered
intellectual curiosity.

It might be responded that while the above comments make
sense in terms of the centers of high culture of the time—Paris,
Rome, Vienna and London—they are not so applicable to provincial
cultures. In eighteenth-century Sweden, as in the more general
Baltic and North German culture of which it was a part, the
intellectual class was not only small but had to be flexible. Outside
such capitals as Stockholm, Copenhagen and St. Petersburg, the
general population lived in conditions which, though not necessarily uncomfortable, were certainly backward. Much of Finland, for
example, was a country of log cabins, and Helsinki, its beautiful
Esplanade not yet built, was a city of wooden houses like the young
towns of North America. Even in the early nineteenth century,

collectors of folklore in Lithuania and Finland were able to collect long lyrics (Lithuanian *daina*) and oral epic poems of ancient type (the *Kalevala*) from the mouths of village bards. In such a culture the Renaissance man, in the rough modern usage of the phrase, could still exist. One such was Peter the Great of Russia; and Swedenborg's own king, Charles XII, the "Lion of the North," had some of Peter's omnivorous curiosity and versatility. The noble Baron Swedenborg, grandson of a successful miner and son of a Lutheran bishop and theologian, travelling all over Europe to study mathematics, physics, astronomy, lens-grinding, mining and salt-extraction methods, reminds us of other perpetual students of the northern countries, unrestricted by daunting intellectual establishments, to whom all knowledge seemed open. To such, as well, the futures of their countries appeared unlimited. Swedenborg was collecting treasures of learning and technique, which his country needed if it was to advance into the eighteenth century.

It is true, then, that Swedenborg benefitted from the freedom which goes with being a pioneer in a vigorous but comparatively undeveloped (if politically important) country. But this does not really explain his contributions to theoretical science, though it does explain somewhat his technical versatility, which was so well-founded in practical experience. It certainly does not explain the physics of the *Principia*, which is in no way a provincial or shallow book. The one figure comparable to Swedenborg in this respect is Roger Boscovich, who as a Serbian had, it might be said, the freedom of a provincial of genius. But Boscovich came later and was, as a Jesuit intellectual, a sophisticated international figure, part of the *avant-garde* of the Roman Church.

There must therefore be something in the nature of Swedenborg's thought which cannot be explained in terms of the culture into which he was born, and which, as a patriotic Swede, he vigorously represented. Nor can it be put down to native genius alone. There must be involved, in some way, a question of method.

Our first impression is that of a practical scientist and man of affairs—a man, for example, capable of presenting very canny memoranda on the public budget of Sweden—who has an aspect which is brilliantly if wildly speculative. This man will write a book of cosmological speculation which at first reads like a science-fiction dream. Some of it anticipates discoveries which would not be made until our time; some of it reminds us of baroque system-spinning at its least disciplined. But this impression arises only from a quick skimming-through of the *Principia*. Closer reading shows us that the book is all of a piece, that it is rigorously argued. Even its "wild" parts are rooted firmly in the practical. Experience, both of the everyday kind and of the industrial techniques of the time, is constantly appealed to. The language is not farfetched or extravagant. It tends more to the homey comparison, as in the following —

> Now nature herself closely resembles this spider's web; for she consists, as it were, of infinite radii proceeding from a certain centre, and connected together, in like manner, by infinite circles and polygons; so that nothing can happen in one of them which does not immediately extend itself to the centre, and from this it is reflected and distributed through a great portion of the fabric. It is by such contact and connection that nature is able to perform her operations, and in this her very essence consists; for wherever this contact is interrupted, wherever a thread of the web is broken so as to dissolve the connection between the centre and its circumferences, there nature itself ceases and terminates.[3]

This is not in the eighteenth-century style. As a rule, the *savants* and *philosophes* of the time scorned homespun comparisons like these. We are reminded more of the ancient Greeks, of Plato's cave-metaphor and his reference to "the spindle of necessity," imagery of a time when the "way of the gods," whether mythologically or rationally conceived, was reflected in the order of everyday things, if more in folk-belief than in philosophy. But eighteenth-century intellectual snobbery is still with us, so it is likely that we shall more or less skip over this passage, taking it to be a rough illustration in the pop-science mode, and hurry on in search of the meaty parts.

And in this we might be disappointed.

For Swedenborg's mathematical equations are extremely simple. His biography tells us that he had excellent mathematical training but he is not interested in evolving elaborate theorems with their proofs and he has none of the brilliance of the mathematical virtuoso. It is not difficult to dismiss him as a man who had remarkable intuitions but whose mathematical learning was distinctly skimpy. "Only in eighteenth century Sweden," we might say to ourselves, "could a man get away with a book like this."

I shall get to the question of Swedenborg's mathematics a little later in this book. Rather than trying to convince the reader in an abstract way that the simplicity of the *Principia* is entirely deceptive (though in no way meant to deceive), it seemed better to me to use an autobiographical approach, to indicate how I found this to be the case. This somewhat removes the taint of special pleading and it also gives a partial answer to the question, "Why should a twentieth-century man, not a historian of science, spend so much time on a completely forgotten eighteenth-century book on physics?" But I shall somewhat anticipate my comments on the criticism in the last paragraph by remarking that Swedenborg's preference for verbal over mathematical argument, for illustrative diagrams over formulas arises out of three major features of his thought. First, he rejected false precision, that is, the use of algebra and other forms of mathematical notation to give an air of rigor to arguments which are actually more precise when expressed in the words of everyday language. Second, most of the mathematical techniques necessary to the presentation of his theories in an adequate notational form, where such would have been useful, had not yet been developed. He would have needed a mathematics capable of presenting purely logical and formal ideas—something like set theory, Boolean logic, topology and modern differential and projective geometry. Third (a continuing theme in this book) he was not an idealist and rejected the search for purely mathematical absolutes which characterized much of the mathematics developed after his time.

My first response to the *Principia* was probably not much different from that of most readers who have attempted to come to grips with this extraordinary book.

Let us assume that we have before us not the text of the *Principia* but a working model of Swedenborg's physical universe.

At first it will resemble a very large smooth ball. We shall make nothing of it. Now let us assume, to make things easier, that the ball is transparent. Inside it we shall see—what?—a universe of smaller balls in constant motion, the motions being primarily vortical (whirlpool-like or turbulent) or orbital (as in a solar system), with many other intersecting motions which we cannot make out. Some of the smaller balls seem to behave like the computer graphics of elementary particles we see in popular science programs on television.

Now let us assume that we can slice into this transparent ball and, by observing the swarm of activity in the slice, form some kind of ordered picture of what is going on in the model. At this stage, if we are really looking, we should experience a sense of baffled wonderment, maybe even a kind of intellectual panic. We shall see every kind of *movement* known to modern physics—probabilistic movement, indeterministic movements of what might be waves or particles, movements in straight lines or flat curves and every other kind of curve, spiral and vortical movement, spin movement...A fully mathematical expression of movements of such complexity would have been, in Swedenborg's time, impossible. Nobody else had even imagined these objects, let alone described them in mathematical form. Yet these particles are not *really* modern, do not *really* look like those we see in our computer graphics or in *Scientific American.* Perhaps they do in a crude or generalized way, in the sense that they are mostly spheres or spheroids, but the movements and forms are arranged in a sort of ideal hierarchy, a kind of chart or functional map. This is not so much a snapshot of some imagined microworld, except by derivation; it is first of all a "canon of forms." We are reminded of such old ideas as the Great Chain of Being. And when these extraordinary forms "come to rest" in a world of recognizable objects, this world is not modern but an eighteenth-century one.

Yet in broadest terms we have a structure remarkably similar to that set out in the following passage, where the brilliant Mexican Marxist logician, Eli de Gortari, describes in modern language the "correspondence between levels" of the physical universe—

The deepest level, whose characteristics we have hardly yet glimpsed, is that constituted by the internal structure of the particles which, a very short time ago, were considered elementary. Then comes the level formed by these particles in the free state, that is to say, where they are not integrated into a structure. There follows the nuclear level, which is the primordial structure formed by the elementary particles, where processes occur at very high energy at very small distances. After this come the atomic processes of distinct classes, in which the nuclei participate as undivided particles, which involve lower energies and greater distances. Then we have the chemical processes, which include interatomic reactions, and which integrate and disintegrate molecules. To continue, we then have the movements and transferences of energy which are produced between molecules constituting the thermodynamic level.[4]

Let me indicate, briefly, what I mean by "remarkably similar."

The deepest level of the Swedenborgian cosmos is constituted by the particles of what he calls "the first elementary." These act in such a way as to form the next level of matter, which is that of magnetism or electromagnetism. Though there is nothing in the Swedenborgian universe which is not integrated into a structure, the area of activity between the first elementary and the magnetic sphere will appear to be one of random and free movement. This is because the movements of first elementary particles are very complex and only apparent indirectly, by the effects they produce. In this process, knots or compact forms of magnetic or electromagnetic energy are developed. From these the first purely material particles emerge, forms similar to our atoms, with comparatively quiescent nuclei and hard or closely-bound particles revolving around them. Swedenborg calls these "ether particles." Inside these nuclei and the revolving bound particles processes occur at high energy and at small distances. The particles of ether then produce the next level, that of the substances we know, but in gaseous form. On this level the nuclei of etheric atoms become hard and resistant, taking on measurable and determined forms, as do the particles revolving around them. We now have the level of matter on which chemical and thermodynamic processes occur.

I have used the phrase "magnetic or electromagnetic" because Swedenborg's "magnetic sphere" either contains or directly generates all the processes we think of as electromagnetic in the naked-eye world. I must of course say "naked eye world" because, apart from some assistance provided by telescopes and microscopes, this was the only world known to science in the early eighteenth century. And I might add, since the above may appear so prescient as to obscure this obvious fact, that Swedenborg bases his theory entirely on intellectual materials from his own time and earlier.

Of course, the Swedenborgian universe is not the Marxist one. It is Divinely created and sustained, and it develops from opposite principles. Yet it is based, as we shall see, on a system of dialectical logic which in many ways resembles (a century earlier!) the logic of Hegel. And it just so happens that dialectical materialism, on which Marxist natural philosophy is based, is rooted in Hegelian logic. As a logical system, Marxism refuses to deny the principle of causality, which is, de Gortari says, "the means of making manifest the dynamic and reciprocal connection existing between each and every objective process, as well as between the distinct levels of existence."[5] Marxist causality ideologically denies the First Cause of religious and Hegelian thought, but since logic itself, though it demands causality, is incapable of defining what a "first cause" might be, this rejection is impotent and without philosophical weight. This is because the definition of a first cause lies outside the system. A chain of causes and effects must, of necessity, have a first cause. Logic cannot tell us whether it is a god or something else. Nevertheless, Marxism accepts causality and also some idea of "correspondence between levels" in the physical universe. Western natural philosophy (the geographical designation is completely inane), which more and more regards the idea of causality as meaningless, rejects first causes from *within* its system and thus paradoxically finds itself more in opposition to natural philosophies based on religion than Marxism does.

Once I had noted this remarkable similarity I could see that my first response, that of wonderment, was in no way an adequate one. A structure which seemed to be related to something as rigorous and closely worked as Hegelian logic could not be approached in this naive fashion. Dutifully I went back to the beginning of the book and started again. This time I forced myself to pause frequently, considering the full implications of every statement. And now, to my surprise, the argument seemed extremely complex. The homey analogies I had dismissed as loose imagery designed to make the reader feel comfortable turned out to be precise and functional. They were still analogies, but they were exact analogies in the sense that every element in the figure corresponded to a precise formal idea. For example, nature is like a spider's web in the sense that it is constructed of straight-line and regular forms which topologically imitate circular and spiral ones, as the spider's web does. It is as if Swedenborg's sentences were sheets or currents of water in a clear lake of great depth, sliding over and around each other in intricate and rhythmically ordered patterns, their outlines almost invisible. They had, furthermore, a most complex mathematical component which I had entirely missed and the arguments in mathematical notation turned out, most unusually, to be mere illustrations of the verbal ones.[6]

By a natural progression I now found myself tracing references to the book through literature, to be astonished by the rarity and inaccuracy of the references to it. Perhaps one bizarre quotation will do. It is from a French writer, Rolland de Renéville, who says that Swedenborg, in his *Principia*, assumes "that the intervals comprised between the particles of matter are the seat of a perpetual movement which can only be God Himself, identified with infinite time and space."[7] If I refrain from quoting other strange misinterpretations, it is only because they are less amusing. Yet I am not implying that de Renéville is an ignoramus. When he is discussing the other "mystics" whose influences on French literature he wishes to trace—the magician Martines de Pasqually and the mathematician Josef Maria Wronski—he makes good sense. It is as if a strange veil of confusion descends over the discussion when Swedenborg is the subject.

Many of the ideas which Swedenborg sets out in his works on cosmology and physics have been rediscovered in our own time. Others appear in the work of better-known natural philosophers, without acknowledgment, in the late eighteenth and nineteenth centuries.[8] Such rediscoveries and adoptions present one with a peculiar problem, which goes beyond the purely historical question of underground influence. Many of the sophisticated ideas of modern mathematical physics are prefigured, as philosophical extensions of the possibilities of differential and integral calculus, in Swedenborg's *Principia*. Such anticipations cannot be ignored, though to forget the time-rootedness of Swedenborg's philosophical thought is more or less to destroy its character.

The following key ideas emerge from the text. They are a bit of a hard gulp in this summary, but I wanted to state them briefly and together, so the reader can refer back to them.

- There is an analogy between geometrical/mechanical and logical form. It is a true analogy, in no way trivial or accidental.
- The universe of the large is built on the same principle as the universe of the small and one great law governs the microworld and the universe of galaxies.
- This law is a pattern, to use modern terms which are not in this case anachronistic, of wave-functions, point-particles and related fields. In the last analysis, wave-functions and point-particles are so closely related that they may be said to be the same. Swedenborg really does deal with the behaviors of waves and point-particles, as an eighteenth century mind could conceive of them; his elementaries correspond to nothing so closely as to the modern idea of a field.
- The operations of this law result in a universe of discrete parts arranged in series, which we may see as successive planes or shells of matter.
- The geometrical and mechanical laws governing each of these planes are fundamentally the same, though the phrase "fundamentally the same" cannot be well understood until we better appreciate what Swedenborg means by "similarity." These laws may be understood in terms of a relativistic Euclideanism revised to include the possibilities of calculus. Paradoxical though it may seem, the almost infinite diversity of nature is the very result of this sameness. Without sameness there can be no

difference, nor can there be variety unless there are universal
laws of transformation between states of relative stability. We
might also say that the greatest complexity necessarily develops
from the greatest simplicity.

- The resultant of these geometrical and mechanical laws is a
  universe which may be apprehended in terms of harmonic functions and other functions which generate transcendental and
  other numbers.

- To refer again to the beginning of our summary of key ideas,
  there lies behind such geometrical/mechanical laws a deeper set
  of laws governed by what may be described as a binary logic
  which is triadic in operation. This logic may take on a probabilistic appearance, by way of the familiar binary "heads or tails"
  image, but it is not to be confused with chance or mere randomness.

- All such laws are really parts of the "great law" referred to
  above, a law which may be understood by human reason, not in
  all the details of its operation but as a generalization.

Much of what initially may seem bizarre or eccentric in this
book actually arises from Swedenborg's constant endeavour to
incorporate, in a structure of high theory, the empirical discoveries
of practical craftsmen. There is nothing of the snobbery of pure
science here, a snobbery which, in any case, was particularly ridiculous in his day. For example, craft acoustics, as practiced by
makers of musical instruments and composers of music, had reached
a near-modern level of sophistication by the early eighteenth century: we cannot surpass the qualities of the best baroque organs
and harpsichords or the violins of Stradivarius. Theoretical acoustics lagged far behind. This example reflects the more general fact
that craftsmen and artisans had practical devices and recipes,
protected by the tradition of guild secrecy, in advance of the notions
of the leisured gentlemen who were founding modern theoretical
science. Swedenborg was intensely interested in craft practices and
other technological applications of science as well as in the anatomical basis of sense perception. It was this interplay between the

practical and theoretical which enabled him to work out an essentially modern theory of sound.

The formal background of the *Principia* (and I use the word "formal" as relating to a systematic doctrine of forms) is biblical and Greek. Swedenborg wishes to demonstrate the rationality of the creation account in *Genesis*, particularly the first ten verses. He believes that "the Mosaic philosophy in some measure coincides with the ancient philosophy of the Egyptians and with that of the Greeks and Romans."[9] In this he reflects the traditional Christian view that Moses had been instructed in the philosophy of the Egyptians. He also believes—again a traditional view—that the natural philosophy of the Greeks was to some extent a rationalization of ancient cosmologies which had been preserved by the priestly schools of the ancient Near East and Mediterranean.

As to the mathematical tradition, Swedenborg attempts wherever possible to explain himself in terms of Euclidean geometry. The entire Euclidean tradition is meant, not only the *Elements* but the work of commentators who had attempted to resolve some of the paradoxes in the initial definitions of Euclid, particularly those related to the point and the line, with the definition of parallels. These same paradoxes give birth in time to what we call non-Euclidean geometry. Swedenborg's own consideration of these gives him relativistic formulations which appear to anticipate modern forms of physics; but it may be seen that he has resolved the Euclidean paradoxes by forms of reasoning found in the Greek tradition itself. Yet neither can Swedenborg neglect the new problem posed by the differential and integral calculus, a technique which seems to be deeply subversive of the fixed relationships not only of geometry but also of number. If we may discover numbers and geometrical figures by approximation or describe a constant as a point where a tangent touches a curve, what happens to the crystalline and static beauty of classical mathematics? His solution is to tuck calculus into the admitted gap in Euclid, the virtual black hole between the definition of the dimensionless point and the generation of the line (e.g. is Euclid telling us that the point is the generator of the line or is the point really the passive terminus of the line?).

Swedenborg's version of classical geometry begins with a notion found in Greek commentaries on Euclid. This notion is attributed to Geminus and Proclus, the latter of whom maintained that Euclid was not only a Platonist but had written the *Elements* to demonstrate the generation of the solid figures so important in the Platonic doctrine of eternal forms—a still controversial statement. Geminus and Proclus have it that the dimensionless point does not merely engender the straight line but *all kinds of lines* including the spiral curve, the curve which engenders Swedenborg's vortex universe. Now "engenders" here is not merely a mathematical metaphor; to Swedenborg Euclidean geometry is also a cosmology. This is one area where he seems to approach Proclus and the Neoplatonists. He was indeed aware of the thought we call "Neoplatonic," but the resemblance is deceptive, since he was in no way an idealist and they were. The formal entities of idealism—Absolutes, Infinites and Ideas with a capital I—are firmly relegated to categories of interior or subtle matter. In this sense he would seem to resemble a dialectical materialist before the time. For Marxist philosophers—it is part of their Hegelian legacy—continually attempt to extract from Greek idealism, even from the Neoplatonists, a logic which they may rework in materialist terms. It results in a Marxist claim on the past. In this they faithfully ape the great religions—Christianity, Islam and a wing of Judaism. Some commentators, even some Swedenborgian ones, have seen Swedenborg's pre-illumination philosophy as materialist or tending that way; but it is rather based on the traditional Christian view that man is "of the earth, earthy." Man's highest self-motivated thoughts do not rise above the material. This is not a materialist doctrine but one of Divine transcendence. Where he does seem to approach Platonic idealism, he is actually reflecting Christian philosophy in the Augustinian tradition, as we shall see.

In order to develop the above points Swedenborg has virtually to invent a kind of proto-geometry and proto-mechanics which takes the form of a dialectical logic. Here again he has some antecedent in Proclus, who holds that Euclid's theorems and proofs belong in the categories of formal logic. This logic is hooked onto the concepts of calculus which he has inserted into the ambiguous space occupied by Euclid's primary point.

We now have a progression of formal categories which somewhat resembles the following. Again, I will briefly summarize some rather knotty ideas, which will become clear later.

Dialectical logic is concerned primarily with *discrete* form. The thesis generates its (not quite) opposite, the antithesis. Thesis and antithesis, working together, produce the synthesis. The three parts of this logical operation, intimately related, are nonetheless separate. Some have compared thesis to the father, antithesis to the mother and synthesis to the child. In a complex fashion, which I will not attempt to explain logically, there is also a line of *continuity* running through this process. In Swedenborg's case, he compares his logic to concepts of the infinite and infinitesimal derived from calculus, which is concerned with *continuous* form once again (the sliding scale). Finally we have classical geometry and related disciplines, which are concerned with the discrete and the continuous together.

Here we do not have to worry *too* much about the terms "dialectical logic" and "calculus." What is important is that we first have *discrete* form, form made up of separate but interrelated parts, like the notes in a musical scale. Then we have *continuous* form, like a sliding scale performed on a slide-whistle or violin played *glissando* or Hawaiian guitar, in which we slide up to each note, stop there a moment and slide on to the next. Then, out of these, we get *discrete and continuous* forms together, as in, say, some old-fashioned gypsy rhapsody for solo violin, in which the performer plays both fixed notes and sliding passages.

Proceeding from such initial assumptions Swedenborg builds up his hierarchy of forms. He believes that the innermost forms of nature must be "perfectly" geometrical and mechanical. His definition of the "mechanical" is derived from geometrical ideas. This is because he believes that mechanics is geometry in movement, while geometry itself is a crystallized form of logic in movement. (This statement may be read backwards, with geometry derived from mechanics.) His creating God is, on the level of Providence as it creates and maintains the material universe, a Great Geometer. In this Swedenborg reflects a traditional Christian idea of great age, stronger in the Byzantine church than in the medieval Western church, but eventually thoroughly acclimatized in Europe.

Swedenborg has seriously considered the traditional doctrine of the four elements (earth, water, air and ether) but finds in the end he must totally revise it. Thus he defines a "universal element," a "magnetic element," ether (not the ether-concept of his day) and air, this last being an idealized gas. To these he adds a fifth element, "aqueous vapor," which we might describe as a transitional stage leading to the formation of liquid and solid substance. This substance is represented by water, "the purely material finite," which he thinks of as a liquefied solid. The breakdown of the "water particle" gives birth to the solid substances we know. Even here we are far from the ancient four elements, at least as commonly understood, because water is a type of all molten matter: "the aqueous vapor is entirely similar to that of a mineral of any kind when melted into a volume or liquefied."[10]

The *Principia* is a hierarchy of ever more complex structures, of idealized waveforms or undulations, whose intersections, nodes or collisions (when the waves take on particle form or vice versa) create the material world we know. The germ of it all is found in his early work, *On Tremulation* (1719): "Tremulation is the most subtle form of motion that exists in nature."[11]

There is one characteristic of the *Principia* which might appear, at least to some minds, to invalidate it as science. This is the absolutely uncompromising theism of its basic assumption, that God is not only the Creator but the Sustainer of the universe. Swedenborg refers to "the nature of that Infinite Being from Whom, as from their fountain, all things in the world derive their existence and subsistence."[12] The above quotation must be taken to the letter: Swedenborg's language is never merely flowery. When a fountain ceases to play it disappears. The entire material universe is like a fountain in relation to the Infinite Being in the sense that, if He ceased to act into it, it would immediately cease to be, leaving no trace behind.

This violates centuries of ideological conditioning, for which Christian philosophers are as much to blame as materialist ones. After the High Middle Ages Christian cosmologies tended towards a compromised theism. God was certainly acknowledged as a Creator, but little attention was paid to Him as a Sustainer, a concept which was becoming much more complicated than it had appeared to be in medieval times. By the eighteenth century the Creator God more resembled a *manufacturer* of universes. At the beginning of time God had started up the cosmos and had then let it run, intervening only for special purposes. This Craftsman God can no doubt be traced back to Greek philosophy—not only to Plato's Demiurge but also to Aristotle's Prime Mover.

It is quite disconcerting to note how this figure is reflected both in so-called "Christian fundamentalism" and its rival deism, both eighteenth-century phenomena. The God of the fundamentalists had created an autonomous self-functioning world, thereafter intervening only by way of miracle and revelation. The deists denied miracle and revelation and some, no doubt, secretly thought of God as a mere "Soul of Nature." This curiously related them, ultramodern though they thought they were, to tribal animists. Yet they assumed the world was autonomous and self-functioning, just like the fundamentalists.

Undoubtedly the older idea of a Sustaining God, which had existed from the time of the Church Fathers to the Renaissance or just before it, was becoming more difficult to defend after the discoveries of Copernicus, Galileo and Newton. The mechanics of heavenly bodies seemed completely self-regulating and so, it could be reasoned, was everything else. After these discoveries, until Swedenborg turned the science of mechanics inside out, the concept of a truly Sustaining God was leading to unsatisfactory results. It was leading either to a concept of *continual* direct intervention, a cosmology of "continuous miracle," such as that of Guillaume Postel,[13] or to the more common form of pantheistic emanationism, that is, of seeing the universe as being in some form the "Body of God," which virtually turned the mechanics of matter into the movements of a person. Such last-ditch archaism would make the cosmos something like a magic spell or would lead, more obviously than deism, to a frank return to the world of tribal animism, where every rock and tree has a humanlike soul.

The universe of Swedenborg is in no way a "dream of God," a very ancient concept implicit in the "sleeping god" of a number of preliterate civilizations, whose inactivity is, again, curiously reflected in eighteenth-century and modern deism. It is not a mere deceptive mask or disguise of His intent, as in cultures with "Trickster" myths, or in modern concepts of God as a being at play, even a sort of croupier in a house where all the games are fixed. It is not an emanation of God, nor, as in some nineteenth-century philosophies, of the Idealist Absolute. It is in a sense a continuous miracle, but in the sense that it is continually sustained, not in the sense that it must be continually tinkered with. It is completely real and it has its own order. Though it may resemble a thought-form in the sense that it has its own logic, which is truly a logic, it is not a thought-form as we imagine a thought-form, because all the thoughts of the Divine Being are completely real. And, finally, it is not a Neoplatonic world, any more than the world of St. Augustine, although, like Augustine, Swedenborg has adopted and developed certain insights of the Platonists and Neoplatonists.

Nevertheless, at some point near the core of the material universe, logic and mathematics shade off into an area which we may if we wish call "protological" and "protomathematical." The combining verbal form "proto-" really serves to mask our ignorance. There is a certain level of natural form which we may only represent to ourselves by analogy, by figure: I do not mean by poetic analogy and figure, which fall into another category, but by what may be called logical and mathematical analogy and figure. Yet this incomprehensible form does not lie only in innermost matter; it extends its ramifications throughout all of matter, for the reason that it has greater motive and forming power than the elements immediately accessible to our reasoning faculty. There is thus a seeming paradox in Swedenborg's vision of the world as a mathematical construction. Our mathematics can only be a model of its real formal principles, known to God alone. At the same time it must be recognized that the real mathematics of the world, which our model thus crudely images, are still a part of the world of matter, not of spirit.

In the next three chapters I am going to explain, to the best of my ability, Swedenborg's idea of what goes on at the deepest level of matter. Even my best explanation will only graze the surface of a remarkably profound argument.

Why so much space devoted to a part of his book? Because this is the most interesting aspect of Swedenborg's theory of matter. "Remarkably profound" is actually a very cautious description of his theory at this level. Here is what is happening: Swedenborg is describing a set of logical and geometrical operations—he is certainly not describing some thing he could see or measure—which eventually results in the physical world which we see, hear, feel, taste and smell. His thought moves in a double fashion: he is *deducing* all of matter from this primary point and at the same time he is *inducing* the mathematics of the primary particle from the behavior of matter as he observes it, particularly fluid matter.

Now to an extent we can again say he is doing what some Greek philosophers did. The Pythagoreans take the fact that natural objects can be numbered and that their parts can be numbered, as their primary or most important characteristic. The Platonists take geometrical form as a primary characteristic, and they say that deep matter is made of certain simple geometrical forms. Their ideas are immensely suggestive, but the problem is that their systems as we presently understand them (that is, without following Geminus and Proclus and including Euclid in the Platonic canon), do not work.[14] Certainly we can generalize them in a way their inventors did not intend and say some such thing as "Pythagoras and Plato both believed that nature is mathematical at the root." But this evades the issue, because they were much more specific than that, and would not have been pleased with such a general word as "mathematics."

Swedenborg's system does work in a generalized and approximate manner. I will not argue it is the best way of solving the problems he tackles. Only a mathematician could answer such a question convincingly. Nonetheless, he does find a way of explaining all the main external behaviors of matter from such abstract beginnings. We shall also see, as we approach the observable world in the later chapters of this first part, that there is much he does not explain. His practical knowledge of electricity is no greater than that of his contemporaries. Yet he relates it to magnetism and, astonishingly, to light, and indeed he has an essentially modern idea of electromagnetism, because he has electricity produced by magnetic forces working on (or inside) his "ether particles." His description of the phenomenon, though, is very knotted and roundabout, because he has never seen such a thing and he must deduce its behavior from his basic geometry. He does not explain the laws of chemical combination, because the chemistry of his day was too primitive to allow this. His descriptions of chemical processes, where they are not plain wrong, are based on simple experiments of the kitchen-stove variety or are drawn from the traditional practices of the technology of his time, which had no theory behind them and depended on the know-how of the craftsman. Yet, again astoundingly, his theory is such that it can be interpreted in such a way as to produce the basic laws of chemistry as we know them. This is to say that, misled by bad data, *he misinterprets his own theory*.

There must therefore be something powerful in his basic assumptions. First of all, they demand the production of phenomena which are real but which Swedenborg could not observe. Second, they are objective, because they indicate that basic laws of chemical combination should be such and such, and do so either correctly (if coarsely) or *correctibly*, while Swedenborg himself introduces confusion by trying to interpret his theoretical conclusions in the light of the crude chemistry of his time.

It then becomes a question of what we mean by "astounding." Two answers suggest themselves.

Astounding Answer One. Swedenborg has discovered basic laws of science which are true for all time, just as he set them out, and the errors of detail are irrelevant.

Astounding Answer Two. Swedenborg has come to an intuitive sense of some of the basic formal ideas, mosty logical and mathematical ideas, which will govern the development of physics in the nineteenth and early twentieth centuries. Basic mathematical forms may be approached in a number of ways and it is a well-known fact that inspired intuition may outstrip mathematical knowledge by many years. To really find out what he has done we shall in the end have to work out his arguments in modern mathematical language. It may well be, since it is much easier to visualize complex vortical behavior than to express it mathematically, that his approach will have to be in part rejected—I mean as science, not as natural philosophy. Perhaps his forms are too general to be reduced to the finely-tuned formulas which physicists and chemists need. Only work by specialists will solve this problem; but it will be a very long time before the *Principia* loses its value as natural philosophy, which deals in general ideas.

I favor the latter answer, because I am very skeptical about the existence of basic laws of science which are true for all time. As knowledge expands, we find that laws we thought were always and everywhere true prove only to apply to certain levels and classes of phenomena. Newton's laws are still valid for the universe Newton knew, the world apparent to the naked eye, but we now know of vast areas of matter where they do not apply or apply only in part.

ENDNOTES

1 Sigstedt, pp. 121 and 83, for the two reviews quoted.

Note that the reviewer of the *Miscellaneous Observations*, despite his antagonism, has hit upon the main point. Swedenborg's primary argument is that nature is geometrical. His choice of circles and vortices as essential forms derives from this and rests upon their geometrical versatility and ubiquity. His argument is first of all strictly formal.

In a very fine book on the philosophy of mathematics, written for the most part in the 1930s, the French mathematician, Albert Lautman, refers to Poincaré's topological study of curves in which he established (in 1881) the ideal or prime importance of cycles closed around a center: "their mathematical importance comes from the fact that an understanding of them determines at the same time an understanding of the curves in their vicinity. In the case of first order equations with real variables it is, for example, the spiral which asymptotically approaches this limit" (Lautman, p. 127).

Swedenborg's initial idea is mathematically sound; but because it is simply assumed that everything Swedenborg wrote had, somehow, to be "mystical," we have such odd statements as that of Professor Sir W.F. Barrett, FRS, in his generally sympathetic foreword to the 1912 edition of the *Principia*, which refers to Swedenborg's repetition of an "error" which led ancient philosophers to argue that the circle is the most perfect of figures (*Principia* I, p. viii). Swedenborg means only that the circle is perfectly symmetrical.

Swedenborg also, in his *Notes on Ontology* (pp. 5–6) makes a distinction between two kinds of circle. There is a "true circle," whose parts are "perpetual circles," and there is a mere model of a circle, which is formed by the rotations of angles. They look exactly the same, but since they are constructed on different bases they are really different forms. In a deeper exploration of Swedenborg's geometrical philosophy this distinction would have to be taken into account.

2 Swedenborg, *Letters and Memorials* II, pp. 676–679. For a detailed biography of Swedenborg, see Sigstedt.

3 Swedenborg, *Principia* I, p. 36. (reference to page number, as in all references to the *Principia*)

4 De Gortari, *Dialéctica de la Física*, pp. 28–28. De Gortari is a Marxist but apparently an independent one, judging by his lack of "party-line" jargon.

5 Ibid., p. 226.

6 Swedenborg is sometimes accused of vagueness or a "merely metaphorical" use of geometry (as by F.W. Very in his appendix to the 1912 edition of the *Principia*) by those who have failed to note the verbal text, in which he indicates the degree of quantitative precision he is aiming at.

7 De Renéville, *Sciences maudites et poètes maudits*, in *Les Cahiers d'Hermès*, p. 160.

8 I cite no examples because in this case it is impossible to distinguish plagiarism from independent discovery. Some natural philosophers would make no mention of Swedenborg, while using his ideas, for fear of being thought gullibly "mystical" or perhaps "heretical" (his *Principia* was placed by the Vatican on its *Index Expurgatorius* in the eighteenth century). In "Notes on the Influence of the Writings in Western Culture" (*NP* Apr/Jun, 1975), Richard R. Gladish discusses a debt on Kant's part (his nebular hypothesis).

9 Swedenborg, *Principia* II, p. 178.

10 Ibid., p. 260.

11 Swedenborg, *On Tremulation*, p. 11.

12 Swedenborg, *Principia* I, p. 38.

13 Bouwsma, *Concordia Mundi*, passim. This excellent study of the life and thought of Guillaume Postel (1510–1581) illustrates the real confusion of thought typical of the "occultist" tradition to which the writings of Swedenborg are sometimes mistakenly related. Postel tries to construct a grand synthesis of "mystical knowledge," from the *Cabala* to what passed in his day for Lullism. For example, he comes up with the notion—quasi-cosmological in the sense that it relates a logical form to the ancient Father-Mother-Child creative triad—that in the syllogism the major premise is masculine and the minor premise feminine, with the conclusion being "the son" (p. 145). This leads him to a form of "sophiolatry" which has been revived from time to time, even in our day, with Sophia/Wisdom as the maternal principle in the triad. However, Postel's notion is a wrenched-about version of a passage in Lull's *Liber de Praedicatione*, a rhetorical manual for the use of preachers, in which Lull suggests that the syllogism may be interpreted as a form of the Trinity, in which the father is the major premise, the son the minor premise and the Holy Spirit the conclusion. Frances Yates (see bibliography) has written at length on this "diffusion" of Lullian thought into European culture, both popular and learned.

14 Many authorities simply reject Proclus' statement. Yet Joseph Ehrenfried Hofmann in his *History of Mathematics*, says that the *Elements* "reveal the masterly skill of the systematist trained in Aristotelian logic and yet standing entirely on the soil of Platonic ideology" and refers to Proclus' commentary as "thorough" (Vol. I, pp. 21–22).

2

Some Definitions

There are six words which Swedenborg uses in a special sense, so special that we must try to define them in a separate chapter. They are the "Active," the "Passive," the "Finite," the "Elementary," the "Similar" and the "Dissimilar." The chapter will be a little difficult and abstract. Again this is not because the ideas are difficult taken one at a time but because the whole *ensemble* of ideas is novel. Some readers may want to skim through it, consulting it when they encounter these terms later in the text. The passages in quotation marks are drawn from various parts of the *Principia*.

The Active

The Primary Active is an entity created by an effort towards motion, but by such an effort as we cannot imagine, because time and space do not as yet exist. It does not in itself *occupy* even an analogue of space, but it automatically and immediately seeks something in which it may project itself. This "something," which is a Passive, then acquires some of the logical aspects of a space, since an event is occurring within it.

In its pure or primary state the Active is not an elementary particle. It has no dimensions and an infinite number of actives may occupy one space and flow within that space without collision. Only when they are enclosed in finites, which are defined by passives, do actives have "determinate place and arrangement" or "upward or downward or directions to any particular quarter." This is as much as to say that the unenclosed Active has infinite degrees of freedom.

Actives are found throughout nature from its origin-point to the "magnetic element." In this element they lose their freedom and become "bound" inside particles of matter. In subsequent massier forms of matter we may say that a particle has an "active component" but not that it is "freely active"; it is now in a Newtonian world. In general, actives "cannot be said to resist but only to act," since they form "nothing contiguous" and "resistance belongs only to what is contiguous." Though actives act "by form, velocity and mass" when embodied in finites, they themselves have "only what is formal; hence they cannot be called material." In regard to the last definition, we have the statements, firmly rooted in classical mechanics, that in external matter "there must always be a proportion between the active force and the mass," that "active force and weight depend upon the quantity of the motion which is the product of the mass and the velocity" and that "the modification of active force consists in velocity. It is by velocity that the state of the active force is determined, so that velocity is thus as it were the limit of the moving force."[1]

Now all this is, I admit, hair-raisingly abstract. It must remain that way, I am afraid. Swedenborg's own words are as simple as they can be and I have found that all my attempts to simplify them further have resulted in a loss of meaning which I have had to make up by a more complicated explanation later on. The abstraction cannot be helped. But the rewards of sticking with the argument will be great, because it is a wonderful mental world we are entering. We will not travel very far into it, but I hope we shall at least be encouraged to explore it further.

It may be noted that though I have quoted the words "weight" and "mass" I have quoted no reference to Newtonian gravity. This is not an omission on my part. We know that Swedenborg studied

Newton but there is not a mention of universal gravitation, not even on the level of massy matter. Since velocity and mass are, in the Swedenborgian system, defined within a universe whose first field or elementary is a space-time continuum (as we shall see later), there can be no doubt that his idea of gravity is much closer to Einstein's than Newton's (though not very close to Einstein's either, at least philosophically). As we shall find, all of Newton's laws are reconstituted in Swedenborg's system. They appear in a different mechanical, mathematical and philosophical setting and sometimes it is hard to recognize them. Yet they are there. For example, the relationship between Active and Passive is closely similar to that between action and reaction in Newton's third law of motion: "for every action there is an equal and opposite reaction." But at the first and most subtle level of matter, where Newton's hard and massy particles may not be found, Action and Reaction must be generalized into philosophical categories. Swedenborg replaces them with the Aristotelian terms Action and Passion.

At the primary level of matter the concept of *limit* must be somewhat redefined. It is not quite the limit of classical calculus, which depends upon ratio, but is rather a logical analogue (a term to be explained later) of this limit. The only ratio we have here is between the Active and the Passive, but neither of these may be seen in ratio to anything else, and neither contains internal parts in ratio. Is there, then, any way in which we may define the Primary Active in itself? It appears there is not, since it only defines itself in relationship to the Passive. The Primary Active looks like a universal force field. This field, since it has in itself no dimensions and no apparent parts in linkage (no contiguity) and since it offers no resistance, is beyond all possibility of perception ("beyond the sphere of the most subtle sense," says Swedenborg).[2] It is not even a featureless sea of energy but rather its antecedent. We should not think of it even as a medium.

That is why it cannot exist of itself. It has only one definable tendency, its search for an otherness, a space, itself only a logical entity, in which it may realize itself. It has, so to speak, a thirst for space. From its self-definition in the Passive there develops *limit*, a single and universal limit. This is limit as the definition of some-thing, as in the case of the remarkably philosophical child who described how he drew pictures: "I have a think and I draw a line around it" (Swedenborg thought children were very logical). This limit is the most subtle conceivable form of motion, an absolute velocity which is the first determinant of space, then of time, or rather of time-in-space, since velocity, as motion in space measured by time, partakes equally of the nature of the two. The first limit of matter is a velocity and this velocity determines time-in-space. Such an idea may remind us of Einstein, though the velocity is not that of light, and time is not formally treated as a fourth dimension in Swedenborg's system.

Thus there is something like a theoretical constant at the root of the Swedenborgian universe. We can only think of it as a bare logical entity, one which may not be defined quantitatively. Yet it belongs in the world of matter all the same. It is perfectly true that Swedenborg says that the Active cannot be thought of as "materi-al," but he is using this word as his eighteenth-century reader would understand it, as meaning something massy, hard and dis-crete. Swedenborg is developing his own much more subtle idea of matter, and the abstract constant of velocity is a part of it. It is not a supernatural entity or measure.

Now I have said that the Active is an *effort* towards motion in the primary point. I am not going to attempt to explain this in physical terms and I do not think I can. Effort has a physical expression as potential energy, but it is also a physical expression of intention. Behind the Primary Active lies the will of the Infinite, which is not God but is in some fashion a manifestation of God, the "Divine Form." It is impossible to determine or to state in philo-sophical language the way in which the Divine Will becomes effort, since the modifications of Will which result in effort are themselves infinite and incomprehensible. But the effort itself belongs in the world of matter. It is a very old idea that physical movement, on which all life depends, must ultimately be referred to God, and we find it in both Descartes and Leibniz, as elsewhere. The advantage of the Swedenborgian interpretation is that it obviates the necessity of spirit's moving matter by something like a manual push, with the resultant universe then operating as a perpetual-motion machine, saved from degeneration by moving in a vacuum.

Swedenborg provides us with a little more help in his *Notes on Ontology*. These are comments on philosophical terms found in the works of Christian Wolff (1679–1754), a distinguished philosopher of Swedenborg's day, and of two now-forgotten but formidably learned scholars of an earlier period, Scipio Dupleix (1569–1661) and Robert Baron (1593?–1639). In these notes he says, "We must conceive of active and motive force...after the manner of substance but (it is) not substance, (it) only so appears."[3] And in another note he says, "There is nothing in physics that is purely necessary but it becomes necessary, certain things being granted or supposed."[4] The implications of the first note are clear and simple but those of the second are more complex, leading us closer to the center of his cosmological thought. In a sense it bypasses the determinism/probability dilemma, but at a certain cost, which is, as always in Swedenborg, belief in a deity. If the physical world were all there is, it would certainly follow that its laws of order and action would be either necessary or probabilistic or combinations of the necessary and probabilistic. But in a monotheistic universe, no matter how God is defined, there is nothing intrinsically necessary but His Will—necessary, that is, in relation to nature, since what He creates must necessarily exist as created. However, He could have willed otherwise. It is only when a certain natural structure is set in place that necessity enters into nature, as a consequence of now-existent chains of causes and effects. But Swedenborg also says, "certain things being granted or supposed," which means to me, unless I am reading too much into a short comment, that if we begin by postulating conditions of necessity we shall determine the world-structure as purely necessary or determined.

Such considerations must be kept in mind when we are considering structures such as this, which begin with a fundamental binary—two entities. A two-entity structure may be interpreted as generating a world which is strictly determined, a world of chance, or a combination of the two.

The Passive

This manifests itself first as a principle of difference, while the Active is a principle of identity, everywhere the same. It seems paradoxical that difference should manifest itself as a principle of definition, but when we think about it we can see that the moment we define something we also define, if only by general exclusion, what it is not. Thus we create a difference. The idea of definition as difference is common to formal logic from the ancient Greeks to George Boole, and in the *Introduction to Arithmetic* by the "Greek" Nicomachus (actually he was born in Palestine and studied in Egypt—in Alexandria), the "Same" and the "Other" engender all number.[5]

As the pure passive is everything the active is not, it takes on the form of pure limit. The active has pure energy in infinite extension, and it is by successive limitings that the active is defined, first in form, then in figure. Figure at this stage is very general, an idea of pure space apart from space. All figure is passive in relation to form, a concept the *Notes on Ontology* again help us to understand—

> Figure differs from form, as, in geometry, a plane differs from a cube; and the property of figure in respect to the property of form, is like the property of figure, geometrically considered, in respect to the entire construction, and hence resulting nature, of a compound. Thus we recede from figure the more we elevate our attention to the higher powers, as to the cubes of the square of a cube and so forth; for these are more removed from planometry.[6]

Swedenborg is referring here to nth-dimensional geometry as he conceived it (there was no clear idea of such a geometry in his time, though it was thought such a thing might exist). This is explained in the paragraph which follows—

> So also with superior forms. These at least cannot be called figured forms, because they are not terminated by space within themselves, but only by imaginary space outside themselves. For, that they may include space within themselves, there must be reference to a centre, a surface, a diameter and many other things; these perish when there are such

(superior...NN) determinations, and with them perishes also the idea of space, of which there is nothing in the form itself, but which can be conceived as being outside the form, and not adjoined to it. For a form which occupies no space, regarded as such in itself, cannot be said to be terminated; but the terminus...must be conceived of as occupying space outside the form.[7]

Swedenborg's idea of nth-dimensionality would correspond closely enough, if developed from the implications of "the cubes of the square of a cube" $[\{(x^3)^2\}^3]$, to modern algebraic modes of representing it. But four important things are to be noted, which remind us of the fact that Swedenborg, who often anticipates modern mathematical concepts, would not necessarily accept all the philosophical ideas we attach to them. Such forms are "superior," which in Swedenborg's use of the word means that they are not only real, but even more real than inferior forms. Second, these more real forms are represented in imaginary space, which means that they are presented to the mind as if they were unreal. The "superior cube" has no quantifiable center, surface etc.: its surface is all perceivable figure, which is to say all that we see and otherwise perceive with our senses. Third, such forms are more interior, which means that we do not arrive at higher dimensions by adding new dimensions in the sensual world of figure. Quite the contrary. *The cube is inside the plane.* Fourth, since only the determinations of such forms exist in space, we never see them as they are, but only so to speak their "shells" and "limits of motion." Very difficult ideas, I admit, but they must be noted.

All this seems to imply that Swedenborg, if he came back to earthly life today, would find no difficulty in, say, four dimensional formalism as we find it in representations of space-time. But he would probably object to what he would see as a confusion, at least in popular accounts of this formalism, between a geometry representing logical ideas and one representing the naked-eye physical world. He would see (again I refer to the layman's perceptions) a confusion between levels of thought.

And here let me insert a parenthetical caution, that the word "real" has two meanings. One of these is something like "authentic" in its root meaning (from Greek *authentes*, one who does things himself). A form which generates another form is more real in the sense that it can exist on its own, while the generated form cannot. But, as denoting objective existence the word "real" cannot be qualified. A thing exists or it does not. In this sense, generating and generated forms, once complete, are equally real. We have to deal therefore with a flaw in the present English language, in which the phrase "more real," which we can intuitively understand, appears nonsensical.

This means that, while in nth-dimensional representation geometrical figure and the idea of space vanish, Swedenborg will allow, in the sensually-apprehensible world of matter (which, of course, we have not yet arrived at in our present discussion), only the three classical dimensions. These, as they are created by motion, necessarily involve time. Nth-dimensional representation does not really add extra dimensions to the classical three, which is impossible. To add another geometrical dimension we should have to imagine a matter more material than matter, a realm of super-solidity. As we penetrate the interiors of matter we first encounter *seemingly* more complex forms of space. Then, as they grow yet more complex, we begin to encounter what may appear, in a crude image, as the leaching-out of space from the figure. Spatial relationships are replaced more and more by logical and functional ones. We are entering a world, not of extended geometry, but of proto-geometry, the binary/ternary logic of primal matter. This is *more real* than material space and time, which nonetheless it unceasingly generates.

We may also say of the primary point formed by the interaction of the Active and the Passive that it exists in a sphere of potential geometry.[8] And we may say, to refer back to an earlier comment, that in the primary point necessity and probability, separately and in combination, have their *single* beginning.

The Finite

It must be admitted, right away, that the Swedenborgian finite cannot be defined adequately in a book such as this. The reason is pretty well indicated in the quotation which follows—

> Without the help of mechanics we cannot conclude anything with certainty. We must confirm our *a priori* observations by mechanics, and thus *a posteriori*. The science of mechanics then confirms the fact, that in the spiral motion (of a substantial) resides all the power of freely flowing from one extremity to another, and that it cannot arrive more easily at any end by any other motion; so that, if anything is to be conceived as continuously in motion, that continuity must be conceived of as spiral. In the lever, mechanics sees its potency and forces; in the inclined plane, its motion; in the perpetual lever, a perpetual potency; in the perpetually-inclined plane, perpetual motion; in the spiral figure, which represents both, it sees concentrated all its capabilities.[9]

This is indeed clearly expressed; but in the last sentence Swedenborg has virtually run through the entire realm of classical mechanics, and thence into an extension of this realm which exists only in his theory. The mechanics of the lever and the inclined plane, which he here assumes the reader fully understands, are far from simple in their full classical development; the mechanics of the perpetual lever and the perpetually-inclined plane are his own developments of the principle of the screw, which is an inclined plane wrapped around a cylinder; and finally, it will be remembered, he is dealing with expressions of these forces in a fluid medium. We have here an eighteenth-century new physics which was without issue and, unfortunately, the mere *starting-point* for its detailed comprehension—which is what we desire—is a complete mastery of classical mechanics as understood in the eighteenth century. This mastery must be complete, because from a partial understanding one will never be able to understand Swedenborg's extension of this discipline, as in, for example, his logical/ mathematical use of such notions as the perpetual lever and the perpetual inclined plane. So I cannot even begin to attempt a satisfying explanation of the mechanics of the Swedenborgian finite. All I can say is that, in the enigmatically smooth swoop of his final sentence, Swedenborg has derived most of classical mechanics from the vortex and in the process developed a completely new definition of equilibrium (though it is not without Archimedean antecedents).

Thus he finds in the vortex the form which unites mathematics and mechanics. In geometry it leads to the cone and then to parabola, hyperbola, circle and ellipse. We may observe this in the form of a spinning and precessing top, such as a gyroscope. If we set a toy gyroscope spinning on a table we can see that its axis, the top of which moves in a circle while its bottom remains fixed at a point on the table, describes the surface of a cone. This is why Swedenborg takes the circle (with the sphere) and the cone as the first regular geometrical shapes created by natural movement. In mechanics the vortex leads to all forms of helical and rotatory motion and ultimately (as forms of torque) to such basic representations of mechanical forces as the screw, the lever and the inclined plane. It even leads to principles which produce a further refinement of Newtonian gravitation. We know that, since the earth is rotating, the true path of an object as it falls in earth's gravitational field describes a spiral, though one little removed from a straight line in the short-path case, say, of a stone dropped from a tower.[10]

For present purposes we may perhaps roughly visualize a finite in the following terms.

A finite may be seen as a closing or bounding curve, inside which we find more active elements which in most cases are complexes of actives and passives. It is a large bubble form, in which these more active elements are smaller bubble forms, which tend to concentrate at the center and the circumference. We may also visualize it as a hollow sphere full of moving points, though actually the shell of the sphere is formed by the motions of the points themselves.

In an illustrative diagram it may take such forms as the following, which are based on Swedenborg's own illustrations.

FIGURE 1

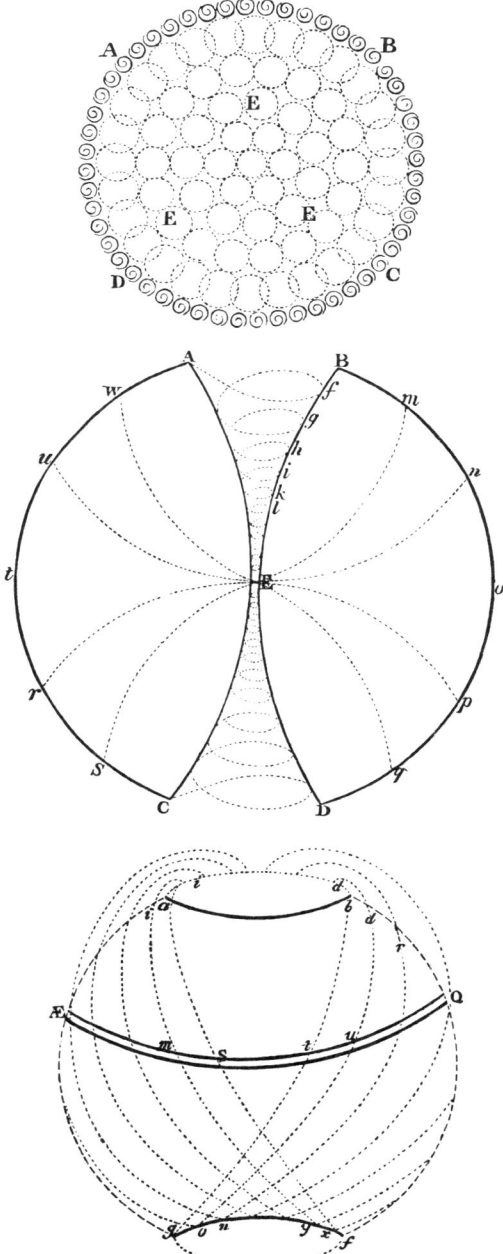

Figure 1
These figures are repoduced from the 1912 English translation of the *Principia*, Vol. I, pp. 158, 173, 191.

From these diagrams alone we may form some idea of the remarkable manner in which Swedenborg extended the applications of classical mechanics.

It should also be noted that a finite may become active and that when it does so it forms one of the internal parts of a finite of more complex degree.

The Elementary

Most people who have read the *Principia* have trouble forming an idea of an "elementary," but this seems to be due to a change of verbal definition since his time. An elementary is not a chemical element as we understand the phrase. The distinction between chemical elements and compounds had not been established in Swedenborg's day. Nor does it much resemble most interpretations of the four elements of ancient and medieval physics—earth, water, air and ether or fire. Swedenborg regards the traditional four elements as four phases of matter—earth or "earths" are matter in the solid state, water is liquid-state matter, air is gaseous matter and ether becomes something for which there was as yet no definition, something like the modern "plasmic matter." True, this phase-concept was included in the old definitions, but they also included much which did not interest Swedenborg in the slightest.

Because Swedenborg's use of the traditional concept of the "four elements" raises problems which can obscure the meaning of his elementaries, I shall discuss this separately, after discussing "the Similar and Dissimilar." In briefest description we may say the following. On the most subtle levels of matter an elementary behaves in many respects like a "field" in nineteenth and twentieth-century physics. As the level of macroscopic and, as we would say now, atomic-molecular matter is approached, an elementary begins to behave like a resistant medium through which motions can travel in the form of waves of the familiar kind. Finally, on the level of "air" and "water" it behaves like a body of gas or liquid. An elementary is made up of elementary particles, which are composed in various ways of finites and their actives. In summary, an element is composed of particles and particles are composed of spaces and forms. An element is then, in the last analysis, a field of spaces and forms.

It is an extraordinary fact that Swedenborg's descriptions of his elementary particles read very much like modern descriptions of atoms and their component particles, though in a generalized form (one atom serves all, so to speak). This is uncanny, particularly since he has constructed his mental objects by a mode of reasoning and geometrical construction which, because of its unprecedented nature, may well, though deceptively, appear homemade. Yet we need not invoke psychic powers. His reasoning is rigorous and we may follow it every step of the way. We may further see—a point to be discussed later—that there is indeed a certain link with modern physical reasoning, through the then-nascent discipline of fluid mechanics and dynamics. The mystery of all this is not a matter of prevision but of method. Swedenborg's mathematical arguments, taken singly, are mathematically obvious, or rest upon Greek and later demonstrations which he does not bother to recapitulate, or are based on common sense and everyday observation. When they are philosophically complex they may be referred to Christian forms of natural philosophy which go back to medieval theories and concepts and, through them, to the Greeks. The mystery lies in his choice, among these simple or traditional ideas, of certain which lead to astonishing results, and, related to this choice, in his ability to refine them and put them together in logically coherent structures which reveal them to be linked in unexpectedly profound ways. The *Principia* is not only science or even only natural philosophy. It is a very deep form of cultural revision. Once refined, and set in such a structure, these ideas cease to be obvious and traditional. They become *avant-garde*, even in our own day.

The Similar and Dissimilar

At various points in the development of his argument Swedenborg insists that his particles are all the same. We may well be puzzled, even a little angered by this. In the first place, his descriptions show them not to be the same; in the second place he frequently insists on the rich variety of nature. Is he making a doomed attempt to ingratiate himself with the atomists who thought of all materials as made up of differently-shaped stacks of hard little balls, like tiny marbles? Or is he separating himself from the atomists of the other persuasion, who imagined atoms of diverse shapes fitted together like marquetry? What *does* he mean?

In a sense he is taking the theories of the atomists into consideration, though tacitly, since he always avoids disputation. What he is rejecting is the inertness of their hard particle atoms. His elementary particles are forms of movement. When we stack up inert objects shaped all the same, we do not get structures, only piles, and usually unstable piles at that. When we pack together objects of different shapes in 3-d jigsaw puzzles we get stability but no fluidity. But when we stack up *movements*—little movements fitted over the larger movements—we get waves, because the movements interact. More specifically we get harmonic waves ("undulations" in his terminology) which reinforce and resonate with each other to produce a quasi-infinitude of secondary waves. Difference emerges out of similarity.

We must devote a fair amount of space to the concepts of "similarity" and "dissimilarity" in the *Principia*, because they relate to a perennial problem in natural philosophy, that of "chance."

Swedenborg's philosophical logic has a structure somewhat like that of probability theory. It begins with a binary (Active/Passive), as does probability theory with its two choices, "heads and tails." Swedenborg does not admit chance into the deep structure of the universe. In his rejection of this idea he does not attack sophisticated versions of probability theory, since these had not yet been developed. Yet I believe his argument against chance-structure is sufficiently cogent to be still applicable. The following is an attempt, based on statements found here and there in the *Principia*, to express his argument in modern terms. I choose this approach to avoid a long discussion of early eighteenth-century theories of chance.

There are two kinds of probability theory, and though they lead to the same or similar mathematical methods, they are based on philosophically opposite ideas.

The first is set out by George Boole in his *The Laws of Thought*. His theory is based on the following statement: "...if p be the probability that an event x will happen, 1-p will be the probability that the said event will not happen."[11] Not only is there a contrariety between p and 1-p but Boolean probability is derived from his *logic*, in which basic or generative logical forms are expressed in the same binary mode as that used in his theory of probability. For his logical system is built upon four symbols grouped in two duads. 0 is the class of Nothing; 1 represents "Universe," and the second duad is set out in his Third Proposition—"If x represent any class of objects, then will 1-x represent the contrary or supplementary class of objects, i.e. the class including all objects which are not comprehended in the class x."[12]

An important aspect of Boole's argument is his undogmatic but conclusive statement that the correct form in which "all questions in the theory of probabilities may be viewed" consists "...in substituting for *events* the propositions which assert that those events have occurred, or will occur; and viewing the element of numerical probability as having reference to the *truth* of those *propositions*, not to the *occurrence* of the *events* concerning which they make assertion."[13] And this, of course, is because his system is not based on an Active/Passive pair but a True/False one.

In other words, the theory of probability is a form of logic, the logic of prediction on the basis of minimal knowledge, and it is based upon the dividing of a complex event into two matching sets of contingencies. In Boole's case, at least one of these events is known, the event x. But when the sequence of cause and effect in an event is unknown we must make rough approximations, and we begin by assuming that all causes are equal and nonessential, that is, that they are equally contingent. For example, we know that the results of tossing a coin are determined by two factors: i) that there are only two sides to the coin; ii) that the result of each single toss is determined by mechanical laws—by the way the coin rests on the index-finger and thumb, by the force and direction of our thumb-flick, by the weight of the coin and by lesser factors, such as wind, atmospheric pressure and so on. However, these mechanical factors, taken one by one, are small and variable. It can be assumed that they will cancel each other out over a run of tosses and that each toss may be seen as the same as every other, that all the tosses are equal. Then the stronger determining element, which is the structure of the coin as a bi-faced entity, will dominate the long-term result. But in this case both sides are equal. "Chance," in the common use of the word, does not enter into the picture. We have one *strongly determined* "event," a manufactured coin which is the very picture of equality. We have a sequence of *weakly determined* "events," the mechanical laws governing each toss, but these cancel each other out and they are taken as equal. The *strongly determined equality* dominates. And if I use "event" in quotes, instead of calling a coin an "object" and the toss an "event," it is that the common description of chance processes rests upon a fallacious, if perhaps pragmatically necessary, distinction between objects and events. In any case, what we have here is a structure of equalities and equivalences.

To follow the approach rejected by Boole, to assert that events *occur* "probabilistically," is to think in the most subjective-idealist of terms, that is, to assume that things are thoughts and vice versa, though outside of any universal law of cause and effect. This is quite different from assuming that the laws of logic are derived from the laws of natural things (Swedenborg's position) or from assuming that the laws which govern things are derived from the laws of logic because the laws of logic are the laws of God or the Absolute (Hegel's objective-idealist position). In the latter two cases, things and thoughts are separated by the very fact that one category is derived from the other, indeed *corresponds* to it. In both cases we have a Divine creator of both thoughts and things, which are therefore different, though related, from the beginning. In other words, to use the phrase "a probabilistic universe" is not only to think as a subjective idealist, which is no sin, but to think clumsily, which is.

The second form of probability theory, the non-Boolean, goes back to Laplace. His initial binaries, as we learn from the first page of Chapter III of his *Philosophical Essay on Probabilities*, are based on the following idea—

Let us suppose that we throw into the air a large and very thin coin whose two large opposite faces, which we will call heads and tails, are perfectly similar. Let us find the probability of throwing heads at least one time in two throws. It is clear that four equally possible cases may arise...[14]

...and he goes on to set out a mathematical theory of probability which is perfectly sound.

But why, if the two sides of the coin are perfectly similar, should we call them heads and tails? I am not quibbling over a merely infelicitous image. Laplace is trying to imagine two primal and perfectly simple events which are the same, yet different. Where in nature shall we find two such events? Where in logic? Here, which is not the case in Boole's theory, there is no real difference between the primal events. Laplace represents Age-of-Reason atheism at its most exuberant and he is trying to prove that religion is nonsense. If the two initial events were unequal in any way we should have a hierarchy in its smallest form—as when we assume that heads is right-side-up and tails is wrong-side-up. We should have in effect an Active/Passive cosmology, and Laplace wishes to avoid this as a relic of ancient superstition.

Boole, on the other hand, has no such intent. For one thing, he believes in God. His theory of probabilities begins with an already existing cosmos, in which x is a known complex idea and $1-x$ an idea much more complex, though unknown. Thus, though both Boole and Laplace develop their ideas in a perfectly sound mathematical fashion, their world-views are virtually opposite.[15]

Now the truth is (see note 4) that Swedenborg's universe *can* be read entirely, though falsely, as a probabilistic structure. This is because the interactions of Active and Passive in the primary point, though we can visualize them in crude diagrams, are innately beyond logical and mathematical description. They appear random, though they are not. For this reason the first particle, the synthesis of Active and Passive, is called by Swedenborg, most strikingly, a "contingency."[16] Were I to explore this it would take us very deeply into intricacies of logic, and I suppose things are complicated enough already. The important thing to remember is that Swedenborg has anticipated the arguments of those who believe in a chance universe, has conceded them their purely mathematical or formal point, and has immediately countered that it may be understood in a contrary sense, as evidence of Divine creation.

Swedenborg's large binary, corresponding after its fashion to the small binary of Active and Passive, is "Sameness" and "Variety."[17] For the Active, as always self-identical, and the Passive, as the principle of differentiation, really do correspond to their macrocosmic cousins. This is sound traditional logic, not at all ahead of its time. Where Swedenborg differs from most natural philosophers—Lull and Hegel excepted—is in his insistence that his binaries are part of nature. They are, in no matter how subtle a fashion, geometrical and mechanical; and the geometrical and mechanical are intimately related, even to the extent that all geometrical figure is created by movement.

In the *Principia* "sameness" means most perfect similarity of function on different levels of the system. This does not result in identity throughout the system because the levels are different, there are so many planes with their own laws, and these planes are related to each other by analogy of function or "correspondence," a term to be considered later. We must not imagine a simple law of geometrical forms, a simple pattern propagating itself from the very small to the very large, from interior to exterior nature. We should imagine instead some thing like the following. First, we should imagine a set of motions or behaviors which completes itself, combining in one complex form as Level One. Since these forms and levels are dynamic, Level One "seeks" further realization, and by a qualitative leap becomes a basic component of what will be Level Two. Here a richer set of motions and behaviors completes itself, combining in a more complex form—namely Level Two as complete—which is a filled-out universe. The dynamic forms of Level Two now "seek" Level Three. The process proceeds through a number of levels, the elementaries. Matter is growing all the time in both complexity and inertial mass, which means that the dynamic energy is slowing down, encountering more and more resistance. Finally the level of solid matter is reached, a state of comparative quiescence and rest.

Two things must be remembered here. The first is that the leaps are *qualitative*. We are not dealing with simple accumulation of mass, as in a snowball, but with the accumulation of discrete planes, or, in spherical representation, of "shells." The second is that our image is a crude one-way representation of a complicated dual process. The outmost layer, that of solid matter, is more complex in measurable components than the "simple" of Level One. It is made up of many discrete bits and pieces or contains, as we should now say, more information. But in a qualitative sense the first "simple" is really the most complex of all, because it contains, in *ordered* ranks of possibility or potential, every quality which will be realized quantitatively on the level of solid matter. In the reality of ordered potential the cube is still inside the plane.

A less technical explanation of the kind of order I am referring to may be found in Swedenborg's philosophical poem, *The Worship and Love of God*, the arguments of which relate directly to those of the *Principia*. In that poem he tells us that Divine Providence cannot be universal unless it is also in the most particular things and that "from these latter things it alone derives the name of universal; or...what is universal derives its essence and actuality solely from the singular things from which it exists."[18] We read also that the single may not be separated from the universal nor the universal from the singular and that in fully realized nature "simultaneous order derives its birth, nature and perfection from successive orders, and the former is only rendered perspicuous and plain by the latter."[19] And we read that "compound things cannot inflow into simple things, but simple things flow into their compounds, such, and no other, being the order which prevails in universal nature, because no other is possible."[20] A somewhat longer quotation may more clearly make the difficult point—

> As to the correspondence itself by the influx of the operation of one form into another, it is first to be known, that the parent or superior form is related to the next inferior form as to its offspring, consequently as to its image, there being no difference between them but in regard to simplicity and perfection. Hence there exists and flourishes such a harmony between the forms, by the mediation of active and living forces, that a change of the state of one, which is effected by a variation

of form, excites a like change in the other correspondently; for a perpetual agreement reigns by mediate active forces, between like forms, especially when all things flow rightly in their order, or when the supreme form, which is the most perfect of all, acts into the next inferior one, and this latter in like manner into the following one, and thus successively.[21]

We thus have—

1) Sameness, or similarity of function between levels, even to the most perfect similarity, but never identity;
2) Variety, which might be called "variety of application of sameness," and results, from the differences between *levels* of application, not only in differences of magnitude but in an immense array of other quantitative differences.

Sameness and variety, then, in interaction, engender qualitative leaps, or subordinate discrete differences within the levels or planes themselves. Such qualitative leaps are particularly apparent on the level of nature which we experience with our senses, most globally in the leaps between the four states of matter—solid, liquid, gas and plasma (or "ether")—and this is the deep basis of four-element theory.[22]

It seems to me that we do not falsify the Swedenborgian idea of variety if we regard it, since we are looking back at it from an age when probability theory reigns, as an *ideological inversion* (*rectification* might be a better word) of probability theory where, nevertheless, the formal properties and aspects of that theory are not changed.[23] The Active and the Passive run through the global series *like* probabilistic binaries; but this is because the pure Active and Passive lie far beyond our perception and furthermore cannot exist apart. Thus, since they are ultimately expressed in such mundane forms as thermodynamic phenomena and even the movements of crowds and the affairs of nations, they can only appear to us in statistical terms.

A more familiar form of variety, as discussed by Swedenborg, appears in the form of "irregularity" of motion. This develops, in the *Principia*, on the level occupied by Actives of the Third Finite,[24] which are magnetic (we should now say "electromagnetic"). At this level we have particles of differing size and elasticity, and their collisions produce irregular movements, as a result of which they lose their active force, becoming passive entities (the Passive is, again, the principle of the Different). This is indeed "probabilistic motion" in the familiar sense and it tends, as in modern theory, to passive equilibrium, uniformity and entropy.

Thus we do have in the *Principia* a form of uncertainty principle, one which runs throughout nature. In the most general sense we may say that it arises directly from the fact that, as before, "simultaneous order derives its birth, nature and perfection from successive orders, and the former is only rendered perspicuous and plain by the latter."[25] In other words a point event (a simultaneity), in fact as well as in perception, can only exist as part of a continuum and vice versa. This, as we shall see later, has deep philosophical implications if we consider the Divine creation of the world, related in *Genesis*, as a "point-event." If at any point in *any* natural continuum we attempt to separate the simultaneous from the successive we encounter a "conceptual blur." This has nothing to do with the weakness of our reasoning powers or the limitations of our senses, whether or not the latter are extended by measuring instruments. It is due to the fact that the two cannot be separated either in logic or in nature. From the logical point of view we may say that if they could be separated there would be no true variety in nature because there would be no inherent principle of change and development. For within nature or within some small part of it there would either be points which could not externally interact or there would be smear-like continua lacking the internal parts which could interact *within* the continua, and in both cases there would be a break in the chain of energy transmission.[26]

Here again we approach a difficult argument of the *Principia*. I certainly cannot elucidate it here. It rests upon Swedenborg's definition of the relationship between the infinitely large and the infinitely small. The definition seems sound to me, but it leads right to an ancient controversy at the heart of number theory.

In the deepest realms of nature the small expands, the large contracts, without, however, ceasing to be respectively small and large. These two motions meet in a non-temporal and non-spatial point. Here, too, there is a meeting of all other complementaries—the simultaneous and the successive, the discrete and the continuous, the end of the world-process and its beginning. This does not mean that they become the same; rather they continually approach each other in a context of perfect similarity-by-analogy. The universe is a point and a point is the universe— and both these statements are true.[27]

The Four Elements

We are now able to return to the idea of the "elementary." In particular we find ourselves better equipped to answer the question of why Swedenborg chose to adhere to the theory of the four elements, a decision which would seem to doom him to darkest obsolescence. It is in the element that the logical/mechanical qualities we have been considering—Active, Passive, Finite, Same and Different—are realized. It is clear that the chemical elements of our periodic table—gold, sulphur, oxygen and so on—cannot be considered as primary forms in this system.

The *measurement-system* of the *Principia* begins with the dialectical unity, itself a synthetic form of Active and Passive, of Ideal Motion in Ideal Space. This runs from the beginning to the end of the book and the fully realized matter at the conclusion of the treatise is still a complex of Motion and Space. A complex of Motion and Space is a general state of matter before it is, say, a chemically-defined substance. Any system so based is bound to end in some form of four-element theory, since the crisis-points (or, as we should now say, the catastrophe-points) are precisely those of transitions between states of matter. These are themselves motion/ space states or *phases*, from the virtually static state of solid matter to the highly active plasmic or etheric state. The chemical elements, the entities which participate in such motions, are *particulars*— parts of the process. I have said "any system so based" because this is a logical outcome, not because it is an accepted idea. Indeed, the rejection of four-element theory by modern science is so absolute that no natural philosopher or scientist could propose a return to it, or a revision of it, without destroying his reputation (at the present time of writing). But the logic of such a development remains, and the old theory is sometimes referred to in a playful way.[28]

By Swedenborg's time the ancient and medieval idea of the four elements had become so inclusive and vague as to lose all definable significance. The difference between element as phase-state and element as substance could not be resolved until the rise of modern chemistry. A choice was made and it was decided to treat chemically-defined matter as primal substance. One who later protested against this was Hegel, in his *Encyclopedia of the Philosophical Sciences*.[29] It is worthwhile to summarize his argument, if briefly and crudely.

His *Philosophy of Nature* is flawed by some serious scientific errors, but much of his reasoning is still valid, though his philosophy of nature is as unfashionable as any philosophy can be. (At any rate, I have not found any who defend it.) He objects, with great vehemence, to the notion, which still persists despite modern physical discoveries which might be interpreted as destructive of it, that ideas of basic matter should be determined only by the criterion of chemical simplicity. He agrees that it was easy to discredit four-element theory in its later and decadent forms, as for example that found in Paracelsus, where the elements become mercury, sulphur, salt and so on, with their philosophical attributes virtually lost in a confused form of practical chemistry. Yet he insists that when we call such entities as gold and mercury "elements" we throw away all possibility of generalization. We have merely adopted a more complicated form of old-fashioned atomism. His argument, similar to Lull's, is that the traditional properties of fire, air, water and earth may be abstracted into purely logical properties of wide application. He adds that when we think of matter only in terms of the differences between chemical substances as defined in the table of elements we have given up serious thought for mere classification.

Hegel's defence of four-element theory, which I paraphrase rather baldly from his discussion of "The Elements" and "The Elemental Process" in his *Philosophy of Nature*, goes roughly as follows—

The principle of differentiation into distinct substances is already present in the doctrine of the four elements when it is rationally understood. Rationality demands that we begin with physical principles before we discuss their determinations in specific substances. Only in this fashion can we link together the categories of logic, mathematics and physical science in such a way that their basic axioms do not conflict. Though it is true that empirical physical science must begin with an examination of the specifically determined entity (e.g. the properties of gold or coal), the philosophical conclusions we draw from such discoveries must have an adequate generality.

The "substantial and invariable" diversity of the elements has a physical representation in the transitions from solid to liquid to gas and vice versa. Underneath such representations, though, lie such logical categories as "latency," "dissolution" or "becoming particular." It is because the theory of the elements has such logical depths that it must be retained.

His own descriptions of the characteristics of the four elements are based—though in a manner closer to the Lullian than the Swedenborgian formulation—on space, motion, activity, passivity, sameness and difference. He defines them somewhat as follows—

Air represents *undifferentiated* simplicity as related to space, presumably because air (or any gas) expands to fill with perfect evenness any space into which it is introduced.

Earth represents *difference*, complexity and individual determination, not only as represented in the differences between all solid substances, but in the friability of earth proper and the fact that every particle of earth is different from any other particle.

Fire represents perturbation or inquietude as related to time ("all-devouring time" in the traditional poetic image), thus by extension all *process* and in particular *fluid activity*.

Water represents *fluid passivity* (neutrality) as continuous equilibrium, in the sense that water finds its own level, seeks a state of gravity-controlled equilibrium and responds passively to disturbance. Water also represents *self-identity* (sameness) in its most general form, i.e. every water-drop resembles the others and the characteristics of a small volume of water are like those of a large volume.

So described, his presentation of the characteristics of the four elements may appear somewhat arbitrary, even merely pictur-esque, but, as with everything in Hegel, they are rigorously de-duced from basic premises. Yet there is an argument against Hegel's imagery, if not his reasoning, and this would be that he selects characteristics of the four elements which happen to suit his logic. His imagery therefore has the same faults as the medieval formula-tion. There is no mention of the facts that air like water responds to gravity and seeks its own equilibrium, though in a different way, that the properties of fire and generalized heat are not the same, that a very fine powder will have many of the mechanical proper-ties of water, and so on.

Swedenborg also rejects chemical difference as a *basic* formal category, but does not regard the search for particular chemical properties, which had barely begun (as science) in his day, as "anti-philosophical." He relates his version of four-element theory to physical facts of a truly generalized kind—the facts now dealt with in phase-theories of matter. This means that his version, no matter what revisions, after more than two hundred and fifty years, it may require, still makes sense. Thus earth or "earths" are matter in the solid state, water is liquid-state matter, air is gaseous matter and ether becomes something for which there was as yet no definition, something like "plasmic matter" (fire is not an element in Sweden-borg but a process, with many of its traditional properties trans-ferred to ether). The purely logical and formal qualities which Hegel later finds in complex substances Swedenborg attaches to the first element and its antecedents in the Active/Passive point. This is to make such formal qualities subtle forms of interior matter, not of the complicated and mixed forms of the sensually-perceived world.

I am not attempting to contrast Hegel unfavorably with Swe-denborg. Much less would I wish to join in the chorus of hearty philistine guffaws which Hegel's system has sometimes aroused. The truth is that, for all its flaws, it now looks better than ever.

Even the empirical science against which Hegel was so prejudiced has shown—particularly in biology but not only there—that the study of nature as a system of formal relations must be added to the nuts-and-bolts study of particulars if we are to make any sense out of it. But the problem with his system is that it allows no transition to the world of particulars. To quote W.T. Stace, he adopts—

> ...the view that particular things cannot be deduced; that nature is governed by caprice and contingency; and that he is to deduce only the universal genera of nature and spirit. We cannot even expect, he thinks, to deduce all natural species, for nature runs riot here too, and blindly multiplies species without reason. In the infinite welter of forms which nature produces reason is completely lost. This endless extravagance of natural production is, according to Hegel, a sort of madness, the absolute unreason of nature. And he observes that this so-called "wealth" of nature, her infinite variety, which is so much admired, is in truth far from admirable. It is the "impotence of nature," her powerlessness to keep within the bounds of reason. This mad productivity on the part of nature is a sort of running amok, a Bacchantic dance in which nature revels uncontrolled by reason.[30]

This is an old and defensible philosophical position, with the most obvious antecedents in Greek and Christian philosophy. It is in Hegel an idealist position, but it is not *necessarily* such. Matter, as containing strong principles of spiritual form ("reasonable" to Hegel means "spiritual") is real; but as containing a principle of riot which leads to decay it has a component which is essentially form-defying and hence "unreal." Matter is therefore dual in nature. We do not have to look very hard to see that Hegel is here setting out his own version of the universal catastrophe Christians call "the Fall," nature in a state of sin.

It does not follow, however, that what is contingent, circumstantial and accidental in terms of a logical system is so in the real world. It could just be that it represents an order too complex for logical analysis. Hegel's confidence in his own vast synthesis is too great to allow him to admit this. As a result his system of natural philosophy is unrealistically schematic, more so than the open-ended logic of Lull, which strongly influenced him, though apparently in the degenerate form given it by Giordano Bruno.[31]

Swedenborg falls into a category condemned by Hegel. He regards the infinite diversity of nature as admirable and as part of the Divine Creative Intent. The principle of variety is essential in his logical scheme, though it arises directly out of basic principles which are also essential to the scheme of Hegel, sameness and difference. In spite of this the two systems come together in a number of respects, and among these we must include the fact that both demand a form of four-element theory. Hegel's form, a revision of the medieval and Greek idea, now appears almost whimsically reactionary, and this makes it easy to ignore its firmly rational basis. Swedenborg's form adapts four-element theory to an ancestral form of the mathematical ideas which modern physics has developed to a state of wonderful and difficult refinement. He begins, as he must, with antecedents of this mode of thought in ancient mathematics and philosophy. These two facts alone help to explain why he appears in many places to anticipate modern discoveries, while in others he seems old-fashioned even for his time.

Finally, if the reader has followed me thus far he has probably begun to sense that the elementary particles of Swedenborg have little to do with the specific particles discovered by modern physics, except to the extent that these are representations of laws. His particles are parts of a ladder-image or shell-image of the cosmos, our choice of images depending on whether we think of the order of nature as a vertical or a sphere-within-sphere structure. As parts of a cosmic structure, and as forms typical of their respective realms or kingdoms, they are more like *connectors* and *generators* of forms than like atoms or their parts. They are, so to speak, the reversed or generative whirlpools out of which elementary fields develop. I believe we may think of them as something like "singularities." Certainly Swedenborg knew nothing of one modern idea of a singularity, in which matter contracts to infinite density and infinitesimal volume, as in a black hole. Yet a kind of singularity is seen even when we draw a spiral and find that our pencil lines, at the tiny core of the spiral, grow closer together until they form a black mass. The explanation of mathematical singularities found in the theorems of differential calculus, which I shall not go into, develops this perception algebraically (see Hurewicz: *Lectures on Ordinary Differential Equations*: bibliography).

Swedenborg does not see the singularity as a sink of the energy of an inflowing vortex, but as the source of the energy of an outflowing one. It must therefore have an organized form, with the singularities of complex elementaries containing within them those of less complex elementaries. Here as always we find that he does not go beyond intuitive extensions of the techniques of basic calculus, which he supplements by observation of forms in nature, such as whirlpools.

There is, perhaps, a very clear traditional rationale behind all this. It would immediately explain why his particles resemble, in modern terms, generic atoms. He does not set out the question quite in the way I now shall. Furthermore, having never seen (directly or indirectly) an atom, he is ignorant of one of the two kinds of particle I shall mention. For this reason the following statement must be treated as my own interpretation. I believe it makes the most sense out of his cosmology and it is amply supported by his arguments elsewhere, but it cannot be said that this support is completely unambiguous if we consider only statements in the *Principia*.

Each Swedenborgian particle is typical of a phase state, not of the components of a particular chemical substance. He is therefore imagining a typical gas-particle, a typical ether particle and so on. So far we are sticking closely to what he says. But (my comment) it also seems to follow from this that such particles of a general kind exist as real entities, while the particles of particular substances, which are also real, are derived from them. Nevertheless, they are unobservable. His elementary particles are form-generating entities. Perhaps we only see their multifarious termini.

It is certainly true that the *Principia* seems to support such an interpretation. Not until we reach the last of his elementaries, aqueous vapor (Part III, Chapter X), do we find an elementary which is "perceptible to sight and touch," and even then we see only the *effect* of the aqueous vapor particle, since our organs of sense "perceive effects but not causes."

The problem here is that, because he could not foresee the development of modern methods of observing microparticles, he does not raise the question of what happens when the capacities of our senses are vastly extended. We do not know if he would say that modern techniques may enable us to perceive causes. But I very much doubt that he would.

Here I must cut a philosophical argument very short. I shall merely say that in the reading I have referred to above his elementary particles, as general causes of physical phenomena, are unobservable. All we shall ever see are particular varieties of them, the "termini" of the cause-and-effect chains they represent. They are like the "exemplars" of St. Augustine, which in turn are not unlike Platonic "types." They are generalities in two aspects. They are real generals, because they are created by God. But, from the point of view of the observing mortal human they are mental ideas, which we form by generalization from the objects we see. Such an interpretation would also fit in well with the earlier quotation from the *Notes on Ontology* in which, it will be recalled, he says that "figure is passive in relation to form."

In this reading his basic forms would be perceived only as they were embodied in specific figures, because the senses can only perceive passive embodiments or figures. Much in the *Principia* can be cited to support the above view, but the closely geometrical and mechanical nature of the argument ensures that his exemplars there take the form of geometrical and mechanical generalizations. A more direct reference to exemplars is found in a note in his later work *The Worship and Love of God*. There he says (italics mine)—

This form, which the stars with their universes determine or co-effect by intermixture and harmony with each other, and which on that account is called celestial, cannot at all be acknowledged as the most perfect of all the forms in the world, if we depend only on the view presented to the spectator's eye on this globe of earth; for the eye does not penetrate into the distances of one star from another; but views them as placed in a kind of expanse, one beside another; hence they appear without order, like a heap without arrangement. Nevertheless, that the *form* resulting from the *connecting series* of all the starry universes, is the *exemplar and idea* of all forms, may appear not only from this, that it serves as the firmament of the whole heaven, but also from this, that the first substances of the world, and the powers of its nature, gave birth to those universes, from which, and their operation, nothing but what is most perfect flows forth; this is confirmed also by the distances of the stars from each other, preserved for so many ages, without the least change intervening. Such forms protect themselves by their own proper virtue, for they breathe something perpetual and infinite; nevertheless, they cannot be comprehended as to their quality, except by lower or lowest forms, the knowledge of which we have procured to ourselves from objects which affect the sight of the eye, and further, *by continual abstractions of the imperfections under which these forms labor*. But let us view these *forms* in their *examples*: the lowest form, or the form proper to earthly substances, is that which is determined by mere angular, and at the same time by plane subjects, whatsoever be their *figure*, provided they flow together into a certain *form*; this, therefore, is to be called an ANGULAR FORM, the proper object of our geometry...[32]

He then goes on to discuss forms other than the angular.

The pattern here is that of a continuing contrast between the true forms of things and the modes in which they appear to the eye. In their inmost or highest forms, their figures, or their aspects to the eye, reveal almost nothing: the form is unreadable. Even the lowest forms, the forms of sensually perceived matter, can only be arrived at by abstraction from figure. These forms are real, even when we only perceive them as mental constructions. Their *figures*, the shapes we see or discover in experiment, are not their true forms, but *examples*, that is, imperfect specimens of forms which we can only arrive at by geometrical generalization.

The shapes of his elementary particles, then, represent forms, not figures.

This is not the common interpretation of the *Principia* by students of Swedenborg. It would make him much more of an Augustinian (I will not say "Christian Platonist," which is an oxymoron) than many will admit. The advantage of this reading is that it indicates that, as we approach the level of sensible matter, form becomes more and more like figure, in such a way that ideal particles are close to individual and particular ones, each of which may be seen to belong to a family whose characteristics may be summed up in a generalized diagram. Deep within sensible matter, however, form and figure are not so easily distinguished. A further advantage is that such a reading makes more sense out of the whole endeavour. In the usual reading of the *Principia* Swedenborg is rashly imagining physical particles from "basic geometrical and mechanical principles." But this would be an unreasonable thing to do. In the above reading he is only and always setting out geometrical and mechanical principles, which he from time to time illustrates by examples from the often-mistaken science of his day and relates to a philosophy we know to be his.

The disadvantage of this approach, for all that it is entirely rational, is that it raises another barrier between the *Principia* and the spirit of modern science. To the scientist, such a phrase as "natural philosophy in the Augustinian tradition" does not have a cheery sound. He would probably be more at ease with the common image of the rash Swedenborg, who has undertaken, to quote the conclusion of the astrophysicist Frank Very's appendix in the 1912 edition of the *Principia*, a "magnificent dash into the unknown."

ENDNOTES

1 Swedenborg seems to avoid the word "acceleration" almost as if it were indecent, though he uses the formulas for it. Instead, he speaks of "changes in velocity." I suspect this arises from his tacit quarrel with Newton, which Hegel seems to echo, in a different way, in his own comments on gravitational acceleration (*Enc.*, No. 270).

2 Swedenborg, *Principia* I, p. 152.

3 Swedenborg, *Ontology*, p. 19.

4 Ibid., p. 47. This is the basis of the very profound idea that finites, the "particles" formed by Active/Passive synthesis, are "contingencies" (*Principia* I, p. 148). The relationships of Active and Passive are so complex in their non-geometrical protospace that they cannot be quantified and appear to be random. Thus they produce, as a synthesis, "contingency," which is the third term of Swedenborg's ternary logic.

5 Nicomachus, *Introduction*, Bk. II, Ch. XVIII, p. 1.

6 Swedenborg, *Ontology*, p. 8.

7 Ibid., pp. 8–9. It should be mentioned that Swedenborg's argument here has marked similarities to one developed by the great Renaissance Spanish architect and engineer Juan de Herrera. Herrera designed the Escorial and other splendid buildings. He was a passionate Lullist and his *Discourse on the Figure of the Cube*

develops a symbolic geometry from Lullian logic. Swedenborg could not have known his *Discourse*, which then existed only in a manuscript copy hidden in a Mallorcan monastery.

8 Perhaps a passive may also be thought of as an attractor, as when Thom says (p. 94): "The most simple attractor of a dynamic system...is the generic closed trajectory."

9 Swedenborg, *Principia* I, pp. 116–117.

10 Cohen, pp. 178–180.

11 Boole, *Laws*, p. 253.

12 Ibid., pp. 47–48.

13 Ibid., pp. 247–248.

14 Laplace, *Philosophical Essay*, p. 11.

15 I do not wish to suggest (it would be unjust to do so) that modern advocates of a probabilistic universe are simple Laplaceans. The Swedenborgian scholar and scientist, Charlotte Gyllenhaal Davis, argues that the laws of chance are laws of order and thus represent the workings of Divine Providence in ultimates ("Chance, Evolution and the New Word," *NP* Oct/Dec 1978). For other New Christian views of probability, see "Providence, Chance and Free Will" by Charles H. Ebert in *NP* Jan/Mar 1984; "Probability: A View of Nature" by Gregory L. Baker in *NP* Apr/Jun 1984; and "Communication on Probability" by Dewey Odhner in *NP* Apr/Jun 1984.

16 Swedenborg, *Principia* I, pp. 148–149.

17 Edward Allen has a good discussion of Swedenborg's doctrine of variety in his article, *Variety* (*NP* Jan/Mar 1971).

18 Swedenborg, *The Worship and Love of God*, pp. 187–188.

19 Ibid., p. 222.

20 Ibid., p. 107.

21 Ibid., pp. 212–213.

22 The transition from quantitative to qualitative change, which occurs in the richest and most complex fashion on the level of matter apparent to our senses, is discussed very well by de Gortari in all his books and by Thom (see bibliography). A deeper study of the Swedenborgian doctrine of the discrete and the continuous, of the qualitative and the quantitative, could well begin with his doctrine of the "contiguous" and the "continuous." His quarrel with Newton, which I have only touched upon, rests upon his rejection of the communication of forces, such as gravitation, across a void. There can be no such communication without contiguity and continuity. His doctrine of the world-structure as one of contingencies rests upon this idea (see *Principia* I, pp. 21–25, 40–41.). His logical/mathematical idea of contiguity and connection may be expressed directly in modern mathematical ideas but a thorough demonstration of this cannot be attempted here.

23 The modern form of probability theory dates from Laplace, but Swedenborg would have been familiar with earlier forms of it, in the works of Pascal, Fermat, Huygens, Bernoulli and others. Swedenborg's belief that chance is an expression of Divine Providence is a commonplace of Christian doctrine, and is particularly well expressed by the Jesuit Baltasar Gracián in his *El Criticón*, where Fortune says (Part II, *Crisi* VI)—"I am of God and of His Divine Providence and so obedient to His orders that not the leaf of a tree nor a straw on the ground may move without His wisdom and direction."

24 Swedenborg, *Principia* I, p. 206 et seq.

25 Swedenborg, *The Worship and Love of God*, p. 222.

26 I am not implying that Swedenborg "foresaw" the uncertainty principle of modern microphysics, which had to be discovered by experiment ("scientific prevision" is a meaningless concept). His awareness of the dialectical inseparability of the continuous and the discrete almost certainly arose from his consideration of the dilemma posed by the discovery of calculus, which made it necessary to think of

numbers both as points at the end of a contracting interval and as discrete integers and fractions. Because he was so musically aware, and also from certain statements in *The Five Senses*, I am inclined to think he was also aware of the musical expression of this dilemma, in which a distinct pitch may be reached either as the endpoint of a *glissando* or slide, or as a discrete entity.

27 The Marxist philosopher-scientist, M.E. Omelyanovsky, discusses this matter in a strangely "Swedenborgian" way, though of course without mentioning Swedenborg and in an entirely materialist context. See his *Dialectics in Modern Physics*, pp. 222–228. Again, the similarities are due to those between certain aspects of Hegel and Swedenborg.

28 In a good popular book on the physics of the vacuum (*Something Called Nothing*), the Russian science-journalist, R. Podolny, referring to the Russian nuclear scientist, M.A. Markov, says, "In one of his papers Markov even tried, extremely arbitrarily, of course, to associate the ancient and modern 'elements'. He assumed that strong interaction corresponds to 'earth', weak to 'air', electromagnetic to 'water' and gravitation to 'fire'" (p. 104).

29 Nos. 281–289 and 316 (1817 edition). I have not found an English translation of this edition and have had to refer to a Spanish one, which I therefore list in the bibliography. The section numbers would of course be the same in any translation.

30 Stace, pp. 310–311.

31 See references to Lull and Bruno in his *Lectures on the History of Philosophy*. It is interesting that he takes Spinoza to task for not learning from them: "...Lullus and Bruno attempted to draw up a system of form, which should embrace and comprehend the one substance which organizes itself into the universe: this attempt Spinoza did not make" (p. 287). Lull is sometimes called "the Hegel of the Middle Ages" (Ovejero y Mauri in his introduction to Lull's *El Libro del Ascenso...*, p. lvii), which seems to put the cart before the horse. For a good early twentieth-century study of Lullian logic, see Bové (1908). There have been many more scholarly studies than that of Bové, but his is of value because he was a Lullist of old-fashioned type, a "disciple" completely convinced of the permanent philosophical value of the Lullian method.

32 Swedenborg, *The Worship and Love of God*, pp. 12–13.

3

The Primary Point
and the First Element

Swedenborg's primary particle is certainly much like some inexplicable prevision of a black hole, of the terrifying whirl pools in space which are said to suck in all matter, even light. But it is a black hole *in reverse*, generating matter instead of swallowing it up. So again we come up with those anticipations of modern discoveries which so trouble and excite us when we read him, emotions which, though natural and commendable (we must admire great minds) actually inhibit our understanding. The "black holes" of modern physics come out of forms of mathematical thought Swedenborg knew nothing of. He arrived at his form-generating vortices by quite another route. This route, though it passes through a forest of ideas as confusing as anything to be found in philosophy, is direct and simple when compared to the dizzying zigs and zags of modern mathematical physics. And again, the question comes down to his method. This is, as we have seen, firmly based on Greek mathematics and logic, though developed in a selective and original way. How could a method which appears so old-fashioned to us produce results so modern in appearance, which are nonetheless (we must always keep this in mind) completely of his time?

I noted earlier a reviewer of Swedenborg's *Miscellaneous Obser-*
vations, scandalized that he should base a complete physical theory
on what looked like a naively literal interpretation of Euclid—

> An exact physicist or mathematician will not readily say that math-
> ematical bodies are actually made up of points, lines and planes, as
> these are described by mathematicians; and in all fairness we are led to
> wonder how the author has come to be of this extraordinary and
> incomprehensible opinion...[1]

The reviewer may have been hostile and his summary of Swedenborg's philosophy may have been very coarse, but he came
closer to the core of the Swedenborgian method than many of its
champions have done. He just happens to object, probably more
strongly than academic politeness allows him to express, to its
basic assumption. The method is indeed a formalistic one.

The classical and eighteenth-century definition of matter was
that its primary quality is "extension," that is, the fact that it exists
in three dimensions. Descartes held to this definition in the most
rigorous manner, maintaining that any body which possesses extension and is inert is therefore material, even if it lacks all other
measurable characteristics such as solidity, form, color and so on.
To such concepts as extension and three-dimensionality, Newton
(with whom Swedenborg always seems tacitly to disagree) had
added those of absolute time and space. These concepts were not
exactly new and had often been accepted as ideas apparent to
common sense. Newton made a complete cosmology out of them (by
adding absolute time and space) but he also introduced a new
problem. For in his universe the scales of measurement by which
extension is determined, namely intervals of time and space, must
now exist either apart from matter or at some level of matter
deeper than the more derivative quality of extension. Newton
thought, it appears, that a universe which had no matter in it could
still have space and time. The laws which determine space and
time intervals now seem to be the primary laws of Divine creation.[2]
All natural constants rest upon them. This is what the too-confi-
dent reviewer of *Miscellaneous Observations* refuses to take into
account. He has made up his mind that geometry and measure-

ment are mere human conventions—well and good—but he errs in assuming his opinion is universal. Even Newton thought they were more than that. There are *constants* in nature, not so much fixed sizes as fixed velocities and things related to velocities—the speed of light and sound, the boiling-point of water at sea-level and so on.

Swedenborg often surprises us by the directness of his reasoning. When confronted with a "chicken-and-egg" problem or paradox he adopts a dialectical solution: the chicken and egg determine each other. One cannot exist without the other and neither comes first. Extension and natural velocity-constants determine each other and neither precedes the other, since one could not exist without the other.

As he knew well, this pushes the problem back one step. The duad, extension/constant, must itself be produced by some thing. We must therefore imagine some quality which, though it is not the extension/constant duad, is capable of producing it. Swedenborg finds this in his answer to another conundrum which exercised the natural philosophers of his day: is movement an essential property of matter, as John Toland (1670–1722) maintained, or is it an external force applied to matter, as Newton maintained? Again, he assumes that matter and movement are codependent. They, or more correctly some analogue of them, exist in a world or sphere anterior to or within the sensually-apparent world or sphere of palpable matter in three-dimensional space.

But again his natural solution has pushed the problem back one step. How to define "matter" or an "antecedent of matter" in a world or sphere where no measurement is possible? How to define such a world or sphere when it has no palpable matter within it?

It seems we have reached some kind of barrier or change point here. It is apparent in the words themselves. "Matter" actually means "substance" and its application to atoms, molecules, stones and stars does not exhaust its meaning. We also speak of the matter of a poem. As to measure, the concept of it cannot be distinguished from that of ratio, which word is linguistically related to "rational." Yet we seem continually to be thinking in ratios the components of which are incapable of measure. We do so every time we make a decision about the problems of everyday life. Most puzzling of all, these three apparently ambiguous uses of terms we would prefer to think of as precise all come together in logic. We have the "matter" of a logical argument; the parts of a logical argument are all "material" (essential) to each other; and the whole and parts of a logical argument are all "rational." Are such connections accidents of language or do they point to deep relationships?

Some philosophers and also ordinary men who like to puzzle their heads about such things have reached the conclusion that the barrier referred to above is actually the barrier between nature and the Divine. As we are now in a sphere whose forms are those of human thought alone (as it seems) and as such thought-forms seem to exist *within* the sphere of sensually-apparent matter, then matter must be made of "mind-stuff." It must be the externalized thought of God, which is the "mind stuff" itself. But "natural reason" says no. Such a philosophy does not match the observed facts. If the non-organic world were directly embodied thought then it would act as if it were not merely organized but actively *thinking*. If we avoid this absurdity by stating, as in our time Teilhard de Chardin has done, that the energy of the microcosmos is an *elementary* form of consciousness, something which matures or flowers in man, then either we are materialists using idealist or religious language, or (same implications) this consciousness is so elementary that it is only energy after all. We are back where we started. We have simply reversed the terms in the equation *consciousness=energy*, which belongs to materialism with metaphysical trimmings. And natural reason rebels against the idea that it is forced to choose between an absurd and a materialist position.

Natural reason, in its presumptuous application of banal common sense to high and mysterious matters, then says, "Well, now, it seems there is some process at the root of matter which is much like logic, but which cannot be thought." And though as an eighteenth-century mind it is not familiar with electronic computers, it knows that logic may in theory be expressed in a form of algebra, an obsession of Leibniz and many others. It even guesses that logical operations may be mechanized, as they are in the Lullian wheel, degenerate forms of which are well known in the eighteenth century. Such concentric wheels match logical questions and answers in such fashion that any turn of the interrelated wheels produces logical statements. So it asks the naive question, "Can we imagine something which has a form very like logic, but is not thought, something whose elements may be moved around mechanically, like the symbols of algebra in a computing system or the questions and answers of a Lullian wheel?"

Let me add a byword here about the word "mechanical," which readers of Swedenborg have often misunderstood. Swedenborg does not here refer to the machine as a concatenation of material parts but to the *design* of the machine. A machine to him is first of all a rational *system*. Our contemporary distaste for "mechanistic thinking" should not blind us to this, but it may well do so.

The reader at this point must be wondering what I mean by "natural reason." I shall give my description of it, and move on to other things. The word "natural" here is not of theological import: "natural" is not opposed to "spiritual." I mean "natural" as opposed to "artificial." The natural reason—this was part of Swedenborg's quarrel with the formal logic of his day—rejects the idea that reasoning by artificial rules is superior to common sense reasoning refined by experience and knowledge. Logic may be mathematised for ease in dealing with intricate chains of reasoning but it must rest, as mathematics does, on experience. Artifice must be based on natural form, in logic as in art.

Natural reason always prefers the easy solution unless it can be demonstrated to be erroneous. It says that subtlety and intricacy of thought is not a virtue unless one is dealing with subtle or intricate things. It says also that although nature is in many places unimaginably subtle and intricate there are always two places at which it appears open to the mind and they are both places of generalization. There is the place of generalization of the infinitely small: when we assume that nature is made up of point-particles or undifferentiated particles of vortical or spherical form we can explain many of its very large forms. There is the place of generalization of the infinitely large: when we assume that the largest natural forms tend to the vortical and spherical we can explain many of its very small forms. But it does not pretend that these are, in logic, other than places of generalization. They may be *exemplars* in the Augustinian sense, but exemplars also present themselves, in logic, as generalizations.

In essence, therefore, this mind assumes that nature is rationally put together. It assumes that truly rational structures, no matter how intricate, have readable surfaces and develop in an orderly way from their bases. It does not mind being "superficial." The intricacies of nature ultimately pass into the form of the readable surface, and "superficial" means "of the surface." It maintains that a truly functional complexity can develop only from a well-ordered simplicity. If not, the parts become tangled up very quickly and cease to work together. This mind is thus the simply rational one, but this alone does not define it—it is also the unpretentious one. For, to slightly modify a statement above, it has little respect for those who affect subtlety and profundity of thought by multiplying quibbles about simple things. It maintains that such never achieve real subtlety and profundity because they are so occupied in complicating simple things that they never do get around to considering what is really subtle and profound. The naturally reasoning mind always arouses the contempt of pedantic, falsely subtle and pretentious minds. Thus it finds itself in continual conflict with academic establishments. It is not easy to be a naturally reasoning mind.

We find a number of statements in the *Principia* which undoubtedly offended the *cognoscenti* of the eighteenth century and continue to offend—

> It therefore follows that he who retains all the natural experience of the world laid up in the storehouse of memory, is not on that account a philosopher...[3]

> Whoever supposes the world to be constituted in any other way (*other than a mechanical or geometrical way*—NN) must take refuge in occult qualities, that he may conceal his ignorance and preserve his reputation as a philosopher in the learned world.[4]

> But if anyone is content with devising principles, and is so indulgent to his imagination as not to look for the evidence of them in geometry and their agreement with physical facts; or if he forms to himself a

distinct theory for every series of phenomena, and for every series of experiments contrives new links of connection, and, when his fragile ties give way, endeavors to restore their coherence with clumsy knots— such a one can never be admitted to these oracles. Surely nature will...laugh at him.[5]

And, finally, he declares his allegiance to "a method of attaining wisdom at once familiar and natural."[6]

These are shocking statements to the wise old men of the tribe. They are proud of their capacious memories and they astonish the young men of the village with them, since to the naive it is the same thing to remember and to know a thing. They are experts in occult qualities, in all manner of things which cannot be explained and must be taken on faith. As to distinct theories, why, the more the better. The phrase "clumsy knots" is intolerable to those who feel their rapid improvisations are preventing the universe from tumbling down (clumsy indeed! it is *nature* which is clumsy!) And— well—as to "wisdom at once familiar and natural," what is it but the opinion of the crowd?

It is no wonder that so few academics take Swedenborg seriously.

We have not yet examined how Swedenborg resolves the question raised above, "Can we imagine something which has a form very like logic, but is not thought?" It is here that his theory enters into its true complexity and it is here that he develops the idea of the material point which so annoyed the reviewer of *Miscellaneous Observations*. The following summary will give only a crude idea of Swedenborg's reasoning; to obtain a better understanding there is nothing for it but to read his books.

To develop this form of natural logic he begins, as we have seen, with two ancient categories, the Active and the Passive. In the categories of Aristotle[7] these are not given any special prominence, but older schools of Greek thought—a topic to be considered in more detail later—considered them to be of primary significance. In the simplest terms, which merely recapitulate the meanings of the words, the Active is that which acts, the Passive is that which is acted upon; but, as we have seen from the definitions in the last chapter, they are much more interesting entities than this would imply. What is of import now is the manner in which Active and Passive resemble the True and the False in more familiar terms of logic. Remember, it is a close resemblance between fundamental binaries which we are looking for, not an absolute identity or a cause-and-effect relationship between Active/Passive and True/False.[8] Indeed, Swedenborg does not compare Active and Passive to True and False in logic, nor does the word "logic" appear in his discussion of the primary point. But this is because a modern dialectical logic of nature of the kind familiar to us through Hegel and the Marxists had not yet been developed.

It does not seem extravagant to say that a dialectical logic of nature in its modern form was invented by Swedenborg. The powerful if cumbersome logic of the Catalan philosopher and poet, Ramon Lull (1235–ca.1313) had by now (outside Mallorca) degenerated into a cultism on the fringes of Franciscan thought or an apology for alchemy. Yet one may also say that this invention was without issue. The Hegelian system, one of the greatest works of the philosophical mind, does show much influence from Renaissance adaptations of Lullism (Hegel gives no indication of direct familiarity with the works of Lull himself) but shows no Swedenborgian influence I can trace. We may find a strong relationship between Hegel and Swedenborg, and between both and Lull, but it arises from thought on a common *double* substratum (Augustinian and Neoplatonic) rather than on a traceable influence of one on the other. In other words, all were doing dialectical logic on a traditional base and doing it well, but in the service of different ideologies. Thus Hegel, in this instance also like Spinoza, relates determination of physical and other qualities to negation. To quote Stace's fine summary of Hegel's thought, "to say that a thing is green limits it by cutting it from the sphere of pink, blue or other-colored things" and "this limitation is the same as negation."[9] In the *Principia*, determination of physical qualities is also the result of limit, specifically the limiting operation of the Passive. Though it would be quite false to say that the Swedenborgian Passive is the Hegelian Negative, the resemblance between the two is not trivial, particularly when we remember that Hegel's use of the word "negative" has very little to do with its use in ordinary discourse, relating rather to such ideas as resistance, the contrary and the different.[10]

Yet Hegel and Swedenborg would have disagreed, and that very strongly, on the position of logic in the hierarchy of thought. To Hegel "logic is the science of the pure idea" and "the absolute form of truth, or, to state it better, the pure truth."[11] To Swedenborg it is a form of mechanics (i.e. systematics) and geometry, so much so that he does not even refer to logic by name but insists, when to our mind he is doing dialectical logic, that he is discussing purer and more refined expressions of mechanics and geometry. And his logical concepts very quickly descend into a form of fluid dynamics, the dynamics of simple fluids. Hegel would have found this an intolerable betrayal of the ideal; more generally idealists (some of whom have been Swedenborgians by allegiance) have found Swedenborg's science as offensive as materialists have done.

To understand how the Active and Passive develop into a world of forms, it is helpful to consider the former as a state of perfect fluidity, the latter as one of perfect viscosity. This is justified because the *Principia*, after the discussions of the first and magnetic elements, which are fluid in a general sense, is entirely a theory of matter in its obviously fluid states—plasmic (ether), gaseous (air), mixed gaseous and liquid (water vapor) and liquid (water). Thus he says: "The elementary kingdom comprehends all those substances which are fluid of themselves and by their own nature, every particle rejoicing in and thriving by its own peculiar motion and elasticity. A group of these constitutes an element, such as air or ether, or others still more subtle, which we shall hereafter investigate in the course of our *Principia*."[12] The development of solid forms is dealt with only briefly, at the end of the book, where a further treatment of this state of matter, which was never written, is promised. In the earlier parts of the book a more general or ideal form of fluid motion is presented. "It is a natural or physical truth," says Swedenborg, "that things finite are generated by fluxion and motion, and that without this nothing which is the subject of geometry could exist."[13] The word "fluxion" here refers not only to the flow of a physical element but to the differential calculus, in his day called "fluxions" as dealing with the rate of variation of a fluent quantity. "Flow" is the characteristic form of movement of all his elements and particles and the word occurs throughout.

Perhaps the rationale of a statement made earlier—to the effect that the *Principia* is much richer than it appears—is beginning to emerge. Swedenborg's diagrams have a static look—tiny balls with smaller balls inside them. But they are complexes of enormous forces, forces which nobody had imagined up to his time.

It is useful, then, to think of the argument of the *Principia* as developing from an early form of fluid dynamics. Swedenborg was anticipating something which would begin to develop much closer to his time than modern mathematical physics. This was classical hydrodynamics or fluid dynamics, which influenced early electromagnetic theory and has developed into modern continuum mechanics. If Swedenborg anticipated new or recently modern ideas on the structure of the micro-world, it seems most fruitful to place these anticipations along the line which runs through classical hydrodynamics to continuum mechanics or the mechanics of continuous media. Any attempt to judge the scientific value of his ideas must begin with his considerable extension of fluid dynamics as then understood. Of course, only a skilled mathematician or physicist could conduct such a study. Yet I do not violate my amateur status by making this statement since the dependence of Swedenborg's theory upon various formalizations of fluid motion is or should be obvious to everybody and he himself points it out. At the same time, since the mathematics necessary to such formulations had not yet been developed,[14] Swedenborg had to rely upon pictures and verbal descriptions of forms seen in the mind's eye. This is probably why some have thought of the *Principia* as a form of scientific poetry rather than as a truly scientific or philosophical work.

There is a sense in which hydrodynamics is a very old science. The measurement of water flow, on which depended the fertility of the land, was a matter of essential knowledge in the great irrigation states of ancient Egypt and Mesopotamia. Nevertheless, modern hydrodynamics in mathematical form could not exist until the discovery, after Swedenborg's time, of an efficient method of measuring the rate of flow of a liquid in the formulas of calculus. The method of his time, which was an ancient one, used geometrical diagrams to illustrate the time it takes such and such a volume of water to flow down a certain gradient.

It is commonly said[15] that modern hydrodynamics is based upon Daniel Bernoulli's general theorem for the motion of a perfect fluid, that is, a fluid in which friction and viscosity are not taken into account. This theorem was discovered in 1738, four years after the publication of the *Principia*; the work of the other great pioneers of hydrodynamics, Euler and Lagrange, was also published after 1734. There are two reasons, however, why we may not make a perfect fit between Swedenborg's form of hydrodynamics and the early classical form of Bernoulli, Euler and Lagrange. The first is that Swedenborg's realism would not have allowed him to accept the simply physical concept of an ideal fluid in sense-apprehended space, influenced by gravity. He would have said that the concept of an ideal fluid must begin in ideal space, where gravity does not yet exist, and that a fluid influenced by gravity, even if only by gravity, is not an ideal fluid at all. The second is that the pioneers of the science were concerned with the flow of water in pipes, canals and natural streams. Swedenborg wished to apply concepts of fluid motion to the inner forms of matter, which he conceived of as flowing in vortices and in sectional and compounded forms of vortices. Fluid vortices would not be mathematically analysed until much later. They are characterized among other things by the fact that they cannot be produced in an ideal fluid, because they are the result of viscosity and other factors which the theory of ideal fluids does not take into account.[16] So Swedenborg's finite forms are not ideal, in the sense of the word in classical hydrodynamics. They have something analogous to viscosity.

Now viscosity in ordinary language is the stickiness or thickness of a liquid. In the language of physics it is the property by which a liquid resists change of shape or of arrangement of molecules, a form of internal friction. We may say that, while the perfect fluid of classical hydrodynamics is based upon the concept of perfect frictionless flow without viscosity, and introduces viscosity as a complicating or inhibiting factor, the perfect fluid of Swedenborg is a duad, in which viscosity and fluidity, like chicken and egg, cannot exist without each other. This increases logical and representational clarity, since we can hardly imagine even an ideal fluid which encounters no resistance, but can easily imagine one which does. Yet it leads to great mathematical problems, since the relationship between flow and viscosity, still difficult to quantify, was practically impossible to quantify with the mathematics of Swedenborg's day.

Swedenborg's idea of an entity which is at once a particle and part of an elementary fluid "field," which seems to anticipate quantum physics and the famous wave-particle dilemma, should similarly be related to antecedents in his time or just after it. The ideal fluid of classical hydrodynamics is infinitely divisible, because it is made up of myriads of identical particles which are in constant movement and collision. It may be treated as a homogeneous continuum because these movements, it is assumed, cancel each other out. Swedenborg's theory is more complex than this but it is based on the closely-related idea that a large body of a homogeneous material may be treated in the same way as a homogeneous particle, the relationship being so close that we cannot say if a homogeneous particle of a homogeneous medium is a separate entity or an inseparable part of the medium. This part of his theory was one of the main causes of confusion among those who read him in his day and throughout the nineteenth century, just as the wave-particle dilemma—the fact that an elementary entity may appear now as a point-particle, now as a wave—puzzles us today.

Yet—and the same comment applies to Swedenborg's theory as to the modern discovery—we are perfectly familiar with such problems in logic. We have the very old problem that when we are considering the whole as the sum of discrete parts we are dealing with a different set of structural relationships than when we consider the part a division of the whole. Yet the entity does not change, only our point of view. If we consider the elementary particle as a sum of discrete parts, like a diagram of detached parts of a flower in a botany text, showing petals, sepals and stamens side by side, it is a waveform made up of a point and the discrete positions it occupies. If we consider it as a point with internal parts, like a blurry picture of the whole flower, we have a continuous waveform made up of superimposed and interacting smaller waveforms, and, because the form is nothing but movement, we cannot find distinct point-positions within it. The conundrum may be put much more subtly and precisely and in terms of the most daunting mathematics, yet it is apparent even on the everyday level. What puzzles us—perhaps "frightens" is not too strong a word—is that the "wave-particle" dilemma presents us not only with a problem which may be *interpreted* as a logical one; rather it seems the very *embodiment* of a logical problem, as if we were looking at a piece of logic illustrated by computer graphics. Some Marxist logicians treat it as just such a problem. Yet we are looking at something real.

A good introduction to Swedenborg's idea of the relationship between the particle and the fluid field of which it is a part may be found in his discussion of magnetic declination.[17] From this discussion we take only a small part of the argument. Swedenborg compares two figures. In the first figure two identical balls roll down inclined planes of differing height, colliding at the bottom. They are flowing down in response to gravity, but the diagram is meant to illustrate a force operating in any direction. The right-hand ball, rolling from a greater height, is less deflected from its course than the second ball. (If we read "particle" for "ball" nothing is changed.) In the second figure the two balls are replaced by identical volumes of water, flowing, as before, down inclined planes of differing height and colliding at the bottom. Similarly the right-hand volume, descending from a greater height and with greater force, is less deflected from its flow-path than the second; but in this case the bodies of water mix and the result is not two entities flowing in different directions but a combined waveform whose flow-path is closer to that of the right-hand volume. Here Swedenborg has arrived at the notion of combining waveforms, which we are familiar with in electricity and acoustics.

FIGURES 2a AND 2b

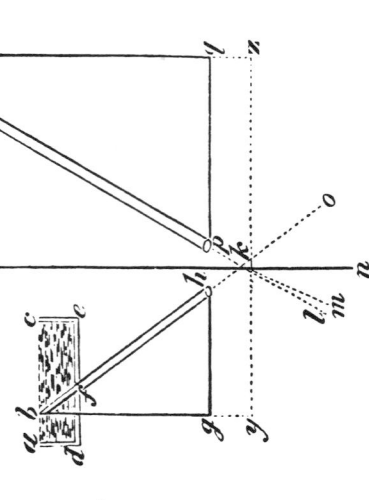

2b

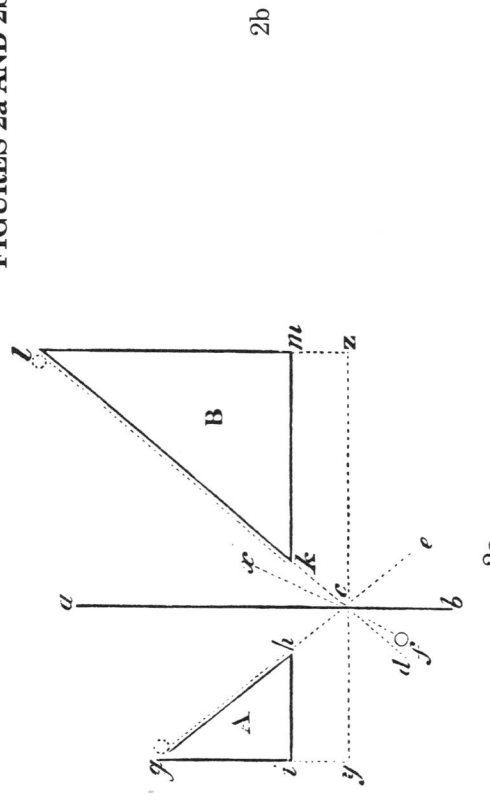

2a

Figures 2a and 2b

From the *Principia*: Vol. II, p. 64 (here 2a) and p. 65 (here 2b). In 2a, A and B are two oblique planes, the vertical of B being greater than that of A. We assume that two little balls are allowed to roll down each of these planes. To simplify the diagram it is assumed that the balls continue moving in space in a straight line after they have left the surface of the incline, rather than describing a parabola, as they would in fact. The ball rolling down plane B continues to move in space towards *d*, while the ball rolling down plane A moves in the same way towards *e*.

Now let us assume that they collide in space at point *c*. Then the ball rolling with greater force (down plane B) will be deflected, after this collision, from its straight-line course and will follow the line *kcf*.

In 2b we have two tanks of water, one higher than the other, and tubes running out of these tanks take the places of the inclined planes. The stream of water flowing with greater force, which by itself would continue in space, having left the tube, along line *pkm*. In this case, however, as the paths of the two volumes of water visibly merge, we get one agitated body of water, with the major force-component moving along line *pkm*.

Swedenborg may compare water (which is a waveform) with a ball (which is a particle) because "water is an element, and it is of the nature of an element that we treat." He means we are dealing with the nature of a fluid and homogeneous medium. It would be completely extravagant to say that Swedenborg has anticipated the wave-particle dilemma of modern physics, but he has encountered something like it on the macro-cosmic level and has assumed that it must exist on the microcosmic level as well. This is an insight of natural philosophy rather than of science proper.[18] It seems that Swedenborg is making a great leap between an early form of hydrodynamics and a transformational logic—a so-called dialectical logic—of nature. But the leap seems more of a reasoned connection when we consider a phenomenon known in fluid physics as the boundary layer, an expression of viscosity and other factors which change the uniformity of liquid flow.

Swedenborg was aware of the phenomenon of the boundary layer in liquids though he describes it in unfamiliar terms: "the particles of water do not possess an even and uniform surface, but one which by contact coheres with those which are in proximity with it."[19] This somewhat archaic mode of description should not deceive us, however, since he has a great practical understanding of flow-phenomena. It is followed by a statement which sounds much more modern.

> For instance, water exerts a pressure proportioned to its depth and also to its area; this pressure is exercised equally in all directions; the particles are put into modulated states and circular undulations; these undulations may be formed within the sphere of another undulation; not to mention many other particulars which we see verified not only in other fluids, but also in every liquid and every volume of every hard and liquefied body. It appears then, that we cannot consider the aqueous particle as any other than a kind of hard body rendered fluid by an extremely small degree of heat; for there are some hard bodies which become liquid by a smaller, some by a larger and more intense degree of heat: water commonly yields to the smallest degree, which softens its rigidity and causes it to flow as a liquid.[20]

This theory extends into a theory of turbulence and may thus be related (in an eighteenth-century context, of course) to what is now called chaos theory, with the difference that Swedenborg's universal vortices are the very form of order, while the vortices of modern turbulence theory are considered to be built up at random.[21] This raises a problem for the modern mind, because Swedenborg approaches the vortex from a philosophical position diametrically opposite to the modern one. In the *Principia* the vortex is a geometrically ordered entity and it develops from the transformational logic of inner nature. It is not a probabilistic or random form, as it might appear when we consider it an *effect*, looking from outside in. The relating of modern chaos theory to information theory has produced the aphorism, "Chaos is the creator of information";[22] but the ordered primal vortex of the *Principia* is also the creator of information. The universe of chaos theory is probabilistic; the universe of the *Principia* was Divinely created. Yet, when such opposition is precise or nearly-precise, analyses proceeding from opposite assumptions often resemble each other as mirror-images do reality. Swedenborg's binary logic produces structures similar to those produced by binary probability theory. Such resemblance of opposites is a very old phenomenon. The Chaos or universal matrix of Graeco-Roman and medieval physics could be and was seen in two different ways. Early materialists could see it as a completely unordered and turbulent ocean of potential forms which came together by chance. Some of these combinations, possessing inherent stability, survived, "the survival of the fittest" on a cosmic level. Others, ephemeral and unstable, lasted only a short time. Ancient Chaos could also be seen as a mysterious and inaccessible realm of primal matter, seemingly without order only because we do not understand its laws. God or the gods, working in this incomprehensible realm, had created the forms we know out of the four elements, the first ordered elements of Chaos which we can perceive by reason. In other words chaos could be pure turbulence or pure potential order.

For his part Swedenborg would hold that chaos was a realm where Divine law operated, though he would also hold that we can at least begin to understand its laws. The thought of the Divine, as it is in the Divine, is and always will be inaccessible, but this thought, as it descends into material form, does become accessible at a certain level. This is because material forms may be apprehended by the senses, or seen in geometrical extensions of sense-observation. The accessible aspect of the Divine creative impulse or intent is a form of natural logic, evidenced in the forms of nature. Thus the following words are no flourishes of conventional piety—

> The philosopher sees, indeed, that God governs His creation by rules and mechanical laws; he may even know what these are; but the nature of that Infinite being, from Whom, as from their fountain, all things in the world derive their existence and subsistence—and what is the nature of that Supreme Intelligence with its infinite mysteries—he in vain strives to know.

> Nature is only a word which connotes all the actuating forces proceeding from the first motion of the Infinite till the world was completed; with this first motion it begins; and as this is produced by the Infinite, so also is nature.[23]

With this in mind we should perhaps be a little less shocked that Swedenborg's picture of the inner principles of nature should combine logical principles with concepts which seem to be derived from a subtle form of fluid dynamics.

The chief characteristics of a boundary layer are much easier to describe than to quantify. Most of us have observed many of them without thinking about it and hydraulic engineers are always dealing with them. When a flowing fluid meets a solid boundary or when it encounters some force or other entity which impedes it or slows it down, there develops a thin boundary layer between it and the boundary, or the impeding force or entity. This layer will move more slowly than the body of the fluid; it will have drag and increased viscosity. There now exists what is called a "no-slip" condition, which means that the part of the fluid which is directly against the boundary has generally the same velocity as the boundary. (This holds only partially in fluids of very low density, so called rarefied fluids, whose velocities are only slowed by the boundary.) This velocity can be zero in the case of a stationary boundary such as a pipe wall; here there is a very thin layer of stationary fluid against the stationary boundary. This is not usually taken into account by the designers of pipe systems: its width is measured in hundredths or thousandths of an inch, but it is there.

The difference in flow between the boundary layer, the layers next to it and the rate of flow at the center of the stream of flowing liquid generates *vorticity* at the boundary layer itself.[24]

Swedenborg, though, is imagining a vortex-form in which the energy of revolution is spreading from the center outwards. His idea is simply and generally expressed, since in his time a detailed mathematical treatment was not possible. He says—

> If the motion is greatest in the centre, and least in the circumference, then it must gradually diminish as it passes from the centre to the circumference. The diminution of this motion cannot be otherwise than according to a simple proportion; because it arises only from the resistance of the moving points, and since there is a consecutive series of these points from the centre to the circumference, the motion is retarded by this series at every successive step; and inasmuch as the cause of retardation and resistance is simple, the variation of velocity is simple; so that the greatest velocity is in the centre, it is less in the circumferences, and least in the ultimate periphery.[25]

It is imagined that the vortical fluid is a series of moving points, each of which offers resistance to motion. This resistance is a cumulative drag on the velocity of the motion, with the effect that this velocity decreases as we move from the center of motion to the circumference. But here, we must remember, he is describing the movement of a fluid in everyday space and time, in which we have friction, gravity and a number of other forces operating to slow down the particles.

In the primary particle and the first element there can be no friction or gravity. Yet there must be *something like* a cumulative drag, *something like* differences of velocity between the center and the circumference. Otherwise the primary movement would not be contained in any way. It would not produce a form. It would instantly fill up whatever space-like thing it was working in. There would be no differences in velocity and therefore no difference between one part of its motion and another. There would only be an

undetermined thing which is everywhere like itself, filling an undetermined thing which is everywhere like itself. It would resemble,
though it would not be, equal nothingness in equal nothingness.

We must pay attention to the manner in which he describes drag
due to friction. He is really seeing it as a generalized force of
resistance which spreads inward from the circumference. It is as if
the circumference were a boundary which was radiating back shells
of "boundariness" into the outflowing fluid, shells which grow weaker
in their constraining effect as they approach the generative center.
The boundary force is strong at the circumference and weak at the
center. The generative force is strong at the center and weak at the
circumference. He has made logical opposites out of center and
boundary, and the effect of their working together is a ratio of
energy and resistance.

Now, as indicated above, Swedenborg was aware of the boundary layer phenomenon, though he described it in such unmodern
terms as the "cohering" of water-particles to the surface over which
they flow. His idea was that the flow of any fluid, no matter how
rarefied or subtle, must have a boundary. Otherwise its velocity
would be infinite, and this is to say what I have already said. That
is, the fluid would not be in flow and would not indeed exist, since
there cannot be flow if a fluid instantaneously fills every space or
analogue of space in which it is. Thus the "ideal fluid" of the
Swedenborgian system, no matter how rarefied, cannot have only
one quality, that of flow; it must have a second quality, that of
boundary, which in the end amounts to resistance to flow. The
Active requires the Passive.

The quality of flow, then, is what he calls "the Active"; the
quality of resistance is what he calls "the Passive." Neither can
exist without the other. Actives, to refer to the definitions at the
end of the first chapter, "have only what is formal; hence they
cannot be called material." (Remember that "formal" does not mean
"emptily conventional" or refer only to mathematical assumptions;
it relates to the Augustinian or Platonic idea of forms as exemplars
or types). The Passive, as pure limit, cannot exist on its own either.
But when the Active flows into the Passive, into a system of

universal limits or boundary layers apart from space and time (space and time do not exist at this stage of the argument) it generates an infinite vorticity.

At this point we encounter one of the most difficult parts of the *Principia*. In the following I have simplified it as much as I can, but at the cost of greatly coarsening a refined argument. Nevertheless, some attempt at visualization must be made, and perhaps no harm will be done if the reader does not forget that, in his discussion of the primary point, Swedenborg is raising questions much more fundamental than I can tackle here. The basic question might be said to be—

HOW DOES A LOGICAL SET GENERATE A SPIRAL?
I

An Active which is finite must by this definition have a limit, because energy must be contained. If it did not have a limit it would be an Infinite Active. It would not only be outside space and time but outside any limitations we may imagine as eventually engendering the limits of space and time.

Let us define this limit as something "passive." A limit just sits there, without any force of its own.

At the very core of matter time and space do not exist. We have only two things. We have the Active and there is only one thing we can say about it, that it flows. We have the Passive, and there is only one thing we can say about it, that it bounds the flow, creates a limit.

There is really no way we can represent this state of primal matter in a picture or a three-dimensional form. Without time and space there is no three-dimensional geometry and pictures are not possible. We can find a symbol, though. In this symbolic representation we shall say that the Active flows in all directions, to use a geometrical analogy, at the same time and with the same force. The limit of this operation is everywhere the same in relationship to the forces of the Active. Therefore the Passive receives the Active at all points, at the same time and with the same force.

Our geometrical symbol now takes the shape of a sphere or a circle. Actually the circle will do just as well as the sphere in our simple representation. In this symbol the center is the source or the Active, the circumference is the limit or the Passive. We now have two things: Active as center and Passive as circumference, and whatever lies between them is a ratio of their relationships, as in the ordinary geometry of the circle, even though we cannot measure the ratio.

II

We are in a world without friction. The Passive cannot absorb the energy of the Active, since it possesses no mass nor any analogue of mass. Therefore it cannot absorb or transmute energy, that is, it cannot act like a physical substance which may change energy into heat. It can only reflect the energy it has received, altering it in terms of the only property it possesses. For "the Passive" by itself is only a name, and when we call it a "limit" we cannot say that it has this quality entirely on its own. It would not be a limit unless there were something to limit. And of the Active we may say the same. "The Active" is only a name. We have said that it flows but this cannot be an isolable quality either, because it does not flow unless there is a Passive, something to limit it. In other words, Active and Passive only exist in relationship to each other.

What then is the *essential logical property* the Passive possesses? It is that of being different from the Active. And the corresponding property of the Active? It is that of always being the Same, of being so much a representation of Sameness that it is, as we have seen, always equal to itself unless it is limited. Unlimited, it would be absolute self-identity, which would show up in all measurements as nothing at all, though really it is the deep root of equilibrium. We say that it flows everywhere with equal force, but on a deeper level of abstraction we should say that it creates a universal sameness of motion. On this deepest level of matter, action and equilibrium ("stillness") are *the same.*

So when the Active reaches its limit, and is redirected by the Passive (it would be something like reflection), every direction of this newly-defined energy, this Active/Passive composite, is different from the direction of the original energy. This is because we are using a geometrical figure, a circle, as our symbol, and in this symbol differences can only be symbolized as differences of direction in the rebound off the wall of the Passive. If we imagine the original force as redirected towards the center it can reach it by any path *but* the path traversed by the original ray. At the same time it must certainly reach the center, since otherwise there is no reflection.

FIGURE 3a

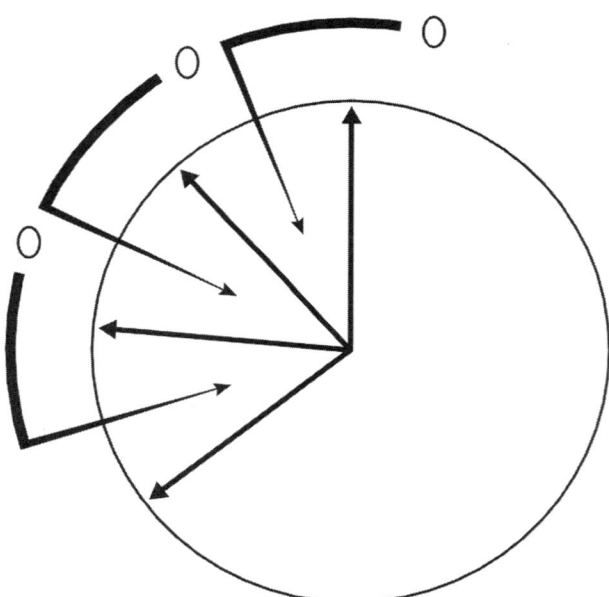

Figure 3a

The crooked arrows are intended to indicate that the observer, O, is moving from one point on the circumference to another, progressively around the circle. He is thus revolving but, as there is no time and all movement is "instantaneous," he appears to be standing still. Note that this diagram (mine, not Swedenborg's) has no mathematical or mechanical significance; it is a crude and illustrative time-space analogy of a "movement" in non-time and non-space.

FIGURE 3b

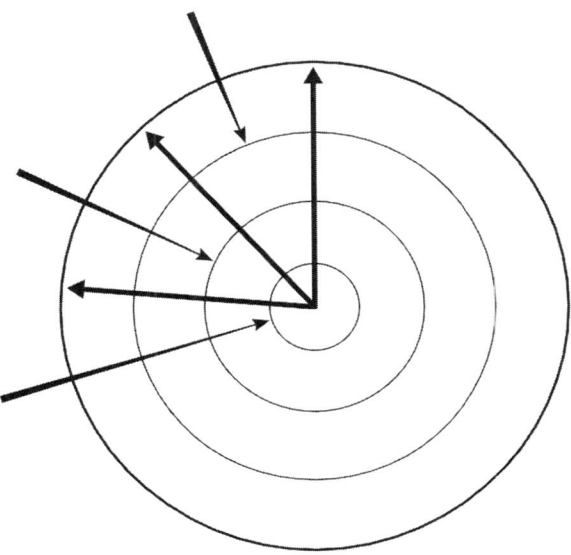

Figure 3b
   Logically, since the paths to the center must be of different lengths, it will seem to the observer that the center is in continual and "instantaneous" motion, so that it actually fills the entire plane of the circle.

In geometrical representation, the effect is therefore as if the returning ray came from a point on the circumference different from that point which was struck by the outflowing ray. The effect is as if the circle were revolving. Certainly it must be in an analogue of motion, since we are dealing with energy and an analogue of velocity.

But note that the reflected ray cannot be of the same length as the original ray, since all the elements of the reflected ray must be different from those of the original ray.

To avoid confusion, since it may appear that we are now dealing with an infinity of possible behaviors, we should again recapitulate the relationship between the Active and the Passive.

III

All we know is the following—

The Active (the Same) is in constant relationship with the Passive (the Different). This relationship we have symbolized as a path or vector of energy going from the Active to the Passive and being reflected.

The Passive reflects the Active in a manner which is totally different, which in effect means that the path of reflection must differ from the original path. This relationship we have symbolized as a returning path or vector which differs in the only ways our circular representation allows, in direction and length of ray. We must not take this representation too literally and imagine that a shorter ray contains more energy per unit of measurement than a longer ray. Difference in energy or intensity is forbidden, as resulting in a diminution of these. We have resistance to flow but not absorption of energy, because the Passive is not matter. The energy cannot be returned with less energy than it had when it was received. Nor can it be transformed, nor, for obvious reasons, can the reflection be irregular or erratic.

The resistance of the boundary here takes the form of a perfect elasticity (a key Swedenborgian term), in which the Active force is perfectly reflected. Differences of energy can only develop later *and they will become the basis of matter*. For matter is nothing other than a complex of differing velocities.

Thus the only imaginable difference is a difference of what we have symbolized as "reflected path."

IV

A difference in the length of the returning ray can only occur if the radius of the circle is continually changing, that is, if the limit or circumference is continually changing. Furthermore, since the boundary or limit is the Different and is all Difference it cannot only be changing in one sense. Nor can it cease to be a circle. The effect of this is that the area of the circle is contracting and expanding at the same time.

FIGURE 4a

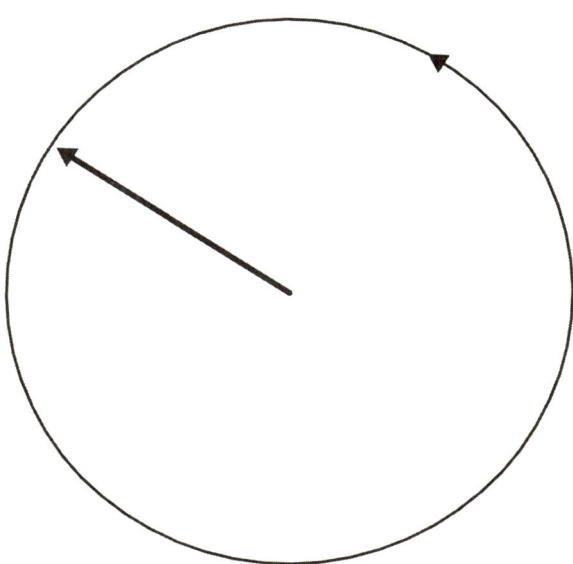

Figure 4a

The arrow indicates at once the observer's "instantaneous" view of the circumference, as if it were a circular wall, and the force flowing out from the circumference to the center, at the same speed as the observer's vector of sight (metaphorically we may say "at the speed of light"). As "force-vector" and "sight-vector" are in synchronization it appears that the boundary is stable and stationary.

But here we encounter a problem.

V

If we place ourselves at the center of the circle and imagine ourselves flowing out to the limit with the outflowing rays, we are entirely in the realm of the Same. Therefore, from our viewpoint at the center of the circle, the boundary also remains the same.

However, if we place ourselves at some point on the circumference, on the limit or border, and look towards the center, we are now entirely in the realm of the Different and the center is also in the realm of the Different. Our position and the position of the center are continually changing and in all directions at once.

FIGURE 4b

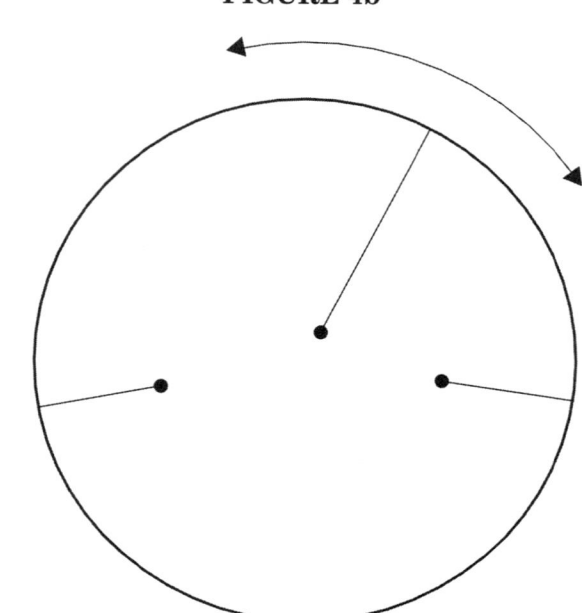

Figure 4b
   We are moving, as the arrow indicates, to all parts of the circumference simultaneously, as in Figure 3a. As in that figure, the center appears to be everywhere at
once, its position to be everywhere "different." The notion that uniform difference
leads to apparent sameness will be familiar to readers of Hegel and other philosophers who begin with a binary pair.

   Those familiar with Greek ideas of Chaos will know immediately where we are in the second case. That is where we are, in Chaos,
But it is a very well-ordered Chaos because we have, conceptually,
two circles which are really one.

VI

   Let us, therefore, imagine two circles. We recognize that our
diagram is taking us farther away from the reality, because there
are not two circles; there is only one. But there is no help in the
matter. We simply cannot imagine how a logical opposition can
turn into a material form unless we imagine the closest material
form it could flow into.

One circle is always the same.

The other circle is simultaneously expanding and contracting. We cannot imagine a circle which does this (at least I cannot). But let us separate the expanding circle from the contracting circle, making a *double circle* or two sub-circles, and first, let us consider the one which is expanding.

VII

What is the best (actually the only possible) visualization of a circle which is continually expanding, whose radii are growing ever longer and striking back at the center at different angles? It is not a circle at all, but a spiral in expanding view (Figure 5a).

VIII

What is the best visualization of a circle which is continually contracting, whose radii are growing ever shorter and striking back at the center at different angles? Again, it is not a circle, but a spiral, in contracting view (Figure 5b).

IX

This is what Swedenborg means by saying that, while the movement of the primary point cannot be visualized, the best way we can think of it is as a form of perpetual spiral, with peripheries unlimited by quantity, whose radii represent pure or total motion which "admits of no degree of velocity." The spiral is "all center" (the Same) and "all periphery" (the Different). He then says (the italicization of "ovum" is mine, and the reason for this will emerge in the second part of this book)—

> But geometry can neither express the effort towards this motion, nor describe its figure, except by similitude. It is incapable of giving any demonstration; for while it is within this point, it acknowledges itself to be not yet finited, nor yet, as it were, put forward or brought forth, in short not yet anything, but only about to become something; and in this

FIGURES 5a AND 5b

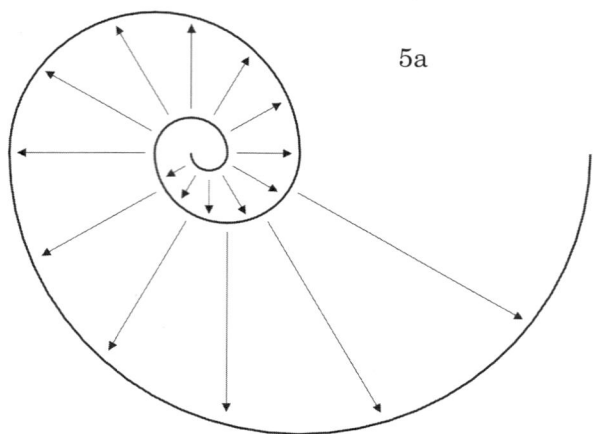

5a

5a and 5b

Again we must note that these are proto-spirals, existing only as conceptual forms. We cannot speak of geometrical or mechanical spiral form in non-time and non-space.

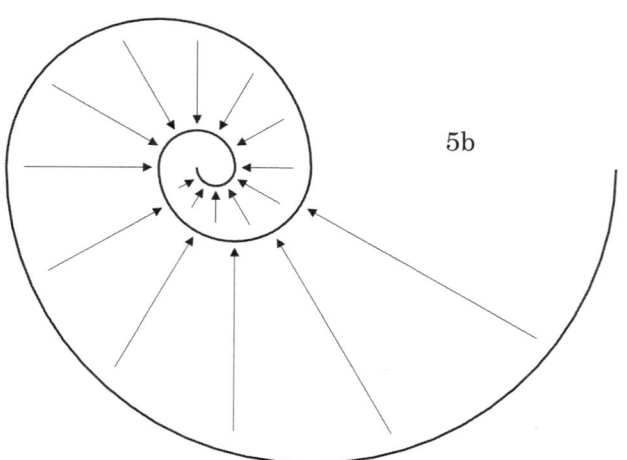

5b

state it lies as it were in embryo till matured; that is, it cannot as yet be analyzed by finite terms or limits, which nevertheless successively arose from this *ovum*. Since, therefore, this point can receive no adequate geometrical demonstration, we must have recourse to the principles and axioms of rational philosophy, and instead of the point substitute an entity, and so proceed to its investigation by the attributes proper to such entity.[26]

All this appears very original, perhaps *too* original. But Swedenborg does not have the conceit of originality. He tells us where his idea came from. It is "the point of Zeno."

ENDNOTES

1 See note 1, Chapter 1.

2 Such a philosophical rather than purely physical belief makes more sense now that we are familiar with the "hidden side" of Newton's thought, that side which led Keynes to refer to him as "the last of the magicians" (de Santillana/von Dechend, p. 9). Newton, interpreting in his own Unitarian fashion biblical passages stating that God created the world "by weight and measure" was one of the first and certainly the most intellectually distinguished of the "pyramidologists." He believed that a "sacred cubit," the ancestor of the profane cubit, was enshrined in the proportions of the Great Pyramid of Gizeh and he set out this belief in a paper, *A Dissertation upon the Sacred Cubit of the Jews* (short title). (Some Newtonians, like the American Jonathan Edwards (*Of Being*, ca. 1719), actually held that space *is* God.) For a discussion of the alchemical roots of his thought, see "Alchemy in Newton's Career" by Richard S. Westfall in *Reason, Experiment and Mysticism in the Scientific Revolution,* ed. Bonelli and Shea, also, passim, *The Foundations of Newton's Alchemy* by Betty Jo Teeter Dobbs.

3 Swedenborg, *Principia*: I, p. 15.

4 Ibid., I, p. 17.

5 Ibid., I, p. 37.

6 Ibid., I, p. 16.

7 Chapter 4, paragraph 1 of the *Categories* (the title was not Aristotle's: he called them "forms of predication").

8 It would be completely illogical to say that the Active *is* the True and the Passive the False. Active and Passive are material primaries, while True and False are opinions or judgments about propositions. But the same binary algebra may be used for both, as we see in the modelling of logical operations in electrical circuits, where the current is "active" when the circuit is on and "not-active" (i.e. passive) when it is off. This binary algebra was invented for logic and we think of it as a "logical algebra." Perhaps a better term will be found in time.

9 Stace, p. 33.

10 Meliujin (p. 106) points out the difficulties which result from the fact that dialectical materialism (but he might also have added dialectical idealism of the Hegelian kind) and formal logic sometimes use the same words in different senses. This applies particularly to the idea of contradiction or negation—contradiction in formal logic signifying the incompatibility between opposing meanings of two logical propositions but in dialectical materialism the *interaction* of objective opposites, as

complementaries. In practice (p. 101) he breaks down the dialectical negative into the three categories of difference, opposition and contradiction, which brings him pretty close, though he does not know it, to the thought of Lull.

11 Hegel, *Encyclopedia*, No. 19.

12 Swedenborg, *Principia*: I, p. 3.

13 Ibid., I, p. 76.

14 A good overview of the state of mechanics in the eighteenth century and earlier may be found in Mach's *The Science of Mechanics*.

15 Russell, p. 74. Russell's text first appeared in 1909 and is closer to classical mechanics in its mathematical procedures than more modern texts such as *Transport Phenomena*, by Bird, Stewart and Lightfoot.

16 Saffman, P.G.: article *Vortices* in *Encyclopedia of Physics*, p. 1097.

17 Swedenborg, *Principia* II, pp. 63–67.

18 Swedenborg here cannot call upon vector theory to help him formalize his idea: it had not yet been discovered. Instead he refers to a "common rule of mechanics" to establish the angles of deflection of right-hand ball and combined flow paths. He does not identify the origin of this "common rule," but it is a version of the mechanics of the inclined plane, still an important part of basic mechanics courses.

19 Swedenborg, *Principia* II, p. 258.

20 Ibid., II, p. 259.

21 Turbulence is described as a "random rotational state of fluid motion" arising from instabilities of momentum in a fluid, and paradigmatically described as "randomly oriented three-dimensional vortex motions." It is said that "turbulence may be considered the natural state of fluids in motion, and indeed most of the fluid of the universe is probably turbulent." (Article *Turbulence* in *Enc. of Phys.*, pp. 1072–1073). James Gleick's *Chaos* is an easily-read study for the layman of "chaos theory" and its relationship to turbulence and other phenomena studied in fluid dynamics. See also an illuminating article, *Chaos*, by Crutchfield, Farmer, Packard and Shaw in *Scientific American* of December, 1986.

22 Gleick, p. 260. The modern scientific approach, which regards "seeing from the outside in" as the only valid one, was attacked by early New Church writers in a vigorous if not always philosophically refined manner. Thus, in a serial publication of 1879, *Words for the New Church* (authors anonymous), it is said that the "hypotheses of modern science are opposite" to the Divine order of things, in which "the true order of creation progresses from the centre to the circumference; that the centre of creation is self-existent, and is an inexhaustible source of life and hence of force, and that from the centre is created the circumference." This is not what Swedenborg says in the *Principia*, where center and circumference are created at the same time. On this basis the authors attack the nebular theory of the elder Herschel and Laplace, according to which "the solar system owes its origin to an atmospheric fluid of vast extent which by successive condensations gave rise to the planets and the sun."

It might be said that "seeing from the outside in" is the scientifically correct point of view if it means proceeding from the known to the unknown. True enough; but the argument here is that the direction of scientific investigation is often confused with the time-order of the universe, as if the known or sensibly concrete existed before the unknown.

Such arguments incite the professorial smile, of course, but this position is an old and respectable philosophical one and is forcefully expressed by Hegel.

23 Swedenborg, *Principia* I, pp. 38–39.

24 The description of the boundary layer is paraphrased from article *Boundary Layer* in *Enc. of Phys.*, pp. 88–89, and Russell, pp. 236–237.

25 Swedenborg, *Principia* I, pp. 118–119.

26 Swedenborg, *Principia* I, pp. 70–72.

The phrase, "except by similitude," probably explains why Swedenborg has been so consistently misunderstood. Only in recent times, with new developments in logic and mathematics, have scientists been able to accept "similitude" as a truly logical category. The confusion over the idea of "geometrical similitude" extends into the past, as we may see in the controversy over the cosmology of the Stoic Posidonius, where we find an Active/Passive circle which somewhat resembles Swedenborg's. See Rist, Chapter 11, *The Imprint of Posidonius*. I find no evidence that Swedenborg had heard of Posidonius and the resemblance is not close enough to indicate direct influence.

4

The Point of Zeno and
the First Element

This is how Swedenborg summarizes the second chapter of his first part: *The First Simple of the World*.

1. There is a primary entity brought forth by the Infinite. Nothing finite can exist of itself; therefore, it must exist by means of that which is capable of finiting, and which is of itself infinite. Therefore composite things originate from simples; and simples from the Infinite, and the Infinite from itself, which is the only cause of itself and of all things. All finite things have come into existence successively; for nothing can be at once what it is except the Infinite. 2. Geometry itself acknowledges a certain simple and primary beginning of its existence, which it calls its own, or the mathematical point. 3. The Holy Scriptures also give us information on this subject and teach us that the world was created by God or the Infinite. 4. Rational philosophy avers that nothing can be or exist without a mode. 5. And if the first simple was brought forth from the Infinite by motion, we are bound to suppose that in producing it there was some thing of Will that it should be produced. 6. The simple is the primary entity existing by motion from the Infinite, and thus, as to its existence, it is, as it were, a medium between the Infinite and the finite. 7. This point is identical with the mathematical point, or the point of Zeno; it is called the natural point.[1]

His reference to "the point of Zeno" is more than a little confusing. At first I believed it referred to the paradoxical geometry of Zeno of Elea, author of such famous paradoxes as that of "Achilles Outraced by the Slow Runner" and "The Arrow in Flight which does not Move." This was the only Zeno whose name was widely known in Swedenborg's day. Surely he could not have intended a more obscure reference, since he does not say which Zeno, out of the four known to us from histories of Greek philosophy and science (the Zenos of Cition, Elea, Sidon and Tarsus), he is referring to. But the following statement forced me to change my opinion.

> With respect to the essential of the first simple, I maintain, that this natural point is the same as the mathematical point, or the point of Zeno. For the world is geometrical or mechanical; nature modifies itself by the laws of mechanism, which are its own laws; wherefore the same beginning is to be assigned to the world, as to geometry. The same point is the first of the world, because it is the first of geometry; or it is the first of geometry because it is the first of the world. Geometry is the law and essential attribute of every individual substance in the world, or of the whole world; and mechanism is the mode by which the world acts or is acted upon; hence the point is common to both, because both flow from the same origin. Thus each acknowledges a certain entity existing before itself, and outside of itself, which it considers as a kind of seed, from which it was conceived, and by which it afterward exists and subsists. Since, therefore, both geometry and the world are derived from the same origin, the same seed, and the same parent, we must conclude that they both proceed from the same point, the difference consisting in this, that the latter point, or that of the world, is called the natural point, while the former, or that of geometry, is called the mathematical point.[2]

This is like a specifically Stoic idea. It was the Stoics, as Sambursky tells us in his fine book, *Physics of the Stoics*,[3] who introduced into mathematics a "dynamic element" which consisted "essentially of a physicalization of geometry by endowing geometrical figures with the elastic properties of material bodies." They held that geometrical figures represent physical tensions and thus they "define the straight line as a line stretched to the utmost." They were condemned by geometers for this: the Neoplatonist Simplicios argued that their ideas "would destroy the essence of mathematics which is static and free from every change and therefore also from tension."

Sambursky says they turned the Aristotelian order upside down "because it was no longer Form that was the ultimate principle which determined and explained everything else, including motion, but motion itself was supposed to explain form. In the 'tensional geometry' of the Stoics the rigid separateness of forms was replaced by a continuum of shapes each emerging from its neighbor through a dynamic principle of variation." This also offended Simplicios, who said, "according to Aristotle tension is not the cause of form (static form: NN), because this would mean that motion and change would become the cause of quality, but quality is considered as having definite measure whereas motion is an indeterminate thing and rather demands to be determined." It is also contrary to Aristotle's doctrine that there is a "primary force which organizes the definite forms and unites them and is at once present in all of them, thus holding the group together."

In this manner, a Greek Neoplatonist, objecting to the Stoic reification of geometry, curiously foreshadows the reaction of the reviewer of *Miscellaneous Observations*, whom we have quoted more than once. And, by the way, it shows how much those have erred who have assumed Swedenborg was a Neoplatonist; here he takes a Stoic position, against the Neoplatonists.

Swedenborg therefore seems to assign a later Stoic doctrine to the founder of the school, Zeno of Cition (his dates are uncertain but he lived somewhat before Euclid). We have little evidence of Zeno's ideas on mathematics, but we do know that he held "that everything that exists must be either active or passive and that it can either act or be acted upon."[4] This notion has a pre-Socratic flavor.

It is possible to find close echoes of some other Stoic ideas in the *Principia* but most of Swedenborg's references to Greek thought are broad and eclectic. His system may not be called "neo-Stoic" either. Only two pervasive trends may be found in his classical references. The first is a bias towards the Augustinian reworking of Greek philosophy. The second is an emphasis on all forms of Greek thought which seem to be "older than Greece," to be derived from the older cultures which were ancestral to Greek culture. Thus Zeno had come from the city of Cition on Cyprus, which contained many Phoenicians, and he was thought to have been of Egyptian origin.[5]

Swedenborg's philosophy is therefore more closely related to pre-Socratic philosophies than to those of the later Greeks. We have no evidence that he went to the surviving fragments. Perhaps his source was unclear as to which Zeno was being referred to. But here ideas are more important than sources. Pre-Socratic philosophy is pervaded by Egyptian and Asiatic influences. Swedenborg is in search of ancient evidences of what he calls "the Mosaic philosophy" and he seeks them out, as did all the learned of his age, in the writings of the Greeks. Thus, for example, we may find an affinity between his thought and that of Parmenides.[6]

Parmenides taught that reality is one and unmovable, with light "as the unmoving heart of well-rounded Truth." We are deluded by the senses into seeing reality as a duad, a network of *positive* oppositions. There is only what exists and what does not. The deeper duad is Being and non-Being, Light and Darkness, which are not too different, actually, from the Same and the Different. Everything—the heavens, the sun and moon and stars—was created out of Light and Darkness.

The cosmos is a vortex, as we see in the following passage.

> For the narrower (rings) are filled with unmixed fire,
> And those that are on them with night, and between rushes a portion of flame.
> In the midst of these is the goddess who guides all things.
> For overall she begins painful death and union,
> Sending the female to mate with the male and conversely again
> The male with the female.[7]

—and again we have the Active and the Passive, often symbolized in tradition as the Male and the Female.

This vortex, as a complete entity, forms a revolving sphere, with the shell of the sphere as the ultimate limit. Yet this sphere contains an infinity of smaller spheres or shells, since there are limits everywhere. To illustrate the first point, in which equilibrium is emphasized—

> But since there is a final limit, it is perfected on every side, like the mass of a rounded sphere, equally distant from the centre at every point. For it is necessary that it should neither be greater at all nor less anywhere, since there is no not-being which can prevent it from arriving at equality, nor is being such that there may ever be more than what is in one part and less in another, since the whole is inviolate. For if it is equal on all sides, it abides in equality within its limits.[8]

And to illustrate the second point, in which interaction of motions is emphasized—

> Parmenides taught that there were crowns encircling one another in close succession, one of rarefied matter, another of dense, and between these other mixed crowns of light and darkness; and that which surrounded all was solid like a wall, and under this was a crown of fire; and the centre of all the crowns was solid, and around it was a circle of fire; and of the mixed crowns the one nearest the centre was the source of motion and generation for all, and this, "the goddess who directs the helm and holds the keys," he calls "justice and necessity."[9]

Some have seen in this Parmenidean vortex-sphere a naive precursor of the Ptolemaic spheres of astronomy.[10] But this would be a mistaken interpretation. We have Parmenides' image of the visible or astronomical universe and it is not like the above. There is no space to discuss it here, but it is well examined by Prier and also by de Santillana (in *The Origins of Scientific Thought*), though the latter would not agree with my argument. What we have here is an archaic form of deep physics, not naked-eye astronomy.

It is not only a form of physics, though, but of logic. Cornford, as summarized by Prier in his beautiful book on the pre-Socratics, says that the sphere of "Being" is graphic and geometrical, lying "between thought—a strongly subjective phenomenon—and objective visual 'reality'." (Prier recognizes Parmenides' belief that thought can be objectively true.)

Swedenborg wishes to show that Greek science is related to the scientific level of Scripture, because both preserved traces of an older revelation, the "Church of Noah." His tendency is to seek out those parts of Greek science which may be harmonized with Scripture, particularly with the creation account in *Genesis*. His vortex theory is of his century, but he is looking back at older versions of it. For example, the Parmenidean account, beginning with the creation of Light and Darkness as a monad in apparent dyadic form— Light as Being, Darkness as Non-Being—is very close to being a philosophical summary of the first chapter of *Genesis*. Some relationship must be assumed, though we lack the historical data to tell us what this relationship might have been.[11]

There is no doubt, then, that the *Principia* has a historical as well as a scientific aspect. Swedenborg believes that at some ancient time there existed a philosophy similar to his, though couched in archaic terms. This raises the troubling issue of "lost knowledge." In their influential book, *Hamlet's Mill*, Giorgio de Santillana and Hertha von Dechend refer to Parmenides' "invincibly geometrical imagination."[12] It is a most attractive turn of phrase but it evades the issue by confusing knowledge and personal idiosyncrasy. We must ask what it means when we find an ancient author "imagining" geometrical ideas which appeared obscure and mystical until the invention of calculus. Is it not possible that he is describing an inherited idea which has not yet been worked out in terms of the geometrical ideas of his own culture? Is the statement from de Santillana and von Dechend not another example of the strange notion that the Greeks, sometimes a single identifiable Greek, invented entire categories of thought?

In this case, we have a description of a sphere which is at once beyond quantitative description and limited in every part (Parmenides) and we can also note an insistence on the formal importance of the infinitely divisible interval (his disciple, Zeno of Elea). Obviously it would be foolish to suggest that the ancients knew Newtonian/Leibnizian calculus as such. But we may ask if they did not have an idea of the limit based on successive approximations. In an interesting old calculus text, the French mathematician, M. Duhamel examined this question from the standpoint of one with a real understanding of the spirit of ancient mathematics. He referred to the ancient technique of reduction to a limit by "exhaustion," and described the particular method of Archimedes, which—

> ...consists of considering, within a quantity, parts of a simpler kind, not fixed like the first, but each capable of decreasing indefinitely in such a way that their sum differs from the quantity in question by a quantity which may become smaller than all given quantities. This is what we express by saying that quantities are considered as limits of the sums of infinitely small quantities, whose number augments indefinitely.[13]

As a mode of calculation, in coarser rule-of-thumb form, this is obviously older than Archimedes, since it is used in calendrical adjustments of the most basic kind, as when the incommensurable cycles of sun and moon are harmonized to yield days, months and years consisting of whole days. The question to be decided is whether the procedure was applied only and always as a "rounding-off" method or was actually formalized to the point where the limit was recognized as a truly mathematical notion. The great scholar, Otto Neugebauer, whose specialty was Babylonian astronomical and mathematical methods (he was less than just to the Egyptians) showed convincingly that the Mesopotamians, at least, must have had some idea of the infinitesimal limit. They had ways of reducing complicated periodic phenomena to combinations of simpler harmonic motions and of determining characteristic constants such as period, amplitude and phase in periodic motions. They understood and used arithmetical and geometrical progressions (which in reverse or diminishing form approach an infinitesimal limit) and "came closer to problems whose importance was again seen only in the early days of the development of calculus."[14] Yet we are not dealing with only one sophisticated system but with at least two. Where the Mesopotamian system was sophisticated in the direction of a very rich complexity, the Egyptian system moved towards a luminous simplicity, about which, and this seems at least partly due to hidden cultural and racial biases, little has been written. Yet without an appreciation of this dual movement of ancient mathematics, its cultural significance cannot be evaluated.[15]

The conclusion must be that some of what we now think of as the theoretical underpinning of calculus was well understood in "ancient times" (we cannot say *how* ancient). It was not gathered together into one discipline and rigorously related to differentials and integrals, which were not used as such. Parts of it were expressed in number theory, much of which we have in Pythagorean form; parts of it were expressed in geometry; parts of it were used in astronomical calculations. Many of these techniques were lost, and some Greek mathematicians (not all of them) were to an observable extent responsible for this regression. Their insistence on a static theory of form (cf. Simplicios, quoted earlier) gave us the invaluable techniques of theorem-and-proof but *also* destroyed or down-graded all mathematical thought of a dynamic kind. The Neoplatonists, with their tendency to think of perfect form as static form, doubtless helped to shore up the Roman Empire as an image of eternal perfection, but they also prevented the development of dynamic thought.

Let us return to the Parmenidean idea that space does not exist as an independent entity, but is formed by the relationships of matter in extension. In this respect, Swedenborg's thought, though not specifically Parmenidean, may be related to it in a generalized way. The primary point, for all that it takes a quasi-logical form, is indeed a form of matter in potency; but the potency is that of generalized necessity (cf. Parmenides' "goddess at the center"), which is to say that it *must* become matter, though not any particular form of matter. It has no extension but inevitably seeks out and realizes forms which have extension. It does not exist in space but seeks to make space. We might describe it as infinitely large and infinitely small at the same time, since it is in a sense neither and both, but out of its workings the infinitely large and infinitely small will emerge. Its realization is the first finite or least substantial. Swedenborg writes of this in terms which have a Parmenidean favor. But, again, his terms are also *avant-garde*, for when he says below that "geometry treats of the variations pertaining to limits" he is anticipating (truly here) the modern idea that geometrical forms may be derived from the operations of calculus.

The least substantial is geometrical; it is limited, but limited in the fewest possible boundaries. This follows from what has been said, since it is the least finite, being finited or limited in its least boundaries. It follows also that it is the least geometrical finite. Nothing is geometrical which is without limits; for geometry treats of the variations pertaining to limits, together with the limits themselves. Geometry, therefore, begins with this first finite; whence this first is also the least geometrical finite.

It fills space, but is the smallest among the finites, or is such that there cannot be anything smaller. Since it is limited, it will, among finites, fill space. If there are more boundaries than one, there must, in this case, be a distance from one boundary to another, or space from one limit to another. This we cannot predicate of a point, which possesses only one limit; unless we predicate it by way of analogy to its internal motion, on which subject we have spoken above.

It is endowed with figure, but figure in its smallest boundaries. This also follows from what we have said. If there is space, there is also figure. If the space is the least possible, then the figure which the space forms, must be a figure in its least boundaries. For a larger figure has several boundaries, since it has to be built up of several points before it is bounded; while a smaller figure is bounded by fewer points. The smallest figure, therefore, is bounded by the fewest and least limits, just as the figure of a point, which is the most simple, has only one limit.[16]

We now have a constant, since the first finites, which are identical, fill space. This constant, however, seems to be unmeasurable. There is as yet no apparent velocity ratio, which can only be determined by the velocity ratios of the first and second finites,[17] and without such there can be no measurement. There are antecedents here which are closer to Swedenborg's time than Parmenides, namely the monads of the later Pythagoreans, Aristotle and Leibniz. To the Pythagoreans the geometrical point was a "monad having position" or "with position added," while Aristotle said "that which is indivisible every way in respect of magnitude and *qua* magnitude but has not position is a monad, while that which is similarly indivisible and has position is a point."[18] Leibniz[19] repeats that the monad has no extension, adding that it has "a certain perfection," but he adopts an idealism which Swedenborg could not accept in calling the monads "souls." Yet we do not learn much in the mere quest for antecedents, since what really matters is whether the antecedent idea is simply accepted or is improved upon. Swedenborg is more rigorous than his predecessors. In effect, he asks the question—How can a monad *acquire* position unless there is a metric ready-made for it to fit into? And if there is such a thing, how is that metric formed? How can a point *acquire* a unique position in space unless space is already defined as a plenum of points? The answer can only be that the point does not "find" a position in space but actually makes space. The primary point—

> ...may be compared to Janus with two faces, who looks both ways at once, or at both universes. On one side is the pure Infinite, into which no human mind is able to penetrate, or in which it cannot discover either a least or a greatest, both being completely unknown, and of themselves identical; on the other side is the finite alone, to which we may have access, through the medium of this point, which partakes in a manner of the nature of both.[20]

A *finite* is an aggregate of active and passive forms. Its passive forms are relatively more concentrated in its massier parts—in its center of gravity and in what we may think of as its shell. It might be said that, in the entire universe, there is nothing but the first finite, since it is the generator of everything else.

The first finite is a geometrical entity because it has limits, but it is limited in the fewest possible boundaries. Yet because it has limits it fills space. The primary point itself has limits as we have seen—boundaries. In the first finite there is a virtual infinity of such points, all related one to the other. When we have limited or bounded things in relationship to each other the intervals between them must also be limited or bounded. For example, if on a flat and featureless plain we erected two circular walls close to each other the distance between the walls would also become a measurable space.

FIGURE 6

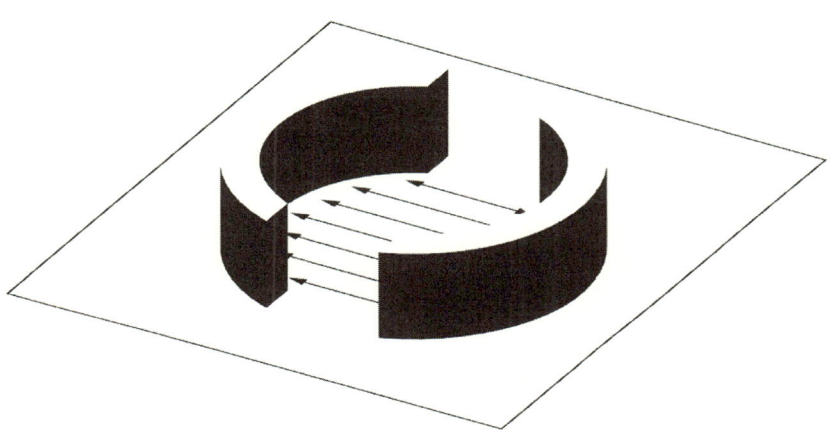

Figure 6
　　We should look at this diagram in two senses. In the first sense the plain can be of any size and the walls can be of any length or angle of curvature. The diagram is then of a purely conceptual or generalizing kind. In the second sense we can imagine that all the parts of this diagram may be measured by size and angle. Once we have done this the entire space becomes measurable, including any element we may choose to add to the diagram—say, towers on the walls or stones lying on the plain.

Of course neither the primary points nor the intervals between them are *in* space. Rather they *create* space. In themselves they are only different from each other and separate from each other and we can define "difference" and "separation" only in logical terms. But when difference and separation become fixed in a material continuum some form of proto-space is created. Also, because everything is in movement relative to everything else, a form of proto-time is created.

Nothing is more deceptive than Swedenborg's description of the first finite. It seems complicated, certainly, but less so than many philosophical arguments. Sentence by sentence it does not seem extremely difficult to follow and we may also assent to it sentence by sentence. But when we have finally worked our way through it we are left with a curiously empty feeling, either as if very little has been said or as if we have understood very little. This seems to be a common experience among those who have tried to understand the structure of the first finite.

In my case I forced myself—it was not easy—to go back over his description. I tried to represent to myself, mentally and on paper, his geometrical argument. The result was disconcerting in the extreme. Sentence by sentence, I had thought I was understanding it because each statement was, by itself, a logical or geometrical statement which nobody could disagree with. But the ensemble was entirely new. That accounted for my feeling of blankness. The argument was leading me into unknown territory, a territory without recognizable landmarks.

The geometrical argument is built entirely on a classical basis. As I have said before, where it is "non-Euclidean" it does not go beyond Greek and later comments on and criticisms of Euclid. Swedenborg's dialectical logic was new but at least it had antecedents in Greek and later thought, and I had the advantage of being able to look at it from a degree of familiarity with the thought of Lull as well as with the more familiar logic of Hegel and his Marxist falsifiers. It was just that nobody had put the two—geometry and dialectical logic—together in quite that way. When they are so put together the elements of classical geometry fall into a new and at first incomprehensible structure.

In other words a truly analytical treatment of Swedenborg's finite would demand a book on its own, and a very technical book at that. Such a book can and ought to be written. But it would serve no purpose to go halfway. A superficial approach would indicate, without proving the point, that the argument is at least broadly logical and self-consistent. An approach in depth would *demonstrate* that it is. But there is no halfway point. One detailed demonstration demands another and if we stop halfway we are left with something most incomplete and unsatisfactory.

Another point I must skip over, with regret, is a crucial point of ideal mechanics. Swedenborg maintains that a revolving primitive point (remember that it makes space but does not in itself occupy space) will not only have an *analogy* of rotatory motion but that parts of it will move at a tilt across the equator, in the shape of an ecliptic band.[21] The argument is clearly set out in terms sufficiently abstracted from the revolutions of bodies in the macrocosmic world but it demands the ideal equivalent of a center of gravity. In this case we have an ideal spiral system with its center to one side. Eccentric motion around this develops an ecliptic form. Again we can see, if we read him carefully, how such would develop out of the ideal mass generated by the ideal energy of the Active and the ideal reflection (difference) of the Passive. But the argument is just too intricate for a generalized study like this.

Perhaps all we need to keep in mind is that the Swedenborgian model demands a form of logical mechanics. In this model we imagine that mental propositions which we now think of in linear terms, that is, as succeeding one another in the horizontal time-sequences of grammatical statement, are somehow revolving around a center. Functionally, though not of course in appearance, the logical form of the model, built upon action and resistance, has analogies with the modern method of representing logical functions in electrical circuits. Swedenborg knew nothing of these, but he had a protomodern idea of the behavior of magnetic currents and fields. And I must add that the "ideal ecliptic band" referred to above is a recurrent theme, and must be kept in mind, at least as a picture.

A detailed discussion of the second finite is also avoided here. It presents the same problem, that of a logical entity which has an analogue of rotatory motion. The necessary points to be made are: i) that measurable ratio begins with the velocity ratios of the first and second finites, as mentioned above; ii) that the second finite, because of the complexity of intertwined Actives and Passives and accumulated limits (we might say it has "more of the Passive in it"), has less velocity than the first finite; iii) that the second finite is formed by the motion of the first finite, in which double rotation (around the equator and around the ecliptic) is a prime factor; iv) that it is still not such a particle as an eighteenth-century person would have called "material."

At this stage of the argument we cannot speak of *the* universe, which has not yet been formed. But we may speak of *a* universe. The quasi-space "enclosed" by the first-element particle (remember that three-dimensional space has not yet been defined) is a universe. It is infinite in the secondary sense of "extending without end," for which meaning of the infinite Swedenborg prefers the word "indefinite." It is nonetheless "enclosed" and there is nothing else. To speak somewhat crudely, we may say that straight lines and their antecedents can exist only on the boundary surface of the quasi-space, where the circumference is infinite (indefinite) and thus appears to have no curvature. This is a crude idea because the case is more subtle than that. Since the sphere does not exist in space we use a figure of speech when we call it "large." It could as well be thought of as indefinitely small. The important thing is that, whether we think of the sphere as large or small or both, it generates an antecedent of straight-line form at the boundary. Swedenborg develops his argument thus, from the vorticity of the component particles—

> There can be no other vortical motion among the particles than such as is in accordance with the figure of each particle, and constantly refers itself to some axis of motion or gyration; likewise the vortical motion forms a certain polar axis. Since all the particles have their poles and axes, according to which they arrange their situations parallel to one another, they also so dispose their general motion that this also shall have a like axis to which to refer itself.

> The circles of vortical motion among those elementary particles which are farther from the centre inflect (*bend*—NN) themselves more and more till they come into a right line with the axis. For if these forms and surfaces, which have a perfectly circular motion, were without an axis, they would then run into circular peripheries and surfaces; since, in this case, there would be nothing dissimilar to drive them out of this course into any other. But if the figures and surfaces are axillary, and if their arrangement is parallel to their axes, they will then recede from

these peripheries, and turn themselves in a direction parallel to their axes; a result which follows from the mechanism of the parts.

This happens until the vortical motion ends in a right line, and so quite vanishes in a direction parallel with the axes of the particles. If the circles, in the course of their progressive motion, gradually turn themselves towards the axes which lie parallel to each other, the motion passes from an oblique to a rectilinear direction, or to an arrangement the same as that of the axes.[22]

The relationship which makes possible this orderly arrangement of continuous parts is that of equilibrium. Two or more ideal or physical bodies, in ideal or physical motion relative to each other, must be capable of arriving at a state of ideal or physical equilibrium. It is the single property of equilibrium, the mean of countless other properties, which enables his ideal figures to extend themselves into the world of space and time we know—

> Equilibrium is the principal means by which two things in motion can be kept in perpetual conjunction. It is by equilibrium that they come into that arrangement, and by equilibrium that they are preserved in it. If this equilibrium is not most perfectly exact, the bond of connection is broken, and the composition, as such, perishes. All concordance, agreement and unanimity is therefore the result of equilibrium. On the most perfect equilibrium depends the perpetual preservation of arrangement and form. Equilibrium is the third or fourth analogue or proportional which results from the degree of motion in two or more bodies. A product of this kind cannot be obtained by the analogies of the antecedent motions except by means of space, extension, arrangement and form; all of which are present if equilibrium is obtained. The essentials, therefore, of equilibrium are the same as the essentials of two or more motions from which is obtained a product which exists only from essentials that as yet have no existence, *nor indeed do exist until the equilibrium is obtained* (italics mine). In two motions there are present potentially extension, space, arrangement and figure; but yet these do not actually exist till each motion proceeds to its equilibrium.[23]

It certainly helps to imagine a set of easily visualized proto-mechanical bodies, with two of each revolving around a common point as a point of dynamic equilibrium. Yet the case is more complicated. We cannot observe these bodies—they do not even

exist as matter (in the "massy" sense). Only their points of equilibrium so exist. The actives which control these particles—

> ...cannot present to us anything really contiguous. They are only
> the similitudes and representations of surfaces, which may apparently
> be in contact with one another, but are not really so. They are only the
> phantoms and ideal forms of sur faces. They are only the active forces of
> certain extremely minute substantials which present themselves under
> the appearance of figure. One of these figures may therefore pass
> through another wherever it may be, and thus a thousand superficies
> may flow through and across a single one.[24]

These bodies, that is, are fragments of hyperspaces, or of dimensions less than three, existing not "above" but "within" ordinary
three-dimensional space. If we could measure these bodies, they
would have an analogue of linear and rotatory motion. They would
seem to move in fractional (and multiple) analogues of the space we
know, since all the dimensions they enclosed, existing in an analogue of dynamic equilibrium, would seem to create, as a composite
resultant, an analogue of three dimensions. To discover, by mensuration, what they are as "things in themselves" (to use an old
phrase of idealist philosophy) would seem, however, to be impossible. We could only detect their points of equilibrium. These alone
can form "extension, space, arrangement and figure," that is to say,
become apparent. As the forces controlling these points of equilibrium changed in the modes of whatever would correspond to direction and intensity at this level of matter, so would these points of
equilibrium seem to dart about, like the places where two search-
light beams cross. They would seem to disappear and reappear.
They would have a quality something like erratic signals. In the
end, a certain pattern would emerge, though it might appear to be a
purely probabilistic or statistical one, as combining average or
mean motion. Yet these moving points of equilibrium or "nodes" are
absolutely real entities. They are not *merely* abstract representations or signals of relationships, but the real results of real relationships. Indeed, if we made the common mistake of assuming
that the entities which are closer to the world of sensually apprehended matter are more real than the farther-away ones, these

relationship-nodes or signals would seem more real than the forces which generated them. And what would they be, in the end, but *information* about an event?

All this sounds modern, if strangely so. Yet, as the reader can see, it is essentially a paraphrase and simplification of the quotations which preceded it, with a few obvious conclusions added. The only new concept I have added is that of the "signal," a modern formalization of what Swedenborg would have thought of simply as information passing through the channels of the senses. Swedenborg had no inkling that it would ever be possible to measure or see (through instruments) even the larger entities of the microworld. He therefore did not concern himself with how information about them would be conveyed to the senses and thence to the brain. Nor, of course, did he know anything about electronic communication. In our case, since we cannot see such entities with the naked eye or optical magnifying devices but only through imaging instruments, what we see is best described as a signal. And there is something quite unmodern at the core of it all. Swedenborg would insist that the randomness is illusory, even when we must fall back on the mathematics of probability to describe it.

In a fascinating article of some years back, the Soviet scientist, I.A. Akchurin, referred to Heisenberg's belief that "the equations of quantum mechanics are precisely equations for different possibilities (characterized by expansion of the wave function over some complete system of states)."[25] "And it is precisely this circumstance," Akchurin added, "that radically distinguished quantum equations from the classical ones, which describe actual motions." He says that the future theory of elementary particles, will, "to put it crudely, be algebraic topology endowed with physical meaning (like the postulates of quantum mechanics are nothing other than the postulates of the geometry of Hilbert spaces endowed with physical meaning). And the principal role in this theory will not be played by equations, but by so-called spectral sequences, specific sequences of groups that characterize the 'organization' (spectrum) of topological spaces: the law of the adjoining of diversified types and varieties of subsets."[26]

All this is complex enough, and the relationships which this distinguished scientist says he is describing crudely are still too sophisticated for most of us. But he puts the matter more simply when he says—

> In the most general form, the concept of information should be related to the philosophical categories of being, possibility and reality. Wherever there are several possibilities, but only one is accomplished and becomes reality (is converted into being) it is meaningful to speak of the information that this realized possibility *carries with it* (Akchurin's italics).[27]

Information theory turned out to be just the useful tool that Akchurin predicted it would become, but this is not surprising since Soviet scientists had always been in the lead in such studies.[28] It is now making a major contribution to chaos theory. But the point we are interested in here is the simple one that a cluster or set of bits of information, whether it is a "thing" or not, is certainly an event before it is a thing. And the statistical and probabilistic laws which were applied to elementary particles well before the possibility of using information theory was raised are also laws of events and relationships before they are laws of things. As the Soviet philosopher, M.E. Omelyanovsky, has said, in terms based on a philosophy of randomness, "A statistical law is realized as an internal tendency making its way through a mass of random events and manifesting itself in them as an average of numerous random deviations."[29]

Swedenborg has his own *pictorial* way of representing similar ideas. What we must keep in mind is—

i) that the particles making up the first element move in an extremely complex multidimensional continuum and thus cannot be observed directly and accurately in three-dimensional terms;

ii) that even the word "motion" must here be understood in a figurative sense. It is not that they are really "still" but that they are "moving" in an undefinable spacelike complex which they are creating by their very "movements";

iii) detectable spaces are directly defined, not by the particles themselves, but by their nodes of movement—the places where their paths cross, the points around which they mutually move—and the tensile intervals between these nodes. It thus follows *logically* (not through wishful thinking on my part) that they create a bi-faced entity: particle as object, wave as event.

The manner in which primary points combine to form an element, succinctly explained in the *Principia*, is discussed at more length in the so-called *Minor Principia*. This is a manuscript which came to light after Swedenborg's death, and it seems to have been composed some five years before the major work, as a first sketch of his theory. It is worthwhile to recapitulate his argument there, even at the risk of some repetition, because it helps us to consider some notions, already mentioned, in another light.[30]

Swedenborg here presupposes two infinites—in motion, the infinite of velocity and, in place, the infinite of smallness. We note here that his two primaries are not space and time, but space and motion, without which we cannot, indeed, conceive of time. From these two infinites the finite can arise, which he says "is proved by the infinitesimal calculus; and geometry also acknowledges the fact that from the motion or infinite fluxion of points something of a finite character is determined, whether it be the line or something else. The science of physics also, which regards matter as infinitely divisible, proves the same."

The rapid rotation of the point produces a hard sphere in the same sense that wave motion produces a plane surface and part of a circular area on the surface of a sphere. If there is no resistance to the motion at any place outside the point, this motion may increase to infinity.

In such a motion there is neither distance nor actualized place, but it contains in potential all distance and place. Yet the word "motion" is itself figurative, because it takes place in a material vacuum where nothing is relative. Thus there is no motion truly conceivable as such (a Parmenidean idea). All the same there are two analogues of geometrical position or place. Several or an infi-

nite number of points can revolve around a common center, which
thus becomes an analogue of a place. They can also encounter one
another in meeting or collision if they are of different "sizes" with
different centers. If points collide they are deflected and follow
more or less curved lines (a straight line being a long or flat curve).
This creates another analogue of place, since a point of collision is a
point of meeting and a summation of specific forces. However, since
there is no space but only its analogue, *what is this but an "information event"*?

The analogue of space which most closely images what we might
call the "functional space" (not a Swedenborgian term) in which the
points move is that of the center with its four quarters. Swedenborg
does not discuss this in any great detail, but the argument behind
the statement develops from the relationship between the equator
and the ecliptic band, noted earlier. The point has become a sphere
of many points, which revolve around two axes, thus creating two
major bands of movement—the equator, which lies in a plane
perpendicular to the axis of rotation, and the ecliptic band, which
lies in a plane tilted in relationship to the equator. We then have a
center and two nodes. The center is the center of the sphere,
through which and out of which, to each pole of the sphere ("north"
and "south"), runs the axis of rotation. The two nodes are the points
where the ecliptic crosses the equator, at the "east" and "west"
positions. (On a terrestrial globe these appear as the points of the
vernal and autumnal equinoxes). Each is a place or a point like a
place; "north" and "south" because they are opposite poles of the
axis of rotation, "east" and "west" because they are nodes where
two lines of force or rotation meet.

I shall now go to Swedenborg's description of the first element,
or part of it. First, I must say two things.

Something must be said about the statement: "...in the starry
heavens we see with the eyes all the stars, as it were, present to us,
yet this presence cannot be effected without contiguity." He is not
saying that the first element transmits light-beams. He means that
without this first element the magnetic element and the ether
could not transmit them, because the first element provides the
base of contiguous parts upon which these "more material" ele-

ments rest. The waves/particles of light are much larger and coarser than the components of the first element, which can hardly be imagined as anything other than particles of space/time, at once discrete and perfectly continuous (an apparent paradox very nicely evaded by the use of the phrase, "most perfectly contiguous").

I have avoided, though reluctantly, any attempt to relate Swedenborg's first element to a known entity of microphysics. In many respects it resembles the vacuum state of modern physics.[31] But any relationship between a Swedenborgian entity and a modern one of which he could have known nothing can really only be explained in one way. This is that the universe is rationally constructed and in such a way that a generalized idea of its structure could have been arrived at by a natural philosopher using eighteenth-century intellectual tools. For, as I have said, we can follow Swedenborg's reasoning, which means that in theory somebody else in his time could have made the same discoveries. But here we overstep the border between theology and Christian natural philosophy.

This is what Swedenborg says of the first element—

> This element is the most subtle, the first and most universal, of our mundane system and of the universe in general. Inasmuch as this element is the first, it follows also that it consists of the smallest elementary parts. That it is the most universal, may be concluded *a priori*; because it is the origin of all the subsequent elements; because also it consists of the smallest constituent parts, can occupy the smallest spaces, and be present where no other element can; therefore it may without doubt be concluded, that it is also the most universal. We may come to the same conclusion *a posteriori*; for in the starry heavens we see with the eyes all the stars, as it were, present to us, yet this presence cannot be effected without contiguity. Consequently from reason instructed by the senses we learn that there is nothing more universal than this element. From reason it follows that, in every system, both the greatest and least spaces are occupied by this element; and that this element is of all others the most perfectly contiguous. As all the essentials of contiguity are latent in every particle; as all the particles may be mutually applied to one another, and in consequence of their form and situation may all conspire to one continuous motion;

as in virtue of their extreme elasticity they may accommodate themselves to every motion; so also by virtue of their simplicity they are the
first and most subtle element, and consequently admit of the fewest
possible modes and variations. Thus, from reason, instructed by the
phenomena presented to the senses, we learn that it is in virtue of this
universal element that all things in the starry system appear, as it
were, present. Whenever they do not appear so, it is only in consequence of our being accustomed to measure distances by comparing the
angles made by distant objects with those immediately near the eye. It
is in virtue, therefore, of this element, that we can contemplate the
remotest stars, as also the planets by their reflected light.

   In this elementary particle, all that had preexisted is latent, such as
the point, the first finite, the second finite, and the active of the first
finite. We have thus in a microcosm the whole of our macrocosm; we
have the entire world, so far as it has developed itself, in each particle,
in which, therefore, we may contemplate a compendium of the whole
world-system. For from a point produced from the Infinite arose the
first substantial; from the first substantial, its actives as also its
passive, that is to say, the active of the first finite and then the other
finite. Thus does this first elementary particle, consisting of the active
of the first finite and also the second finite, comprise within itself all
that as yet is active and passive in the world. Thus we have the world
concentrated in a single particle. I entreat the indulgent reader to
pardon me for venturing to speak so positively of the elements and
entities of the *natura prima*, which are so unknown and occult, as if
they were objects well known and familiar to the senses. It would
indeed be rash in me so confidently to lead him through an unexplored
region, a region of so many clouds and shadows, were I not aiming,
through the medium of the principles explained, to arrive at an element
in which we are able to make experiments, and which, by help of these
and geometry, may be subjected to the most rigorous examination.
When we have arrived at this stage, if it appears that there is a
geometrical harmony between the experiments and our principles, if a
connection is pointed out between the first entity or simple and the
aforementioned element, I then flatter myself that I shall have won the
assent of my reader; more particularly as, in the present age, there is no
other way left for us to open the secrets of nature.[32]

Swedenborg is therefore about to propose a means by which his theory may be tested. He has in mind an experiment which will either demonstrate or fail to show a "geometrical harmony" and a "connection" between the forms which go to compose his first element and those belonging to an element in which it is possible to conduct experiments. This will be the element he next considers, the "magnetic element." Did he show this "geometrical harmony" and this "connection"? We shall consider this question in the next chapter.

ENDNOTES

1 Swedenborg, *Principia* II, pp. 551–553.

2 Ibid., I, p. 56.

3 The following is summarized from Sambursky, pp. 85–88.

4 Rist, p. 152. I say "seems" because Swedenborg's primary point is obviously related to the Active/Passive cosmology of Zeno of Cition. At the same time, by using some logical ingenuity, we could draw more remote parallels with the philosophy of Zeno of Elea. Neither case can be proved.

5 In *Anteriorité des Civilisations Nègres* (Présence Africaine, Paris, 1967, p. 39) Cheik Anta Diop quotes Diogenes Laertius as saying Zeno was very big and black, "whence the fact that some called him a branch of the Egyptian vine."

6 The following comments are based on Prier, pp. 90–111.

7 Prier, p. 105.

8 Nahm, p. 117.

9 Nahm, p. 121. Cf. also the "whirlwind cosmology" of Empedocles, discussed by Bollack (p. 177 et seq.).

10 It may be argued that this complex is a succession of discrete revolving rings, but this would be to forget—

i) that the rings cannot be discrete: first of all because Parmenides does not admit empty space into his scheme; second because between each of the rings or crowns is a mixed crown which joins them, yet the rings revolve separately and do not make a single wheel; third, because the whole makes a sphere, so the rings do not all have the same diameters;

ii) that the motion of the crowns is directed from the center by justice and necessity, which means that motion is communicated from ring to ring.

We do not have Parmenides' complete argument and the case is therefore ambiguous, but I opt for the vortical interpretation for the above reasons.

11 Those who have read in the *Cabala* will note a similarity between the last quotation and parts of the Cabalistic doctrine of the creation, with its wheels, spiral whirlwinds, crowns and shells—see Schaya, Ch. V. The Parmenidean resemblances are clearest in those parts of the *Cabala* which are supported most strongly by the literal sense of Scripture. These resemblances indicate the error of those who assume Swedenborg was influenced by the *Cabala*. We know from his philosophical notes that Swedenborg knew almost nothing about the *Cabala*. But the *Cabala* is

based on Scripture and upon pre-biblical religions and also includes elements reminiscent of pre-Socratic philosophy. Inevitably, therefore, there will be fugitive resemblances between Cabalistic and Swedenborgian thought.

The mystery is that, while no Cabalistic text is very old, the doctrine may be related to some aspects of the physics of the Stoics and pre-Socratics and to Orphic cosmology. These in turn have roots in Phoenician and Egyptian thought. Is the doctrine, in part, as old as this implies, or are we looking at an archaising tendency in Jewish thought which gravitated towards ancient doctrines preserved in later Greek thought? Patai's *The Hebrew Goddess* is an excellent study of syncretistic elements in the *Cabala*. He does not discuss a possible Punic (Carthaginian) influence on Cabalistic thought, though the imagery associated with *Binah*—mirror, hand raised in blessing, description as "face of God" (Schaya, p. 41)—are all characteristics of the great goddess of Carthage, Tanit. Other North African elements of late date (Egyptian, Romanised Carthaginian) may be found. But the Cabalistic tradition refers the "preservation" of the *Cabala* to Palestinian and Mesopotamian rabbinical schools, with no mention of such sources.

12 de Santillana and von Dechend, p. 200.

13 Duhamel, p. 24.

14 Neugebauer, p. 108.

15 Extant Egyptian mathematical papyri consist largely of quick-calculation formulas for practical use, based on a binary concept of number. As Gillings wrote (p. 3) "...their mathematics was based on two very elementary concepts. The first was their complete knowledge of the twice-times table, and the second, their ability to find two-thirds of any number, whether integral or fractional. Upon these two very simple foundations the whole structure of Egyptian mathematics was erected..." From this, a number of historians of mathematics have drawn the truly astonishing conclusion that Egyptian mathematics was simple and naive. Yet is it not obvious that such simplicity can only be achieved by prolonged mathematical thought over a long period of time? Undeveloped mathematical systems are universally distinguished by cumbersomeness.

Gillings is an honest and thorough analyst, yet he must bow to academic pressure (which in this respect tends to racism, "innocent" or not) by concluding that, though the Egyptians "reached a relatively high level of mathematical sophistication," they "did not think and reason as the Greeks did," and "if they found some exact method (however they may have discovered it), they did not ask themselves *why* it worked." But this is to forget that mathematical order was thought of as the expression of the divine order (the gods here being Thoth and Maat). So it is not the case that the Egyptians did not ask "why"; it is rather that we reject their answer to the question on philosophical grounds.

Perhaps, when we have related Egyptian modes of calculation to their geometry, and have managed to reconstruct their *theory* of mathematical form, we shall discover some remarkable things. Example: how did they arrive at a "strange" formula for discovering the area of a circle—subtract from the diameter its ninth part and square the remainder—which is in error by less than 0.6 of one per cent (Gillings, p. 140)?

The evidence of Egyptian mathematical sophistication is apparent to all—in their architecture, city planning, public works and public accounting. A civilization of this complexity and durability cannot be maintained by rule-of-thumb methods.

16 Swedenborg, *Principia* I, pp. 82–83.

17 Ibid., I, p. 112.

18 Euclid, *Elements* I, (ed. Heath), p 155.

19 Leibniz, *Monadology*, in *Selections*, pp. 533–537.

20 Swedenborg, *Principia* I, p. 59.

21 Ibid., I, pp. 96–101, 136–138. In the *Minor Principia* (*Principia* II, pp. 311–313), Swedenborg defines the equatorial line as arising from the bisection of the spiral lines which flow from one pole to another, while the ecliptic line is that which cuts these spiral lines at right angles. The statement may appear extravagant yet it is true that a symbolic geometry of logic may as easily be erected on this structure as it now is on a Cartesian graph.

22 Ibid., I, pp. 180–181. "Axillary" is a strange word here, since the *axil* is the hollow where the base of a leaf joins the stem, or where the branch leaves the trunk. Unless Swedenborg's Latin has been mistranslated, there is a pun here. Swedenborg is not only referring to movement about an *axis* but to the spiral pattern found in the leaves of plants. See *Phyllotaxis and the Fibonacci Series*, by G.J. Michison, in *Science*, 15 April, 1977, also Huntley (bibliography).

23 Ibid., I, p. 160.

24 Ibid., I, p. 163.

25 Kuznetsov *et al*:, pp. 445–446.

26 Ibid., pp. 454–455.

27 Ibid., p. 437.

28 Gleick, p. 261; Akchurin in Kuznetsov *et al*, p. 439.

29 Omelyanovsky, p. 162.

30 The following discussion is drawn from *Principia* II, pp. 299–359.

31 In *Something Called Nothing*, which has the merit of mentioning both "Eastern" and "Western" discoveries in this field, the Soviet science-journalist, R. Podolny, refers to the theories of the American physicist, John Archibald Wheeler, on the nature of vacuum. He quotes Wheeler as saying that any elementary particle is "not a foreign and physical entity moving about within the geometry of space, but a quantum state of excitation of that geometry itself; as unimportant for the physics of the vacuum as a cloud is unimportant for the physics of the sky." And further, Wheeler says of Einstein—

> Einstein, above his work and writings, held a long term vision: there is nothing in the world except curved empty space. Geometry bent one way here described gravitation. Rippled another way somewhere else it manifests all the quantities of an electromagnetic wave. Excited at still another place, the magic material that is space shows itself as a particle. There is nothing that is foreign and "physical" immersed in space. Everything that is is constructed out of geometry. (Podolny, p. 175)

The physicist Fernando Caracena's comments on the vacuum state in "The Finer Things of Nature" (*NP* Jul/Sep 1974) and the resultant discussion, are of great interest in this context. See also "Does Physics Equal Geometry?" by the mathematician, Gregory L. Baker (*NP* Jan/Mar 1974). Baker's approach is cautious and most commendably so, since much Swedenborgian thought has been too rash in the statement that this or that modern discovery "confirms" the science of the *Principia*. This is to confuse science and natural philosophy. Nevertheless he says, while pointing out the speculative nature of both Swedenborg's and Wheeler's arguments, that geometrodynamics (Wheeler's theory) is highly consistent with the general spirit of Swedenborg's philosophical works. "The fluctuating geometries are reminiscent of the first natural point motions, and one is hard put to describe physical phenomena at any deeper level" (p. 33).

As early as 1928, Sir James Jeans had at least anticipated the bare ideas of black holes, white holes and singularities in the following statement about galaxies, then called "spiral nebulae." He wrote—

> Each failure to explain the spiral arms makes it more and more difficult to resist a suspicion that the spiral nebulae are the seat of types of forces entirely unknown to us, forces which may possibly express novel and unsuspected metric properties of space. The type of conjecture which presents itself, somewhat insistently, is that the centres of the nebulae are of the nature of singular points, at which matter is poured into our universe from some other and entirely extraneous spatial dimension, so that to a denizen of our universe, they appear as points at which matter is continuously being created. (Quoted by Sullivan, p. 198)

32 Swedenborg, *Principia*, I, pp. 187–189.

The statement, "Thus we have the world concentrated in a single particle," may seem to be an unwarranted logical leap. Yet it follows inevitably from his description of the primary point, in which all of time/space is generated.

Perhaps we can imagine that, by way of an immensely long chain of evolutions and involutions, the primary point eventually turns into the banal and typically eighteenth-century diagram which nonetheless combines all measurable time and space into a single image with a unified metric—the clock face. On the clock-face, where the point of the moving hand becomes like a planet revolving around a sun, the complex movements of the radii of an infinite spiral become a single radius sweeping out a circle; the peripheries of the spiral collapse into a simple circumference. Such an image of what happens in the *Principia* is certainly very crude. For we should certainly find, if we looked further into the matter, that we have always taken the familiar "clock-face image" too much for granted. To begin with, as twentieth-century persons, we should have to rethink the idea of a "clock" in terms such as physical relativity uses (e.g. it can be an atom: cf. Weyl: pp. 7, 307).

See Herbert Dingle, who said (1938, p. 18), "The physical world of Einstein is even now beyond the grasp of many able minds, yet the essential ideas embodied in it were apprehended by Swedenborg in 1734."

5

The Magnetic Element

There is something uncanny in the way the *Principia*—so often laid to rest as a mere prevision of whatever scientific theory prevails at the time—returns, like a loquacious guest just after the party is over, to insist that it has more to say. Thus, in 1912, Professor Sir William F. Barrett, FRS, gives it a splendid and sonorous farewell—

> The second part of the *Principia* deals with magnetism, and is chiefly occupied with a transcript of Musschenbroek's experiments on magnetism. Whilst we may dismiss Swedenborg's idea of a magnetic element and magnetic spheres, we find a remarkable prevision of the molecular structure of a magnet. "Magnetism," Swedenborg remarks, "consists only in the regular arrangement of the minutest parts of the magnet:—
>
> Indeed, what proof could be plainer than the one derived from iron filings sprinkled around a magnet, which in a continuous line follow the course of the magnetism and dispose themselves into the same situation and path as the smallest parts of the iron; and if we could see the latter with the help of lenses or with the naked eye, they would seen to be arranged in a similar manner. In filings, therefore, we see the effigy of the parts in the iron which are brought into a regular order at the will of the magnet. If we could artificially combine steel dust into a solid mass and move the magnet over it, we should have ocular proof that every atom took up that position, which the smallest parts of the iron

assumed when rubbed; that is to say, a regular arrangement. If this arrangement of the parts of the iron be disturbed either by too frequent bendings or by too hard blows, or by fire, then the iron immediately divests itself of its magnetism and assumes its original character."

All this might have been written by a student of the present day and is perfectly correct.[1]

Professor Barrett's remarks were just and generous—for 1912. But now, some eighty years later, we may no longer "dismiss Swedenborg's idea of a magnetic element and magnetic spheres." Not only do we know that electromagnetic forces move in the fundamental core of matter, we now know that most of the sun's energy takes the form of electromagnetic radiations.[2] The very word "magnetosphere," as applied to the earth, is routinely used by scientists and laymen interested in science, along with the phrase "interplanetary magnetic field" to describe the effect in our solar system of the sun's magnetic field.

When we read the first chapter of the third part of the *Principia*, *Comparison of the Starry Heavens with the Magnetic Sphere*, we find that Swedenborg sets out a close analogy between the vortical structure of the magnetic field and the force-fields around the sun (or any star). The validity of this view was confirmed in 1878. In that year there occurred a total eclipse of the sun. Astronomers were able to photograph the corona, a tenuous mass of plasma or ionized matter surrounding the sun. This had to be done during a total eclipse, when the disc of the moon hid the sun, because the light of the sun is so great that it actually whites out the corona. It was then observed that "the corona's structure strongly resembled the kind of pattern that iron filings made when sprinkled over a magnet."[3] Investigation of the implications of this observation eventually led to the conclusion that the sun is a gigantic magnet.

Yet it is obvious to every reader that there is nothing visionary in Swedenborg's discussion of what he calls "the magnetic element." A very large portion of it is taken up by the experiments of the Dutch physicist and mathematician, Pieter van Musschenbroek (1692–1717).[4] The quotations make for rather dull reading, since Musschenbroek's discoveries have been common knowledge for a long time. But they show us, as do the more everyday technological works with which the *Principia* was bound in its first edition, that Swedenborg had a very great respect and appetite for the available physical data, in no way preferring speculation over hard fact.

Like most scientific writing of its time, the *Principia* refers to ways of measuring and comparing quantities and phenomena which we no longer use. We have retained the words Swedenborg employs in common speech, but often with changes of nuance. He will refer to "subtle" and "gross" matter, using the former word to refer to light, delicately-structured and fluid substances or their "effluvia," the latter word to refer to heavy and massy substances, such as iron. Such words apply not only to the relative tenuity of substances but also to their relative nobility, their places in a hierarchy of values analogous to the values of thoughts and emotions, social structures and the like.

The magnetic element is the first "subtle element" which may be observed and analyzed both on the very large scale—the earth is a great magnet—and on the very small. As Barrett observed in 1912 (above), Swedenborg realized that magnetism extended down to the molecular level. But he does not use the word "molecule" nor, though he creates models of elementary particles which greatly resemble the atoms and subatomic particles we know, does he use the word "atom" to describe them. In his day an atom was a hard tiny particle resembling the smallest bit of a substance obtainable by a process of perfect pulverization or by continually cutting it up with an ideally tiny knife. It would have resembled an infinitesimal pebble or crystal. When he does use the word "atom," what he means is something like our "molecule." He could not accept an image which, for all its contemporary respectability, appeared naive to him. Thus he approvingly quotes Musschenbroek, who says that the magnet "cannot consist of some fortuitous collection of mere atoms."[5] His own quasi-atomic structures, complexes of fluid motions, are much more like superstrong bubbles than eighteenth-century atoms.

A force which controls the tiniest particles of iron, particles so small that anything smaller would not, strictly speaking, be iron at all, must have its origin in a sphere or conceptual area beneath the smallest particles of iron. And here again we must note that Swedenborg's conceptualization of what we call the "microworld" is different from our own, so much so that the word "microworld," though we must use it, is really misleading. We imagine ourselves as penetrating, with our instruments both physical and mathematical, first into the molecule, then into the atom, then into the parts of the atom, thus into a world which grows smaller and smaller. It is a sort of tunnelling process. We form the picture of the most elementary particles as enclosed in the structure of the atom, which in turn is enclosed in the molecule. By "we," of course, I mean those of us who have studied a little physics as part of a nonscientific education; the concepts of high mathematical physics are not like this.

Though our image of the atom itself is enormously more sophisticated than the classical one, this is still traditional "atomism" because it moves only one way, from the large to the small. But Swedenborg has a dual view of the microworld. It is very different from our own, and I know of nothing to which I can compare it. It is a world in which magnitude, size, is viewed from a dual perspective. This arises from his view of the *infinite*, in which the greatest and least entities are the same. This is mathematically sound but extraordinarily difficult to visualize. All I can do is describe the picture I have of it, which is very crude. We must have some mental picture of this seeming paradox as we move into the grosser realms of matter described in the *Principia*. Otherwise his descriptions of magnetic and more obviously material particles are exceedingly difficult to follow.

Swedenborg has imagined a series of world-planes, which are really shells as flat curves of an infinite onion-sphere. If we were to think in this way we could imagine—

A mass of iron, visible to the naked eye
The molecular plane
The atomic plane
The subatomic plane of elementary particles
The "vacuum" plane

And in considering this model it would be incorrect to say of any level that it was really smaller than the level above it, since the sphere, including every one of its shells, is infinite in the spatial sense. The mass of iron, which stands in here for all the sense-apparent matter in the universe, is larger than its individual constituent molecules, which are larger than their atoms and so on down to the vanishing point. But the molecular "field," which extends through all solids, liquids and gases, is larger than the "field" of solid objects; the "field" of atoms includes solids, liquids, gases and plasmas; the "field" of subatomic elementary particles includes all these, plus etheric and electromagnetic forces which extend through all space. Finally, the "vacuum plane" not only fills all space but is a precondition of the existence of space. Yet its "infinity" is within every molecule of iron.

In such dualistic thought, smallest entities may be embodiments of the most widely extended fields. It is actually a reflection on the plane of the observer of the infinite vortex structure of Swedenborgian matter. I cannot imagine an infinite vortex, but I can imagine a dual one. In the dual vortex, tunnelling towards the center is a form of narrowing of vision if we think of the visible world as very large and the particle at the bottom of the hole as very small. But if we think of ourselves as living in a field of microparticles and wishing to work our way into the world of tangible matter, we are not tunnelling in but rather tunnelling out. The cone narrows as we ascend and the particle of destination, a particle of solid matter, is at the point of the cone, thus very small.

In the following quotation we have a dual movement—

> The primitive force in a point continually produces similitudes of itself, by the multiplication of itself into itself, whenever occasion offers and the force can go out into act. It has been above shown, that by the mechanism of its motion and perfectly regular and geometrical figure, the primitive force in a point cannot but produce similitudes of itself, and continue to produce them in their sequents; consequently, that a substantial thus arising cannot but be perfectly similar to the point, and possess a perfectly similar power of producing sequents in like manner. There may, therefore, be substantials which by their multipli-

cation into themselves, and thus by being frequently compounded, are elevated into high powers. So that if the first point were considered as one, and 100 points constituted one smallest substantial, the second substantial would consist of 100 first substantials, or of 10,000 points; the third finite would consist of 1,000,000 points; the fourth finite or substantial of 100,000,000 points; the fifth of 10,000,000,000 points; and so on by a continual multiplication of the substantials into themselves. And since the actives are the same with the finites or substantials in a free state, it follows that one active must consist of the same number of points. Hence the third active consists of 1,000,000 points or 10,000 first substantials; and so on. The number I have fixed upon only by way of example; for we cannot tell what may be the number which at first has to be multiplied into itself.[6]

Things are certainly getting bigger here, by leaps of powers of ten (the number being illustrative only). So the particle which emerges at the end of all this multiplication—say a molecule of iron—is immensely larger than the primary point. But we know two things about the primary point. The first is that it is successively limiting itself by growing in this fashion. The second is that it contains within itself the real potential of every form it takes in its successive limitings through the fields of matter, from the most subtle to the least. If we lived in the sphere of the primary point (imagine yourself as floating around a stratosphere-like realm of "infinite possibility") then this process would be seen as going on *beneath* us, like some whirlpool spiralling down to a tiny iron particle at the center.

Again we have the image of the double vortex or, more simply, the double circle. It is a process like this which, on its way to producing hard particles like those of iron, produces, as a stopping-place along the way, the magnetic element.

And something like light is with us all the way.

For the first elementary particle, the particle of the first element, is compounded of the second finites and the actives of the first. And the active of a finite is the same as the action of the finite itself in a free state, a state in which it has the ability to act or move freely.[7] Only one possibly measurable entity performs work in the first element. This is a "something" whose velocity must be *in ratio* to that of visible light. For the first element is universal and "perfectly contiguous," this property of contiguity enabling us "to see with the eyes all the stars, as it were, present to us."[8]

Yet this velocity is certainly greater than that of light, though it must be some rationally derivable multiple of the speed of light. Any fundamental of velocity must be at the first motion in the first space/time continuum, that is, at the level where space/time is defined. Swedenborg maintains that visible light travels in the ether, in the same continuum as heat or electricity, and the ether is a "grosser" medium than the space/time continuum, with slower waves moving in it. Yet his argument necessarily defines visible light, though the point is made in somewhat muted fashion in the *Principia*, as the sense-apparent part of a complex vibration whose hidden or interior part is in the first element. He is more specific in *The Five Senses*, where he says that light is generated by a movement of the solar ocean,[9] which begins, according to the *Principia*, in "active solar space." And this consists of "the actives of the first finite."[10]

It therefore follows that his universal ratio is not visible light but some more rapid entity whose velocity is in ratio to, or is some multiple of, the speed of visible light. This cannot be the velocity of the primal Active, since that is literally infinite (the Active has no mass). The speed of visible light would be, however, the boundary constant of velocity *in the ether*, which is where (see next chapter) space/time *as we know it* is generated, being a direct effect of the ratios of movement in solar space.

It may seem that in this discussion we have moved to a much more subtle or deeper level of matter than is represented by magnetism, but Swedenborg's idea of magnetic force is wider ranging than our everyday idea and much more so than that of his contemporaries. It is not restricted to iron but is rather a universal force to which iron, because of its internal structure, responds particularly well. Thus he holds "that bodies of every form are magnetic" (if we take all aspects of magnetism into account this is true) and that magnetic forces run through them in straight lines in the form of "subtle elementary particles."[11] "Magnetism" is the only word available to him; but he makes it a universal force of which iron-based magnetism is only a form. He further describes electricity and light waves as wave-particle movements in an ether which contains magnetism and therefore responds to these internal magnetic forces. It is clear, then, that he has passed far beyond the definition of magnetism common in his time and has imagined, though not in descriptions we easily recognize, some of the essential properties of electromagnetism.

The magnetic element, he says, is "the first in which elementary nature presents herself as visible to the eye." And he adds, in the same passage—

> Here it is that she begins to emerge out of her hiding place, and from darkness to issue forth into light. Here it is that she discloses to view many of her mysteries; that she presents an image of herself as a whole; that at the very first glimpse of herself, she overwhelms, as it were, and confounds our senses by the forces with which she has invested a rough, dark, common and heavy body. This body is the magnetic stone; which may well be called the *lapid lydius* or touchstone of the learned; which to the minds of philosophers has been as much a source of perplexity as it has been to their senses one of delight, and to both a subject of wonder.[12]

By saying that here elementary nature "presents an image of herself as a whole" he is referring to an essence, a kind of soul which animates this image. Not a conscious rational soul but something like it, a rational *form*. The "essence" in this case is the first element, which we have already discussed. And, however scandalous this may be to the modern mind, he *means* it. This is no flourish of fine writing; such may not be found in the *Principia*. For all its "previsions" of modernity, this book, committed to the doctrine of the Great Chain of Being, is in some important ways quite old-fashioned for its time. It possesses ideological if not scientific links to the Renaissance and High Baroque. These links go back even farther, to the ideas or exemplars of Augustine, which are also images which possess "a kind of soul."

The true link between electricity and magnetism would not be discovered until the nineteenth century. It had indeed been known since the day of William Gilbert (1570) that materials other than amber (our word "electricity" comes from the Greek word for amber, *elektron*) can attract other objects if rubbed with a cloth; thus Gilbert said that "a lodestone attracts only magnetic bodies, electrics attract everything." A year before the *Principia* was published, that is, in 1733, Charles Francois de Cisterney du Fay had discovered the fundamental law of electricity: "like charges repel and unlike attract," a law which could be related to the attraction between the opposite poles of a magnet. Some formal relationship between the two forces could be, vaguely, sensed.

Now it is in Swedenborg's magnetic sphere that rectilinear geometry is, so to speak, "born," because magnetic particles are capable of arranging themselves in rectilinear patterns. "All motion between the elementary particles, which we have called magnetic, runs round a centre in a spiral direction, and when it has arrived at its state of rest, comes into a rectilinear arrangement, and into the same with the arrangement of the parts at rest."[13] If it were not for the magnetic element, from which the more obviously material elementaries were developed, if the universe consisted only of the first element, then the sun's "...active space would be a centre without circumference, an active without passive; a soul without a body; a space without place; an eye with no quarter toward which to look; there would be no upwards, downwards, or sidewards; in a word, without a termination in elementaries nothing would exist; but everything would relapse into its original emptiness."[14]

Let us return to the concept of the vortical movements which are shared by the magnetic field and the stars. These vortices are generated by the motions of elementary particles which are made up of "third finites and of the actives of the second and first finite."[15] But the third finite is "a simple or point multiplied into itself or raised to its third power" (a conventional exponentiation, as we have seen), and it contains within it second finites which contain first finites. Each of these entities has parts and all of them exist in an unmeasurable pre-geometrical continuum. Yet they contain the basis of all geometry, in the binary form of active and passive or (to

use a Pythagorean concept) "likeness" and "unlikeness" or sameness and difference. It is altogether to be expected that this binar-
ism should be reflected in the bipolar forms of the magnetic sphere.
Two quotations will illustrate what I mean.

> The third finites which had entered into the world, and of which we
> have spoken in our former chapter, were near the sun or the large
> active space of the vortex; consequently they cannot remain finites,
> because they are near the active space, but must necessarily be convo-
> luted and aggregated into new surfaces, in the same manner as are the
> second finites into first elementary particles.[16]

> This finite (*i.e., the third finite*: NN), therefore, derives its origin
> from the elementary particle; for it is the same as the elementary
> particle in its most highly compressed state, in which the actives have
> vanished in consequence of the compression. Let us return to the theory
> of the elementary particle. We have said that these particles may be
> expanded and compressed; that under a state of compression they
> become very similar to finites; that they ultimately cease to be elemen-
> tary; and that actives, when banished from their localities or reduced
> within a narrow compass, become finites or substantials. With regard
> to the way in which this is done we have said, that by means of
> compression the elementary particles retreat into a less space, and, as
> it were, into themselves; that their surface becomes multiplied three or
> more times, and ultimately into as many series and orders as there are
> spiral surfaces in the finite; that in their highest state of compression
> they more and more divest themselves of their elementary nature, and
> become more and more like a finite; until the whole of their elementary
> nature becomes changed into that of a finite, their elastic into a hard
> nature, and their highly compressible into a stubborn resisting nature.
> Now this can occur in no other place than round the large active space,
> in its vortex.[17]

What is happening here? We are in the first part of the eighteenth century. Swedenborg, a man with the most remarkable
geometrical imagination and tenacity of inward visual representation, is imagining the evolutions of a set of shapes. These are
images of fundamental forces, which by compression acquire inertia and become the massy forms of our world of straight-line geometry. The most elaborate techniques of modern topology and

differential geometry (structure of manifolds and vector and tensor analysis included) would be required to express these evolutions in mathematical terms. But the calculus has barely been invented.

All the same, the reader may by now be growing tired of reading about particles which may neither be seen nor measured. Nobody has ever questioned Swedenborg's *gifts*, he might say, but could the *Principia* be, in the end, a vast structure spun out in the air—a spider's web in the pejorative sense? Could it be one of those slippery "wisdom works," common in occultist literature, which can never be disproved because they contain no verifiable statements, but cleverly hover around the edges of logical paradoxes or deny all distinctions in a muddy transformationism—"What is above is as what is below," "all is nothing," "all is all" and so on. It is essential that there be errors in the book if we are to take it seriously—and this is not a paradox. The presence of error in a work of natural philosophy—even a work of theology, even a sacred text—shows that the author is paying due attention to the facts, the facts of his time, which is the only time he knows or can understand. The interpretation of fact will always be proved erroneous in some way, because every age errs in the interpretation of physical fact. The absence of error, on the other hand, shows that the facts are being ignored, that no clear statements are being made. Nonsense is never in error.

Swedenborg knows this. That is why he will propose a test of his theory, in the form of an experiment in the "magnetic element." He will partially succeed and partially fail, and a consideration of this mixed success and failure will help us to get a handle on this puzzling and daunting book.

The need of an adequate theory of terrestrial magnetism was, in his day, a pressing and practical one. Navigation depended upon it and, given the mercantile economy of the time, the prosperity of Europe depended upon it. The magnetic compass and the ship's clock or chronometer were the only navigational devices which could be used in all weathers. Navigational astronomy was well developed and mariners would shortly be able to make use of the reflecting quadrant, which was either invented or perfected by

John Hadley in 1731 and was the immediate ancestor of the modern sextant. Nevertheless, such instruments used for shooting the sun, moon and stars, were not of much use in cloudy weather or in turbulent weather when the ship was rolling so badly that a fix could not be obtained. Making an observation under the latter conditions was as difficult as focusing a telescope on a distant building when one is on an amusement-park ride. And even when conditions of observation were excellent, celestial observations only gave one the latitude, not the longitude.

What this meant was that the compass was more reliable, most of the time, than other navigational instruments. At least it always pointed roughly the same way. But there were many problems with it.

For one thing, it did not point to true north but to somewhere vaguely close to it. Before the North Magnetic Pole was discovered it was thought that this "bad north" might be somewhere in space (as the Spanish navigator, Martin Cortes, speculated). Some even thought it did not exist objectively, that it was only an anomaly of magnetism that compasses should point in a certain direction and that it was therefore a pure accident that this direction should be to the north (in 1581, Robert Norman, a true relativist, called compass-north the *Point Respective*). It was not until 1600 that William Gilbert discovered that the earth was a magnet, with opposite magnetic poles. A great theoretical discovery this, but it left much practical work to do, and navigators were still struggling with it in Swedenborg's day.

Because magnetic north was different from true north, a difference called "variation," every compass reading had to be corrected for this difference. This may appear merely pedantic—why not simply take magnetic north as "effective north" and forget about true north except as a nicety of land based astronomy? The trouble was that compass observations could not give you your latitude or longitude; they could tell you where magnetic north was, but could not tell you where you were on the earth's surface. For that you needed to make celestial observations based on the positions of sun, moon and stars. There were no celestial coordinates corresponding to magnetic north; to use celestial coordinates to line up earth positions you had to take into consideration the position of earth in space and only the *true* poles of the earth, the two ends of its axis of rotation, could be used to relate earth to sun, moon and stars. There was just no way around it. To reconcile compass readings with the celestial observations necessary to establish the position of the ship you had to make a certain calculation to determine how far true north was from magnetic north, so that compass and celestial observations could be interpreted in terms of a single set of coordinates.

This correction of the compass reading has been for a long time now a matter of simple arithmetic and trigonometry. At every point on the earth's surface not on the longitude of the magnetic pole, a line running to magnetic north will point in a different direction. If I am in London and point the index finger of my right hand at magnetic north, and the index of my left at true north I will be indicating a certain angle between them. If a friend in Kingston, Jamaica, does the same the angle between the two directions he is pointing in will be different. What we need is a world chart and a set of tables derived from it enabling us both to find, from the single compass-finger pointing at magnetic north, the angle which will give us true north. These charts and tables are now available to every hobby-sailor and the professionals and wealthier yachtsmen have passed on to navigation by computer.

It was not that easy in the early eighteenth century. Compasses made in Baltic countries indicated on their cases that true north was about one quarter of a compass point (2°49') to the east of the direction in which the compass pointed; English compasses placed it one-half of a point to the east; and so the differences ran through Europe. Compasses indicated true north only in the cities where they were made, which led to great error when they were used at sea.[18]

There were other problems too. There was "deviation," in which the compass needle was deflected by iron in the ship itself, and "dip," in which the compass needle tilted from the horizontal, pointing below the horizon—but these were not so important, because they could be corrected. The main problem was variation. Navigators could not relate magnetic north to true north unless they knew where they were and could work in the appropriate correction for the place on the earth's surface where they were.

To quote Henry Raper's *Practice of Navigation*, used by almost all British navigators in the last century, and a direct continuation, though it was first published in 1852, of much older manuals: "The first attempt to give a comprehensive view of the direction of the compass needle, in all parts of the world, was made by Halley, in a chart published in 1700,"[19] thus only 34 years before the publication of the *Principia*, which makes reference to Halley's chart. By this time it was well-known that variation itself varied. For, as Raper says—

> The first good determination of the variation, in England, was made in 1580, when the direction of the north end of the needle was about one point to the eastward of the meridian. Since that time, the variation has been observed with increasing frequency and accuracy. The following is an outline of the change of the variation in England.
>
> Commencing in 1580 at 11°15' easterly, the north point of the needle moved towards the meridian, and crossed it in 1657, moving westward at the rate of 10' annually. The north end of the needle continued to move westward, with a diminishing rate, till 1818, when it attained the limit of its western range, 24°38' westerly. Since that date the north point of the needle has moved to the east with an increasing rate. The variation in London is now 17°30' westerly, diminishing at the rate of 8' annually.[20]

The magnetic pole itself seems to be shifting; but nobody knew, in Swedenborg's time, if it followed a regular cycle or moved erratically about; nor did they know, assuming it did follow a regular cycle, what the rate of movement was. We still do not know.

Swedenborg was interested in problems of oceanic navigation, as advanced a technique in his day as space navigation is in ours. And if I seem to linger on this point it is because this interest ran very very deep; the problem of *orientation*, in the broadest possible sense, lies at the root of much of his science and is even reflected in his theological writings. He invented an intriguing method of determining the longitude, which throws an unexpected light on ancient mythologies.[21] But at the moment I want to show how the

Principia, which appears to be so speculative, centers around an entirely practical problem, the variation of the compass.

I must use the word "astonishing" once more. This is the only word which can be applied to the part of the *Principia* devoted to the problem of determining the movements of the magnetic pole. Working, as we have seen, from an abstract model of the deepest components of matter, Swedenborg attempts to solve this highly macrocosmic problem. His attempt was an overall failure with a most significant element of success. This element of success gives us a very rough and general but nonetheless real indication of how seriously we should take his general theory. His theory of the magnetic pole is based entirely on his general theory of vortical motion, which is based in turn on the unprecedented logical mechanics of his primary point. That is why he proposes it as a test of his theory.

For data he has only Halley's magnetic map, referred to above. This map was an achievement for the time, but it bore little relationship to reality (Fig. 7).

Apart from this he has only what Musschenbroek refers to as a "rude chaos of observations,"[22] very few of which could have been accurate to the extent required.

Swedenborg begins with a diagram of the earth as a spherical magnet (Fig. 8).

He then launches into an analysis of the available data, which need not concern us, but which, again, shows his great respect for physical fact. There follows a chapter, *On the Causes of Magnetic Declination*, in which he step by step develops a theory of terrestrial magnetism from his theory of the magnetic element. The development of the argument is fascinating but we do not have the space to recapitulate it here. At the end of this chapter he comes up with a formula for determining the rate and extent of movement of the magnetic pole, which is further developed in the next chapter, *Calculation of the Declination of the Magnet for the year 1722, at London*.

Now he is certainly performing a useful service for the sailors of the world here, and particularly for his own maritime nation,

FIGURE 7

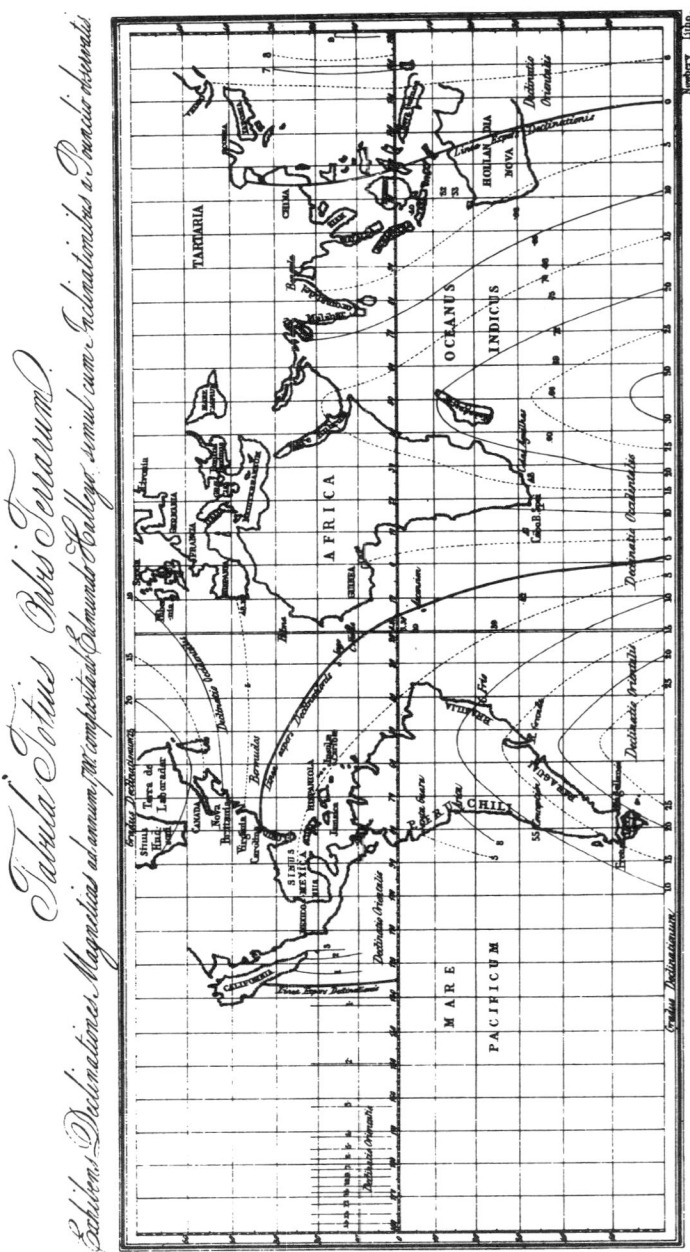

Figure 7
The Magnetic map of Dr. Edmund Halley, used by Swedenborg (*Principia*: Vol. II, facing p. 54).

FIGURE 8

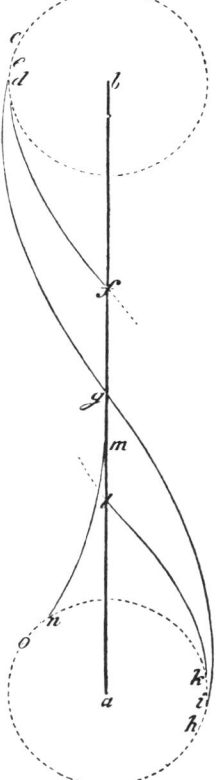

Figure 8
Swedenborg's schematic map of terrestrial magnetism. The north magnetic pole is in the upper circle *c,* the south in the lower circle *h*. From *Principia*, Vol. II, p. 72.

Sweden. But few people have a taste for two-hundred-year-old trigonometry, and the reader might tend to nod off until he is awakened with a start (he should be, anyway) by the following diagram (Fig. 9a)—

He has discovered something not known until the last century, that lines of terrestrial magnetism are not circles but sinuous lines around the earth (Fig. 9b, 10a, 10b).[23]

This is an excellent illustration, in the world of everyday and common sense observation, of Swedenborg's "mean-motion" method. All movements are assumed to be regular and so, of course, are the curves derived from them. No "line of magnetic declination" has the simple beauty of the diagram (Fig. 9a), but the lines taken together tend towards it. If the movement of the magnetic poles is regular, then Swedenborg's predictions, based on his calculations, will never be far from the truth though never dead on.

We have more apparently prophetic statements to explain here, if we can. He comes to this conclusion—"the declinations at Paris can scarcely be greater than about 37 degrees, and this very rarely; nor will the period when this is the case occur oftener than once in 20 or 30 ages."[24] It has recently been discovered by the method known as "counting varves" (which I need not go into) that the limit he roughly sets out can be applied to ancient times as well. "It has been established," says the English physicist, E.W. Lee, "that in

FIGURES 9a AND 9b

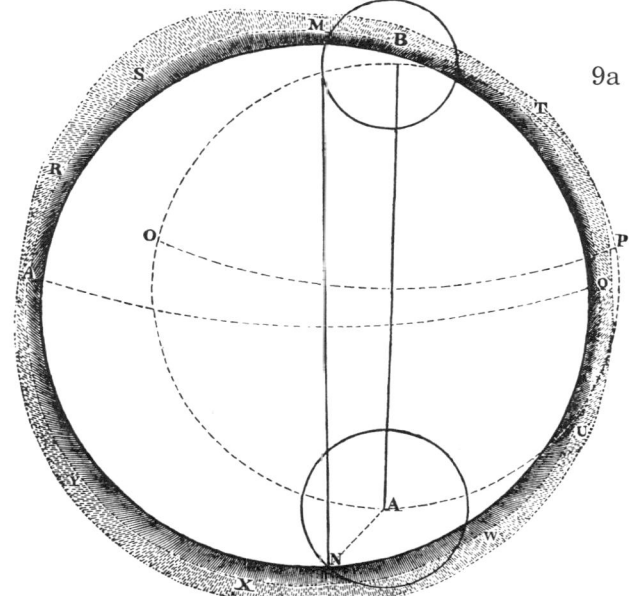

9a

Figure 9a

Figure 9a is another of Swedenborg's schematic diagrams of terrestrial magnetism. From *Principia:* Vol. II, p. 5.

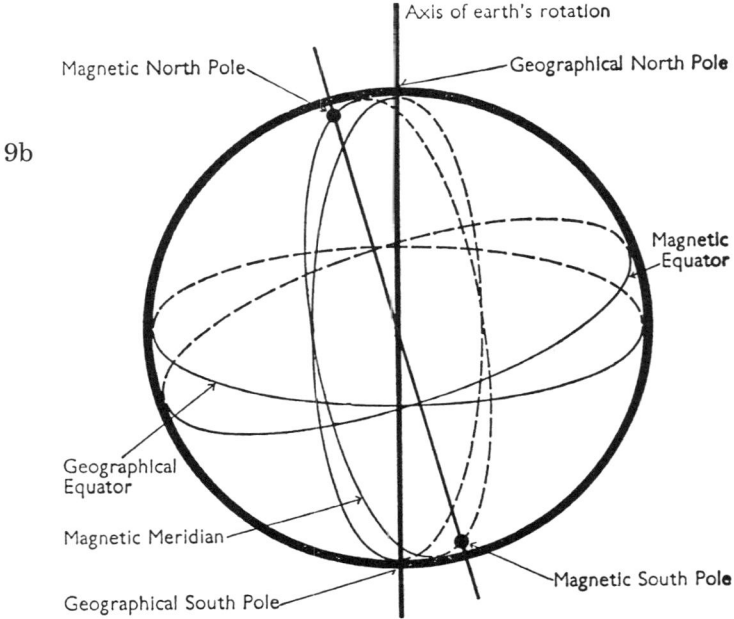

Figure 9b

Figure 9b illustrates a modern idea of the relationship between magnetic and
geographic coordinates. Redrawn from Lee, p. 241.

FIGURE 10a

Hemisphere from 60° W. to 120° E. Longitude.

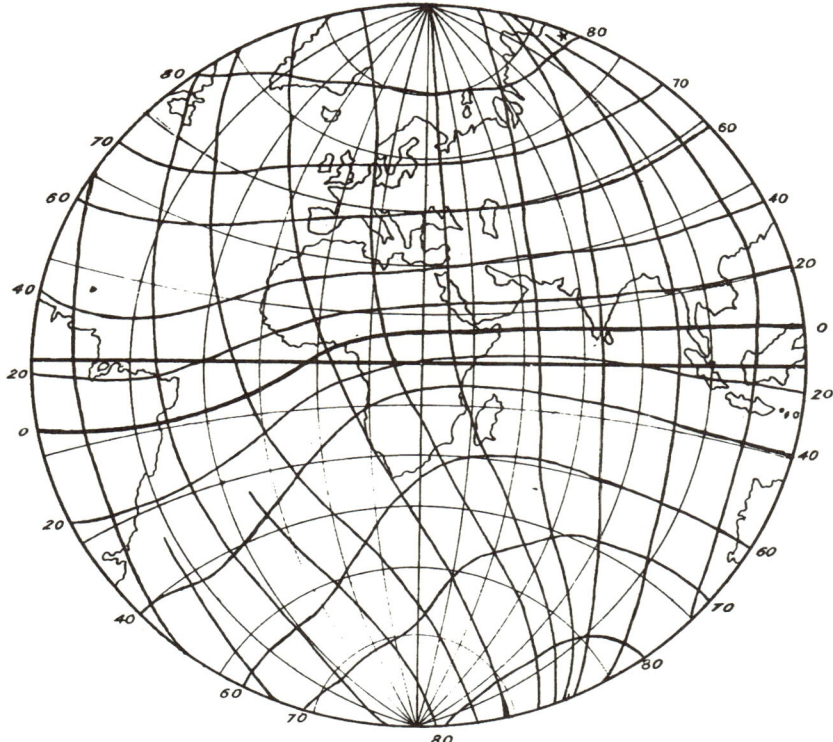

Maps showing the **Magnetic Equator,** line of **Equal Dip,** and **Horizontal Direction** of the **Compass Needle.** The parallels of latitude and the meridians are drawn at every fifteen degrees of latitude and longitude; the figures at the circumference denote the dip in degrees along the respective magnetic parallels; and the direction of the magnetic meridians, compared with the direction of the geographical meridians, shows the variation.

Figure 10a

These maps were published at the end of the last century and still bear some relationship to Swedenborg's. Modern methods, using more refined instruments of measurement, reveal more irregular patterns. From Raper, p. 82.

FIGURE 10b

Hemisphere from 120° E. to 60° W. Longitude.

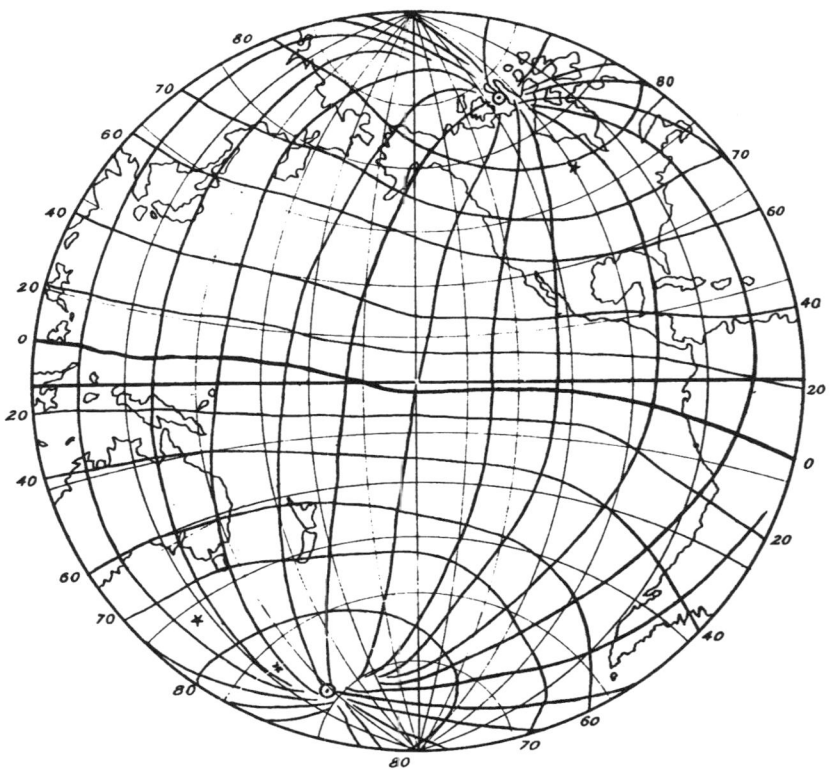

The points (O) to which the magnetic meridians converge are the magnetic poles, sometimes called, from the dip thereat being 90°, the poles of Verticity. The points (✳) show the approximate position of the foci of maximum force. It is remarkable that these six points are within 160° of longitude.

These maps, and the following table of horizontal force, are based on the good work on this subject done by the late Sir F. Evans, R.N.

Figure 10b
  From Raper, p. 83.

the last 12,000 years or so the earth's field has been that corresponding to a magnetic dipole at the centre, with a secular variation in declination of between 30° east and west of the geographical north pole."[25]

Swedenborg further says that the magnetic pole describes a *circle* about the north pole, completing its circuit in about 386 years.[26] Here we see the faulty result of his dependence on regular and harmonious figure. In fact, the circuit of the north magnetic pole is an irregular *oval* and takes about 500 years.[27] At the same time, we must marvel that he came so close. We may find another example of error resulting from his dependence on simple geometrical figures. His main source, Musschenbroek, had found that the declination of the needle varied continually by a few seconds either way. Swedenborg was convinced that the tiny errors noted by Musschenbroek were due to errors of observation—

> What ground then, I would ask, is there for believing that within a
> few minutes of time the needle or its declination is liable to so many
> mutations, when after all it may possibly be an error of observation; a
> contingency which I consider to be unquestionable.[28]

In the strict sense Swedenborg was partially right: many of the fluctuations reported by Musschenbroek *were* errors of observation. But not all of them were and Musschenbroek was objectively correct in guessing that the north magnetic pole may be continually fluctuating over a small range. By the nineteenth century navigators knew that readings can vary from day to day.[29]

Swedenborg now proceeds, with the greatest confidence, to predict the direction of magnetic north in the future and to test past readings by the same method. His tables[30] cover the period from 1610 to 1920. Since his data for the period 1610–1700 are very incomplete, I will reproduce his tables for the period 1700–1920. Column A, "By Calculation," represents Swedenborg's calculations based on his new principles; Column B, "By Experiments," represents actual readings not based on calculations and ends at 1728. The assumed center at which measurements are taken is Paris.

FIGURE 11

Years	By Calculation.		By Experiments.		Years	By Calculation.		By Experiments.	
	Deg.	Min.	Deg.	Min.		Deg.	Min.	Deg.	Min.
1677	2	57			1707	9	47	10	10
1678	3	7			1708	10	1	10	15
1679	3	18			1709	10	15	10	15
1680	3	29	2	40	1710	10	28	10	50
1681	3	41	2	30	1711	10	42	10	50
1682	3	53			1712	10	56	11	15
1683	4	5	3	50	1713	11	10	11	12
1684	4	17	4	10	1714	11	24	11	30
1685	4	29	4	10	1715	11	38	11	10
1686	4	41	4	30	1716	11	52	12	20
1687	4	53			1717	12	6	12	20
1688	5	5			1718	12	20	12	30
1689	5	17			1719	12	34	12	30
1690	5	30			1720	12	48	13	0
1691	5	41			1721	13	3	13	0
1692	6	1	5	50	1722	13	18	13	0
1693	6	17	6	20	1723	13	33	13	0
1694	6	34			1724	13	48	13	0
1695	6	51	6	48	1725	14	3	13	15
1696	7	7	7	8	1726	14	18	13	45
1697	7	24			1727	14	33	14	0
1698	7	40	7	40	1728	14	48	14	0
1699	7	56	8	10	1729	15	2		
1700	8	12	8	12 ←	1730	15	17		
1701	8	26	8	25	1731	15	30		
1702	8	39	8	48	1732	15	43		
1703	8	53	9	6	1733	15	56		
1704	9	6	9	20	1734	16	9		
1705	9	20	9	35	1735	16	22		
1706	9	33	9	48	1736	16	35		
					1737	16	48		

Years	By Calculation.		Years	By Calculation.	
	Deg.	Min.	1772	23	30
1738	17	1	1773	23	41
1739	17	14	1774	23	52
1740	17	27	1775	24	3
1741	17	40	1776	24	14
1742	17	53	1777	24	24
1743	18	5	1778	24	34
1744	18	17	1779	24	44
1745	18	29	1780	24	54
1746	18	41	1781	25	5
1747	18	53	1782	25	5
1748	19	5	1783	24	58
1749	19	17	1784	24	48
1750	19	29	1785	24	40
1751	19	42	1786	24	30
1752	19	55	1787	24	20
1753	20	8	1789	24	12
1754	20	21	1790	24	2
1755	20	34	1791	23	56
1756	20	46	1792	23	50
1757	20	58	1793	23	44
1758	21	10	1794	23	38
1759	21	22	1795	23	32
1760	21	34	1796	23	26
1761	21	44	1797	23	20
1762	21	54	1798	23	14
1763	22	4	1799	23	8
1764	22	13	1800	23	3
1765	22	23	1801	22	50
1766	22	31	1802	22	34
1767	22	40	1803	22	16
1768	22	49	1804	21	54
1769	22	58	1805	21	36
1770	23	8	1806	21	18
1771	23	19	1807	21	0

Years	By Calculation.		Years	By Calculation.	
1808	20	42	1843	5	0
1809	20	34	1844	6	0
1810	20	12	1845	7	0
1811	19	50	1846	8	0
1812	19	25	1847	9	0
1813	19	0	1848	10	0
1814	18	38	1849	11	0
1815	18	4	1850	12	4
1816	17	30	1851	13	6
1817	17	0	1852	14	9
1818	16	30	1853	15	12
1819	15	50	1854	16	15
1820	15	19	1855	17	12
1821	14	30	1856	18	0
1822	13	50	1857	18	50
1823	13	10	1858	19	45
1824	12	30	1859	20	40
1825	11	40	1860	21	32
1826	10	50	1861	22	20
1827	10	0	1862	23	0
1828	9	10	1863	23	40
1829	8	25	1864	24	20
1830	7	38	1865	25	0
1831	6	40	1866	25	40
1832	5	50	1867	26	20
1833	5	0	1868	27	0
1834	4	10	1869	27	40
1835	3	0	1870	28	18
1836	2	2	1871	28	44
1837	1	0	1872	29	10
1838	0	0	1873	29	36
1839	1	0 East	1874	30	2
1840	2	0	1875	30	28
1841	3	0	1876	30	54
1842	4	0	1877	31	20

Years	By Calculation.		Years	By Calculation.	
1878	31	56	1900	36	21
1879	32	21	1901	36	22
1880	32	45	1902	36	23
1881	33	0	1903	36	24
1882	33	20	1904	36	25
1883	33	40	1905	36	26
1884	33	55	1906	36	27
1885	34	8	1907	36	28
1886	34	20	1908	36	29
1887	24	32	1909	36	30
1888	34	42	1910	36	31
1889	34	52	1911	36	28
1890	35	4	1912	36	25
1891	35	14	1913	36	22
1892	35	23	1914	36	19
1893	35	32	1915	36	16
1894	35	40	1916	36	13
1895	35	47	1917	36	10
1896	35	52	1918	36	7
1897	35	59	1919	36	4
1898	36	6	1920	36	0
1899	36	13			

We know Swedenborg did not fudge his figures—he explains his method at length so we may check on this—and we find a remarkable coincidence between his calculations and the declinations observed for the period 1700 to 1728. What about the years following? Here both the limitations and the strengths of his method are well indicated. We know from Raper[31] that in 1818, as measured from London, "the north end of the needle...attained the limit of its western range, 24°38' westerly. Since that date the north point of the needle has moved to the east with an increasing rate." (There

would be a difference of something between less than one degree
and two degrees between London and Paris readings, depending on
where the magnetic pole was in its movements.) Swedenborg esti-
mates the western range limit will be reached in 1781 *and he puts
it at 25°5'*, which is certainly not bad when we consider that none of
the observations available to him indicated what this limit would
be. And of course there are factors affecting the earth's magnetic
field of which Swedenborg could know nothing—magnetic storms,
the influence of sunspots and the electrical conditions of the atmosphere.[32] But he is twenty-seven years out in his prediction of when
this limit will be reached. His calculations decrease in accuracy
from this point. Thus he has the magnetic pole at 36°13' East in
1899, while it was actually (from London) at 16°34' West.[33]

The next figure shows the movement of the magnetic pole from
1580 to 1958.

FIGURE 12

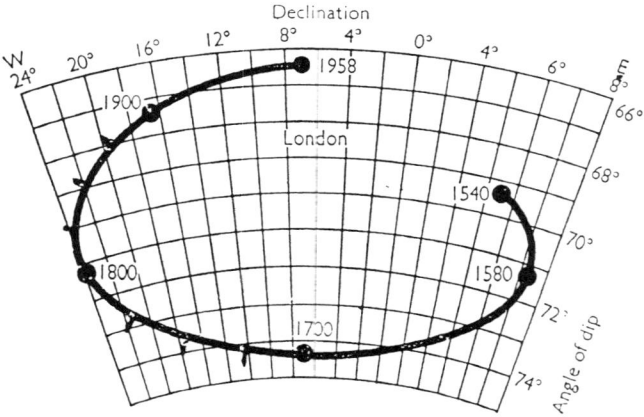

Figure 12
    Long-range variation of the declination and dip at London from 1580 to 1958.
Redrawn from Lee, p. 246.

It may be seen that it is irregular within certain limits and that no clean and harmonious curve can or could have predicted its movements with precision or near-precision.

Swedenborg expects his calculations will support his general theory. He says "...I see no reason to doubt that experience will bear them out because the calculation is based not only upon theory, but also upon experience itself. I am not indeed vain enough to put forth these speculations, without the sanction and consent of experience; for unless experience imparts her light to theory, the latter will only blind the understanding, and cause it to wander in the mazes of error."[34]

Swedenborg resolves all irregularities in nature into images of harmony and order. In this process he develops some remarkable mathematical ideas—

> Nature is always the same and identical with herself. If in the least things she is most perfectly geometrical, so also is she in the greatest. That which is most perfect in a smaller form gives rise to nothing dissimilar to itself, and consequently there is nothing dissimilar to it in the larger. All dissimilarity implies imperfection. Were nature dissimilar to herself in her large productions, there would be something imperfect in her least productions, and this would also generate something dissimilar. But since in the first entity, as in the natural point for instance, every thing is most perfectly geometrical, so the same perfection is contained even in the greatest entity; that is to say, similarity is maintained throughout. The infinite itself is the cause and origin of the whole finite world and universe: this infinite is a unity in which greater or less can have no existence, and in which there are simultaneously all things that ever can be. According to our idea, what is infinitely great and what is infinitely small are, as it were, two things; but because the infinite is in the highest perfect and most perfectly identical, it follows that such as it is in its greatest, such also is it in its least entity: nor is it possible to think of such an intermediate between the greatest and the least in the infinite. According to our finite senses we are apt to conceive that the finite is intermediate, stretching in the infinite from the least to the greatest; but because what is finite is nothing in respect to what is infinite, the intermediate between them must also be regard-

ed as respectively nothing; so that in the infinite the greatest and least entity are one and the same. For a finite difference between two entities implies no other state in the infinite than that of its being one and the same. Nature, the offspring of the infinite, derives from its origin this property also, that it is most perfectly similar to itself, for the reason that nothing perfect or dissimilar can spring from the infinite. Since however nature is finite, it follows that in the state of perfection and similarity to herself to which we have referred, she derives this peculiarity and this only, as it were, from herself, that she is susceptible of degrees and times, of dimensions, modes, ends, and boundaries, and also of variety in her state, which is not the case with the infinite.

With respect to the nature and series of finites we observe that man is introduced into the world and its mechanical order, as an intermediate between its least and greatest things; for his senses perceive such things as are, in general, equidistant from the extremes of nature. He does not comprehend everything that lies around him. His wonder is excited both by what he sees and by what he does not see. Wherever he looks he is filled with astonishment, one extreme of nature being above his senses, the other being below them; he aspires, however, to a knowledge of both. Now since nature is most perfectly identical with herself, both in what is greatest and in what is least, we may, from what we see and feel, arrive at a knowledge of what we neither see nor feel. Thus has nature designed that we should be instructed through the medium of the senses. But man possesses a soul as well as senses; and the soul has the power to reason and analyze, so that by reasoning and analysis, or by comparison of similar things, we may arrive at some knowledge of those things which do not come within the scope of the senses.[35]

His extraordinary intention has been to trace a pattern which runs through the whole of nature. This, we may say, he has done. The pattern he detects in the motions of the north magnetic pole actually does exist. He has derived this pattern from the invisible forces within the primary point. These he has described in terms of a "logical mechanics" which he has himself invented, for all that he has some precedents in early Greek thought. This is where he has succeeded. But he has failed to take into account—actually, there was no way in which he could take into account—the irregularities, the kinds of turbulence which run through all of nature. For the pattern he detects in the motions of the north magnetic pole, though it does exist, is so perturbed by what information theory calls "noise" that it can no longer be seen as an absolutely dominant and controlling factor. This is where he has failed. In philosophical terms he has predicted (not in the passage just quoted) the existence of "wobble," "perturbation," "turbulence" and "noise." He has done so by making nature a structure of contingencies. And certainly if, at the very root of the system, active and passive were perfectly reciprocal, they would persist in the blissful state of the primary point. They would have no tendency (no "desire," so to speak) to produce anything beyond themselves. But he has no way of measuring "wobble," "perturbation," "turbulence" and "noise." Thus the reality he sets out is that of a mathematical approximation.

He had actually set himself (nobody could set it for him) a dual test. The first test was the prediction of the movements of the magnetic pole to 1920, the results of which we have just considered. The second test (see the end of the last chapter) was whether or not he could succeed in showing a "geometrical "harmony" and a "connection" between the forms which went to compose his first element and those belonging to the magnetic element. In this, as it seems to me, he has succeeded. When we disregard perturbations of the earth's magnetic field caused by external influences—solar effects, electromagnetic storms and the like—considering only the innate magnetic field, then the movements of the pole can be related in a generalizing sense to his pattern. This is considered a legitimate abstraction. Thus, "In 1839 Gauss showed that the field of a uniformly magnetized sphere (which is the same as that of a geocentric dipole) is an excellent first approximation to the Earth's magnetic field."[36] Here is the Gaussian sphere,[37] developed more than one hundred years after the *Principia* was published.

Its relationship to the Swedenborgian diagram of the earth as a spherical magnet, illustrated earlier (see Fig. 9a, p. 136), is obvious, and all the more so when Swedenborg's comment on the diagram is added.

FIGURE 13

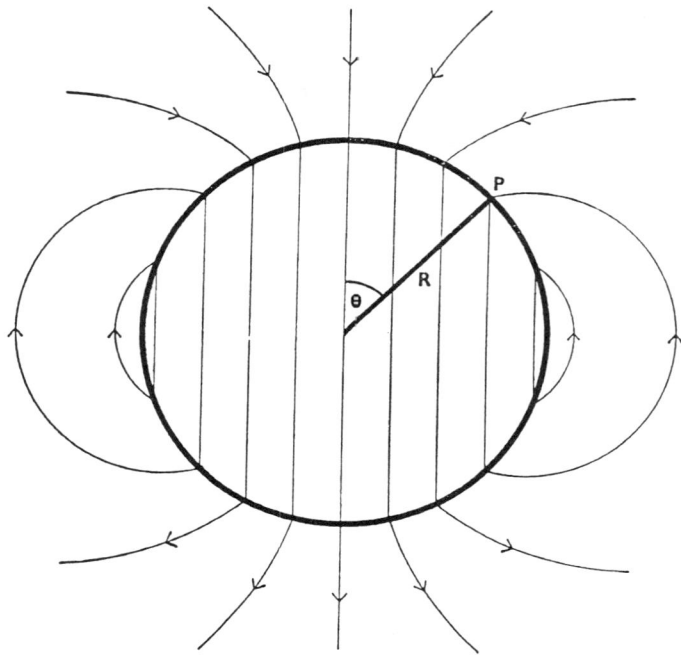

Figure 13
   The magnetic field of a uniformly magnetised sphere, after Gauss. Redrawn from Lee, p. 246.

Swedenborg says, "In fig. 84 (Fig. 9a here: NN), let BOAP be the earth; B and A the two poles of the earth; OP its equator; M the north magnetic pole; N the south pole; AEQ their equator; MAENQ is also the earth; but this circle passes through each magnetic pole. Near the poles M and N the particles of the element are erect, or are perpendicular to the horizon. But at a distance thence, as at T or S, they are in an oblique position, that is to say, oblique in regard to the earth; and this obliquity is the same with the magnetic inclination. Near the equator in AEQ, the particles of the same element lie horizontally; whence again they gradually become erect towards the other pole in N, and so on."[38]

If the Gaussian sphere is "an excellent first approximation," which nobody would deny, then clearly the Swedenborgian sphere, which preceded it by roughly a century, must be too. And in the second test, that of "geometrical harmony" and "connection," an excellent first approximation is all that is required.

We may go further yet. In a geometrically generalizing cosmology, or "canon of forms," which is what Swedenborg's cosmology is, an excellent first approximation is all the proof the theory requires. His theory indeed has all the faults of one based on mathematical generalization. But note where it begins. It begins at the primary point, the point where the ratios of material relationships are so subtle and obscure that they can only be represented as logical opposites. And from this he has deduced a real world *with a measurable degree of inaccuracy*. Where, in the history of science, shall we find an achievement such as this?

ENDNOTES

1 Swedenborg, *Principia* I, pp. ix–x.

2 Herman and Goldberg, *Sun, Weather and Climate*, p. 24.

3 Bova, p. 31.

4 In addition to his magnetic studies, Musschenbroek discovered the principle of the Leyden Jar, an early form of electrical condenser which built up and stored charges of static electricity. He was largely responsible for introducing the natural philosophy of Newton into Holland.

5 Swedenborg, *Principia* I, p. 543.

6 Ibid., I, pp. 206–207.

7 Ibid., II, pp. 156–160. See also I, p. 89 and I, pp. 111–112.

8 Ibid., I, p. 187.

9 Swedenborg, *Five Senses*, p. 117.

10 Swedenborg, *Principia* I, pp. 224 et seq.

11 Ibid., I, p. 246.

12 Ibid., I, p. 233. It might be said, by the way, that the question of when man first became aware of the properties of the lodestone is of considerable importance in the study of ancient science (see Part II of this book). Studies of a worked lodestone object found in Mexico indicate "that the Olmecs may have discovered and used the geomagnetic lodestone compass earlier than 1000 BC—predating the Chinese discovery by more than a millennium" (John B. Carlson, "Lodestone Compass: Chinese or Olmec Primacy?," *Science*, Sep. 5, 1975, p. 753). Carlson believes it possible that Olmec sites were oriented by use of the lodestone compass. Greek knowledge of the lodestone is commonly set back to the sixth century BC, the time of the philosopher Thales, a Phoenician of Asia Minor. *Lapis Lydius* means "Lydian stone," referring to Lydia in Asia Minor.

13 Ibid., II, p. 575.

14 Ibid., I, p. 216.

15 Ibid., I, p. 217.

16 Ibid., I, pp. 216–217.

17 Ibid., I, p. 213.

18 The above account of the development of the theory of the compass is from Hewson, Chapter II.

19 Raper, p. 71.

20 Ibid., p. 71.

21 Edmund Halley, when Swedenborg met him in Oxford in 1712, acknowledged that Swedenborg's method was the best of its kind and another famous astronomer, Flamsteed, had started to work on the lunar tables the method required (Sigstedt, p. 23).

The method is described in *Swedenborg's Work on Longitude*, by Wertha Pendleton Cole, in *NP*, April, 1933. Although the perfection of the chronometer eventually resulted in the disappearance of lunar methods for ascertaining the longitude, a process which was beginning at about the time Swedenborg developed his method (which was thus never adopted by the seamen of the world), it was the best and simplest of lunar methods developed up to that time. This work still retains great historical interest because of the possibility that ancient navigators used such methods. Basically the system generalized the old method of finding the longitude by observing lunar eclipses; the Swedenborgian method observes the position of the moon, not at the eclipse point, but in relation to the stars. The method is so simple that if, say, story-like accounts of the travels of the moon among the stars were used instead of accurate lunar/stellar tables, a coarsely effective determination of longitude would be possible. There are many myths which seem to be concerned with the position of the moon among the stars and in relationship to places on earth. The best-known is the Greek myth of Io. By putting together what one knows about ancient navigation and methods of tracking the moon, along with the "moon-myths" mentioned (strictly speaking, they are not myths but mnemonics), one may arrive at a possible ancient mode of navigation which would explain the confidence of ancient mariners, based as it must have been on an ability to determine their positions with at least fair accuracy. This would have had much to do with the spread of ancient culture patterns.

A highly speculative but fascinating attempt to reconstruct ancient systems of navigation is found in Gilbert Pillot's *Le Code Secret de l'Odyssee*. Following the scholar, Jean Richer, he finds the "Greenwich" of this ancient system in the temple of Amon in the oasis of Siwa in Egypt.

22 Swedenborg, *Principia* II, p. 54.

23 Raper: insert between pp. 82 and 83. The nineteenth-century magnetic map was drawn by Sir F. Evans, R.N.

24 Swedenborg, *Principia* II, p. 132.

25 Lee, p. 262.

26 Swedenborg, *Principia* I, p. 60.

27 Lee, p. 245.

28 Swedenborg, *Principia* II, p. 13.

29 Raper, p. 72.

30 Swedenborg, *Principia* II, pp. 127–131.

31 Raper, p. 71.

32 Here, as often in this book, Swedenborg's errors in one place point to accuracy in another. In his theory the sun is a great magnet. As he says, "This magnetic element exists chiefly in the solar vortex" (*Principia* II, p. 58). It follows then that the magnetism of the sun should influence the magnetism of the earth, as we now know it does (NASA, *Sun, Weather and Climate passim*). Yet with his philosophical belief in the complete orderliness of the physical universe he cannot imagine that

the magnetism of the sun should *perturb* the magnetism of the earth. One indication of the potency and objectivity of a theory is that its author cannot grasp all its implications or misses some of them.

33 Raper, p. 103A.

34 Swedenborg, *Principia* II, p. 127.

35 Ibid., II, pp. 151–152. Note that the phrase "as respectively nothing" can only refer to zero as an infinitesimal, not as being absolutely nothing.

36 Jacobs, J.A., article *Geomagnetism*, in *Enc. of Phys.*, p. 355.

37 Lee, p. 236.

38 Swedenborg, *Principia* II, pp. 5–6.

6

The Ether and the
Solar Vortex

It seems that we can feel fairly well at home in Swedenborg's magnetic sphere. In 1912 his description of it appeared in large part "perfectly correct" and we can now see further that much which appeared to be speculative in 1912 is also correct. What is not "correct" is not inexplicable either, since we can see where he went wrong.

After the magnetic sphere, though, he discusses the ether—and here we shall at first find ourselves quite lost. We might attempt to orient ourselves by saying, "Well, this is an *old* idea. People believed in the ether from Greek times up to about the time of the First World War, didn't they? Then Einstein proved it did not exist." Yet this does not help, because when we start to read Swedenborg's description of the ether we find it has very little to do with the classical ether, either Greek or Victorian/Edwardian. For one thing it is made up of things which look like atoms in Swedenborg's illustrations and it behaves in a very unclassical fashion, like a subtle gas. What is he talking about?

I would like to show that Swedenborg's ether does indeed have little to do with the classical ether. It is something much more up to date. What he is describing is like what we now call a plasma or an ionized gas, or what some in his time called a "fire-mist." If it is hard to recognize as such it is because Swedenborg had no experimental or sensual experience of an ether. He had to imagine something between the magnetic element and air, and his geometrical theory gave it certain characteristics.

As I indicated in the imaginary quotation above, it is now a commonplace that we have no need of the ether. From about 1814, when Augustin Fresnel imagined that light travelled by displacing an invisible substance, pervading the entire universe, which was at once highly rigid and very tenuous, experimenters had tried to find some evidence that it actually existed. None could be found. The famous Michelson-Morley experiment of 1881, which I need not describe since it has been discussed so often, showed that light did not behave as if it travelled through such an ether. It also showed that the earth and its atmosphere did not travel through a resisting and stationary medium. Finally a paper of Einstein, written in 1905, "On the Electrodynamics of Moving Bodies," declared that there was no need at all to postulate the existence of a luminiferous ether.

We may say, however, that it was impossible to prove that the ether did not exist, since it had been defined so multifariously that a standard of proof or disproof could not be set. The ether-concept originally arose out of the perceived necessity to postulate some element more subtle than air, which could fill all of space and yet provide some substance through which God or the gods could act in the world of space and time. If one did not believe in gods one still needed a substance which could, at least, be the most subtle of all.

We find that the idea of ether already exists in ancient India.[1] There the Vaiseshika school of unknown age believes that though ether cannot be perceived directly we can demonstrate its necessity logically and can also sense it indirectly, because it is the bearer of sound. In this theory, ether does not have an atomic nature but combines with atoms in the substances of the phenomenal world and also fills the spaces between atoms. In the system of the Greek Anaxagoras, who was born at the beginning of the fifth century BC the "ether" (the Greek word is derived from the word *aitho*, to light up, to burn or blaze: it is already connected with fire) appears as a substance more tenuous then air, being the stuff of which the sky is made. Whether Anaxagoras' idea was more refined than this we cannot know because we have only seventeen fragments of his treatise on nature. In Plato *(Epinomis)* it is a substance intermediate in nobility or subtlety between fire and air. In Aristotle it is the substance of which souls are made.

We need not proceed farther, since from the time of Aristotle the concept branched and rebranched, possessing no internal consistency because it was intended to fill gaps in a number of logically separated fields of inquiry, such as the gaps between—

i) the soul and the body, a medium being required which enabled the soul to communicate with the body;

ii) God or the gods and matter, a medium being required which enabled divine forces to act upon matter;

iii)air and the substance of the whole universe: it was known, perhaps from mountain-climbing experiences, that the air grows more rarefied as one rises above sea level, and therefore it could not be assumed that air filled all of space;

iv)wave/corpuscular phenomena, such as sound and light, and the human sensory (a medium was required to connect them);

v) atoms and the space in which they discretely existed.

The ether, then, was really concocted to solve a problem, or several problems, and its assumed properties were from the very beginning (as in Swedenborg) those which it was assumed would solve the problem or problems. It never really existed as a positive idea, but only as a set of positive assumptions to fill a gap or negative interval, and so its existence could neither be proved nor disproved experimentally. What the Michelson-Morley experiment really disproved was a single formulation of the ether-idea, that it was a stationary medium which could offer resistance to the earth's movement through it, thus producing friction or drag. The problems the ether idea was intended to solve never really disappeared, and they have not been solved in our time either.

It is not necessary that the ether be a material substance as ordinarily understood. Max Born pointed out that in his later years

Einstein proposed that the complex consisting of empty space and the gravitational and electromagnetic fields could be called the "ether." In this medium there would be no determinable points, and it would not be meaningful to speak of motion relative to it. Born says, "Such a use of the word 'ether' is of course admissible, and when once it has been sanctioned by usage in this way, probably quite convenient."[2]

Now Swedenborg's ether does resemble such a complex, though it is indeed a form of matter or substance as Swedenborg defines substance. The manner in which he describes its components is inevitably not a modern one. The first component of space (which is not, however, an "emptiness") is defined by the first element; electromagnetism is defined by the second; and both are contained in the ether.

What then of gravitational fields? Swedenborg's theory retains some relevance to Born's statement even here, since it is in the etheric medium that gravity becomes fully apparent, though it has deep antecedents in preceding stages of the argument.

From his published works (but see Appendix E) it does not appear that he has his own theory of gravitation, but rather an attitude towards the theory of Newton. Unfortunately, his very refined manners—at this stage one wishes that he had been less of a Swedish gentleman—forbid his engaging in pointed dispute. He nowhere attacks Newton; he merely does not mention him (Musschenbroek does, in the sections quoted in the *Principia*). We therefore have nothing to go on except a point of view implicit in Swedenborg's entire cosmology, which seems to be as follows.

Newton's theory of gravitation is perfectly correct in the empirical sense. It works. It is good mechanics. But it has the great disadvantage of postulating the transmission of mechanical force across a void, which is unreasonable. And there are other unreasonable aspects of Newton's natural philosophy, such as his assumption of the existence of absolute space and time. How can a space with nothing in it be measured, and, if it cannot be, how can something which is nowhere measurable be called a space?

Swedenborg has his own philosophical definitions of all the elements which enter into the Newtonian equation: mass, velocity and so on. He does not dispute Newton's equations or any well-established mechanical law, but refers to them casually as well-known. He does not deny in any way the empirical formulation of Newton's gravitational law which says that "any two bodies of masses *m* and *M*, which are at a distance *r* from each other, will attract each other with a force *y(mM/r2)*, where *y* is the constant of gravitation."[3] He takes it for granted. He reproduces Musschenbroek's praise of Newton as "the prince of philosophers," and in his *Miscellaneous Observations* he says that to Newton's researches "all other observations cannot but be inferior." But he does not accept Newton's philosophical framework. To Swedenborg, mass is an infolding of motions and components of pure space as geometrically and logically conceived; all forms of velocity are developed from vortical spin; and space as we know it is full of "fields" (my term: his is "elementaries"). A gravitational constant must be a particular expression of the order of the universe as a whole, which manifests itself at the level of bodies with perceptible weight. It is not an elementary force or a simple one, nor is *any* component of the sensually perceptible world. It is an abuse of language, therefore, to describe gravitation as a "fundamental law."

In the *Principia* he does not describe gravity as a separate force. He speaks of "centres of gravity," another term for which is "centres of mass." Every massy body has such a center of gravity, but so does an elementary rotatory system. A center of gravity itself is a form of compacted motion, that is, something like a particle. He tells us that the center of a primal vortex is somewhat removed from the axis of rotation and thus from the geometrical center. It is the wobble caused by the double rotation of the vortex—about the axis of rotation through its geometrical center and about the center of gravity—which is most deeply responsible for the complexities of natural form. Because of this, the tiniest particle has the form of motion of a precessing celestial body, since the center of gravity moves in the plane of the ecliptic. And, of course, since this form of movement is supposed to be found in every entity from the primary particle to the largest complex of suns and planets, it seems to be a universal, and in macrocosmic terms a measurable universal. It is also, since it binds the centers of gravity of small bodies to the center of whatever large system they compose, a *force of attraction*. Thus the formulas of Newton are not denied but fitted into a different universal context, in which the troubling anomaly of action across a void does not appear. This context centers on the notion of the primary point in a philosophically subtle way which cannot be adequately discussed here. But the key idea is that gravity is a constant, or more or less of a constant, because of the complex interactions of the entire well-ordered universe. It is in one sense a statistical constant, the accumulation of smaller attractions.

By the time we get to the ether or Third Element, all of "infinite space" (not a Swedenborgian term) is full of movements derived from the vortex. These movements are related one to the other by the mechanical relations between their centers of force—in this case, centers of mass, since they are massy objects. We must not imagine spaces full of tiny whirlpools. The vortex is the formal and summary origin of all curves and straight-line movements. This is a difficult aspect of Swedenborg's argument, one which seems to mislead all who consider his theory. Yet, as we learn from the opening chapters of the *Principia*, it is the essence of his "new geometry." When he talks of a "vortex" (say, of the "solar vortex") he is talking of the central and primary motion form which generates all the forms and motions a body can exhibit. Had he wished, though it would have aroused deafening hoots of derision in his time, he could have called all the forms analyzed in Euclid's *Elements* "forms developed from a Euclidean vortex." It is a great mistake to imagine, as so many have done, that he is constructing a universe of tightly packed vortices. This would be geometrically and mechanically absurd. In his system the space of everyday observation is Euclidean, containing straight lines, curves and shapes which approximate the Platonic solids.

As we have seen earlier, the case is not dissimilar from that of one who would generate all geometrical entities from conic sections. We might remember from our school mathematics that we can obtain such figures as the ellipse and circle by sectioning or cutting a conical surface into various slices. But the cone is a static, not a dynamic figure. Swedenborg must therefore look for a dynamic interpretation of the cone, and the result of this is that "conic sections" are seen as static models of what might be called (coarsely and avoiding many mathematical problems) "vortical sections."

The gist of this, then, is that Newton's laws, including the law of gravitation, are in no way denied as empirical facts. Rather they are fitted into a different philosophical and particularly a different geometrical framework.

Swedenborg's ether is a very active thing. It is not that paradoxical jelly, the nineteenth-century "luminiferous ether," which is both rigid and highly rarefied. It is, as we shall see, something close to what we know. It is, to quote a modern authority, something which is "the most widespread state of matter in the universe."[4] It is a generalized form, the speculative ancestor, of what we now call a "plasma."

A plasma can be called an ionized gas. All or most of its atoms have lost some or many of their negatively-charged electrons, and the result is the conversion of these atoms into positive ions. This leaves us with a mixture of three kinds of particles: free electrons, positive ions and electrically neutral molecules or atoms. The sun and the stars are composed of very hot plasma, and the ionosphere around the earth is an envelope of plasma, as are also the radiation belts lying beyond the ionosphere. When natural discharges of gas occur—in the action of lightning or of sparks or arcs produced in the laboratory—plasma is also generated. It is generated, too, in the very hot parts of an ordinary flame. Thus, in the simplest way of looking at it, plasma is the state of matter beyond gas on the scale of temperature. When any natural material is heated beyond the stage at which it becomes a gas, it then becomes a plasma. Even the plasmas thinly diffused in space have a very high temperature in the technical sense, since their particles move very rapidly and are thus "hot," but the temperature of such a plasma as a whole is very low. Plasmas are found in metals at room temperature and have been studied in large atoms.

Swedenborg's ether does not at first appear much like a plasma; but this is due to his mode of argument which appears, to our kind of scientific reasoning which proceeds "from the outside of matter inwards," to be logically inverted. We still define a plasma as a collection of atoms which have lost some of their parts, thus conceptually or in logical sequence placing particles of plasmas *after* those of gases ("Big Bang" and related theories are somewhat changing that now). Swedenborg defines his ether as a collection of elementary particles which have *not yet* acquired the parts which will make them the atoms of the materials we know.

There is no doubt that his ether is much closer to our idea of a plasma than either classical ether or the luminiferous ether of the nineteenth century. It should be clear by now that I am not saying that his ether is a plasma or that he has discovered plasma. I mean that his theory led him to postulate the existence of something so much like what we call a plasma that no more appropriate modern word may be found. Obviously, also, it possesses qualities which are nothing like those of a modern plasma. I am not crediting Swedenborg with quasi-miraculous prevision, only the close reasoning of a natural philosopher of genius, building on the ideas of his time. Leibniz, in a letter written in July of 1671 (Swedenborg quotes it in his *Philosopher's Notebook*), has ether as a weightless substance, whose movements cause gravity, "elastic force and magnetic direction." He also says that light causes it or its particles to gyrate. Leibniz is building on Aristotle, as he says. In the most general of senses, the ancient Greek association of ether and fire, which has always been puzzling, anticipates the idea of a plasma. When Swedenborg adapts such non-systematic insights to his own highly systematic world-diagram, he comes up with a recognizable sketch of what we now call a plasma. His procedure is perfectly rational and we may follow it in detail. He has so closely defined the magnetic sphere and the generic behaviors of gases that the space between them can only hold particles of a certain kind. Yet these particles do not only resemble plasmas. Indeed, they have qualities which have not been observed and probably never will be, because they embody all the logical and geometrical possibilities of the interval they occupy.

Naturally our overview is going to be a coarse one. Also, I shall not concern myself with the areas in which his ethereal particles resemble nothing known to modern science. Such detail would not be appropriate in this book, and, in any case, it would have to be undertaken by a professional scientist thoroughly familiar with the *Principia* and sympathetic to its philosophy. But there is another reason. As I have stated earlier, it is my view, though not that of the majority of students of Swedenborg, that his elementary particles are Augustinian *exemplars*, of which individual particles are particular realizations. This has been missed, I believe, despite what appear to me to be clear statements in the text, partly because many students of the *Principia* have tended to underplay traditional Christian elements in Swedenborg's philosophy, regarding them as inert remnants of "old thinking" which he would later discard. If this "strong view" of the traditionally correspondential nature of his cosmos is not accepted, we still have the "weak view," which is very amply supported by the text, that the *Principia* is not so much science in the modern sense as a "canon of forms," a geometrical vision of matter. What is valuable in it rests upon the principles by which the argument is organized. Swedenborg's observations and measurements are often flawed. In few cases are they superior to the standards of the time, and it can be convincingly argued that as a practical scientist Swedenborg was not among the greatest figures of his age. He himself admitted, not from false modesty, that his forte lay not in experimental science but in "contemplating facts already discovered and eliciting their causes."[5]

It is the same principles which result in some of his failures, as we have seen in the last chapter. But it is the power of his logical method which interests us, and not its particular failures, since the latter are in no way remarkable, while the successes are.

Swedenborg's ether particles are bundles animated by an energy which he calls "magnetic." I shall call it "electromagnetic." This is in line with modern usage and also with the fact that Swedenborg's description of magnetism includes many phenomena we now label "electromagnetic." By way of a complex of geometrical/mechanical forces which he describes, but which I need not go into in this summary, these energy bundles have quiesced into free material particles, particles of "ether." In examining his description of their behaviors we note that these particles, uncannily, exhibit some behaviors roughly typical of particles of plasma. Sometimes they resemble free atoms, sometimes ions, sometimes electrons. But all these behaviors are related to a single particle-form, which resembles nothing so much as a huge conventionalized atom (see the figure farther on in this chapter).

Their motion is like that of free planetary bodies, in that they revolve around their axes and move "from place to place," though the notion of space is still vague in this sphere of matter. Nevertheless, ethereal particles are very definitely a form of matter, though they are not fixed forms like particles of metals or salts. That is why we may legitimately call Swedenborg's ether a phase of matter. In his mode of thought, the logical inverse of ours, ether particles, by complex interfoldings and interactions, may generate the particles of gases, while we say, inversely, that particles of gases may dissociate in plasmas.

His explanation of how this occurs is intricately geometrical, but it may be simplified in this manner. Ether particles originated in the sun. The parental forms of earth and other planets were made of nothing but ethereal particles. These folded into each other, acquired subsidiary particles from each other, and thus formed themselves into the substances we know. This transformation occurred first at the surface of the infant earth, which in effect had the form of a great plasma ball cooling from the outside in, its surface first turning into gases, then liquids, then solids.

The ether particle, then, possesses an internal space full of electromagnetic activity in the form of specific internal particles. These electromagnetic particles contain in their turn particles of the "first element," which I can only describe as bundles of nonspecific space/time. It is for this reason that Swedenborg's gigantic ethereal particle so resembles, in its curiously generic way, a modern representation of an atom. A modern atom also contains within it electromagnetic particles and yet smaller ones, whose behaviors, while they occupy something like a space and move in such a fashion as to simulate time-governed behavior, do not seem to be controlled by the laws of space and time we know.

The resemblances between the Swedenborgian and modern particles indeed go farther than my summary can indicate—but the question does remain, *how* far? His description of their behavior is couched in terms of the only mechanical analogies available to him, terms drawn from the behaviors of bouncing balls, bubbles and other naked-eye phenomena. Thus he refers to such concepts as elasticity, compression, centrifugal force, tension, rarefaction and compression. He is precise, if not quantitatively so, in his use of these concepts, which we find strange. But to relate such concepts to the quite different ones we use to describe the behaviors of microparticles could only be done by somebody completely at home in modern mathematical physics, who could translate one set of concepts to the other and develop equations containing both. This would be difficult, demanding a novel *conflation* of logical and mathematical notations (individually, these already exist).

To give an example of how strangely close to laboratory reality Swedenborg's speculations can be, we might note that he says the particles adhering to the outer surface of his "ether-atom" (my word)—

> ...may be broken up, and cease to be elementary; but nevertheless the finites, inhering to their surface, and which are now escaping by reason of the disruption, cannot actuate themselves, but must fall into some of the surfaces of the neighboring particles, and there like finites continue their motion as before in some other surface...[6]

Just such an event occurs when a gas is ionized, that is, becomes a plasma. Its electrons tear free and begin to dart about independently, impelled by electromagnetic forces. With a drop in temperature or removal of the laboratory apparatus which is causing ionization we have what is called "recombination," the electrons and ions joining together in new forms like their original ones. But there is more yet. He says, supporting his statement by an intricate argument, that "the motion of the volume of the ethereal particles is the same as the motion of the particles individually." This is a motion which "is perfectly equal in all directions; differing in this respect from the motion of the volume of the first and second elements."[7] What he is imagining is something remarkably like the "collisionless behavior" found in plasmas, in which the collisions of plasma particles, at certain critical densities and temperatures of the plasma mass, become assimilated into a general movement of the mass, a movement which we know as "collective plasma oscillation frequency."[8]

Let us now return to a point made earlier. It may be said that Swedenborg satisfies the Einsteinian conditions for an acceptable ether in this sense, that his etheric element contains within it and is built upon empty space and electromagnetic fields (which latter are fully realized in the ether proper), and that it is itself the plane on which gravitational forces come observably into play.

But what of the demand that there be no determinable points in this medium? This seems to be justified, since if there were determinable points, with space between them measurable in naked-eye terms, we should have a fully material three dimensional space. In such a space ether would have to be a gas, liquid or solid. Ether or forms of it would enter into decomposable chemical substances. For if ether were fully in space and time as we know them sensually, then by chemical operations on a substance, we should be able to extract a portion of ether, which would now be a chemically specific substance like oxygen or nitrogen.

It is difficult to arrive at Swedenborg's meaning here, and one of the chief causes is that, since he has no mathematical tools to formulate what he has imagined, he must continually use analogies and comparisons from the naked-eye world. This produces an impression of *fully realized* materiality which he did not intend. The first set of attributes we should note, however, is that the ethereal particles are entirely spherical, move perpetually, touch one another only at one point, "can subsist under any kind of motion and with perfect aptitude to it," can expand and contract according to heat, and meet with no mechanical resistance. They are also subject to pressure according to the altitude of the ether column and then, but only in the highest degree of compression, cease "to be both elastic and elementary, becoming hard and similar to a kind of material finite" Also, "in a single volume in motion, there may exist innumerable other volumes, even indeed equal to the number of centres or causes of motion, or to particles," and "the volume is, as it were, a large connected whole, whose motion is that of its particles." A volume of ether particles may flow through any hard body and the refraction of the direction of flow determines the color of the body.[9] In summarizing certain aspects of his argument, we may say that the earth, in passing through such an ether, would encounter even less resistance than a sieve passing through air. "As seen from the ether," the earth would be a purely conceptual network, without solid parts. Ether would freely flow through it— more accurately yet, would behave as if the earth had no existence. For an elementary is complete in itself, and it forms the "next most material" element only when it reaches a state of plenitude—one might almost say when it "buds" (a response to pressure, quiescence of movement and other factors) into a new form.

The answer does seem to be that there are indeed no determinable points in this medium since the only motion of its parts is curvilinear and ethereal particles can only touch each other at one point. These would then be "tangent points" but they would not be observable. There would be no collisions and strong interchanges of forces and thus no "sparks" as it were, interchanges of energy which would form nodes. Nor would there be points of mechanical resistance. Ethereal particles are only still when, under great pressure, they cease to be such and turn into something like gaseous particles. In his sphere of plasma-like ethereal particles we do have space and time of a non-quantitative sort, because we have bodies with centers and these bodies move. But space is indeterminate because the bodies have no fixed outlines, being in a continual expansion and contraction which would appear random. And time is also indeterminate, because no body or portion of a body moves in a fixed and measurable cycle. There can be no time measurement without cyclical motion.

Swedenborg's language here is in no way modern. The condition of space/time indeterminacy he refers to as the "universal chaotic condition" and he relates it to the Chaos of the Greek poets and myth-makers. Nonetheless, Swedenborg's ether particle, when we see a picture of it on page 215 of the second volume, looks like a complex and generalized atom, a rough sketch of something which would not be "seen" until our century. Compare it, for example, with a modern visualization of atomic nuclei.

FIGURE 14

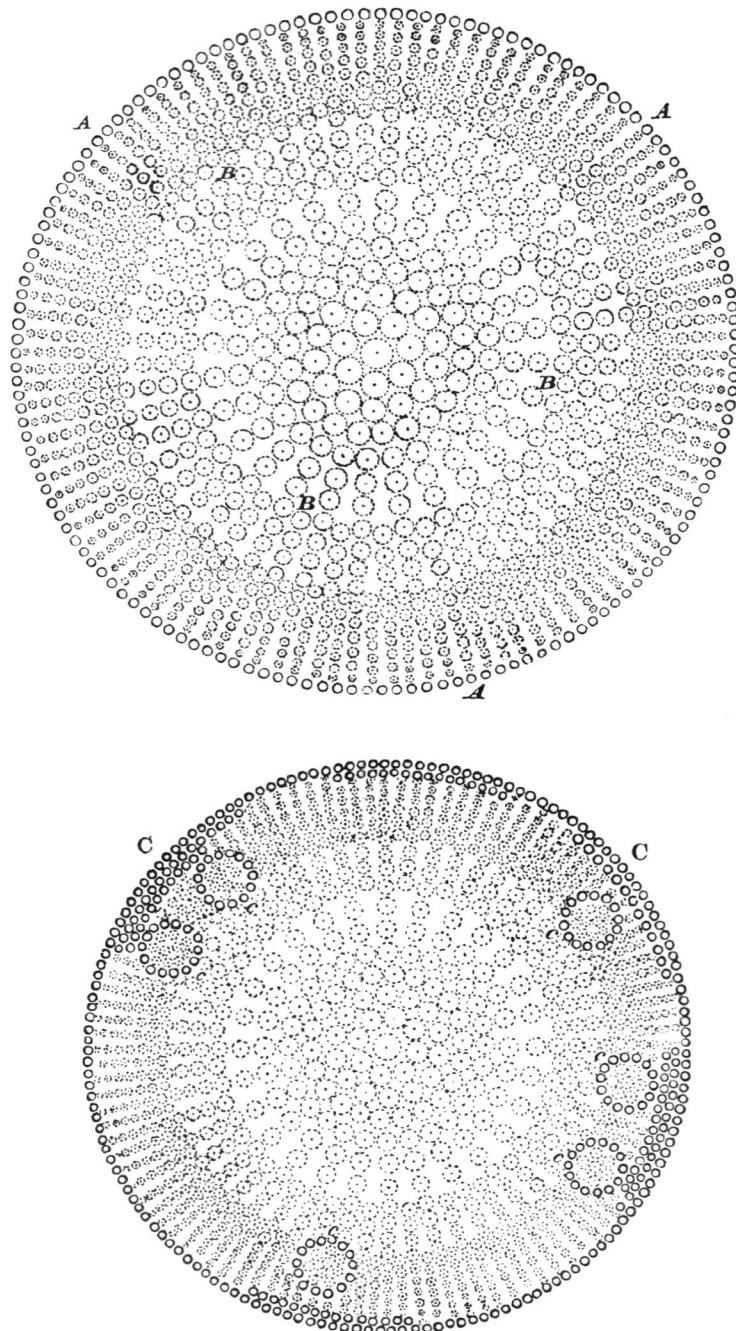

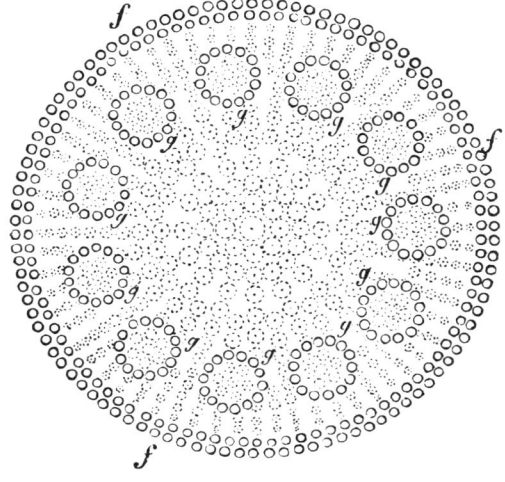

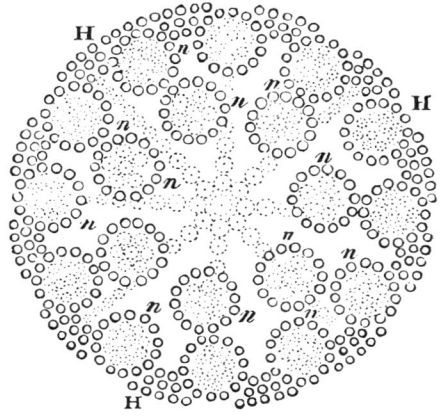

Figure 14
    Ether particles in various states. From *Principia* II: pp. 215–217.

FIGURE 15

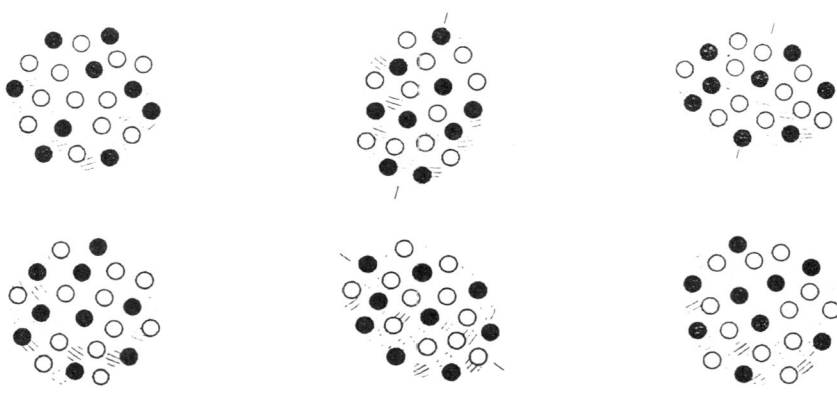

Figure 15
    Diagrams of atomic nuclei of various shapes in modern representation (compare Swedenborg's visualization: Figure 1). The protons are shown as dark circles, the neutrons as open circles. Redrawn from "The Size and Shape of Atomic Nuclei," by Michael Baranger and Raymond A. Soresen, in *Scientific American*, August, 1969, p. 58.

There are also non-etheric particles in his etheric realm. Thus he talks of—

> ...minute corpuscles which resemble a kind of effluvia, and which are so small as to be able to move only a volume of ether, but not a volume of air; these, if spontaneously moved, excite light to a certain distance. If they are not spontaneously moved, but put in motion by means of the tremulation of the parts in any hard body where they are, then light also is produced, and also electricity, so long as the tremulation continues. That the motion of the ether, when diffused in all directions from a given centre, or when diffused to equidistant circumferences, produces the phenomenon of light, is evident from what we have stated.[10]

He has come pretty close to defining the work done by photons and photoelectrons. When photons, which are both wave-like and corpuscular in form, strike a reflecting surface, photoelectrons are emitted from the surface and light is seen. Also, a modern scientist tells us, the exchange of photons generates the electromagnetic force and "the force of static electricity is also generated by a flood of photons."[11]

The "Swedenborgian photon," then, is not an ether particle, but it inhabits the etheric realm like a tadpole in a pond. This again seems to make it legitimate to think of his etheric realm as composite in one sense, but dominated by his single-formed version of atoms and their parts free or bound.

We should now look more closely at three aspects of the etheric realm which are most important in understanding its functional relationship to the rest of the *Principia*. These are—

i) The relationship of light and heat to the ether;
ii) The relationship of fire to the ether;
iii) The role of ether in the relationship between sun and earth.

In the etheric sphere he places some but not all of the properties of light. As we have seen, he has imagined "minute corpuscles which resemble a kind of effluvia" and which are something like modern photons. But these are not the sole originators of the complex phenomenon of light. He says—

> Motion diffused from a given centre through a contiguous medium, or volume of particles of ether, produces light; for as a result of this motion the ether is reflected from every particle it meets with, and thus the form of an object is presented to the eye. The central motion of the particles of the ether produces not only a rigid expansion of every particle, but also heat; and if this motion be urged from the centre to the circumference, it causes light together with heat. If, however, it be urged from centres to circumferences so as to become a local motion, but without the central revolution of every particle, it occasions light without heat.[12]

There are two kinds of motion involved here, more fully described in a portion of his argument which I have not quoted. In the first case we have a wave motion propagated through a medium in which the particles are in double motion, whirling about their axes and also in longitudinal motion. This produces both light and heat.

In the second case, the wave is propagated through a medium which is still except for its response to the wave motion itself; this produces light without heat. Let us look at the second case first. The particles in a medium or elementary cease to move, either about their axes or in a longitudinal direction, when they are in a compressed condition. It is true that all the elements may exist in a compressed condition, even to the most material: a solid with its nearly-still molecules is in such a condition. However, since the phenomenon of light is fully realized in the etheric realm, light, and its companions heat and electricity, may run *through a solid*, because the interior parts of solid particles are not so compressed. In the etheric realm itself light may run *along* or be reflected by the quasi-hard electromagnetic shells of the etheric particles, which are the compressed parts of the magnetic sphere. Inside the magnetic sphere is the non-dimensional space/time sphere, and this also has its compressed parts: indeed, these form the comparatively still and static components of the magnetic sphere. Is it possible, then (quickly to recapitulate an earlier argument), that there exists some wave motion, ancestral so to speak to light, in the space/time sphere? We shall look at this in a moment.

But first we must note that Swedenborg's theory calls for heat to be generated on the same level as light. We now know heat to be generated by the movements (generally considered random) of molecules and of the single atoms, which in effect act as molecules, of monatomic gases. Yet even here we find something remarkable since we may say of molecules in a gas that "apart from travelling about they are also capable of rotating about their centres. As a result of collisions they are in general in a state of rotation. Kinetic energy is also associated with this rotation."[13] This is the "double motion" referred to earlier.

As this kinetic energy is the cause of heat, we may say that Swedenborg, who has said in the earlier quotation that heat is transmitted by spinning particles, has correctly, if schematically, identified the main component of the mechanics of heat generation and transfer. And, furthermore, since his etheric realm is the interval containing the equivalent of our free electrons and other free particles (its "sign" the conventional "ether particle"), and since the smallest molecule is the free atom, it is correct in terms of his particular formalization to place the generation of heat in the etheric realm. And of course it is well known that heat is also transmitted by electromagnetic radiation, as infrared rays.

Let us then look again, if briefly, at the idea that there exists some wave motion, ancestral to light, in the first elementary or space/time sphere. We know that in his system wave-like motions of two kinds may be propagated through this first elementary, one through a medium of apparently self-moving particles, the other through a medium of apparently still or passively movable particles. This is because he tells us that its particles may exist in quasimotional and quasistill or compressed forms. He has also defined the first element as perfectly contiguous and has said that "motion diffused from a given centre through a contiguous medium...produces light." Such a wave motion as we have mentioned is therefore proposed in the most subtle parts of what is ancestral to the thing we call the space/time continuum. We have the tremendous biblical (and Parmenidean) image of light as the very foundation of the universe, the invisible light which animates the Active/Passive field, making it productive of fields above itself and thus of the analogous waves which animate the first element, the second or magnetic element and the third or etheric element, where they become visible. When we consider the date of the work we must find this a splendid and troubling image.

We must now consider his theory of fire,[14] which is extremely (to me inextricably) complicated. In this phenomenon, in "the nature of that fire which is subtle and penetrating or elementary, as also the nature of that which is less subtle, or the common atmospherical and culinary fire," there participate the active principles of all his elements. Fire in his system is the generator of movement in the sensually perceived world. His language resembles that of some of the pre-Socratic philosophers. He pays tribute to their idea of fire as an element, without admitting it to be such—

> Without fire all things would be torpid, neither the air nor the ether would be stirred into motion, consequently without fire or something like it, new series would not be produced to bring the earth to its

ultimate perfection, no production and secretion would be effected; there would be no growth of plants from the mineral kingdom; there would be no living creature partaking of the elementary, mineral and vegetable kingdoms...

We can no longer think of such concepts as archaic, though, since the modern combination of ecology and general systems theory has brought them back with a rush. Thus, in a useful but easy introduction to the new sciences of global events, a book entitled, appropriately, *Le Macroscope, Vers un Vision Globale*, Joel de Rosnay tells us how what began as the physics of heat, thermodynamics, now provides a model for global processes of the most diverse kinds.[15] It is from thermodynamics that we obtain the idea of *entropy*, which is so important in the theory of information. And because heat and energy are so closely related, the cycle of heat exchange may be considered as a symbol of all cycles of energy exchange. The theory of heat may, finally, be related to the processes which govern the making of all organized forms: order and disorder, or improbability and probability.

I will not go into a comparison of modern and Swedenborgian ideas of heat in relationship to probability theory. They are quite different. In Swedenborg heat is the *productive transformation of energy*. We encounter once again the philosophical impulse which generates his system. This is the opposite of the modern materialistic one, because it is based on the assumption that physical energy comes from the *interiors* of matter, that nature is like a fountain and that the center of the material universe is a form of energy created by God, if certainly not to be identified with Him. Thus in Swedenborg's concept of fire we have to deal with continual transformations running from the most subtle to the most macroscopic of forms—

It follows that finites of every power and dimension may put themselves into activity, provided they have space for so doing; provided also they are not implicated in any elementaries flowing around, and become convoluted into surfaces or new globular, superficial or elementary particles...Consequently, the fourth and fifth finites cannot put themselves into activity in a volume of the elements of the first and second, without immediately being converted into new elementary, or ether and air particles. For they have no space for their movements, because elementaries are present to impede them, and convolute them, while in the condition of themselves becoming active in new surfaces; as in the case of ether or air when converted into water or other fluids.[16]

We may see then that the two chief characteristics of fire, according to Swedenborg, are activity and transformation. In our modern point of view the most obvious form of transformation would be that of chemical change. Swedenborg is not concerned with that here but with a more generalized form of transformation—that of change from one phase of matter to another, as in solid to liquid to gas to ether.

It would seem that a discussion of "Swedenborg's nebular hypothesis" should end this chapter. In some modern books on the history of cosmology, Swedenborg is credited as one of the pioneers in the formulation of the nebular hypothesis—most often by mere mention of his name. Somewhat more attention was paid to him at the beginning of the century, as in a 1910 edition of *The World Almanac*, where its astronomical editor, J. Morrison, wrote—

> The cosmogony of our solar system rests on the nebular hypothesis first propounded by Swedenborg, but not generally accepted in his time; it was, however, subsequently revived and partially confirmed by the researches of Sir William Herschel. At a later date it was examined by the celebrated Laplace, and it is erroneously known as the nebular hypothesis of Laplace. It should, however, in all justice, be called the nebular hypothesis of Swedenborg.[17]

Splendid! Yet it turns out that, while it is true that Swedenborg's cosmogony of the solar system resembles, in a generalized sense, the nebular hypotheses referred to above, the resemblance vanishes on closer examination. Frankly, while the *pictures* in the *Principia* seem to be illustrating a form of nebular hypothesis, the text speaks of something quite different. This is true even though the title of Chapter IV of Part III is *The Universal Solar and Planetary Nebular Matter, and its Separation into Planets and Satellites*. His theory of the formation of the solar system, of which the following quotation presents only a summary fragment, is

greatly more complex than a nebular hypothesis. It is a vast structure which has never been explored, and no part of it can be under
stood unless his entire system is. I can merely set out some of the
more striking aspects of his theory. To begin, I will quote his
summary of the chapter, so densely reasoned and so dependent
upon ideas that are strange to us, that it appears opaque and closed
in on itself, like some gigantic monolith fallen from outer space.

> The second elementary particles...are most highly compressed near
> the solar active space; and, in consequence of this compression, they
> cease to be elementaries. Finites exist in the same manner as first
> elementaries; but these finites of a higher dimension exist from second
> elementaries, and are the fourth in order, the former being third in
> order.
>
> Although all finites possess this power of self-activity, nevertheless,
> those which have their origin near the sun are not capable of becoming
> actives, nor of entering into the solar space to its actives, in conse-
> quence of a difference as to velocity, circles, and mass. But the actives
> which may have been casually made, at once cease to be actives, and
> necessarily remain mere passives around the solar space of the actives;
> consequently the functions they there perform are those of a guard, to
> prevent the other finites of the same kind from penetrating into the
> solar space, and thus from any longer projecting themselves into it.
>
> In this manner the number and quantity of finites of the fourth kind
> increase more and more, by reason of the successive compression of the
> elementaries; and they also become compact round the solar space.
> These finites thus formed an immense volume, and crowded around
> and enclosed the sun in such a way as to form an incrustation; nor do
> they cease to act till the vortex is fully formed.
>
> Nevertheless this crust, formed round the sun, and consisting of
> fourth finites, is carried round by a kind of revolution. It is thus
> representative, as it were, of an active centre in forming and perfecting
> the vortex, round which, consequently, the elementaries could never-
> theless flow in a vortical current, but with a potency and force different
> from that which they would possess in case the solar space acted simply
> and contiguously upon the circumfluent elementaries. The whole of
> this immense crust, together with the enclosed solar space, is not
> unlike an elementary particle; for in each elementary particle there is
> an active space, exteriorly to which flow the finites. Thus, both as to

figure and motion, this chaos is, on an immense scale, an effigy of each individual part of an elementary particle. Thus nature is similar to herself in her largest as well as her least production; and thus she appears in her most stupendous proportions, as well as in her most minute.

This incrusting matter, being endowed with a continual circular motion round the sun, in the course of time removed itself farther and farther from the active space; and in so moving itself, occupied a larger space, and consequently became gradually attenuated, till it could no longer cohere through out, but burst in some part or other.

The solar crust, being somewhere broken up on the admission of the vortical volume, collapsed upon itself; and this toward the zodiacal circle of the vortex, or conformably to the situation and motion of the elementary particles; so that it surrounded the sun like a belt or broad circle. This belt, which was formed by the collapse of the incrusting expanse, revolved in a similar manner; removed itself to a greater distance, and by its removal became attenuated till it burst, and formed larger and smaller globes; that is to say, formed planets and satellites of various dimensions, but of a spherical figure.

This incrusted expanded matter might subside partly into itself, and thus consist merely of a volume of finites. It might partly subside inwardly, or toward the solar space, and thus revolve round some active space. It might partly subside exteriorly or towards the vortex, and thus enclose a volume of elementary particles. Thus there might exist bodies of three different kinds, namely, planets, satellites, and erratic bodies straying round the sun, such as we are accustomed to call sunspots. It therefore follows, that these bodies, separated into globes, consisted of fourth finites; that they directed their course into the vortical current according to their size and weight; that they continued more and more to increase their distance from the sun, until they arrived at their destined periphery or orbit in the solar vortex, where they are in equilibrium with the volume of the vortex.[18]

The argument here might appear to be quite impenetrable. But it may be disentangled if we adhere to the meaning of his philosophical categories, which he has explained for us in earlier sections of the work. In quick overview, he is describing something like the following—

FIGURES 16a–16e

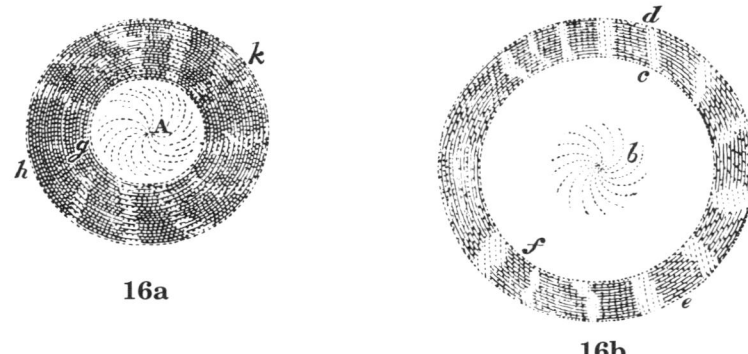

16a

16b

Figure 16a and 16b

In Figure 16a we see the solar space, A, surrounded by crust *kh*. In Figure 16b the crust is pushed outwards by the solar activity and becomes thinner, with stresses (light areas) developing in the ring. From *Principia:* Vol. II, pp. 185–189.

16c

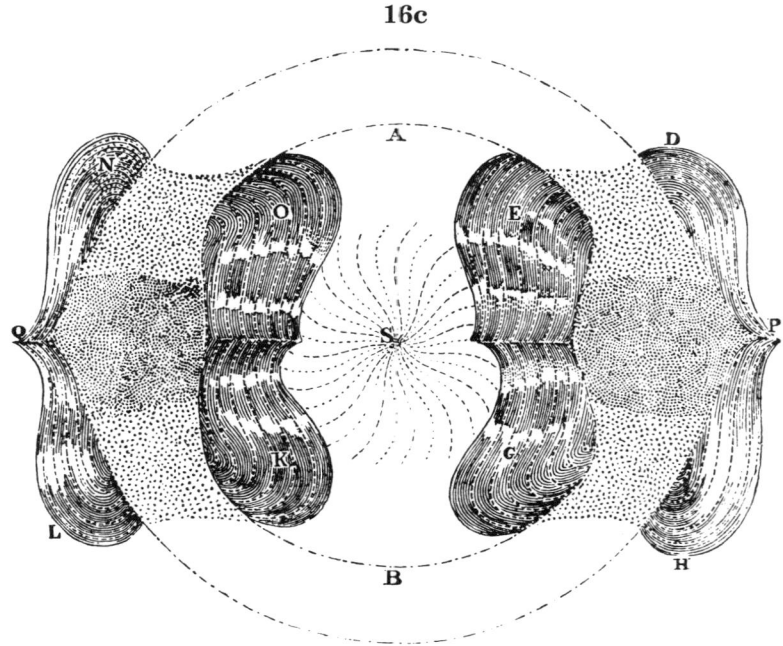

Figure 16c

In Figure 16c the crust collapses. Parts of it (EG and OK) collapse into the sun, and these parts surround themselves with fragments of internal solar matter. Other parts (such as DPH and NQL) explode outwards and enclose part of the material for the crust. From *Principia:* Vol. II, pp. 185–189.

16d

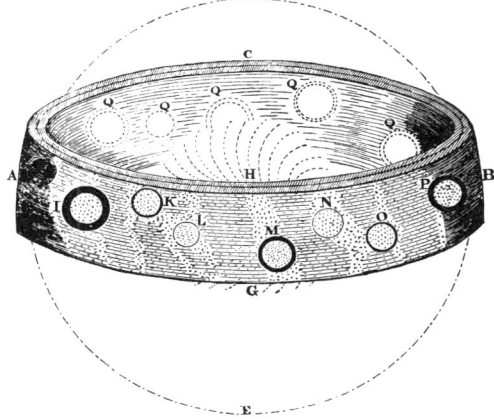

Figure 16d
After the disruption of the solar belts its materials form themselves into globes. These are fluid bodies, but the globular elements enclosed in them are of lighter or more rarified fluids. From *Principia:* Vol. II, pp. 185–189.

16e

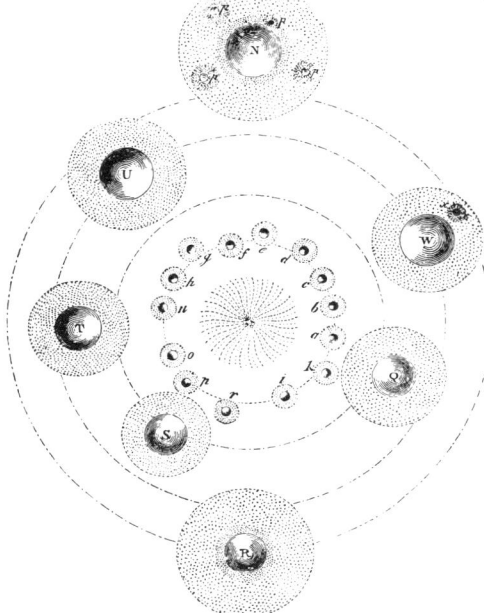

Figure 16e
The globes (outer ring) will become planets, in some cases with moons. The enclosed globules of lighter elements have separated from the planet-globes. These will sink back into the sun, some of them becoming sun-spots. From *Principia:* Vol. II, pp. 185–189.

His fourth finites are the "surfaces" of ether particles, which enclose magnetic (electromagnetic) forces.

His solar chaos is something so close to a plasmic state that we may simply describe it as such, with no more anachronism than may usually be found in the translation of old natural philosophy into modern terms. His sun is therefore a "plasma energy generator."[19] The sun throws out a plasma ring (more properly a sphere), and this is held in place by the magnetic forces within the sun. For it is within the sun that ethereal plasmic bundles are formed, by interactions and infoldings of electromagnetic forces. We now know this to be close to what really happens.

In time the plasmic bundles (my word) inside the solar ring quiesce into tiny particles—ancestors of ethereal particles properly speaking. These form a crust around the sun, a crust made up of a potential form of the matter we know and observe. The crust revolves around the sun, but it also takes the form of a magnetic field, or, as Swedenborg says, of a form "not unlike the effluvium circulating round a magnet."[20] Due to a combination of forces—centrifugal force, various vortical motions and so on—the crust is gradually attenuated, losing its density in an irregular manner. As a result it begins to break up and collapse upon itself, separating into clumps, which then reform around the sun in the shape of a belt. This aspect of the theory, or, more strictly, the part I have extracted, is consistent with modern knowledge.

In this belt the planets begin to form. In their first condition they are small balls of plasma or ether particles. They cool as they gradually revolve outwards from the sun. Eventually, by a process of interfolding of surfaces, stages of expansion and contraction and by the passing of surface particles from one "ether-atom" to another, the planetary plasma ball freezes into the sphere of gases, liquids and solids we know, their first forms being aqueous vapor and water.

This is certainly more than a nebular hypothesis[21] and more modern in style than anything suggested in the standard cosmologies of the nineteenth century. Swedenborg has told us things about the sun we have only learned in the past few decades. Yet his is not the theory favored by modern cosmology. This theory does indeed describe the sun as a ball of plasma but says that it was formed from a great cloud of dust and gases which collapsed on itself as an effect of gravity. It was the turning of gravitational energy into heat, during this collapse, which created the hot ball of plasma we call the sun. A dust of ices and earthy particles, vaporized by the heat of the sun, gathered around it in the form of a revolving cloud. The mechanics of rapidly revolving spheres flattened this cloud into a disc. The temperature of the disc now began to drop and did so rapidly, since the disc had a large surface area and thus quickly radiated its heat into empty space. As the temperature dropped and the materials in the cloud turned from gases to solids, they came together in clumps of irregular shape. These clumps formed the cores of what would later be planets.

We note that the essential difference between Swedenborg's theory and the modern one is one of order and direction of formative movement. The modern theory works "from the outside in." It begins with a heterogeneous collection of space dust possessing virtually no innate energy, existing at a temperature of about -370° Fahrenheit.[22] The collapse of this cloud into itself produces the ball of energy we call the sun. Swedenborg works "from the inside out." Energy pouring from the most internal parts of matter expands *outward*, taking more and more complex forms, and in this fashion the sun is born. Nor does the modern theory see early planets as plasma balls.

Now, modern cosmology is such an arena of conflicting ideas, all of them changing very rapidly, that it is possible that the theory I have called "modern" will be out of date by the time this book is published. It will probably still be true that the Swedenborgian and *any* modern theory will deal with entities and concepts which, taken one by one, are at least roughly similar. Yet the theories in most respects are respectively inverted one to the other, and this to the extent that one almost seems the mirror-image of the other, even though the great difference between eighteenth-century and modern scientific knowledge makes the mirror-image seem cloudy and distorted. Such an inversion is due to the very great philosophical differences between Swedenborg's approach, which is based firmly on the belief that God created the universe, and the modern one, which claims to be theologically neutral but implicitly and often explicitly rejects any such belief.

It should be noted, finally, that Swedenborg believes that the events he describes as having created our solar system arose from conditions common to all stars. He ends his chapter on "solar and planetary nebular matter" with an account of several stars which have come into and disappeared from view from the late 1500s to the beginning of the eighteenth century. He believes that such disappearances are due to their having become encrusted by incipient planetary matter in just the way he describes for the sun, though not all such incrustations result in the formation of planets.

Deeply buried in the massive architecture of his theory is the notion that the universe was once a single great particle, though indeed both "great" and "single" are completely inadequate words. They are inadequate because this particle had no size, nor can we truly say whether it was one or many, because space and time did not then exist. It would therefore be illegitimate to talk of the universe as having had a "beginning" in the temporal sense. We may only use the word in a logical or philosophical context, as meaning that the universe had a *cause*. For a "very long time" (though there was no time and we mean by this phrase only to point to a long chain of causes and effects) the universe existed in some fashion we cannot visualize, with all of the Nature we know hidden inside it in a form of real latency. There was no such thing as measurable time until the material universe we know—with its chemical elements, its large and small bodies in gravitational interaction, its organisms which grow and decay—was fully realized. We see again that, while the cosmology of Swedenborg has even more modern resemblances than those examined above,[23] while it even has a strange similarity to "Big Bang" theory (which we have not looked at), these resemblances are in the deeper sense illusory, because they spring from a philosophy radically different from that which animates modern cosmologies, Marxist or "Western."

ENDNOTES

1 Arjiptsev, pp. 26–27, 30.

2 Born, p. 224 (footnote).

The Swedenborgian ether is a system of space-like relations apart from space, in which there is no preferred direction. The centres of ether volumes have attractive force but there are innumerable such volumes in fluid equilibrium. Thus the ether as a whole has no centre. In such a continuum we cannot distinguish vertical from horizontal. Yet as there are centres there must be axes, thus mutual perpendiculars. Furthermore, since spaces cannot be defined metrically time cannot be measured. We fall back on the bare idea that time is different from space and can only represent this difference graphically as another perpendicular, this time to all of space.

Swedenborg uses his preferred bubble-models rather than a Cartesian graph, but I believe that the above accurately represents his concepts.

3 Peierls, p. 24.

I should say that this book is now out of date in many respects but it has the virtue, not found in many more recent popularizations, of integrating the physics of elementary particles, as then understood, into an overview which includes classical mechanics and electrical theory. It is also clearly written. It should be read in conjunction with more recent texts.

4 Artsimovich, p. 9.

5 Swedenborg, *Economy of the Animal Kingdom*, Part I, No. 18, quoted in *Words for the New Church*, p. 508 (author or authors anonymous).

6 Swedenborg, *Principia* II, p. 208.

7 Ibid., II, p. 213.

8 *Enc. of Phys.*, pp. 765–766.

9 Swedenborg, *Principia* II, pp. 211–218.

10 Ibid., II, p. 219.

11 Trefil, p. 82.

12 The discussion here, and the quotation, come from *Principia* II, pp. 219–223.

13 Peierls, p. 112.

14 The following is summarized from *Principia* II, pp. 235–254.

15 de Rosnay, pp. 135–138.

16 Swedenborg, *Principia* II, pp. 235–236.

17 Isaiah Tansley, in his introduction to the *Principia* (I, pp. lxxiii–lxxiv).

18 Swedenborg, *Principia* II, pp. 592–594.

Swedenborg's theory appears even more modern when we consider that his sun is formed by a spiralling inrush of finites, which have developed to the point of being "particles or compounds," into an "immense sphere or volume" (see *Principia* I, pp. 226 et seq., II, pp. 408 et seq.). The reason I do not mention this in the text is that this degree of anticipation of the modern theory appears so incredible that the reader would probably not believe me if I stated the case so baldly and simply, and the necessarily detailed explication would be very complex.

19 Bova, p. 31.

20 Swedenborg, *Principia* II, p. 182.

21 The renowned Soviet cosmologist, Otto Schmidt, wrote in the 1950s that "Scientific cosmogony begins with the well-known works of Kant (1755) and Laplace (1796). They were the first to propose hypotheses concerning the formation of the

solar system out of scattered matter; they regarded it as a regular development of matter that follows the laws of nature and did not need the help of divinity" (Schmidt, p. 11). Note the concluding clause. Schmidt is completely in accord with his Western fellow-scientists in the assumption that a cosmogony which requires "the help of divinity" is not to be considered true science *even if it is scientifically correct.* The laws of nature are, implicitly but irrevocably, to be separated from the creative intent of any divine being.

In an illuminating article in *The New Philosophy* (*NP*, July/Sept. 1990 (pp. 378–379), W.R. Woofenden quotes the following distressed statement from the Leipzig edition of Kant's works—"...the system of Swedenborg is unfortunately very similar to my own philosophy...We must either suppose greater intelligence and truth at the basis of Swedenborg's writings than first impressions excite, or that it is a mere accident when he coincides with my system." Plagiarism or not? As Woofenden remarks (p. 372) this consideration "in no way invalidates the claims of good scholarship, that Kant and the others had at least the opportunity to be aware of the theory published in 1734."

22 Bova, p. 44.

23 Because the following is a speculation of my own, I put it in a footnote.

Swedenborg acknowledges a certain incompleteness in his account of the ether when he says: "If we could reduce all these things to rules, we should then know the nature of the organs of sight, and the definite entities from which, as from centres, the ether directly, obliquely and reflexively turns itself" (Principia II, p. 218). What he wants, therefore, is a form of geometry and mechanics which at once explains the nature of vision and the movements of his particles. In the same paragraph he describes what he is looking for, a geometry and mechanics which can take in motions "more or less curvilinear," "similar and dissimilar" and "more or less harmonious," motions which "may pass at the same time through the organs of the eye, and simultaneously present themselves to the mind." He further defines the desired discipline in a footnote beginning on p. 269 of *The Worship and Love of God*, where he says that "the eye...resembles a *camera obscura*" and that if we examine the structure of the eye "it will be manifest to us, by the help of the sciences, of what quality is the ether and its modifications."

What he needs, it seems, would be (in modern terms) a form of projective geometry (with a related mechanics, not part of the discipline as we know it), one which may be adapted to his theory of the vortex as a generator of forms (perhaps by way of conic sections). Everybody who has studied even the mere basics of projective geometry knows that it is based on the geometry of sight (the eye as camera), that its techniques allow the treatment of lines of all curvatures (including the straight line seen as a flat curve) and that it deals in sufficient generality with all forms of harmonic ratio. Also, affine geometry, which is a subgroup of projective geometry, is an important tool in modern physics.

Certain theorems of Pappus and Pascal, which we now think of as the foundations of projective geometry, were proved in Euclidean terms in Swedenborg's day. There was no obvious indication that they would lead to a new geometry. The theorems of Desargues, also foundational elements, had been forgotten. Nonetheless, perhaps some sense that a new geometry was possible could have occurred to an acute mathematician such as Swedenborg, particularly one who was looking for a link between logic and mathematics.

7

Earth, Air, Water and Fire

Swedenborg is now about to deal with measurable material substances—gases, liquids and solids. There are two ways of looking at these. There is the experimental physical and chemical approach based on the nature of particular substances. We begin with a known material like lead and we observe its behavior as it is melted and vaporized. The other approach is a generalized one based on the idea of phase-states. We begin with a general idea of how solids, liquids and gases behave, and we fit the behavior of a particular substance like lead into this model. In a well-developed scientific culture like our own, the behavior of lead appears or should appear to be the same in both models. The two methods are not irrelevant one to the other and they do not or should not give different results.

The science of Swedenborg's day had almost no notion of the inner structures of specific substances and what few ideas it had were almost all wrong. The generalized "forms and forces" view had yielded remarkable results in the theories of Descartes and Newton, and Swedenborg would carry it farther. But how to bridge the gap between the general and the specific? Swedenborg had constructed an astonishing natural philosophy, so precise in its generality that it was able to describe generic atom-shapes, which we now recognize as similar to real things. Yet he could not develop the atom-forms of specific substances from these. His theory could only predict that there would be many such forms. In the discussion of ether, air, water, aqueous vapor and fire he shows that such variety of forms is possible. This is the best he can do. He promises us a further development of his theory at the end of his discussion of the ideal liquid mineral he calls "water"—

> Many other facts remain to be noticed with regard to water; but inasmuch as its particles are not elementary, nor constitute any portion of the elementary kingdom, the proper place for noticing its phenomena will be where, God willing, we come to treat of minerals; for the aqueous volume is entirely similar to that of a mineral of any kind when melted into a volume or liquefied. Our remarks on the subject of water would extend to great length were we to enter into all its phenomena. We should have to show, for instance, in what manner and for what reasons the connections of its particles could be resolved; in what manner after the dissolution the enclosed globules occupied the interstices between other and aqueous particles; in what manner, consequently, new terrestrial and saline parts originated; what were the figures of these parts, and the nature of their motions between the aqueous particles; in what manner these particles convey them through the fibres, stems, and pores of plants; how it is that they organize them into the plant form; how again they carry with them the superfluous parts in the plant into the external atmosphere; how it is that water hardens into ice and its vapor into snow, and how, as a result of this, forms like plants are produced; together with many other particulars pertaining to the material kingdom of nature, both vegetable and animal.[1]

The promised volume on minerals never appeared. Yet we can see from the above that Swedenborg had no way of distinguishing between water as a chemically specific substance and the general liquid state. The notion of water in the part just quoted shifts uneasily between the two concepts.

It is very probable that the promised volume would have contained much which we should now perceive as erroneous. It would have contained some remarkable insights but these would not have resolved the errors, only compounded them. The theory he proposes to develop is, it appears, essentially the same as that proposed in his *Chemistry*, a work published in 1721 and thus thirteen years before the *Principia*. It is the theory that the chemical substances we know were formed by the break up, under immense pressure from the water and air of which the early earth was made, of water particles at the bottom of the column of pressure.

When we look at the *Chemistry* we see that he has anticipated a great variety of forms which modern research has found in the arrangement of atoms in molecules and of molecules in crystals. His early geometrical/mechanical version of four-element theory, a phase-state version in effect, has led him to assume that such forms must exist in the minute forms of matter. Some of his diagrams of elementary particles resemble forms we may encounter in scientific journals of the present day. But the relationships are random. We often find that the forms Swedenborg attributes to a substance are not truly characteristic of that substance but may be found in some other. The reason for this is that his elementary particles, "quiesced" in solid and liquid matter, inevitably create such forms. In some cases the disconcertingly familiar shapes depicted in the plates of the *Chemistry* are crystals; in other cases they are abstract representations of known forms of movement; in yet other cases they are concocted to illustrate an explanation which happens to be incorrect. Such resemblances only indicate the truth of Swedenborg's theory taken in its most general formulation, that nature is geometrical and that it is straight-line geometrical in solid matter. For that matter even the polyhedral forms Plato gives to elementary particles may be found in molecular structure. Linus Pauling and Roger Hayward refer, in their book *The Architecture of Molecules*, to "the importance of these polyhedra to molecular architecture."[2]

I shall quote one example of a remarkable individual insight in the *Chemistry*, which nonetheless compounds an error. Take the following observations on salt, which occur almost casually—

> When the salt water of the sea is in motion, it scatters a kind of faint fire or light, which is a sign that the saline particles are broken by the motion. In fresh water the appearance does not occur.

If a mass of common salt be broken in the dark, a feeble light is visible, indicating the fracture of the particles...The fracture takes place at the weakest parts, or the joining of the points in the cubes.[3]

In this case he has observed a known form of luminescence in salt crystals. It is found among "complex molecules, in vapors and solutions and for impurity centres in solids" and we now attribute it to "imperfections of the crystal lattice, such as vacant lattice points, interstitial atoms or ions, slip due to plastic deformation, fissures etc."[4] We know that "like vacancies and interstitials, impurities may trap and donate electrons or holes and alter the electronic and optical properties of the crystal. In addition, they may introduce some of the characteristic atomic optical absorption or luminescent spectra to the crystal."[5]

Swedenborg's observation of the luminescence of fractured salt-crystals is an important factor in his theorizing, incorrectly, that new solid substances may be generated by the breakup of water particles at the bottom of the sea. He has no way of distinguishing between a salt-crystal and a molecule of salt. All he knows is that the luminescence he observes is due to the fracture of the salt particles. He reasons that such light-energy could not have been released unless the salt-particles had been cracked. He then assumes that what happens to the particle of salt could happen to any material particle, even such a cohesive one as that of (chemical) water. Great pressure at the bottom of the sea would have broken up particles of water, forming particles of metals, salts and other solid materials. This process would have continued until, as in the *Genesis* account, solid land emerged from the primeval waters.

Such a theory is not part of the *Principia*. It seems that he later abandoned it, apparently with some regret. In his *The Worship and Love of God*, published eleven years after the *Principia*, we read that in its first form, while it was still close to the sun, our globe...

...was not as yet earth but an uncovered wave, the whole without a shore or slime, and being thus a large fluent heap of the principles of inert nature, operated upon by the rays of a neighboring burning focus, effervesced and boiled from its depths. To the intent, therefore, that these principles or elements of inert and heavier nature might coalesce into secondary and new principles of water, salt, earth and the like, and in order that from these principles foetuses of an infinite variety might again finally be hatched, this globe must of necessity have undergone innumerable vicissitudes and changes...[6]

And a little later we read that after the formation of the first terrestrial atmosphere a crust appeared on the surface of "our liquid orb," which was still "boiling from its very bottom" and that at this stage, while it was still a simple sphere without hills or valleys, rivers and streams broke through from the interior of the orb.[7]

Water as we know it is now a *secondary* development or "principle," along with the other chemically-defined substances and mixtures we know, "salt, earth and the like." The "ideal water" referred to in the *Principia* as constituting the surface of the earth in its first stage is rather "a large fluent heap of the principles of inert nature," a cooling plasma. We have already encountered these principles of nature in considering the more subtle elements: they are inside what we now call atoms and microparticles. He has imagined a chaos made up of something like nuclear matter which is, so to speak, cooling down into a globular form and which is beginning, through "innumerable vicissitudes and changes," to turn into the chemical substances we know. Water is the most directly tangible and visible *representation* or *image* of this quasi-nuclear matter; molten matter in general is a less direct one.

This is a proto-modern theory. We cannot say it has been "proved by modern science" because theories of the formation of the earth and other planets are still in dispute; but it is, even if wrong, modern in type. We see that even the most generous interpretation of Swedenborg's cosmology, which makes him one of the pioneers of the nebular hypothesis, actually does him scant justice. He was on the verge of an enormous scientific breakthrough. The only obstacle in his path—a very large obstacle—was the primitive state of chemistry at the time.

There is also a biographical implication here. It is of the utmost importance, but I can only hint at it here, because its importance is of a theological kind. *The Worship and Love of God* was written "two years after the opening of his spiritual vision."[8] It was never completed. Swedenborg abandoned his scientific and philosophical career as it was approaching an extraordinary peak, when he was at the height of his powers. The pain of this sacrifice, in a man who was not only ambitious of fame but would certainly have achieved it, is (the mildness of the term is almost ludicrous) hard to imagine.

I shall devote little space to his discussion of air, water and aqueous vapor. The truth is that at this level of his argument his theory becomes, to the modern mind, dense and almost impenetrable, demanding very detailed explication. Let me illustrate this by way of one argument we *can* understand. He is explaining why water flows—

> Aqueous particles are the more mobile and fluid, in proportion as the circumfluent ether particles are the more mobile, extended and rigid; and the less mobile and fluid in proportion as the circumfluent ether particles are the less mobile, extended, and rigid, but soft, as it were. In proportion to the want of mobility and tension in the ether particles, the aqueous particles are torpid and languid, uniting and forming into a hard mass. That finites of this kind, or aqueous particles, owe their fluidity or mobility to the interfluent ether, which in its own nature is mobile because it is elementary, is evident a priori, or from the principles already laid down.[9]

Pre-scientific gobbledygook, it would seem. Yet we should know by now that every word in the above quotation, words such as "mobile," "fluid," "circumfluent," "rigid" and "soft," has a strict meaning in his formal vocabulary.

In this isolated case a translation of concepts is easy. We have seen that his ether contains movements which closely resemble the behaviors of free electrons, thus of electrons in clouds. A recent theory of the structure of liquids and gases, based on a theory developed in the 1870s by the Dutch physicist, J.D. van der Waals, expands on the following idea of the forces between molecules. J.A. Barker and Douglas Henderson, who developed this theory, say of these—

The only significant forces are electromagnetic ones; they arise from a distortion that develops in the cloud of electrons surrounding a molecule when another molecule is nearby. Because an electron is much lighter than a molecule and moves correspondingly faster the configuration of the electron cloud can be described only in the methods of quantum mechanics.[10]

In this theory the fluidity of the mass is determined by the state, among other things, of this electron cloud surrounding the molecule. Swedenborg is saying much the same thing, but is referring not to clouds of electrons but to circumfluent and interfluent ether particles. Of course he knows nothing of quantum mechanics. His theory is constructed out of non-quantitative and verbally described entities. But the result is a logical model of a fluid which is truly analogous to the modern theory.

I believe the word "striking" is not an exaggeration here. I could give more examples of the same kind; but to explain the relationship between Swedenborgian and modern concepts—a necessary procedure in this case—would result in another book as long as this one. And, because his theory is all of a piece, I should also have to give many examples of places where the fit is crude, or where Swedenborg is in error and this would be tedious. Also I do not have the slightest doubt that among the errors I so confidently pointed out, there would be found statements which future scientific discoveries will show to be true. This has been the case with the *Principia* for more than two hundred years.

Perhaps the reader will forgive me, then, if I say only this. Even on the level of naked-eye matter Swedenborg's theory often holds true, when we consider it a phase-state theory in the most general sense. The fit with fact is, so far as we are able to ascertain now, erratic and imperfect. It can be very close, but it can also be remote and in many cases there is no fit at all. Both the successes and the failures arise from the same kind of theoretical modelling. In the case of a theory developed more than two hundred years ago there can be only one conclusion: the theory must be taken seriously. And since it is a development of ancient four-element formalism that system, too, must be taken seriously.

Perhaps this is a good place to stop, catch our breath and look about us before we continue our climb. Swedenborg's *Principia* is a great mountain. It has its crevasses where thought turns giddy, its precipices which seem impossible to scale and its streams with dangerous rapids which we dare not cross. It also has many beautiful meadows and caverns glittering with crystals. We have taken the easy path up the mountain and have missed much, but even this path has had its steep ascents which have left us out of breath, its rickety bridges and its places where the road has been washed away. Most of this chapter will be taken up with discussion of a key question, that of why Swedenborg chose to develop a theory of matter based on the traditional four elements; but at this stage of our climb let us glance quickly over the territory traversed so far.

Swedenborg's theory is entirely of its time. If we consider his root concepts singly, we find nothing without some antecedent in the Graeco-Roman and Christian traditions or in the thought of his day. The ensemble is nevertheless remarkably novel and in many cases, which we can in no way explain away as lucky guesses, he anticipates or seems to anticipate discoveries made long after his death, sometimes only in the past few decades. This must be due to his method, his way of conceptualizing things. It is certainly not due to his abilities as an experimental scientist or to the abilities of those he quotes. In some cases (as particularly in his extensive references to Musschenbroek's studies of magnetism) his physical data are reliable and still sound; in others they are coarsely observed or simply wrong, and this results in erroneous conclusions and predictions.

We may sum up his overall approach in this way. He considers nature to be a physical realization of logical and mathematical ideas, ideas which are, at their source, the Ideas of God. This assumption leads him to develop his own form of fluid mechanics, in which primary physical notions may be most clearly and simply embodied. In his view we proceed incorrectly when we imagine the smallest parts of nature as tiny massy particles which cannot be subdivided. We know nothing in nature or mathematics which may not be cut into smaller and smaller parts. We also observe that the more matter is refined the more subtle and fluid-like it appears to be.

The first form of nature, the primary point, he imagines as an entity made up of two components, an Active and a Passive. We may call this a quasilogical entity. The point behaves like a problem in logic in which there are, so to speak, three "degrees of freedom," the True, the False and the Contingent. The possibility of logical algebraisation is clearly indicated though I do not pretend the process would be easy. Before we begin this process the entities are different. The Passive is not the False. Once we do begin it, logical and material categories closely parallel each other, because the same symbols can be used throughout without falsification of either sequence. In this respect he seems to anticipate the assumptions of Hegel and, in a formal sense, he actually does so. But he rejects the Hegelian idea of the universal adequacy of logical thought and indeed, because of the meaning of the word in his time, does not characterize his formalization as "logical."

The pattern of Active and Passive runs through his system from beginning to end. It is the foundation of the geometry and mechanics which manifest themselves throughout his vision of nature. For, by a daring combination of Active/Passive logic and of a mathematics which combines the new discipline of calculus with geometrical constructions as old as Archimedes and Apollonius of Perga, he has shown how relations of Active and Passive may generate a primary form of movement—a vortex—and, from this, a knot of energy, his Primary Point. As the vortex is at once an enclosed wave and a point we may legitimately call this a wave-particle, without fear of anachronism.

The Primary Point must, of its intrinsic nature, generate new points. Because the initial binaries of Active and Passive run throughout nature, constituting a principle of separation and distinctness, the points thus generated must rank themselves in orders of complexity and relative energy. Thus nature arranges itself in a hierarchy of fluid "elementaries." These are very much like discrete "fields," to use a modern term, of decreasing energy and increasing massiness.

The three primary elementaries are as follows—

A First Element. Swedenborg's description of this element is highly abstract and could only be set out, apart from his own words, in a form of logical/mathematical notation. The most important idea to be retained from the discussion is that the first element contains, in germ, all the attributes which we shall later find realized in three-dimensional space and successive time. On this level of matter, space and time take forms analogous to purely logical descriptions of their parts, descriptions which also lie at the basis of mathematical thinking. Thus, while mensuration is impossible here, the element possesses such qualities as universality, contiguity, continuity, simplicity and interaction of parts.

A Second Element, the magnetic, which, considering the range of phenomena Swedenborg includes in this category, should nowadays be called "electromagnetic." This embodies the first element.

A Third Element, that of the ether, which in many respects though not in all, resembles what we now think of as the plasmic state of matter, but also embodies the electromagnetic forces of the second element.

Despite the faultiness of much of the physical data, the argument is developed in a rigorous and self-consistent fashion. This is so much the case that the weakness or inaccuracy of the data may be corrected by the philosophical arguments, which are on a much higher level.

The best modern description of Swedenborg's theory would probably be that it is a theory of the phase-states of matter. Yet, this granted, it must further be granted that his phase state theory goes far beyond anything found in most modern theories of phase-state, which develop from thermodynamics. As a universal theory it is a late development of the system of the four elements.

It is customary now to think of four-element formalism as completely outmoded, belonging to the prehistory of science. Swedenborg obviously did not believe this. If we are to understand why he took this attitude, which even his age considered a backward-looking one, we must now examine this element-symbolism in more detail.

The history of four-element formalism is, in one sense, that of all natural philosophy up to the birth of experimental chemistry in early modern times. Yet the subject remains deeply mysterious and confused. A primary reason for this, no doubt, is that the idea of a nature composed of four, some times five elements, is used to support natural philosophies of very different kinds. It is a form, almost, of rhetorical type: it provides a framework of discourse; and though it is an image of a world-system it cannot truly be called a theory, though it may accommodate several. The four-element systematics of Plato, Aristotle, the Stoics and others are quite different and in much irreconcilably so.

The system, if we may call it that, is certainly older than the speculations of the pre-Socratic Greeks,[11] though it is to these that we owe the first purely formal and philosophical definitions of the four elements, which were formerly the departmental abodes of deities. Yet in their works, which have come down to us only in fragments, it is impossible to be sure whether the elements are primary substances of a physical kind or pre-material essences from which such substances are formed. We have, for example, the well-known fragment of Heraclitus: "Fire lives in the death of air, and air lives in the death of fire; water lives in the death of earth, earth in that of water." We may extract from this an idea of the phase-transformations of matter; but is that what he meant? Was he referring to entities which are in a sense both physical and nonphysical, to an ideal fire and air and water and earth which exist in some fashion as deep embodiments or symbols of meta-physical principles, but nonetheless exist *objectively* so? In what, for instance, shall we find the generality of fire, when the fire of burning oil is certainly different, as he knew well, from the fire of burning wood and both from the heat of the body? What does he mean when he says: "The sea is the purest and the foulest water; it is drinkable and healthful for fishes; but for men it is unfit to drink and hurtful"? Taken to the letter, this is a statement of childish banality. Yet we could also take it, not necessarily in an anachro-nistic sense, as implicitly denying the basic philosophical impor-tance of any idea of chemical purity, such as would have been known to metalworkers, familiar with impurities in metals. The deep reality of a substance is to be defined, not in terms of the complexity of its components, since all substances are complex, but in terms of its role in natural cycles, which is multifarious. That is to say, the sea is pure from the viewpoint of a fish and impure from the viewpoint of a man and this statement better sums up the nature of "sea" than would a statement which imagined the sea as distilled water to which various impurities have been added. Nature is not a laboratory or its ancient equivalents (say, the workshops of the metalworker or glassblower or alchemist). Symbolically or parabolically it becomes a poetic statement about human experience on different levels ("fishlike," "truly human"), much as in his, "In the same rivers we step and we do not step; we are and we are not," which is often taken to refer to the human experience of time.

Our puzzlement is not due to cultural distance or cross-cultural incomprehension. Later Greek and Roman writers were as bemused as we are, and the ambiguities of the pre-Socratics were only amplified in succeeding cosmologies. It seems that the pre-Socratics deliberately spoke in images so framed that they included physical and psychic categories in one continuum. We are familiar with this as an exalted mode of poetic speech, not as philosophical and scientific discourse.

Then too, because of the gradual usurpation of scientific and philosophical discourse by materialists, we now associate materialist thought with discursive and reasoned prose, religious and idealist thought with lyrical or symbolic language. We forget that every culture has its atheists and materialists, even those in which highly figured speech is the literary norm. In considering ancient texts we might easily read an idealist or religious meaning into them when it is not intended. The Phoenician Sanchuniathon, a pre-Socratic before the pre-Socratics, openly declares that man has created gods in his own image, but then proceeds to give us a thumbnail history of the cosmos using the image-language of a syncretic Phoenician-Egyptian religion. He debunks myth in the language of myth. It seems that myth-laden discourse is the only kind he knows, or perhaps considers worthy of an educated man, and that the most he can do is to ask us to consider mythical formulations from a materialist perspective.

Four-element formalism never quite shakes off the ambiguity of a mythical belief without context. By "without context" I mean that this belief, though clearly related to some myth-system, cannot be fitted into any known one.

There is no doubt that Greek four-element formalism is related, but at one remove, to a very old and widespread system. In this ancient system gods (I am conflating several mythical schemes) are governors of the four quarters—east, north, west and south. The four quarters also have, in many such systems, colors and musical tones assigned to them. The gods also govern the major parts of nature: there are gods of the air, the sea and other bodies of water and the earth.[12]

Four-element formalism is a little different. It may be attached to both theistic and atheistic doctrines and is much more like a form of natural philosophy than like a theology or part of one. Analogies of the Greek system are found in India and China and all three systems have this theologically neutral quality. In some cases they are overtly atheistic; it is well-known that a number of Greek philosophers came under attack from pious worshippers of the gods. Though we do not know its age or where it originated, the local forms of four-element theory are so alike that they appear to have had a common origin. There are usually four but sometimes five elements. These emerge from a chaos which embodies or generates a principle of binary order—Creative/Receptive, Love/Strife, Male/Female and so on. There are other common characteristics but I need not mention them here.

Although the system is like a form of natural philosophy, it is also like a mythical account of creation. The four elements are often described in language appropriate to accounts of gods or at least to godlike things. We are never far removed from the spirit of epic cosmogony. What is puzzling is that the first literary expressions (known to us) of this form of thought appear to have a long history behind them. They are not of the temple and sometimes they are antagonistic to the temple; nevertheless, they seem to have come, in some way, out of the temple. This may only mean that they bear the imprint of a time when the sacred chant was the common standard of literary style; it may also mean that they are secularized religious teachings. But there is none of the humility of the temple here. The pre-Socratic philosopher speaks with a mystical authority; often he has the air of an intellectual sorcerer, eyes afire, hair and robes streaming in the cosmic winds, as he chants his poetic equations.

The four-element system never quite loses this quality, that of something one-third hymn, one-third spell, one third dialectical logic. It carries an air of ancient mystery from the pre-Socratics to the seventeenth century. A faint trace of this archaic splendor can even be found in the degenerate jargon of alchemy. The mystery is real, not a mask of the charlatan. For the most puzzling thing of all is that, despite the great age and durability of the system, nobody really knows what the four elements are. The pre-Socratic philosophers of Greece, the first to enunciate the system in the European tradition, begin with a common set of verbal ideas, but cannot agree even on the meanings of the words they are using. It is as if they had been handed some ambiguous ancient text and each had come up with his own reading.

Many of these ideas, as individual notions, can be traced back to specific ancient sources. Thales, born about 624 BC, was of Phoenician origin, according to Herodotus. His theory that the first principle of matter was water does indeed remind us of the Phoenician cosmology of Sanchuniathon, which we shall consider later. We are also reminded of Greek myth, most particularly of its aspects which reflect older non-Greek myths. Aristotle, who was as puzzled as we are, says, in discussing Thales' theory—

> ...there are some who think that the ancients, and they who lived long before the present generation, and the first students of the gods, had a similar idea in regard to nature; for in their poems Okeanos and Tethys were the parents of generation, and that by which the gods swore was water—the poets themselves called it Styx; for that which is most ancient is most highly esteemed, and that which is most highly esteemed, is an object to swear by. Whether there is any such ancient and early opinion concerning nature would be an obscure question...[13]

When the Greek and Roman writers are considering the origins of natural philosophy there is often some reference, direct or indirect, to mythology and the learning of the temple. When there is not a mythological reference, we may be told that the philosophers studied under guru-like figures such as the gymnosophists of India, or in the temple schools of Egypt, Phoenicia and Mesopotamia. The pre-Socratic philosophers themselves remind us of gurus, each with his school of devotees, but they are also, in many cases, practical mathematicians and engineers. Four-element formalism is, by modern standards, a mixed phenomenon in every way, but it did not appear so to the Greeks.

Even in the medieval period, with its obsessive search for a purely linguistic precision of terms, there is no consensus on what the elements actually are. At times earth, water, air and fire are only the earth we stand on, the water we drink, the air we breathe and the fire which cooks our food. At times they are phases of matter, part of an early thermodynamic theory. At times they are powerful but vague images in a quasipoetic cosmology. At times they are logical categories. At times confusion itself takes on the appearance of definition, and they become magical entities in an occultist philosophy. Not only is there no consensus, there is little argument. Medieval doctrines of matter can be of great philosophical refinement or very crude, but such doctrines exist side by side, without any attempted reconciliation.

Perhaps the real problem is one common to traditions which have some idea of divine incarnation in human form. Such traditions pose the question of the relationship of earthly matter to divine substance. In the Old Testament God can take on apparent physical form, as when He wrestles with Jacob (*Genesis* 32: 24–32); the Greeks and Romans had many stories of gods who had taken on human flesh, if not in an identifiably historical context; Christian belief held that the Incarnation had taken place, in strictly historical not mythological time, in Jesus. How had divine substance put on flesh without being sullied or debased by it? For human flesh is animal flesh. Christian philosophy shrank from examining this question, treating it as a "Divine Mystery." Yet, while the descent of God into a human form is indeed a Divine mystery, of which we can at best form only a remote and ineffectual logical model, the nature of matter is not such, but the proper subject of natural philosophy and science. We must therefore have some idea of matter which shows how it could be responsive to a divine act. If we shun such an investigation matter also becomes a "Divine Mystery," and we are halfway towards deifying it, which deification is itself a way-point on the road to materialism. The incarnationist theological tradition did not resolve this dilemma.

It is perhaps for this reason that we find that Islamic philosophy, in the medieval period, has a clearer and more unified idea of matter than does Christian philosophy. It is not a case of absolute philosophical originality or superior learning, though Islamic natural philosophy is among the glories of culture. Islamic scholars were part of an international intellectual community of learning. They knew the Greek philosophers and Christian interpretations of them, having avidly absorbed a great deal of the civilization of the orthodox Christian East, and they were also familiar with Jewish learning. But Islam rejected the idea that God Himself was incarnate in Christ. It accepted the Virgin Birth and believed that the spirit of Christ was in some fashion the "Spirit of God and His Word which He cast into Mary" (*Koran* IV: 169), Muhammad being the *Paraclet* or Comforter prophesied by Christ, "the Spirit of truth, whom my father will send in my name" (*John* XIV: 26). It believed in visionary *appearances* of incarnation. But it did not believe in direct and unmediated contact between Divine Substance and natural matter, a real paradox into which Christian philosophy had wandered. It is true indeed that Christian philosophy *could* have produced a philosophical solution to the problem. It was there in the Augustinian system of "descending exemplars," an orthodox system of *mediated* contact. Christianity had, however, a deep fear of anything which suggested "emanationism," the idea that all things are outflowings, in some kind of successive materialization of substance, of the essence of God. Emanationism had been the basis of scores of heresies. Unless the hierarchy of descending exemplars was treated with the greatest logical care, it seemed, it would become an emanationist system, spawning heresy after heresy. Augustine had to be accepted, but his philosophy was, in effect, frozen. It cannot be said that, excepting the Lullian system, Augustinism advanced beyond the stage of ordering and clarifying Augustine's philosophy, which he himself thought of as a beginning, not a final summation. It is interesting that Lull's first purpose in developing his system was to answer objections to Christian philosophy raised by Muslims.

One Islamic belief is summarized thus by the Iranian scholar, Seyyed Hossein Nasr...

> The natural matter consists of fire, air, water and earth. All that is found in the sublunary sphere—the animals, plants and minerals—come from these constituents and by corruption return to them. Their creator is Nature, which is one of the forces of the celestial Universal Soul.
>
> Universal Matter is the Absolute Body. From this Body is drawn the entire corporeal Universe, that is, the celestial spheres, stars, the elements and all other beings whatever they may be. They are all bodies and their diversity comes only from their diverse forms.
>
> Original matter is a simple and ideal substance which cannot be sensed because it is none other than the form of unique existence; it is the primitive foundation. If this foundation receives quantity it becomes by virtue of that reception the Absolute Body about which one affirms that it has three dimensions—length, breadth and thickness. If this foundation receives quality, as, for example, the form of a circle, triangle or rectangle, it becomes a special body which is determined as being such and such. Thus quality is equal to 3, quantity to 2, and the primitive foundation to 1. Just as 3 comes after 2, so does quality come after quantity, and just as 2 comes after 1, quantity comes from the primitive foundation. In its existence the primitive foundation precedes quantity and quality as 1 precedes 2 and 3.
>
> The primitive foundation, quantity, and quality are simple, ideal forms which cannot be sensed. When one of them is united to another, the first is matter at the same time that the second is form. Quality is form with regard to quantity, and quantity is matter for quality. Quantity in its turn is form for the primitive foundation, and the primitive foundation is matter for quantity.[14]

This doctrine dates from the eleventh century AD, if not earlier. It has an archaic sound and because of this we might easily forget that we, unlike our nineteenth-century ancestors, now think in a similar if formally more sophisticated manner. The simplicity of the mathematical concepts deceives us into forgetting the weight of implication, resting upon the entire Euclidean and Pythagorean traditions, which they bear. When we posit a matter which consists of various infoldings of space and time or which is generated by fluctuations of a vacuum state we are much closer to this mode of thought than we are to the hard atomism of the seventeenth to early nineteenth centuries. Note, for example, that the "Absolute Body" is nothing other than Euclidean space. What we have here is a threefold evolution of matter. The first component of matter is something as yet unrealized in space. The second component is the Absolute Body, which is the realization of the first component in undifferentiated, space-creating and, simultaneously, space-filling form. The third component is the realization of the second in differentiated and individual forms. Finally, we have the change-able world of natural matter, the sphere of fire, air, water and earth. This Islamic theory appears remarkable for its time, yet we can trace its origins in pagan Greek, Christian and other sources. The Christian world could have produced such a simple and coher-ent theory but it did not. The reason, I suggest, is the difficulty of reconciling any then-known theory of matter with the theology of incarnation. A descent of the Divine into flesh had to be *through* the most subtle realms of matter, and this was almost impossible to imagine. If it could be imagined it was difficult to reconcile it with what was then considered orthodox Christian theology.

In the most abstract form of four-element theory fire, air, water and earth are composed, in differing proportions, of the four quali-ties of hotness, wetness, coldness and dryness. These might sound like the categories of naive minds unless we remember that this school of thought insists that all hidden categories, no matter how subtle, must "come to rest" in categories manifest to the senses. The cycle of fire, air, water and earth must therefore have another cycle within it. For example, in one interpretation, which we shall return to shortly, heat is a form of energy (to use a modern word), with cold being a lack of energy, while wetness is continuity of substance and dryness (friability) is discreteness of substance.

The above over-schematic discussion necessarily gives the appearance of simple unity to a thought-system which never took on an absolute or orthodox form. To take two philosophers closely connected in time and place, the English Aristotelian, Robert Grosseteste (?1169–1253) thought, and argued with a depth which can still astonish us, that the true essence of matter was light flowing into the form of a sphere, while his pupil, Roger Bacon (?1214–1294) thought that primal matter was a mathematical substance, made up of number-relationships. The point, from a modern perspective, is that, while they were both right in an admittedly crude fashion, the mathematical tools to demonstrate the correctness of their generalized views were not developed until the nineteenth century, or fully employed until the "Einsteinian revolution" of the early twentieth century.

The formulation of Ramon Lull (c. 1235–1316) seems to be the most daring and complete medieval development of four-element structure. All questions of natural genius aside, part of this must have been due to his deep knowledge of Arabic philosophy. In his formulation, cold belongs properly to water, while humidity belongs properly to air. This surprises us; we would naturally have assigned humidity to water. But humidity here is not everyday moistness; it is thought of as the power of an entity to extend in space and to permeate or penetrate another, a quality better exemplified by air than by water. Furthermore, these qualities divide into pairs. Heat, which is virtually the same as positive energy in a society which lacks machinery run by inputs of regulated and measured power, has as its opposite cold, which is like negative energy. The opposites of the power of air to extend in space and to penetrate, that is, to extend itself as a continuum through a substance or medium, are the qualities of friability, inertness and particularity, as symbolized by earth, which now becomes the bearer of "dryness" and the opposite of air. We have, then, an active/passive cosmology, with heat and humidity being the actives, respectively, of the passives cold and dryness. As a result, to quote Lull, the elements cannot be separated from one another, "because all the elements are mixed, and each is in the other."[15]

From a modern viewpoint it is not too great a philosophical step to think of the scale of increasing cold as one of loss of energy or entropy, and of that of increasing heat as one of increase of energy or negentropy. The scale of humidity as a continuum then becomes a scale of "successivity," while that of dryness, as representing lack of continuity and inert particularity, becomes a scale of simultaneity. Thus our four elements become negentropy/entropy and successiveness/ simultaneity, and we have a logically pleasing representation of the phase-states of matter.

This final step was not taken nor could it have been. Such a logical and mathematical formulation, though Lull sensed the need of it, was not possible in terms of Aristotelian logic and Euclidean geometry, which could not cope with sliding scales. Lull could not set out his logic in an economically algebraical form, but had to illustrate it with revolving wheels and combinatorial matrices. They give his books an odd appearance. His diagrams look like something between navigational tables and board games. What was needed was a new form of dialectical logic and also the calculus, which latter made it possible to think of a number as both a discrete entity (simultaneity) and an entity reached at the end of a scale of growing or diminishing quantity (successiveness) sliding to an infinite or infinitesimal. The medieval system could not develop a mathematical logic of nature. Lull himself, who carried the forms-and-forces world view to its highest development before Swedenborg,[16] could not do this.

Since four-element theory was still, in Swedenborg's day, an accepted if often disputed part of the theory of matter, and since a degree of Lullian influence could be found everywhere in it, we need not bother to trace this influence too precisely. As I have indicated earlier, it is most likely that it came to him through Leibniz. In any case, he goes back to beginnings, and apart from contemporaries or near-contemporaries, depends mostly on Greek sources, chief among them Plato, Aristotle and "pseudo-Aristotle."[17] What we question is why he should have continued to develop it, though very much in his own way, when the advanced minds of his time were abandoning it. There seem to be two answers. The first would be that, as we have seen, he wished to preserve and develop the insights of the past. The second would be that he was firmly in opposition to the growing trend, which eventually came to dominate science and still does, to develop all large forms exclusively from the combined activities of small ones. This mode of thought, even in a Christian or deist context, would lead inexorably to the idea of a universe without God. For it was impossible to conceive of a Supreme Intelligence who would create the minute particulars of a universe before He had an idea of the universe as a whole. Either He would be making up the universe as He went along, by a process of guessing and improvisation, or He did not exist at all and large forms were created exclusively by the activities (which could not be, if the analysis was pushed far enough, anything but random) of tiny entities or microparticles. Swedenborg could not accept this. He needed the concept of large forms as already existing in the intent of Providence; and there was no more inclusive concept of nature in the large than that which was found in the system of phase-states—etheric, gaseous, liquid and solid. When the order of nature in the large is as "primary" as its order in the small, the necessity of randomness (though not of the mean motion which we measure statistically) disappears.

There was yet another reason for denying that the whole was exclusively engendered by the parts. This was that the whole-part dilemma was certain to exist as much in the small as in the large. As Swedenborg saw it, the smallest particle of matter which could be obtained by mechanical division (say, by cutting up matter with a very tiny knife), must inevitably be a complex entity, perhaps as complex as, though much smaller than, an entire world. How could it be otherwise? Elementary geometry told him that a line may be infinitely subdivided, and that each of the tiny lines thus created still contains an infinity of points.

Such were his guiding principles. In the details of the discussion, he could not free himself entirely from the limitations of his age and we do not expect this. Yet we may now ask whether, in reality, anything is left of the traditional four elements in Swedenborg's theory. Could it be that his reworking is so complete that his reliance upon them is no more than a series of unnecessary genuflections before a tradition, gestures which only obstruct our understanding of what he is trying to say? This is a difficult point to answer because there is something of truth in it. We can understand phase state perfectly well without references to ether, air, water and earth as "elements." His contemporaries could have done so as well, since four-element theory, though it had not yet been abandoned, was a virtually inert body of thought, considered by advanced minds to be archaic and incapable of development. For example, in his very advanced *Theory of Natural Philosophy*, published in 1758, Roger Boscovich refers only to the "so-called four elements," coolly describing them as heterogeneous substances.[18] And while, in our time, Swedenborg's theory of a phase-state universe developing out of logical/mathematical forms can still appear new and exciting, we balk at his apparent demand that we accept the archaism along with the novelty.

The complete answer must be that there is more involved here than mere traditionalism. When we talk of the phases of matter we imply the question "What remains constant when an entity passes through solid, liquid and gaseous states"? We should now say the atomic/molecular structure remains constant; a medieval Aristotelian philosopher would have said "primal matter" does. But to Swedenborg the atomic/molecular structure of a particular entity (as he understands it) is not truly basic. His fluid-dynamic cosmology is such that the doctrine of phase comes first, in sequence of argument at least. Atomic/molecular structure develops out of crystallized or infolded phase states. The particular chemical entity is the last structure to develop in his canon of forms and it can in no way be "more primary" than the field of sense-perceived matter as a whole. Nor is there a bare-substratum primal matter, in the Aristotelian sense, unless it be bare space/time itself, which is not primary in the *Principia*.

What *is* primary is the Active/Passive point, a quasilogical entity in which the Active is pure successiveness and the Passive is pure simultaneity, with both seen in logical rather than temporal terms. Each elementary, itself a complex of actives and passives, is relatively more active than the elementary which develops from it, hence more fluid and hence containing within it more of the "successive" or "continuous" than its descendant, while the elementary which it engenders contains relatively more of the "simultaneous" or "discrete." So consistently is this worked out that we may say that his entire system, from the Active/Passive point to solid matter, is a steady progression from high to low energy and from almost pure successiveness to almost pure simultaneity. For "simultaneous order derives its birth, nature and perfection from successive orders, and the former is only rendered perspicuous and plain by the latter."[19] This progression could also be visualized (crudely) as the gradual freezing or crystallization of a perfect fluid, the independent active.

Through this entire process there run four kinds of movement.[20] They are *tremulation*, which is the vibration of the small particles at the surface of a large particle of composite form and a similar motion at the centers of particles; *undulation* or wave motion in a volume of particles; *movement caused by pressure*, which includes pressure-of-weight and thus contributes to gravity, and *local or translatory movement*, along a line or curve. Such forms of motion are found in every element and one engenders another: tremulation causes undulation, which causes pressure, which causes local motion.[21] It is in these four forms of motion, perhaps, that we should seek his most abstract version of the ancient four elements. And there is an implication here which Swedenborg could not himself develop but which may further explain his curious silence on the question of Newtonian gravity, which we noted in the last chapter. If gravity is in some fashion a derivative of pressure, and if all pressure is engendered by undulation, then it follows that gravity can be nothing but a wave engendered by a vortex. But though this is a necessary conclusion, there was no way, either mathematical or experimental, of demonstrating it. The Newtonian theory was (and of course still remains "on its level") demonstrable in both ways. (See also Appendix E).

Nonetheless, it is not extravagant to say that the *Principia* is all about universal gravitation. Newton says that the gravitational attraction of two bodies is directly proportional to the square of the distance between them. The gravitational constant is thus "a constant of proportionality." He further proves that the attraction between two masses is between their centers of gravity. The question is then to define what mass is and what the center of gravity is, and to do so in terms of energy and inertia. For only energy and inertia can produce energy and inertia. Therefore it seems energy and inertia must produce mass, must define distances and spaces and must be responsible for material proportionality itself. This is the root of Swedenborg's vorticism. The general argument is actually irrefutable, though we need a rigorous modern study to determine how well he has worked out the details.

A simple logic governs the entire intricate system. When we think about it we can see that such entities as Active and Passive, if skilfully evolved into particular forces and forms, will not yield the particles of particular substances. They will give us complexes of energy and mass, or force and inertia, or kinetic energy and potential energy. When represented in diagrams these may indeed resemble textbook illustrations of electrons, atoms and molecules. Yet they are not "snapshots" of real and imaginary particles but schematic diagrams of microsystems.

In other words we shall never find, by physical experiment, particles exactly like those of Swedenborg's. Rather, if his theory is correct, we shall find forms which cluster around the generalized norms he sets out. And here—there can be no doubt about it— modern experience supports him. Unless we wish to evoke chance or miracle his theory is, to make a minimal statement, a good one. And it is a good theory in the manner of other good theories of his time, if on a superior level. For we also find, though it would be tedious to list them here, protomodern elements in the works of Descartes, Euler, the Bernoullis and, of course, Leibniz and Boscovich.

Swedenborg seems to have believed that the inner structure of nature is logical and mathematical well before he wrote his *Principia*. I do not only mean that he thought this was an efficacious way of generalizing natural processes. He thought that logical and mathematical entities were physically if very subtly real. He believed that when we think logically and mathematically we think from and with our senses, *sensually*. That such thought may be mechanized, as we know now in the computer age, is an adequate proof of the validity of this viewpoint.[22] When we construct a triangle or a syllogism we do not merely operate *in* the world of sense and thus of matter. Our ideas are themselves physical; we actually manipulate sensual and physical entities in the form of "brain waves." Not only that, but we "discover" logical and mathematical truths because they were already there in the delicate physical tensions of thinking, just as the tensions of subtle matter are there, whether we know of them or not.

Though the idea of "discovering" mathematical forms which are "already there" sounds quite Platonic, most Platonists would have been horrified by this. Swedenborg has demonstrated that Plato's World of Forms exists, but at the same time he has ruthlessly demythologized it. Whether Plato himself would have been horrified is much more difficult to determine since (there is no consensus on this) it is at least possible to interpret his world of visible mathematical forms as belonging to the sphere of sense-appearances and of "becoming."

I say Swedenborg seems always to have believed this. The conclusion emerges from a reading of his *Algebra*, published in 1718, when he was thirty years old. This is an elementary text, published for the use of students in a Sweden where the level of ordinary mathematical education was low. The worked problems are in gunnery, mechanics, and private and public accounting, and it is possible that Swedenborg had in mind the forced-march development of a cadre of trained engineers, military men and civil servants, to the greater honor of Sweden. To me there seems to be something radically novel about this text, though I could not substantiate this statement without an extensive study of early eighteenth-century textbooks on a similar pedagogical level. One is astonished to note how rapidly Swedenborg moves from the simplest arithmetical concepts to the discussion of practical problems in, for instance, ballistics. There is no apparatus of theorem-and-proof. Every mathematical entity is described as much as possible in terms of familiar objects: a circle is "a little ring," a parabola is "a line made by bombs or anything cast out," a globe is "like a ball or shot," a cylinder is "a roller of equal thickness" and the horizontal line of a Cartesian graph "follows the even water's edge." We seem to move very quickly from the level of *Sesame Street* to one of practical mechanics. The reason, of course, is that the book was written in a century when ordinary people barely knew basic arithmetic. Calculus was still very arcane: he solves problems we now handle with calculus by methods of arithmetical and geometrical progression.[23]

The book is remarkably easy to follow; but his reduction of mathematics to problems in mechanics and accounting has more than an immediately pedagogical purpose. It arises from a rethinking of mathematics which was in his day quite *avant-garde*, and is somewhat so even in our own. This emerges from two of the definitions in his short preface—

Of algebra he says—

> Whatever contains any likeness or proportion, let its species be what it may, is embraced by this science. It treats of everything which relates to an equilibrium or an analogy. And as it appears that in reality nothing exists in the world which is destitute of some likeness, or incapable of being equalled or compared with other objects, so it is the province of algebra to investigate the degree of similarity. This science is still in its infancy; but it continues to increase; and will speedily extend itself to the comprehension of subjects, with which, at present, we are but imperfectly acquainted.

Not only that, but algebra may be compared to physics in a direct sense, not only as a mathematical technique. For, as he says further, "Physics relate to motions, times and other analogies; and thus extend to everything in nature which has any similarity or proportion." The use of the word "analogies" here is striking and unique. Motions and times are related to each other as analogies are, by *similarity* and *parallelism*. This is the basis of his early doctrine of correspondences, which we shall consider in Part Two of this book, and it demonstrates the hidden relationship between this doctrine and the cosmology of the *Principia*, a relationship which, once sensed, is gradually seen to embrace a vast network of linked ideas. It is also, I believe, a very good reason in favor of my view that the *Principia* is a system of, to adapt the Augustinian term, "natural exemplars."

I have been concentrating in this chapter on some medieval and ancient links, perhaps to the point of making Swedenborg appear an archaic figure in his time. This should be corrected. His belief in exemplars and types was unfashionable but his vortex theory was not. He would have agreed, though not in all details, with the following quotation from Leibniz—

> Aristotle's primary matter is the same as Descartes' ethereal matter. Each is infinitely subdivisible. Each inherently lacks form and motion, and each acquires forms as a result of motion. In each, mind is the source of motion. Whirls are produced without solidity in Aristotle's as well as in Descartes' vortices. The cause of solidity in each is a motion greater than any which can break it up, though this is not how Descartes explains it. Each whirl propagates any action it receives through motion to another whirl because of the continuity of matter. For Aristotle, as well as Descartes and Hobbes, makes all particular motions depend on the universal circular motion of whirls. Hence, the principal circular motions alone possess intelligence for Aristotle, because it is their action which produces all other action. Aristotle fell into error when he made the earth the centre of the universe and all its rotations. But this was a pardonable error since natural philosophy had not yet been sufficiently guided by observation.
>
> My emendation is that *primary matter is nothing if considered at rest*. Certain Scholastics have expressed this more obscurely when they said that form gives existence to primary matter. But a proof can be given of this. For whatever is unthinking is nothing, and whatever lacks variety is unthinking. Now if primary matter simply moves in one direction in parallel lines, *it is uniformly at rest*, and consequently is nothing. But *all things are full* in so far as primary matter is identical with space. Hence, *all motion is circular*, or composed of circular motions, or those returning unto themselves. Many of the circular motions oppose each other, and many blend into each other. Many try to unite in one, tending to make bodies come to rest or annihilation of motion...[24]

I have said he did not accept the above argument in all details. He rejects Aristotle's idea of motionless and formless matter. He accepts Leibniz' emendation that primary matter at rest would be nothing. But he rejects the simple vorticity of Aristotle and Descartes. He makes the vortex a generator of Euclidean geometry, thus making it in a sense invisible and, indeed, a geometrical "exemplar." The idea may be archaic but he has arrived at it by geometrical and mechanical means which are, in his time, advanced.

Ideas such as the above, with the other factors we have considered, led Swedenborg to adopt the bubble as the model of his elementary particle. It is not difficult to see how vortical movements in a fluid could generate bubbles. The bullular model had many advantages, among them the following—

i)   The pressure inside the bubble, which maintains its shape, is always in some measurable relationship to the pressure outside the bubble. In the floating soap-bubble, for example, this outside pressure is provided by the air, as what we would now call a "field," as also the inside pressure. When this image is generalized and applied to the microparticle it is possible to form some mental image of forces within the microparticle and to relate them to external forces. The "hard pebble" picture of the microparticle common in his day did not permit this.

ii) The bubble is typically spherical, but it can take any curved shape and even a straight-angle shape with rounded corners and edges. Thus it can be the basic shape of a versatile geometry and of a mechanics too, since all kinds of movement can be related to such shapes and their derivatives.

iii) As bubbles can form inside bubbles, figures of microparticles can be made as complex as one wishes.

iv) Because the bubble is a form of fluid matter it can be related to the forms of hydrodynamics and thus to an early form of continuum mechanics.

The bullular model is still useful, it appears. For, according to a recent article in *Scientific American*, by Hans Gutbrod and Horst Stocker,[25] a newly developed "plastic ball" model of atomic reactions is now being used. As described in the article the model has certain similarities to the Swedenborgian one. It is a hydrodynamic model in the sense that the nuclei of atoms are imaged as being much like droplets of water. There is even an analogue of phase theory. Thus solid phases are represented by "condensates of the nuclear fluid, such as particles called density isomers." Massive nuclei, containing many protons and neutrons, represent the liquid phase. And, say the authors, "The vapor phase would consist of a dilute gas of light nuclei and free nucleons," while "an assembly of free quarks and gluons corresponds to the plasma phase." We even find such phrases as "nuclear viscosity." It appears, then, that we have analogues of the phases of matter even in the interiors of atoms, and that the analogues are close enough to permit construction of models of the atom. As the authors say, after describing the phases of water—ice, liquid, gas and plasma—"nuclear matter exhibits similar 'phases'."

Since this chapter deals with one of the most controversial aspects of Swedenborg's theory, let me repeat, even at the risk of boring my reader, the five main points I have tried to make—

i) Four-element formalism, in the modern form of phase theory which Swedenborg anticipates, is capable of modelling material processes from the most elementary to the most complex.

ii) This theory proceeds from generals to particulars. By itself, it cannot provide a complete picture of reality. Swedenborg's generalizing power is so great that he can invent or discover some behaviors even on the very complex level of naked-eye matter. But a general theory cannot evolve true particulars, only finer and finer generals. He cannot fix the behavior and form of any single entity. Formal deduction must be balanced by experimental discovery, and we cannot say that we have arrived at a scientific truth until both meet and reinforce each other. He was himself perfectly aware of this and regretted the lack of sound data which in his time prevented this "double motion."

iii) Swedenborg was attracted to four-element formalism because, in spite of its erratic and unsatisfactory performance up to then in the world of hard matter, he perceived a deep rationality within it.

iv) He also valued it because it provided a link with the past, not only the immediate but the ancient past.

v)   He wished to retain this link with what was valuable in ancient philosophy for one overriding reason: it was more compatible with a doctrine of Divine creation than anything else in his time.

I refer to a link with the *ancient* past. I doubt that he knew, at this stage in his life, how far back the implications of his theory ranged. His image of the spider's web, referred to earlier, is our clue to what is happening. A passage from René Huyghe's *Formes et Forces* may help us in our transition to an ancient world, very different from that which Swedenborg knew of through his classical studies. In the following quotation, Huyghe shows us how the spider's web is based upon a triangle and a double Archimedean spiral.

> The completed web of the spider also describes a spiral. The American engineer Bert E. Dugdale has attentively studied the successive phases of the work of the spider in the course of its construction. The basic structure is a triangle, conformably to the geometrical postulate which teaches the engineer that "three points suffice to define or stabilize a plane." On this triangle a set of threads radiating from the centre relates it to the framework, completing the sustaining network on which the animal then deploys two spirals: the first, which is provisional, is destroyed in the course of the execution of the second; it departs from the centre, extends towards the exterior framework and attaches itself there, after having reversed by a loop the direction of the final orbit; the second, much tighter spiral is made of the sticky thread which serves as a trap and winds from the periphery towards the centre, where the spider awaits his prey. These are Archimedean spirals, thus with parallel turns, and are not logarithmic, as some have written; in fact, in making them, the animal is by its very dimensions constrained to maintain equal spacing.[26]

The image of the created world as a spider's web, or, more generally, as a piece of woven stuff, is very old and widespread. It can be as ambivalent as nature itself, since the spider is an image both of predation and of patient craftsmanship. This symbol is best preserved in Africa. Thus, in Yoruba myth, the first marshy world, a form of Chaos, was visited by the celestial gods "coming down spiders' webs," and central and southern African peoples say God ascended and descended from and to earth by way of a spider's thread. In West Africa, the cunning spider-spirit Anansi (Annancy in America) is, so to speak, God's "chief official." Among the Dogon, we have an elaborately developed image of the creation as both a spiral and as "woven stuff," in a fascinating form of mythological philosophy revealed to Marcel Griaule.[27]

Some such system of belief probably existed in the ancient Mediterranean and Europe. In the Mediterranean it seems to have been associated with an ancient form of cardinal-direction (four-quarter) cosmology which was replaced by the Olympian system headed by Zeus. It would have been a "transformational" ideology, related to that found among Amerindians, in which animals, plants and prominent geological features are transformations and meta-morphoses of the "first men" (often because they sinned in some way).

Ovid, whose sense of the ancient past was very acute, presents a modern (i.e. Augustan Roman) version of this ancient cosmology in his *Metamorphoses*. I shall quote the translation of Dr. Samuel Croxall, not because it is particularly faithful and certainly not because of its poetic quality, but because it gives us an "eighteenth-century Ovid" and also because it is more fun to read rhymed couplets than prosy modern versions.

The low-born Arachne, renowned throughout Lydia and even neighboring countries for her skill in weaving, has dared to challenge Pallas, the very goddess of the art. So Pallas, disguised as an old woman, descends to earth to teach Arachne a cruel lesson. First, still in disguise, she attempts to dissuade Arachne from her rash challenge. Then, when Arachne refuses, she appears in her true form, "cloth'd with heavenly light," to accept it.

Straight to their posts appointed both repair,
And fix their threaded looms with equal care:
Around the solid beam the web is tied,
While hollow canes the parting warp divide;
Through which, with nimble flight, the shuttles play,
And for the woof prepare a ready way;
The woof and warp unite, prest by the toothy slay.
  Thus both, their mantles buttoned to their breast,
Their skilful fingers ply with willing haste,
And work with pleasure; while they cheer the eye
With glowing purple of the Tyrian dye;
Or, justly intermixing shades with light,
Their colourings insensibly unite.

Minerva paints a well-composed Olympian scene, in which gods
appear as denizens of a heavenly court—

Pallas in figures wrought the heav'nly powers,
And Mars's hill among th'Athenian tow'rs.
On lofty thrones twice six celestials sate,
Jove in the midst, and held their warm debate;
The subject weighty, and well-known to fame,
From whom the city should receive its name.

And Minerva further indicates her commitment to an anthropo-
morphic idea of the gods by, all too self-revealingly, including
herself (as of course she has every right to do)—

Herself she blazons with a glitt'ring spear,
And crested helm that veiled her braided hair...

The older transformationist cosmology is alluded to, by way of
warning to Arachne of her own fate, in the corners of the tapestry—

And then, to let her giddy rival learn
What just rewards such boldness was to earn,
Four trials at each corner had their part,
Designed in miniature, and touch'd with art.
Haemus in one, and Rhodope of Thrace,
Transform'd to mountains, fill'd the foremost place;
Who claim'd the titles of the gods above,
And vainly us'd the epithets of Jove...

Nevertheless, Arachne insists on representing the gods in their nonhuman forms: Jove as a bull, eagle, satyr, shower of gold and snake; Neptune as a steer, stream and ram and so on. Or she shows them as shepherds, images of the "Golden Age." Minerva, outraged, condemns her to animal form—

> Then, going off, she sprinkled her with juice,
> Which leaves of baleful aconite produce.
> Touch'd with the pois'nous drug, her flowing hair
> Fell to the ground, and left her temples bare;
> Her usual features vanish'd from their place,
> Her body lessen'd all, but most her face.
> Her slender fingers, hanging on each side,
> With many joints, the use of legs supply'd:
> A spider's bag the rest, from which she gives
> A thread, and still by constant weaving lives...[28]

Ovid is always subtle and ambiguous, and perhaps we are reading too much into this fable when we see it as a conflict between the Olympian view of the gods and an older system, a system of shepherds, in which, as in the religion of Egypt, the attributes of the gods took on animal forms. Yet there are other and more obvious challenges to the Olympian hierarchy in Ovid's book which, as an account of the metamorphoses of gods and men, seems to take the side of Arachne. We have, for example, the great speech of Pythagoras in Book XV, where Pythagoras says we (including the Roman reader) have given the anthropomorphized gods our own human vices, by inviting them to share in the blood sacrifice of helpless creatures. It is the Golden Age Ovid loves—

> ...when man, yet new,
> No rule but uncorrupted reason knew...[29]

Arachne's tapestry shows nature in perpetual and fluid transformation. The tapestry of Pallas shows it hard and fixed, with fragments of (formally unresolved) transformationism at the edges. It could also be that Ovid, in this little vignette, and throughout the entire poem, develops a most subtle dialectic of the relationship—sometimes a battle, sometimes a marriage—between the fixed and the fluid, a dialectic implicit in the natures of the ancient gods.[30]

ENDNOTES

1 Swedenborg, *Principia* II, p. 260.

2 Pauling and Hayward, facing plate 12.

3 Swedenborg, *Chemistry*, pp. 58–59.

4 Yavorsky and Detlaf, *Handbook of Physics*, pp. 487, 870.

5 Watkins, George D., article *Crystal Defects* in *Enc. of Phys.*, p. 174.

6 Swedenborg, *The Worship and Love of God*, pp. 22–23.

7 Ibid., p. 24.

8 Sewall, Frank, notes in *The Worship and Love of God*, p. 284.

9 Swedenborg, *Principia* II, p. 258.

10 Barker and Henderson, in *Scientific American*, Nov 1981, pp. 131–132. See also D. Chandler, J.D. Weeks and H.C. Anderson: "Van der Walls Picture of Liquids, Solids and Phase Transformations" in *Science*, May 20, 1983, p. 787.

11 In *Civilization and Barbarism* (pp. 353–361) Cheik Anta Diop makes a very good case for the Egyptian origin of pre-Socratic concepts.

12 It was easy enough for those who did not believe in ordinary polytheism to reverse such reasoning. In Cicero's *The Nature of the Gods*, Balbus, a rational deist and Stoic who believes in the existence of gods but rejects mythology as superstition, says, "A great number of gods have also been derived from scientific theories about the world of nature" (Book II, pp. 62–64), and he later identifies Jupiter and Juno, respectively, with ether and air (ibid., pp. 64–66).

13 Nahm, p. 61.

14 Nasr, pp. 58–59. The phrase "Absolute Body" seems to have affinities with Cabalistic notions, though the *form* of the thought has not.

15 Pring-Mill, p. 64. Lullian logic is tetravalent on a binary base. This is why it can lead to such a formulation as Herrera's "cubism" (see note 7, Chapter Two).

16 Heer, p. 307. Lest I be considered a Lullian fanatic I shall quote his description of Lull's "cybernetic machine": "Here in rudimentary fashion were anticipated the great universal formulae of Einstein and Heisenberg, which have provided man with the mathematical keys to the problem of matter, light, energy, and the fundamental laws of the cosmos. A miracle machine: or, as later scoffers were to say, a wind machine, tossing empty words about. Leibniz however was not among the mockers; Lull's vision came too close to his own dream of finding a universal, scientifically viable language, which should enlighten all men impartially: the prerequisite of universal peace."

17 The pseudo-Aristotelian work (probably by some Platonist) entitled (Eng. tr.), *Divine Wisdom According to the Egyptians* (see Swedenborg, *Philosopher's Notebook*, pp. 508–509).

18 Boscovich, p. 160. The theory of Boscovich is another example of an eighteenth-century philosopher's producing a proto-modern theory of the microworld.

19 Swedenborg, *The Worship and Love of God*, p. 222.

20 These four forms of movement are discussed by Erland J. Brock, in his article, "Observation, Induction and Myth," *NP*, Jul/Sep 1978, pp. 249–250.

21 See Swedenborg: *On Tremulation*, pp. 11–12 and 20; *Minor Principia* (*Principia* II, pp. 456 et seq.) and *Principia* I, pp. 139, 181 and 240, also index refs. in *Principia* for passing references to the subject footnoted.

22 Swedenborg's thoughts along these lines are not fully developed until the theological period, but are sketched out in the psychological works. See Hugo Lj. Odhner's fine study, *The Human Mind, Its Faculties and Degrees*. They are implicit in *On Tremulation* (1719), where thought and nonhuman nature are both said to be forms of undulation.

23 Unless the translation I have, a photocopy of a very old, anonymous and handwritten manuscript, is itself incomplete, it would appear that the book was published without its two concluding sections, which would have dealt with differential and integral calculus.

24 Leibniz, ed. Weiner: *Selections*, pp. 90–91.

25 *Scientific American*: Nov 1991, pp. 58–67.

26 Huyghe, pp. 277–281.

27 Griaule *passim*.

28 Ovid, *Metamorphoses* (translations ed. Garth): quotations from Book VI: lines 77–209.

29 Ibid., Book I: lines 113–114 (translated by Dryden).

30 It seems from Otis' *Ovid as an Epic Poet*, particularly from his comments on the speech by Pythagoras but also passim, that it is generally considered old-fashioned to regard Ovid as a philosophically profound poet. But consider the figure of Janus, at the beginning of the *Fasti*, who *was* Chaos, but became, with the formation of the material cosmos, a two headed (binary) god who has "the guardianship of the vast universe." If this is not philosophy, I do not know what is.

PART TWO

1

Towards the Doctrine of Correspondences

The "doctrine of correspondences" is the best-known of all the ideas Swedenborg put forward, either as a philosopher or as the bearer of a Divine revelation. This doctrine was not understood and a false image of Swedenborg entered the literary history of the nineteenth century. It is still with us, the image of a strangely prosaic and banal mind (who is nonetheless wildly imaginative), who vulgarizes ideas he has taken from the works of Boehme and the *Cabala* (neither of which he knew), who is quintessentially bourgeois (though an aristocrat and a courtier) and whose thought is basically irrelevant (though it had a great influence). This absurd image perpetuates a widespread confusion found among the poets of the early nineteenth century. A mistaken notion of "universal correspondence" had been seized upon by certain poets, among them some of the most talented of the age, in an almost desperate response to a crisis in their art. This misunderstanding must be discussed, because it colors every reference to "Swedenborgian correspondences," creating a thick fog of error. But it is also true, misunderstanding or not, that only the poets realized the significance of this new idea, if only because they had to. They recognized in the doctrine of correspondences a new rhetoric. They were right in this, though the doctrine is much more than that, and though, in the end, this something more proved to be something they could not accept (see Appendix A).

What we have in the nineteenth century is a crisis of the image. Poets can no longer claim, as they had roughly up to the seventeenth century, that poetic comparisons are based on real relationships in a Great Chain of Being. The philosophical basis of this assumption, tied to the traditional social hierarchies, had disappeared with the Old Regime. Yet poetry is nothing if it is not an art of imitation, representation and comparison. The poet imitates and represents an action when he sets out words in such fashion that they describe an external or mental event, along with the flow of emotions and emotion-bearing images which accompany it. He compares images and events one to the other, not only when he uses simile and metaphor but when he uses almost any figure of speech. The science of rhetoric, as related to poetry, is an objective study of the way this is done. Rhetoric is to poetry what harmony and counterpoint are to the composer, what perspective, color theory and the anatomy of human, animal and other forms are to the painter, what the sciences of proportion and weight-bearing materials are to the architect. In the end, as a science of imitation, representation and comparison, it rests upon a philosophical foundation. Imitation is not meaningful unless there is a real relationship between the poet's mind and the world outside it. Representation is impossible unless the poem enters the world it is imitating, that is, becomes an artifact. Comparison is arbitrary and entirely flimsy if the likenesses among things in the external world do not correspond, in some way, with the likenesses among the thoughts in the mind of the poet.

Classical rhetoric is hardly taught anywhere these days, though many of its categories appear (in denatured form, as it seems to me) in semantics and semiology. The techniques of music and visual art I referred to are still taught in conservatories and art schools, but they are taught reluctantly and in truncated form by professors low in the academic hierarchy. In some fashion they are considered outdated, even though their bases in the sciences (acoustics, geometry, optics, anatomy and linguistics) have never been effectively challenged. The rejection is an ideological one. It cannot be supported by any objective idea of progress, since, again, nobody can point to any objective discoveries which have demonstrated uncorrectible errors in the scientific or philosophical bases of these disciplines. Undoubtedly there is continual progress to be made, but here we have simple rejection, not the desire to progress.

When entire disciplines come under prolonged attack, then slide out of existence like discredited bodies of political opinion, we cannot treat this as an event with a simple cause. The causes of the overthrow of rhetoric, particularly the part of rhetoric which deals with the formal classification of images, lie very deep. I am not sure that they do not have something to do with a profound and obscure change in the relationship in the developed countries between man and his environment. It is certainly a fact that modern literary critics in these countries are periodically swept by waves of admiration for literature produced in countries where classical rhetoric, or some non-European analogue of it, is still strong. We need only consider the spasms of enthusiastic praise for Russian poetry just before and immediately after the Bolshevik Revolution, for the Spanish group of 1927 (Lorca the most famous among them), for the neoclassical novels and stage plays of France in the 1930s and 1940s, and for the neobaroque novels of Latin America in our own day. We have also had shorter periods when African, Indian or Arabic works were in vogue, works arising out of non-European rhetorical traditions. In all these literatures we find a use of poetic figure which is, in terms of Western literary culture, quite out of date. It is as if we had a deep longing for what we had abandoned.

One may perhaps find a philosophical reason, though it is not the deepest reason, for our abandonment of the science of rhetoric. This would be in the rise of subjective idealist philosophies, dominant nowadays in various forms. There is one esthetic belief which unites the nineteenth and twentieth centuries, and this is the notion that the inner experience of the artist, when the idea of his artwork first occurs to him, is the *true* work (obviously there is a paradox here in the word "work"). Since the true work of art is internal, the external artwork is at best a dull simulacrum of the true work. To quote Shelley's *A Defence of Poetry* (but I could as

well have quoted the twentieth-century Italian philosopher, Benedetto Croce, or even an art-critic in yesterday's newspaper), "All
things exist as they are perceived: at least in relation to the percip-
ient"; (poetry) "...makes us the inhabitants of a world to which the
familiar world is a chaos," and "when composition begins, inspiration is already on the decline." There are today art-ideologies of
non-idealist kind, even disguised liberal or Western forms of Social
Realism. But subjective idealism dominates. Certain artists of the
present day, telling us we should regard their works as process not
product, that the objects they present us with are mere traces of
deep perceptions which they cannot communicate, live in the de-
bris of the subjective-idealist world built by Shelley and his contemporaries, a world which once had its own beauty.

It is true that there is a case to be made against rhetoric, but it is
an old case.

If we look upon rhetoric as a study of common word usage,
attached to an empirical set of prescriptions for using language to
achieve certain effects, then it is more of a manipulative craft than
a science. To the extent that it is a science, it is difficult to argue for
its autonomy. For to the extent that it studies the use of figures of
speech it is a subordinate category of the sciences of language; to
the extent that it studies the emotive effects of language it is a part
of psychology; to the extent that it studies the science of the logical
manipulations of meaning it is a branch of philosophy and formal
logic. Thus as a science it seems eclectic and ill-organized with no
internal principles of its own. This slighting description of rhetoric
may be modern in form, but it goes back as far as Plato and may be
found, in different expression, in his *Gorgias*. It is a justified
criticism. The science of rhetoric as we have it is a mere bundle of
loosely related studies, from the banalities of the style manual to
some very subtle examinations of verbal figure. The science of
verbal figure is called *tropology*, from a Greek word for a figure of
speech, meaning "to turn." But we should never guess that such a
dynamic idea, which reminds us of the turns in dance steps, lies
behind the static classifications of the rhetoric manuals.

There is another way of looking at rhetoric, in which it is seen as
a true and autonomous science because it deals with real and

autonomous things. All prescriptive ideas of "tasteful" or "effective" style are not treated as science, but as something like a derivative technology, eclectic and oriented by need and fashion. Most of us know something of the history of taste in English poetry. The age of Pope and Dryden reacted against the preceding age, in which poets often felt themselves obliged to work in every poetic figure which had ever been discovered, the more bizarre the better. This reaction in time resulted in the verse typical of the late eighteenth century, in which there was a very narrow repertoire of figure and that adhering closely to the pedestrian canons of common sense. Among the romantic poets, who by and large professed to disdain rhetoric as a science, the density of figure went up to almost the Renaissance and Baroque levels; they strangely aped, in the name of spontaneity, the productions of rhetorical *virtuosi*. Canons of taste, then, fluctuate. The true science of rhetoric, on the other hand, deals with words and images as they embody ideas. And, since it is a science, one may argue these ideas are as real as material objects, if only as true generalizations. Such a view is consistent with any religion based on sacred oral traditions or texts. It is consistent with objective idealism, which grants the material object the reality of the embodied idea. It is even consistent with the Marxist form of materialism, with some adaptation. It is not consistent with subjective idealism, which turns the objective world into a world of shadows or unknowables or a chaos on which we impose an order which really exists only in our own minds. Thus the objective idealist Plato, when he attacks the manipulative and ill-organized rhetoric represented by Gorgias, is simultaneously advancing the claims of what he considers to be a true rhetoric, which will be the basis of a new art-language prescribed by the censors of the State. This will be the rhetoric appropriate to the Platonic system of Ideas, Ideas which are real and which will take the place of the gods of the polytheistic theology of his day. (In a Platonic state, Shelley, who thought of himself as a Platonist, would be one of the first to go to the wall.) In religion too ideas are real—yet not autonomously so, but rather because they all, even human ideas which may be fleeting and illusory, relate in some way to the Divine mind or to the minds of the gods. Only a divine being may have completely true ideas, and they are true because all the operations of a divine mind are absolutely real.

In the ancient (pre-Greek) world rhetoric is also a science in the physical and mathematical sense.[1] This is a very large subject and I shall return to it later. We are concerned now, however, with the historical resonances of the Swedenborgian doctrine of correspondences, first in relationship to the theory of poetry in the early nineteenth century, then, though in very general terms, in relationship to ancient cosmologies.

The first thing which must be pointed out is that the doctrines expounded in the works of Swedenborg have actually very little to do with poetic correspondences as set out by literary historians and critics. They should rather be related to biblical exegesis. In France, where the theory of poetic correspondences is most clearly expressed, we have to deal with a revival of occultism and gnosticism on a frame derived from Renaissance (once Byzantine) Neoplatonism. This revival is manifest both in the rituals and dogmas of secret societies (largely masonic in structure) and in writings available to the general public.[2] Swedenborg, whose works are rarely studied, either by the secret societies or by the literary critics who will later echo their errors, becomes one figure in a cloudy procession of initiates. If he is distinguished among them, it is because he carries with him the prestige of an adept in the physical sciences who has gone beyond science. He is supposed to have proved, both in theory and by direct experience of the spiritual world, that there is a link between matter and spirit, which expresses itself in the form of symbols. Yet here the imagined link and favored symbols are not those of the Bible. What they are can hardly be defined, but they have little to do with Swedenborg. He becomes part of an eruption of every kind of occultist and symbolic system, or rather of fragments of systems: cabalism, symbolic alchemy, seventeenth-century Rosicrucianism, Alexandrian gnosticism, magical or truly philosophical Neoplatonism and neo-Pythagoreanism, and new versions of Alexandrian and Renaissance misconceptions of the "wisdom of the Egyptians and Chaldeans." There are forms of symbolic mathematics, but they owe more to the magical tradition than to Swedenborg.

Indeed, where there is a truly philosophical background to the doctrines of poetic correspondence, it is to German idealism and romanticism that we should look, rather than to Swedenborg. The idealism of Hegel and other German idealists—not a Hegel carefully studied but one whose thought had spread into general literary culture—is found in the *Vers Dorés* of the exquisitely talented Gérard de Nerval,[3] who lost his reason and hanged himself (was murdered, some say) at the age of 47, in 1855.

> Souvent, dans l'être obscur habite un Dieu caché;
> Et, comme un oeil naissant couvert par ses paupières,
> Un pur esprit s'accroît sous l'écorce des pierres.

A god hidden in obscure things; a spirit which grows "within the crust of stones" like the eye of a growing thing hidden by its eyelid—symbols such as these are often taken as poetic correspondences and in a sense they are. But the image relates to the God-in-Nature of German idealism and also to some extent to the Renaissance emblem or pictorial allegory; it has nothing to do with Swedenborg.

In short, the Swedenborg of the literary critics is a person who never existed. The poetic correspondences of de Nerval do not have Swedenborgian roots but arise out of a complex personal synthesis of updated Renaissance Neoplatonism (in which Swedenborg appears as a sort of dimly-glimpsed magus) and philosophical idealism. We may say the same of poets who publicly evoked the name of Swedenborg, such as Baudelaire. The appeal of German idealism, even in the Hegelian formulation, was that it too could be interpreted as stating that physical nature is a diaphanous structure of symbols. This is not what Swedenborgian correspondences mean. Strictly speaking, Hegel also defends himself against such an interpretation, since he sees physical nature as dense and hard, the opposite of diaphanous, and as completely though not autonomously real; but this was not understood then and is sometimes missed even today.

The theory of poetic correspondence is largely an underground movement. It does not penetrate the academies. It is to be found in the letters and occasional journalism of the poets themselves—

particularly in the criticism of Baudelaire—and it is doomed to remain fugitive, alluded to but never explained. The theory remains underground not only because it is anti-academic but because it is also anti-scientific—both for very good reasons, of course. For these poets, the major intellectual currents of the age were represented by the growth of a materialist, capitalist and scientific establishment appealing to hard logic, and by the increasing domination of intellectual life by the bureaucracies of universities and state school systems. They judged these trends to be anti-poetic in the extreme. Science, in particular, would have nothing to do with any theory of correspondences, whether Swedenborgian or not. It would be naturalistic prose, not poetry, which would claim to be scientific. Academic literary canons would move from dead classicism to a prettified naturalism with barely a nod to poetic correspondences. Worse yet, the establishment had swallowed German idealism in one great gulp, and Hegel had become the philosophical bulwark of the Prussian state.

What this meant was that there was no coherent world view, now that Hegel was gone, to which a theory of universal correspondences could be attached, unless it was the philosophy and theology of the *real* Emanuel Swedenborg (that is, not the absurd illuminé and cabalist of the secret societies). Yet this virtually demanded complete religious conversion. It is naively thought that poets are more spiritual than scientists and philosophers, because they are not so cursed with intellectual pride. But there is also a pride of the imagination, which the new poetic theory, overturning the old psychology, elevated above the reason. Poets accept Christianity no more easily than rationalist intellectuals, because Christianity demands a recognition that the unregenerated imagination is corrupt. The greatest and most ruthlessly honest recognized the corruption of the imagination; they could see it in themselves. Baudelaire certainly did, as did Rimbaud; but the first could only waver tentatively to and away from the Roman Catholicism of his mother, and the second gave up poetry entirely, to embrace the vigorously amoral life of a gunrunner in Africa. Furthermore, the rational aspect of poetry, always vitally present up to the eighteenth century, was scorned by the romantic *avant-garde* at least publicly (some were acutely rational in secret). Didacticism and philosophizing were certainly to be found in the popular poets of the time, but the advanced spirits, those whom our age thinks of as its poetic ancestors (Hugo and Tennyson need not apply), had little use for them. Poets were not supposed to think consecutively, except in their off-hours, when they wrote criticism. Shelley, who knew more about logic and classical poetic theory than he admitted, had said in his *Defence of Poetry* that "Reason respects the differences and the imagination the similitudes of things" and that "Reason is to the imagination as the instrument is to the agent." If this is so, and arguably it is so in poetry, then the two are still related. It does not matter which is superior to the other or which includes the other. For if a theory of correspondence is not also logical it cannot be universal.

There is a hidden factor in all this, for which some nineteenth-century Swedenborgians themselves must bear the blame. This was the peculiar notion, held by many of them, that the science of correspondences was something like an easy code which made the believer the master of all knowledge, that it was a key which fitted all locks, and which enabled any earnest student of the Writings to unfold the inner meanings of not only the Bible but ancient mythologies as well. Generally, they were misled by a failure to distinguish between logical categories and living forms; in extreme cases one found them manipulating "Love" and "Wisdom" as if they were mere counters on some abacus ordered on a binary principle. In this error they resembled, though less conspicuously, certain rash Lullists of earlier times and Hegelians of their own. To outsiders this appeared both presumptuous and silly—sometimes innocently blasphemous when Swedenborgians were expounding Scripture. Applied to the study of ancient mythologies, this pseudo-method could result in simplifications as grotesque as were to be found among those who tried to demonstrate that all myths were forms of astronomical code.

However, some forms of myth *were* in astronomical code. (And, indeed, since Swedenborg's logic is efficacious, some Swedenborgians have produced interesting insights into mythology, erring mainly in applying Christian theological ideas to mythological systems in full polytheistic decadence.[4]) In an illuminating article on the myth of Perseus, called *The Gorgon's Eye*, Jerome V. Lettvin[5] relates ancient rhetorics and arts of memory to sky-mapping. Referring to a first century BC "art of memory" called *Rhetorica ad Herrenium,* Lettvin says—

> We are instructed, for example, to imagine a walk through a temple, quiet and alone, during which we keep several feet from the wall. The argument that we wish to remember becomes associated with a sequence of things we see on the walk within the temple; and indeed the English word "topic" derives from *topos*, or place—a topic is the place in the temple to which we have attached an idea in the course of our walk. In effect, the temple comes to embody a kind of cross-mapping, in which something that we wished to remember superimposes itself upon something that we already knew very well. The temple is thus a stable and well-known ground on which the new set of facts is arrayed: the temple serves the purpose of a theory, to the extent that you can derive from a theory a great many facts, that, although seemingly unconnected, can nevertheless be related by the mapping you have made.

> We have, therefore, an art of memory in which a well-known universe can serve as a ground upon which other universes can be mapped. But when you do such a thing, the world is no longer held together by what you might call conventional reason or logic.

Later, applying the argument to astronomy, he says—

> Still, let us assume that the ancients spoke in parable, namely that what was said was put in rhetorical terms because of not having a language with the modern exactness—not having, that is, the terms in which to express even simple trigonometric relations, such as the position of the sun along the horizon on the day of summer solstice.

Lettvin belongs to a flourishing modern school which interprets myth, sometimes with an exclusivity which simply cannot be defended, as a form of calendrical and astronomical symbolism. Yet myth was that too.[6]

It is very probable, since the art of memory was considered a part of rhetoric,[7] that we can find here the answer to the puzzling question of the quasimathematical nature of most rhetorical terms. They are almost topological (pun intended) in that they seem to refer to operations in a geometrical mental space, the parameters of which can be described in logical but not quantitative terms. For although I am not sure what Lettvin means by *conventional* reason or logic, there is no doubt that the cause-and-effect sequences of many myths can be described in terms of *dialectical* logic: Hegel does so describe them. They can also be represented in logical algebra, as Lévi-Strauss and other structural anthropologists have shown.

The origin of the figures of rhetoric, as we have them, is mysterious. The terms are Greek and the system is pervaded by the Greek mathematical spirit. They are concerned with deep operations of the human mind and have obvious philosophical implications. Yet, when rhetoric appears in Greek culture as an organized system, it is associated with the suspect arts of the political demagogue. It is an art of persuasion, even of making the worst appear the better cause. One would say from its structure that it *should* have had about it some aura of the sacred or at least the philosophically profound, yet it is associated with the profane, the equivocal and the shallow. Various persons are said to have "invented" it, among them Empedocles (ca. 492—death sometime after 440 BC) and his follower, Gorgias (ca. 485—death sometime after 427 BC); but no single person could have invented such a system, much less one which first appears before us in a state of decadence.

What shall we make of such attributions? Clearly, neither Empedocles nor Gorgias (who emerges in Plato's perhaps unfair portrayal as clever, but shallow and easily flustered) could have invented the figures of speech we know. Nor could they have been the first to organize them into systems. They are all found in the Bible and are organized there in such freely intricate and fruitful complexity that unaided human composition seems impossible. Egyptian, Mesopotamian and other ancient literatures—often rigid, lifeless and conventional in a manner which seems the epitome of the "official" style of totalitarian states—are rhetorically organized in the highest degree. If Empedocles and his followers invented or discovered anything it might have been the secondary form of "correspondence" we think of as particularly Greek, the form which is the ancestor of our own science of tropes. In this form, figures of speech are described by words which refer, in many cases, to logical, permutational and mathematical processes. For example we have terms such as "sequential yoke" (*zeugma*), "word-folding" (*ploce*) and "circular repetition" (*cycloides*). Yet on analysis it appears that this system, too, could not have been invented by one man or small group. We know the classification of figures of speech in this manner took place over a long time. A single man or group could not therefore have invented it, though he or they could have had the initial insight which led to the classification.

The Greeks did not invent personal or occasional poetry, of course; they are as old as man. They do seem to have invented, though, the figure of the autonomous poet-sage, who speaks out of his own authority and personal inspiration, in images peculiar to him. He may indeed claim to be possessed by a god, but it is not the god of a particular cult (Apollo is much more than a god of poetry) and he is not a temple-poet. Nor is his own personality supposed to be rendered insignificant by his utterance, as in the case of the Hebrew prophets, who bear the Word of the Lord. Nor is he the quasi-anonymous voice of a tradition, as in the wisdom writings of the Hebrews and other more ancient peoples. The effect of this, simply, is that universal correspondence becomes part of subjective technique, of a personal art-language. It becomes, that is, a rhetoric.

It is for classical scholars to comment upon the value of Empedocles' poetry as poetry. We have only fragments and most of them were selected by philosophers who wanted to illustrate this or that philosophical point, not to exemplify his poetic genius. Raymond Adolph Prier, whose *Archaic Logic, Symbol and Structure in Heraclitus, Parmenides and Empedocles* I have found particularly enlightening, says[8] that his extant corpus "reveals a conscious systematic use of symbols that in themselves draw the clearest possible structure the archaic mind could proffer." Prier says some very valuable things about the "dyadic" nature of Empedoclean thought and about his "considerable use...of the circle and the sphere,"[9] but such geometrical imagery is also typical of Parmenides, as Prier points out. He refers to Empedocles' number symbolism, as in his statement, "I shall speak double."[10] It turns out that the imagery of Empedocles is shot through with mathematical symbolism, and, as Prier concludes, "The geometrical or structural simplicity of archaic logic, expounded through the symbolic content of a universal order, finds no better spokesman than Empedocles."[11]

There can be little doubt that not only the structure but the imagery of Empedocles' poetry is deeply influenced by his geometrical view of the cosmos. The four elements which make up his physical world, ruled in their movements by Love and Strife, are also found in the mind. The four fundamental colors correspond to his four elements: White/Fire, Black/ Water, Red/Earth, Yellow/ Air,[12] in the style of the ancient tradition which associated colors with the four quarters or cardinal directions. It is also said that Empedocles had been a pupil or disciple of Pythagoras.[13] Yet the world-view of Parmenides is as geometrical as is that of Empedocles, though his cosmology is quite different.

Our question is, however, "What evidence can we find that Empedocles invented a mathematical way of organizing figures of speech, a mathematical tropology?" The answer must be that the only available evidence hits somewhat to the side of the answer we need. All we can say is that his approach to the art of poetry, along with that of Parmenides (with other less conclusive evidence from writers of the time) indicates that such an approach might well have arisen during this period. It was a time in which the old sacred imagery was being reworked into world-pictures of a geometrical kind, in the context of an avowedly personal world-view. The old images might well have been classified in just such a spirit. Certainly the art of memory, whose age we do not know but which has an air more archaic than that of formal rhetoric, had a certain geometrical quality by virtue of its use of imaginary temple space. Plato in the *Phaedrus* (from 274) says, in a rather ambiguous way, that the Egyptians had invented it. Yet "might well" is hardly a conclusive phrase. No Greek writer (known to me, at any rate) unequivocally describes such a process. The process obviously occurred, but we do not know if it took the form of a conscious program.

All we know is that by the time of Plato (c. 427–347 BC) the world is, as he tells us in his *Phaedrus* (266–270), full of rhetorical manuals. Teachers of public speaking divide speeches into preamble, exposition and direct evidence, indirect evidence, probabilities, proof and supplementary proof. There is Evenus of Paros, "the inventor of covert allusion and indirect compliment." Not to mention Tisias, Gorgias, Prodicus, and Polus, author of "The Muses' Treasury of Phrases," with its examples of reduplications, maxims and similes. Protagoras, we learn, has produced a book on *Correct Diction*. One suspects that if Empedocles had been responsible for this, he would have regretted it. But Plato says that *true* rhetoric— the "art of letters"—was discovered by Thoth of Egypt (*Philebus* 18b); Thoth was, among other things, a measurer, numerator, the god of equilibrium and, according to the Egyptologist Maspero, the chief of the gods of the four quarters, as the "center."

In any case, the origin of the Greek rhetorical system, particularly that aspect of it called "tropology," or the science of figures, is to be sought in the bare realization that mental space, as set out in words, may be described in terms of a non-quantitative geometry. The rhetorical use of specifically geometrical terms, such as those derived from the geometry of conic sections (ellipse/elliptical, parabola/parable) is a mere development of this idea, an application almost on the level of careful mental drudgery. Given the initial idea that this could be done, it takes only knowledge and careful labor to work out the details. It is probable, also, that the craft of melodic variation in musical composition contributed to this mode of formalization.

Now the realization of the possibility of this endeavour is very ancient. It goes back to the first forms of scientific myth. To all intents and purposes, the basis of the theory was worked out when men discovered they could model astronomical movements in verbal images. Let us say I want to express the idea of opposition in relationship to the zenith, to describe, for example, the positions where the sun rises and where it sets, as two opposing points on a line drawn over the zenith. Then I can say the constellation marking the place where the sun rises is "at war" with the constellation in which it sets. Or, if I do not like the battle image, which implies conflict, that is, if I wish to stress the harmony of the cosmos, I can say the eastern constellation is to the western one in a relationship of "fruitful opposition," the creative complementaries of male and female; I can say that the eastern constellation "marries" the western one.

We are here dealing with a set of non-quantitative relationships. We can use number-words in our myth, of course—numbers representing days or years, for example. But the parts of language lack implicit number above the ternary. We cannot say that a verb is bigger than a noun, only that it is different, some "other." Two nouns may represent objects of different sizes—apple and mountain, say—but unless we add number words we cannot say how much bigger the mountain is than the apple. On the other hand, the principle of duality and the principle of trinity which develops from it is everywhere present in language. We have "this" and "that," "presence" and "absence," "active" and "passive," "synchrony" and "diachrony." We also have trinities when we place a "present" between "past" and "future"; and when we create or imagine this intermediate point we have the beginnings of a non-quantitative geometry. For example, when we put the present between the past and the future we create a "time-line."

We do not have to get much more specific to create a model of the heavens. Let us say it is noon when I write this. Then the past is the dawn, the future is the dusk and noon is my present, between dawn and dusk. But the marker of noon is the sun at its highest point in the sky for that day, its "noon-position." Thus I have modelled the path taken by the sun.

We have here the beginnings of a dialectical and algebraical logic. A complete dialectical logic, from which an algebraical notation may be developed, can be built up from three elements: the Same, the Different and a third element which may be seen either as a point between the two or as the result of their working together. This third element might, for example, be the Contingent as combining likelihood (the Same) and unlikelihood (the Different). If I am thinking in terms of the kind of myth-making described above, then I can call the *same* the "Bridegroom" and the *different* the "Bride." The Same and the Different—and this is just a pictorial form of a tenet of Pythagorean philosophy—engender distinct (and contingent) qualities as so many children.

Yet the point between them may also be seen as the place where they come together, the "marriage-bed," and this takes us back to our first diagram, but now in a quasi-spatial rather than a quasi-temporal form.

Given the nature of language, which is, if not natural in the sense of being innate, at least second nature to man, there is nothing particularly complicated about this way of thought, though it can be deep. It becomes complicated as it is elaborated, of course—and in abstract notation it becomes as complicated as any equation in relativistic physics—but so does any simple system. So-called "primitive" peoples think this way all over the world—or used to. They divide their villages into "male" and "female" sides; they divide their tribes into clans bearing the names of animals and plants with opposed or markedly different characteristics; they classify foods as "hot" or "cold." This has nothing to do with the subconscious, except in the secondary way that the sense of duality is also in the subconscious, as everywhere in the mind. It is a form of rationality particularly well-suited to non-literate cultures, and really it has much more to do with the nature of memory (that is, with the construction of mental complexes which may be remembered easily) than the subconscious as modern psychology defines it. There is an unbroken line extending from this primitive mode of thought to the logics of Hegel and Boole, to set theory, binary arithmetic and the computer flowchart. Logic is a mysterious and ancient procedure.

Let us backtrack a little. I have established a line between dawn and dusk, with noon in the center. This is a time-line. If I express it in terms of space, I have (roughly) a line between east and west, with the position just under the noon sun, the place where I am standing, as the center. But to really *orient* myself (orient=east) I need a map, a grid of lines which cross each other. To form such a grid I need, at the very least, a north-south line. Not only that: if I am going to make a calendar it is not enough to mark spring=east and autumn=west (again, I speak schematically, so far as horizon observations are concerned). I also need to note the summer and winter solstices, and these give me a north-south line.

This is the beginning of cardinal-direction symbolism, which is so vitally important to all civilizations whose main repository of knowledge is in myth-systems.[14]

I confessed uneasiness, a little earlier, about Lettvin's statement that the "memory-theatre" of astronomy on a mythical base is not "conventionally" logical. It is perfectly logical and even, in its internal relationships, conventionally so. One may relate it to Aristotelian as well as to Hegelian logic, though more immediately, because of its dynamic nature, to the latter. It is logic in pictures and stories. If I give logical categories names, if I invent little stories showing their interactions, I invent a form of scientific myth. Despite modern prejudices on the matter (as in Robert Graves' *The White Goddess*, where such prejudices are scored for the entire brass choir) ancient scientific myth is not opposed to some imaginary thing thought of as "true myth" but is only a specific form of myth. This is a fact repugnant to both logicians and to nineteenth century and modern poets. Yet it is demonstrably true, and the historical conclusion to be drawn from it is that logic and rhetoric are interrelated very closely, that they always have been, and that both are thus very old and have their roots in ancient ideas of universal correspondence.[15]

Swedenborg's attitude to the formal logic of his day is very revealing. It gives us an intimate glimpse of his habits of thought.[16]

He notes approvingly a statement by Rydelius, a Swedish philosopher of the time: "The thing of value in the ancient logic now lies concealed like a diamond in the midst of chaff, or rubbish." What then would be the diamond and what the rubbish? This is explained by quotations from Malebranche and Descartes. Malebranche is quoted as follows—

> General ideas and the ideas of logic never beget anything but a vague, superficial and barren science. Therefore so far as possible, we must consider these distinct and special ideas of things with attention; that so we may learn the properties which they include. It is in this way

that nature must be investigated, dismissing all those chimeras which exist only in the brains of certain philosophers.

By "distinct and special ideas" Malebranche is referring to what he has earlier defined as the "clear and distinct ideas of extension, figure and local motion," as contrasted with "the general and confused ideas" of the metaphysician and logician. Descartes is quoted as saying—

> I have often noted that philosophers fell into the error of trying to explain by the definitions of logic things which, by themselves, were exceedingly simple and well known. Thus they made them obscure.

We may see here the roots of the kind of logic we have considered in our discussion of the primary point of the *Principia*. And there is a degree of self-criticism here. Swedenborg is aware of what we have discussed at the end of Part One—that general ideas can never beget particulars, only "smaller generals." That form of traditional logic which concerns itself with the definitions of words, the kind of logic Malebranche and Descartes are attacking, is of little use in the discovery of truth. Logic is to be related to geometry and mechanics in their most general forms. The application of traditional logical procedures to arguments about the nature of things often reduces the simple and obvious to confusion and obscurity.

The chaff or rubbish then is the form of logic which endlessly disputes about and chops up the meanings of words, without concerning itself about the nature of *things*. Obviously, words are meaningless unless they refer to things and events. Swedenborg does not reject the art and science of logical thought. His notebooks reveal him at study, carefully working out the forms of the traditional syllogisms (*Barbara, Celarant, Darii* and the like) and his logical sense is exquisite. Yet the logic he believes to be the diamond in the chaff is the kind of logic sought by Leibniz, as in his quotation of the following statement by this philosopher—

> The whole doctrine of logical consequences is no less capable of demonstration than is arithmetic or geometry; and long ago, when I was a young man, I experimented with this in many ways. Herein,

surely, is contained, if I may use the expression, a universal algebra. For ordinary algebra is the doctrine of quantity in general, or of indefinite number; but the true characteristic algebra, furnishes a kind of Analysis, if I may use the term, which pertains to all accurate reason.

The moment logic is related to arithmetic, geometry and algebra in this way, as being "capable of demonstration" and a "universal algebra," it necessarily takes on the apparatus of theorem and proof. We have here the beginnings of modern symbolic or mathematical logic. To Swedenborg, however, it becomes apparent that if logic is to be related to arithmetic, algebra and geometry it must also be related to mechanics, which he sees as "geometry in motion." Thus we find him taking note of the famous ten categories of Aristotle: Substance, Quantity, Relation, Where, When, Situation, Possession or State, Action and Passion.[17] At another point in his notes he transcribes a number of basic mathematical theorems and equations, and these transcriptions are sandwiched between examples of parabolic and allegorical correspondences and typical biblical correspondences. If we follow his mode of thought through we can see how he is attempting to relate logical and rhetorical categories to forms and determinants of motion.

These notes are, it should be remembered, largely retroactive and confirmatory. He has already worked out his theory. For the *Principia* is based, as we have seen, on a form of logical mechanics.

We may say that the concept of correspondences links up with traditional or Aristotelian logic through the category, "relation." An orderly understanding of relative mechanical motion is best come by, in Swedenborg's view, through a theory of harmonic motion. This is in no way an original insight; it is a standard assumption of the theorists of "universal harmony" of his age and earlier. Thus Marin Mersenne, in his *Traité de l'Harmonie Universelle* (1627), relates music, verse and the mechanics of pulleys and levers to the proportions of geometrical figures, in an argument which is certainly simple and approximate but could be pursued profitably in modern terms. Swedenborg, for his part, translates in his notebooks large sections of *A Musical Dictionary* by James Grassineau (1740), paying particular attention to his acoustical and mathematical arguments, a number of which are based on Pythagorean theory. There are also many notes from Scripture, illustrating what Swedenborg calls "harmonic correspondence." They do not differ significantly from traditional exegeses of biblical figures of speech, and thus need not be set down here. What is noteworthy is the rubric, their being classified as *Harmonic* Correspondences.

We may, by studying the development of his thought in these notes, see how the syllogism of analogy develops into the system of parallel or tiered statements which we find in his *Hieroglyphic Key.* Here is a quotation from this work—

EXAMPLE VI

From effects and phenomena judgment is made concerning the world and nature, and from the world and nature conclusion is made as to effects and phenomena.

From actions and inclinations judgment is made concerning man and the rational mind, and from man and his mind, when known, conclusion is made as to actions and inclinations.

From works and the testimonies of love judgment is made concerning God, and from God conclusion is made as to His works and the testimonies of His love.

HARMONY OR ANALOGY

As the world stands in respect to man, so stand natural effects in respect to rational actions.

As man stands in respect to God, so stand human actions in respect to divine works.[18]

There are logical gaps between the three tiers of this structure; they are what Swedenborg will later call "discrete degrees" of a system. There is no purely logical way of relating the effects and phenomena of nature to the actions and inclinations of man, though once this relationship is accepted its implications may be worked out logically. The validity of the comparison rests upon observations, and the observations may be interpreted according to a number of ideologies, even, as in ancient Egypt, according to a polytheistic and "hydraulic" one. We may say that the actions and inclinations of man are specific forms of natural effects and phenomena, and in this judgment we speak according to a strict materialist ideology. We may say that mental and natural things are innately different but are alike in the sense that they exist together in the mind of God as parts of His creation, and many theistic ideologies make some such assumption. We may say further that they belong to structures which run "parallel" from creation, and this is Swedenborg's view.

Swedenborg combines a great respect and even a love of logical procedures with a realistic sense of their limitations. How shall we interpret the idea that logic cannot close the gaps between "discrete degrees"? There are some very well-worked-out theories, strictly logical, which demonstrate that it is formally impossible to penetrate to final or ultimate truths by logic alone. The limitations of logic are implicit in the system and can be demonstrated by the rules of the system. The better the formulation of the system, the clearer its limitations are. We need not recapitulate these here. Most of us have at least heard of Godel's "Incompleteness Theorem" and other arguments which show that any logical system is limited by its axiomatic base, and that without such a limitation logical thought is impossible. We are so aware of the limitations of logical thought, of the paradoxes it encounters when it is pushed too far, that we are inclined to forget what a potent and beautiful tool it is.[19] Yet such gaps, the gaps between discrete degrees, not only wind around systems of logic but between their parts. They are not faults but structural necessities. There would be no logic without them— no definitions, for one thing. Logic is a structure of relationships across gaps.

In the above case, that of the three levels of Swedenborg's EXAMPLE VI, we can say that each statement is simply and almost trivially true in terms of the logic of its level. The statement about "effects and phenomena" is a truism in terms of the logical method as applied to the physical sciences. The statement about "actions and inclinations" is a truism of psychology and the sciences of behavior. The statement about "works and the testimonies of love" is a truism of theology. Reason tells us that they are related and must be if we are to think connectedly about the world. Observation tells us that the first two tiers, those of mechanics and human action, are related. If they were not, the brain could not function. It is true that unaided common sense cannot see God. It is also true that materialist philosophy denies any reality to the subject matter of theology, though it does so only to insist all the more strongly on the relationship between the first two tiers.

From this example, Swedenborg sets out what he describes as some *Rules*. *A Hieroglyphic Key* was not written for publication and Swedenborg does not bother with all the niceties of logical demonstration in his personal notes. Nevertheless, the argument is completely logical and could be worked out in an acceptably formal manner.

> From the several examples that have been adduced, a certain analogy may be formed, and from the analogies an equation, which may again be reduced to its own analogies; as in the following: as the world stands in respect to man, so stand natural effects in respect to rational actions; and so likewise in the other examples. And if the world be denoted by w, man by m, effects by e, and actions by a, they may be joined together in the form of an analysis, to wit w:m::e:a. That the manner in which these terms should be associated with others (may be) multiplied, and from them an analysis (may be) formed, will come for demonstration elsewhere. These are the first rudiments of that universal mathesis of which mention was made above. There is also a continuous ratio or analogy; for example, As the world is to man so man is to God. From which analogy it follows that God passes over into the world through man; or that God has nothing in common with nature except through man; also, that the perfection of nature depends upon the perfection of man; for God, the founder of nature, disposes the world no otherwise than in accordance with the quality of the medium or man whereby He communicates with the world.[20]

Let us now return to the "primitive" correspondences discussed above, those related to astronomy and calendar-making. How far may they be extended? This really depends on how far we are willing to trust evidences of internal consistency in mythological systems. In the systems discussed above we find an enormous wealth of imagery associated with the four cardinal directions, the corresponding seasons and times of day, and the heavenly bodies.

There are two extreme ways of interpreting this. The first is that these associations, which include almost all the key symbols of the cultures in question, and that to the extent that the astronomical and calendrical system seems to have become a virtual encyclopedia of spiritual and material entities, were basically formed by accidental accretion. There seems no philosophical or scientific reason, for example, why the chief of gods, Jupiter, should be associated with the planet of that name, or why the god of the planet Mars should embody all the attributes and appurtenances of war. The second is that the system is thought out to the last detail, that we have a complexly organized "philosophy in pictures." Very few contemporary students of myth would adhere to either of these extreme positions. Most occupy a position close to the first but admitting an element of the second—that is, that myth-complexes form largely by accretion and are mostly the results of the accidents of history and the vagaries of opinion, but that the wise men of the tribe will always try, sometimes in a very tortuous manner, to give a semblance of rationality to this fundamentally incoherent system. A few such wise men, men of naturally synthetic genius, will succeed, by accepting some images and rejecting others and by carefully interrelating the imagery they have selected, in developing religions with theologies of rational construction. (There are some other ideas, such as those based on Jungian archetypes, but I can not discuss them because they are beyond my comprehension.)

Swedenborg's position is quite different from either of these. No matter how novel it may appear in expression, it is, at this stage in his life, Christian in the entirely traditional sense. More precisely, it is that of a Lutheranism which has not forgotten its patristic and catholic roots, and particularly favors the Augustinian tradition. He accepts the story of Adam, while leaving open the question of whether Adam (Man) is a particular or a collective noun. Adam and "his" immediate descendants had a direct and God-given intuition of natural and spiritual reality. They were not mathematicians and scientists and their understanding of the world must have been in the spirit of naive realism. Nonetheless, the fit with reality was so close that any true explanation of the natural and spiritual worlds, no matter how theologically and philosophically profound, would meet, if it could be expressed in "naked-eye" symbols, with their immediate and intuitive assent. This primitive concept of reality developed into the first theologies, philosophies and rational cosmological systems, including, of course, astronomical and calendrical systems. However, with the degeneration of man as recorded in the first chapters of *Genesis*, beginning with the very sin which resulted in the expulsion from Eden, these systems became corrupted. Men began to worship, as the old Phoenician Sanchuniathon (we shall meet him again) says, the heavenly bodies, the fruits of the earth and the spirits of dead kings and heroes.

At this stage Swedenborg's argument joins the modern positions referred to above. We have the growth of myth-complexes by accidental accretion and the development of philosophies and theologies from these systems by rationally-minded men. But, and here is the profound difference, such begin from a philosophical position which is already fully developed. It is certain that the main trend of modern thought in the West, which is entirely anti-Christian and materialistic, rejects the traditional view which Swedenborg here embodies (much more will it reject his later theology), yet it cannot be said that it does so on logical grounds. Nothing in logic or in what we know about prehistory can either support or deny the idea that a form of early man existed in such a state of integrity, the state of the "wise child." Of ourselves we can neither imagine nor reconstruct the first forms of human rationality. We cannot say whether they were in the form of obscure glimmerings, of innocent clarity, or of some mixture of both.

We do, however, confront systems whose degree of rational organization seems to be massive and all-pervasive, no matter how strange their logical procedures may appear to us. The Mayan system as we now know it, tied to fixed cycles of symbols, seems to have this quality. It is certainly true, as our ability to read Mayan texts improves, that we discover much more of the accidental, the fortuitous and the historically determined than we once perceived. We are already discovering that the placid Utopia of the older anthropological texts was a scholar's dream. Systems always appear most rational when they are understood in most general terms. Yet the result of such increased knowledge can only be that the system will appear somewhat less pervasively organized than it now appears to be, as if it does not live up to its own idea of rationality.[21] The Egyptian system—schematic and rigid to a fault— now appears more not less organized than it appeared when we knew it only from Greek accounts. When we consider the visual aspects of hieroglyphic symbolism (leaving out its phonetic aspects), we find that a constant array of symbols—feathers, crowns and other ceremonial regalia, stylized animals, the *ankh* and *ma'at* figures—march through it from the beginnings of high civilization to the decline of the Ptolemaic period. The rhetoric of religious and cosmological poetry remains always the same. Philosophies and theologies come and go; the symbolic language, within a small range of variation, does not change. Unlike the Babylonian and Assyrian systems, which are more mysterious and terrifying in their emotional content, the Egyptian system seems to lie open to the reason, even when it is magical.

I have referred to *A Hieroglyphic Key*. We should expect a relationship with Egypt. Indeed, Swedenborg says—

> It follows then that there is some correspondence and harmony between all things, that is, between natural things and spiritual and *vice versa*; or, that in universal nature there is not a thing that is not a type, image and likeness of some one among spiritual things, all which are exemplars. Otherwise no spiritual intelligence could ever know such things as are below itself; and yet it knows them both of itself and in itself. The Egyptians moreover seem to have cultivated this doctrine, and to have signified these correspondences by hieroglyphic characters of the utmost diversity, whereby are expressed not only natural things but also and at the same time, spiritual things.[22]

Those who have looked herein for a short guide to the "mysteries of Egypt" have been disappointed. *A Hieroglyphic Key* is nothing more than a set of notes for a study of the syllogism by analogy. But that is the whole point, of course. It is much the same point as that made by Hegel in his comments on the symbolism of Egyptian art and architecture. The symbolism of Egyptian hieroglyphic writing is based on the notion of universal analogy. The system has been influenced by the accidents of historical change, but it is on the whole a rational and ordered one.

The study is called *A Hieroglyphic Key* because (so Swedenborg believes) the real key to Egyptian symbolic thought lies in the logical formulation of universal analogy, its basic form being the syllogism by analogy. The logic is pictorial, expressed in myths. The "mysteries of Egypt" are rational mysteries. It would be about a century (1822) before Champollion would begin to decipher Egyptian writing and Swedenborg could know nothing of the specific characteristics of the system. His comments are therefore generalized and abstract. He knew, as did all the learned of his age, that the symbols of the Egyptian writing system were the same as those of the temple art. The Greek authors testified that the system was symbolic in an ordered fashion. He needed nothing more. If the same symbolism was found in the writing system and the temple art then natural objects must have been used to represent spiritual entities. All temple art, unless it is simply historical painting (as in much Christian art) does this. If the symbolism was well-ordered, then the Egyptian logic of analogy, the logic which related natural objects and spiritual entities, must also have been well-ordered. We may say that his "key" may be applied to any such system, no matter what its culture of origin, because it is, in essence, a universal symbolic algebra. Indeed, in a sense, all pictographic writings are nothing else. It goes without saying, of course, that it can only be applied by those deeply familiar with the culture being studied and the results must be carefully checked against the facts. Any algebra must in the end refer to known quantities. Otherwise we only read back what we have put in. In any case, it no longer appears strange to us to read mythologies in terms of a symbolic algebra. Structural anthropologists such as Claude Lévi-Strauss do just this, though they save themselves from accusations of "mysticism" by insisting on the materialist basis of their theories.

The universal vortex of Swedenborg is also found in ancient thought. It is found, in particular, in the pre-Socratic philosophers, and that in a form which unmistakably recalls a certain ideological line we have traced earlier. This begins, as we shall see, with the Egyptian/Phoenician cosmogony of Sanchuniathon and runs through the Orphic and Pythagorean cosmogonies of Greece. The cosmogony of Sanchuniathon has, itself, a long series of ancestors, particularly in the Egyptian tradition, but here we find ourselves overwhelmed by a plethora of data. The Egyptians had many cosmogonies, each attached to the school of a particular god—there was a Ra-cosmogony, a Ptah-cosmogony, an Amen-cosmogony and others. No matter how strong our desire for a rationally simple outline of Egyptian cosmogony, it seems we shall never have one. There were *several* rational cosmogonies, as is often the case in polytheistic cultures: Hindu India provides a modern example. The ideological unity of Egypt has been greatly exaggerated. We have been misled by the rigid coherence of art-language and verbal symbol, by the immense age and rocklike durability of the government and social system. Egypt, which in *some* respects resembled a modern totalitarian state and in others a sacred monarchy such as that of Japan before the Second World War, was not totalitarian as a whole. Those who worshipped a particular god were free to claim universal status for him (in one or two cases her, but goddesses were usually consorts of gods) and to develop an appropriate world-system, provided they did not transgress the bounds considered necessary for the maintenance of the state, or violate theological ideas considered essential, as Akhnaton did. Thus when we stand, say, at the time of Sanchuniathon (ca. 9th century BC) and look towards the past, we do not see a clear and definable stream of ideology—his ideology—running from that past. We see rather a large lake, whose outlet river, at the very point we are standing, runs through a narrow gorge. Put another way, the system of Sanchuniathon is a sort of ideological sieve, which lets through only a little. It is this narrowed stream which feeds the Greek tradition. (It should be remembered, by the way, that the foreign influences on Phoenician civilization at the time of Sanchuniathon were not only Egyptian: it is just that the Egyptian influences concern us here.)

This stream, narrowed in its passage through the Egyptian/Phoenician cosmogony of Sanchuniathon's time, widens into a great lake on the *other* side, which is our own scientific and cosmological tradition, beginning with the pre-Socratic philosophers of Greece[23] and developing into the more widely influential Aristotelian and Platonic traditions.

In his *Metaphysics* Aristotle says (and here I repeat and expand an earlier quotation)—

> As to the quantity and form of this first principle, there is a difference of opinion; but Thales, the founder of this sort of philosophy, says that it is water (accordingly he declares that the earth rests on water), getting the idea, I suppose, because he saw that the nourishment of all things is moist, and that warmth itself is generated from moisture and persists in it (for that from which all things spring is the first principle of them); and getting the idea also from the fact that the germs of all beings are of a moist nature, while water is the first principle of the nature of what is moist. And there are some who think that the ancients, and they who lived long before the present generation, and the first students of the gods, had a similar idea in regard to nature; for in their poems Okeanos and Tethys were the parents of generation, and that by which the gods swore was water—the poets themselves called it Styx; for that which is most ancient is most highly esteemed, and that which is most highly esteemed, is an object to swear by.[24]

Thales of Miletus was, Herodotus tells us in the First Book of his Histories, "Phoenician by descent."

We know of the other opinions referred to by Aristotle; some argued that the first principle was earth or fire or air. However, the idea that matter was formed by a motion among the four elements is more or less universal at that time. No matter which element is considered primary, their coming together is usually seen as something like a rotatory mixing, as of stirring a thick fluid substance in a mixing-bowl or building up a pot from clay and water on a stationary or rotating base.[25] There is also a secondary image, that of weaving, or forming a network of matter from threads of substance.

The mixing-bowl image of creation is immensely old, and it is only one of a long series of spiral or vortical images found all over the world. Let me give a few examples, which will indicate at once the richness of the data and the difficulties of interpreting it.

In many cultures the serpent, which takes a spiral form in repose or attack, is a symbol of universal cosmic forces. The symbolism of serpentine forms, as related to fundamental cosmological ideas, is most highly developed in MesoAmerica. A free-lance Mexican scholar, José Diaz-Bolio, has published a number of books in which he claims that the natural proportions of the rattlesnake— the arrangement and number of its scales, for example—are the basis of MesoAmerican geometry and canons of artistic propor- tion.[26] Undoubtedly he has some of the monomania of the amateur who has made a discovery; yet he makes a good case, for all that it could be argued that the proportions of the rattlesnake were most important but not an exclusive base. So adapted, his proposition is rational and defensible. Amerindians in general most often re- ferred geometrical forms to nature. Thus the Indians of the North- west Coast of America, who developed one of the finest geometrical arts of any people, gave their form-elements such names as "flicker- feather," "head of the salmon trout," "eye," "raindrop" and so on.[27]

In Mayan culture the spiral conch-shell or the shell of the sea- snail takes the place-value of zero in the numerical system, but should more properly be read as "completion." It may also be read as the generator of number.[28]

The Yin-Yang symbol of China can be related to the spiral form, and the importance of the spiral in Japanese cosmological symbol- ism has been explained by Nahum Stiskin in his book, *The Look- ing-Glass God*.[29]

The use of the vortex or maelstrom as a universal symbol of creation and destruction, particularly in an astronomical sense, has been examined by de Santillana and von Dechend in *Hamlet's Mill*.

This is to list only a few of the entry-points into a vast field of ancient cosmological symbols related to spiral and vortical forms. Another territory, almost as large, is added when we consider labyrinths, whirling crosses such as swastikas and squared spirals such as fretwork or meander designs. And we must also add "earth- diver" myths, in which a symbolic animal or god carries up the beginnings of earth from the depths of the primeval sea, creating an "earth-mound"; this image is closely related to the image of the earth formed from a mound of clay on the potter's wheel. Finally, the "secondary image" referred to above, that of weaving, is to be related to the image of the spider weaving his spiral web. These ancient variants of the vortex-myth, most of which may be found in

Egyptian and Mesopotamian myth, funnel into Greek mythology, and thence into pre-Socratic philosophy, where they take on non-mythical forms. This is not at all an arbitrary set of correlations, as we can see immediately when we reduce these images to geometrical forms.

At times in pre-Socratic philosophy we see what looks like a strangely distorted version of a nebular hypothesis, in which rotatory motion produces a disc which surrounds the *earth*, not the sun. Thus Plutarch tells us—

> Anaximander says that at the beginning of this world something productive of heat and cold from the eternal was separated therefrom, and a sort of sphere of this flame surrounded the air about the earth, as bark surrounds a tree; then this sphere was broken into parts and defined into distinct circles, and thus arose the sun and the moon and the stars.[30]

This is an extraordinary statement, when we think about it. Anaximander, who believed that our world and others were eddies in a universal fluid vortex,[31] has the earth throwing off a sphere of flame. The sphere eventually breaks into the sun, moon and stars. This does not make sense even in terms of campfire physics. If a cosmos-generating heat is coming from the earth, then the surrounding ring should be cooler, not hotter, than the earth. In addition to this, Anaximander's earth is not a sphere but has the shape of a cylinder, floating in space and "keeping its position because it is the same distance from all things";[32] the part we inhabit is one of its two flat ends. But how should this strange shape throw off a *sphere* of flame?

Indeed, the theories of the three famous Milesians—Thales, Anaximander and Anaximenes—all have this very strange quality, that they violate common sense perception. They have nothing of the quality of naive realism. We can not imagine how we might come to similar conclusions, if we were looking up at the heavens and wondering how it all began.

Now it is an absolute truism that the earliest Greek philosophers had learned from the older civilizations. It is not denied even by diehard believers in the "Greek miracle." But there it rests, as a reluctant admission forced out of them, because the idea of the "miracle" must be preserved, it appears, in *some* form. So the obvious question is never asked. It goes something like this—

The theories of the Milesians, at least as they have come down to us, have a disconcertingly piebald quality. We have profundity mixed with nonsense; we have mechanical notions which make no sense even on the naive level but which nevertheless contain fragmentary ideas which are, though ancient in style, remarkably coherent and sophisticated; we find Thales and Anaximander and others using practical mathematical, engineering and astronomical techniques which have clearly come from elsewhere. Is it not very likely that the patchy nature of their cosmologies arises from their imperfect assimilation of theories which were, at their points of origin, more coherent? Note I do not say "more correct," only "more coherent."

This is, as I say, an *obvious* question. It cannot be answered by saying we cannot judge their philosophies because we only have them in fragments. Those who preserved the fragments for us, who had the original texts before them, found the pre-Socratics quite baffling. If there is no conclusive answer to it, it is because the philosophies of Mesopotamia and Egypt (and other cultures of their time) are embodied entirely in the symbolic language of myth and ritual, which we are reluctant to examine. On the practical side we have evidence of highly-developed crafts, of a sophisticated mathematical astronomy in Mesopotamia, of the splendid architecture and engineering works of Egypt, of the navigational skills of the Phoenicians. On the level of theory and philosophy we either have nothing or we have the symbolic language of myth. It is, however, inconceivable that there can or could be nothing on this level. There can be no highly developed crafts, no mathematical astronomy, no splendid architecture and engineering, no extensive navigation without theory. And there can be no theory without philosophy.

It follows therefore that the high theory and philosophy were embodied, just as the Greeks said they were, in the mythology, ritual and religious symbolism of these peoples. Indeed, the evidence that this was the case is overwhelming.

Nevertheless, writers on pre-Socratic philosophy still assume confidently that thinkers such as Anaximander—naively but splendidly framing hypotheses—were speculating "into the future" of science when they imagined cosmological events such as that described by Plutarch above. We have here the humanist version of the innocence of Adam; the pre-Socratics, nobly intoxicated by the possibilities of the rational tools they have invented, are dreaming the dreams which gave birth to modern science. But it could just as well be that the pre-Socratics began with the imperfectly absorbed fragments of ancient cosmogonies. These, if translated into an abstract logical notation, out of the concrete symbols in which they were written (we have more than enough texts from the ancient civilizations to do this) would reveal a level of logical thought higher than that we find among the pre-Socratics themselves. In that case the earliest Greek philosophy would still be representative of a high and necessary endeavour and it would still be the ancestor of our science. Instead, though, of the image of an originality which appears miraculous and is certainly unprecedented in the sense that it is not to be found in any other culture, we should have a more mundane and comprehensible mixture of original speculation and reconstruction.

Certainly the notion of the Greek miracle may not be found among Greek writers themselves, despite their very natural feeling that they represent the crown of civilization to date. They trace the ideas of the pre-Socratics back to the age of myth and to secrets held in the temple schools of Egypt, "Babylonia," Phoenicia and even India. Their assumption, furthermore, is always that there is more to be learned from the temples, that they have not yet absorbed all the lessons of "the East." They continue to travel restlessly even after the civilizations they alternately revere and despise have fallen into intellectual decay and are capable of giving "the earnest student of ancient wisdom" nothing but astrology, magic and distorted or syncretic forms of Greek philosophy itself. We have known such intellectual travellers in our own time. They return, breathless with excitement, from the East, bearing new "secrets of ancient wisdom" which turn out to be Indian or Japanese versions of older European versions of a "perennial philosophy" based on traditional Asian thought. Or like the nineteenth-century student of Mayan culture, Augustus Le Plongeon, they bring back stories of Atlantis from village wise men in Yucatan, who have learned them, by trickledown, from Mexican occultists affiliated to Anglo-Saxon Rosicrucians.

Yet it is the Greeks who give us the sciences of beauty and proportion, who virtually invent the autonomous poet and musical composer and "fine artist." Included in all this is the "invention" of the science of rhetoric. Correspondences have been denatured. It is a great loss, but the age-old Eastern concept was too decadent to survive. The images of poetry no longer cohere, except inasmuch as the poet is thought of as "inspired" in some fashion which does indeed reflect the order of the universe, but in a lesser way—in mimesis, in the harmony of the verse line, in the coherence and tastefulness of the imagery as related to the subject matter of the poem. It is now logic and mathematics, particularly geometry, which reflect the universal order as it is, without mediation. Of course, only some Greek intellectuals think this way. To many, dominated by the commercial and industrial spirit, which is also Greek, mathematics is a purely practical matter. Yet when the fine arts wish to lay claim to representing, not only thinking about or describing, the universal order, they will fall back on the claim that they embody "deep form." The language which describes art forms begins to resemble that of mathematics. The terms describing rhetorical operations in poetry and imaginative or persuasive prose become geometrical.

We ought to recognize this state of affairs. Something similar has happened in our own time. We may see it reflected in the microcosmic world of the fine arts. The crumbling of the tradition of musical harmony after Wagner; the modern decay and collapse of a tradition of poetic image-making which began with the troubadours; the decadence of representational art at the beginning of the twentieth century—these are objective facts. Furthermore, the poets of the first part of the nineteenth century had already seen, as noted in the beginning of this chapter, that a catastrophe was at hand. Out of this crisis emerged, though not clearly or singly, an obsession with purely mathematical ideas of form. We see it in the music of Schonberg, Stravinsky and Hindemith; we see it, though less clearly, in the replacement of consecutive poetic argument by the juxtapositional mode typified in Pound's *Cantos* and Eliot's *The Waste Land*; we see it, very clearly indeed, in the geometrical forms of abstract painting and sculpture. This is not the place to argue whether or not such a response to the crisis was inevitable or rational. Probably it was. What matters is only that it appeared inevitable at the time. It was not accompanied by highly reasoned critical thought. Many of the writings of Schonberg, Pound, the cubists and so on now appear to contain a mixture of acute perceptions and puerile or shallow formal analysis. But that is unimportant. The tradition was discarded because—such imagery occurs continually in these writings—it was "dead" and "putrid."

At the same time, however, the artists cannot reject the *lessons* of the past. Schonberg evokes the counterpoint of J.S. Bach and actually refers once again to the distorted image of Swedenborg found in the Martinist tradition to justify his non-dimensional polyphony;[33] Pound returns to the troubadours and Eliot to the "metaphysicals"; the cubists and other abstractionists reach far back to Egyptian and "primitive" art. They claim, that is, to be restoring the permanent values of the putrescent tradition which, in disgust and horror, they are fleeing.

Of course no age is like another. Furthermore, art is not philosophy or cosmology. But there are certain universal patterns. The pre-Socratics, the modernists of their age, reflect the same pattern of rejection and attempted revitalization.

ENDNOTES

1 The sense of rhetoric as an ancient science had been obscured, by Christian times, by occultist speculations about the meanings of Egyptian hieroglyphics (see Wind, passim). These speculations were based on Alexandrian and Hellenistic writings (now rejected as uncritically as they were once accepted). The idea that a science of imagery might have physical, mathematical or logical implications had become, in this way, associated with magical thinking. Ramon Lull had a better idea. As he says in his *Doctrina Pueril* (Chapter 73, No. 12): "Time, place, truth, state of being, quantity of time relating to these, necessity and other things similar—all these relate to rhetoric."

2 A perverted Swedenborgianism, in which the philosophical and theological doctrines of Swedenborg are crudely violated and in some cases so twisted as to

proclaim the opposite of their true sense, enters the secret societies through rites set up by the Abbé Pernety, Martines de Pasqually, and Louis Claude de St. Martin. Blake's very intricate world-view (see Ault, bibliography) is best seen in this context, though his synthesis is entirely his own.

3 In a letter to Alexandre Dumas, de Nerval defends his *Les Chimères* as follows: "They are hardly more obscure than the metaphysics of Hegel or the *Memorable Relations* of Swedenborg, and would lose their charm on being explained, if such a thing was possible" (A. Rolland de Renéville, in *Les Cahiers d'Hermès*, pp. 161–162.)

4 See books by J.J.G. Wilkinson and C. Th. Odhner (bibl.)

5 Brecher and Feirtag (eds.), pp. 133–151.

6 This form of interpretation goes back to the ancient Greeks but was revived in the 1890s by Sir Norman Lockyer. It achieved modern respectability with de Santillana's and von Dechend's *Hamlet's Mill*.

7 For a splendid study of arts of memory, see Yates, *The Art of Memory*.

8 Prier, p. 120.

9 Ibid., p. 131.

10 Ibid., p. 134 and developed thereafter. Bollack has a fine study of Empedocles' imagery in his *Empédocle*, which illustrates further the logic which lies behind it.

11 Ibid., p. 145.

12 Bollack, p. 238.

13 Brun, p. 121.

14 Swedenborg maintains, in the theological works, that four-quarter orientation is one of the deepest elements of human perception and rationality. A non-measurable form of it is found in the heavenly world, which is indeed civilization and the human domain in the only true sense. The reader is referred to these for insights on a level infinitely superior to those which he will encounter in Swedenborg's philosophical and scientific works.

The (converted) Islamic scholar, René Guénon, has written a beautiful little book on some of the matters discussed above, *Le Symbolisme de la Croix*. Guénon was a Martinist (see note 2 above) but showed true responsibility and good faith in abandoning the rootless encyclopedic gnosticism of this cult and embracing a real religion.

15 The demonstration may be found in the works of Ramon Lull, whose parables, stories, poems and literary prayers are so many incarnations of his logical system.

16 The following comments are drawn from passages in *A Philosopher's Notebook*, a record of his readings in philosophy during the period from 1740 to 1741. The pages referred to are 110, 113 and 239, where the specific quotations occur.

17 Swedenborg, *A Philosopher's Notebook*, p. 112.

18 Swedenborg, *Psychological Tracts*, pp. 166–167.

19 One interesting and entertainingly written consideration of the boundaries of logical and mathematical thinking is Rudy Rucker's *Infinity and the Mind*. Rucker's notes and bibliography guide the reader who wishes a deeper understanding to the appropriate sources. Swedenborg discusses these limitations in *The Infinite and the Final Cause of Creation*.

20 Swedenborg, *Psychological Tracts*, p. 168. I have not examined the idea that "God has nothing in common with nature except through man." It is part of his theology of the Incarnation and has nothing to do with modern ideas of "immanentism."

21 For useful studies of MesoAmerican thought, see Girard, Séjourné, León-Portilla and Westheim (bibliography).

22 Swedenborg, *Psychological Tracts*, pp. 183–184.

23 Again, it is not difficult to relate pre-Socratic and Egyptian thought, as Cheikh Anta Diop has shown.

24 Nahm, p. 61.

25 The creation of man on a potter's wheel by the Egyptian god, Khnemu, is relevant here. Odhner (pp. 71–73) has an illuminating discussion of him. Budge discusses him in *The Gods of the Egyptians*, Vol II, pp. 49–55.

26 Diaz-Bolio develops this idea in all his books.

27 Boas, pp. 253–257.

28 Thompson, pp. 138–139.

29 Stiskin *passim*.

30 Nahm, p. 63.

31 de Santilla, p. 27.

32 Nahm, p. 64.

33 See p. 132, Boulez. Schonberg's idea of "Swedenborgian" space" was derived from Balzac's *Séraphita*, a work more Martinist than Swedenborgian. His idea (a false one) is that such space is entirely relativistic in the *subjective* sense and this forms a small part of his argument against the necessary rootedness of a harmonic tonic. Nevertheless, Schonberg realized the relevance of the Swedenborgian idea of space in formulating a new esthetic, and I intend in no way to minimize the importance of his discoveries.

More generally, it is sometimes argued that abstract art (also non-tonal music) is not geometrical in the true sense, because much of it is based on occultist and symbolist diagrams and the aim is only to create what is pleasing to the intellect or senses, without reference to theorem and proof. This is only to say that the mathematics is "bad" or "intuitive," which is not the issue. In any case, in the thought of some constructivists, vorticists and musical serialists, "respectable" mathematical thought is clearly at work.

2

An Ancient Rhetoric

I n the last chapter we glanced at a troubling phenomenon—the ubiquity of certain cosmological symbols. Perhaps "troubling" is too mild a word. It raises the deepest problems of cultural history, of psychology, and ultimately of religion. How shall we interpret the fact that peoples who, it seems, can never have been in contact with each other—people separated by half the globe and living on all imaginable levels of material culture—should have had such similar ideas about the way the world was formed?

Most attempts to answer this question fall roughly into three categories. The first—the answer of the three great monotheistic religions of Judaism, Christianity and Islam—is that God granted such a degree of wisdom to the first man or men that he or they were able to formulate elaborate cosmological ideas. These, communicated to their successors, were the first forms of natural philosophy and they spread all over the world. The second, the "diffusionist" hypothesis, has it that these cosmologies spread from one or more centers of high urban culture, ultimately reaching the ends of the earth. The third, favored by psychologists and anthropologists of many schools, holds that these myths arose out of two givens—the innate nature of man and the environment he confronted—and are in this sense "natural products."

I will resist the temptation to compare these ideas in terms of their implicit logic. They rest upon three different notions of the nature of man which, as *a priori* assumptions, can neither be proved nor disproved.

Swedenborg's answer to this question is, as we might expect, a synthetic one. The first humans were given wisdom from God and their ideas about the world were communicated to their descendants. The descendants of these descendants formed centers of high culture, centers of diffusion. And all this was possible because man thinks symbolically. He thinks symbolically because his environment, taking the word in its broadest sense, demands it. This is the doctrine of correspondences, and it develops from what I have called "natural wisdom." A theistic interpretation of this is found in the philosophical works but is a firm declaration of faith and is not in strict logic (I do not say "reason") necessary. Philosophy can only reach the Infinite or the Absolute. In the theological works a theistic interpretation *is* absolutely necessary. Here the doctrine of correspondences will be applied to (rather, drawn from and then applied to) the language of Scripture and will take on a living and organic form. In *The Worship and Love of God*, that beautiful and unfinished work which gives warmth and richness to the doctrines of the *Principia*, it is expressed in poetic and logical form. We turn to this work now to help us visualize the transpositions of a logical statement, transpositions up and down a ladder each rung of which is a different plane or level of being.

> It is said that the heavenly paradise is opened, and that whatsoever is in it is shadowed in the earthly one; consequently that one is represented in the other, as will be seen confirmed more clearly in what follows; for such is the established correspondence, that we are introduced by natural and moral truth, by only transposing the expressions that signify natural things, into spiritual truths, and *vice versa*, and thus, as it were, from one paradise into another. By way of illustration, let one or two examples suffice; as first: *Light reveals the quality of its object, but the quality of the object appears according to the state of the light, wherefore the object is not always such as it appears*; as in the case of beautiful things, if they be objects viewed in varied light. Now if instead of light we take intelligence, the quality of whose object is the

truth of a thing; since intelligence is admitted by all to be spiritual light, this conclusion follows: *Intelligence discovers the truth of a thing, but the truth of a thing appears according to the state of the intelligence; wherefore that is not always true which is supposed to be true.* In like manner, if instead of intelligence wisdom be called into correspondence, the object of which is good, (it then follows:) *Wisdom manifests goodness, but the goodness of a thing appears according to the state of the wisdom; wherefore that is not always good which is believed to be good.* To take another example, for correspondences of this sort, as of all things, are infinite: *Harmony flowing from the union of natural entities is not given without a principle of harmony from a superior union in nature, which conjoins single things universally, and the universe singly.* If instead of harmony we say concord, and instead of union, love, and instead of natural entities, human minds, then this truth results: *There is no concord flowing from the love of human minds without a principle of concord in superior love, which may consociate single minds universally, and their universal society singly.* But if instead of this love we take another, it will instantly appear what kind of union thence results, for as the quality of the love is, such is the union. From these and an infinity of similar cases, we see how there may be a transition from an earthly paradise into a heavenly one, and how from the one we may be instructed concerning the goodnesses and truths of the other; but from propositions not true result falsities, and thus we are not introduced into paradises.[1]

A similar transposition of logical terms is found in Hegel, though his difficult and knotted style of expression could not be farther removed from that of Swedenborg, and they are not philosophically similar except in this. The terms of Hegel's and Swedenborg's logic ascend and descend through planes of meaning from the Absolute through animate nature to inanimate nature. And such patterns are not found only in Hegel and Swedenborg. Each is describing in his own terms the Great Chain or Ladder of Being, a form of which is found in most religiously based natural philosophies.

The near-universality of this "diagram"—there is not enough space here to illustrate how widespread it is or the many disguises it takes—affords a *partial* answer to the problem of the ubiquity of certain religious symbols. This would be that the similarity comes from their being organized on a similar framework—this very ladder or chain. The answer is partial in two senses: i) that it does not tell us why this hierarchical ladder/chain is itself universal; and ii) that it does not tell us why rhetorical images and figures of speech, supposedly arbitrary inventions,[2] fit naturally on a ladder whose rungs are logical categories. It is easy enough to see why the first question cannot be answered; no system can explain itself. As to the second question, it is perhaps badly phrased. What do we *mean* when we say that rhetorical images and figures of speech are arbitrary inventions?

Disconcertingly, the very terms of rhetoric indicate that it deals with a form of non-quantitative but quasi mathematical thinking, something between projective geometry and musical analysis. Most of these terms are Greek in origin and they indicate a very high level of formal thought which would be well worth analysis from a mathematical point of view. For what are we to make of such terms as *ellipsis* (as in "an elliptical statement"), *hendiadys* (two for one) or *anabasis* (gradual ascent?). Such words define manipulations in abstract mental space, in which the rhetorical figures are seen as on some huge graph. There is a sort of horizontal, the "ground" of the base or logical sense, and there is a sort of vertical, the rhetorical figures themselves being like plants or buildings in the way they extend above or below the horizontal "ground."

Since the terms are Greek, it might well appear that the science of rhetoric was a Greek invention or discovery. But this cannot be the case. The biblical scholar, E.W. Bullinger, published around the turn of the century a massive book, *Figures of Speech used in the Bible*. He finds every one of the known Greek figures in the Bible, all of them used with conscious art. And he demonstrates, over the 1100-odd pages of his book, that the figures, though they are often rough and homely in appearance, are used with an utterly astonishing elegance, power and precision. Such figures are not universal or instinctive: we may search the entire body of Chinese or Amerindian or other literatures, oral and written, and we shall find only a fraction of the figures identified by Bullinger. To find the full repertoire of these figures we must turn to Egyptian and Semitic literatures, and literatures which have learned from them, such as the classical Greek and our own. (The literature of India might be added, but this raises a historical problem which I am not equipped to consider.)

We also have another book by Bullinger, *Number in Scripture*. Like *Figures of Speech Used in the Bible*, which works from earlier forms of rhetorical analysis of Scripture (chiefly seventeenth and eighteenth century), *Number in Scripture* has a line of ancestors, both Christian and Jewish. He is discussing a phenomenon which has been commented upon for many centuries.[3] But Bullinger has the clear if narrow rationality of the Protestant evangelical tradition at its best, and he ignores the numerological and even magical excesses which often marred this type of study in the past.[4] Here, too, Bullinger shows that symbolic numbers were consciously and poetically used, to a degree we now find incredible. The Bible is a dense network of such,[5] resting upon the structure of the Hebrew alphabet, in which each letter stands for a number.

I say he "shows" this, but Bullinger would reject such an idea. He believes it to be impossible that mortal man could have composed such an intricate book or collection of books as the canonical Bible, and that every word was directly inspired by the Holy Spirit. I too believe this. It would have been impossible for any group of men to construct a work with such intricate patterns of number-relationships, though of course it would be foolish to base a religious faith on the mere complexity, even the miraculous complexity, of a sacred text. But one must ask the further question, "What is in the mind of a writer when he is writing down words dictated by the Holy Spirit?" The idea that the biblical writers were "possessed" by God, losing their own consciousness in the process, is neither Jewish nor Christian. We are not dealing with the Greek oracles, possessed by gods or spirits while in a state of trance or narcosis. The First Letter of Peter says: "(The salvation by Christ)…was the theme which the prophets pondered and explored, those who prophesied about the grace of God awaiting you. They tried to find out what was the time, and what the circumstances, to which the spirit of Christ in them pointed, foretelling the sufferings in store for Christ and the splendours to follow; and it was disclosed to them that the matter they treated of was not for their time but for yours" (I Peter: I: 10–12: *New English Bible*). This means that the proph-

ets were conscious while they wrote and pondered the literal significance of what they wrote as ordinary writers do. At the same time
they followed the dictates of the spirit within them, attempting to
discern the precise application of the message it delivered. They
"questioned the Spirit" on the level of ideas and weighed the words
they were given. They must also in some way have been aware that
they were dealing with symbolic numbers and proportions.[6]

What we have, then, is not oracular possession but some thing
which takes the form, though it does not have the content, of that
inspiration of which poets have always been aware, that inspiration which is so strong that it seems the voice of "some other"
within the mind. The content in the prophetic case is in some mode
divine and the Inner Voice is real, not an objectified part of the
poet's mind, so much so that it is heard sometimes as an external
voice (as the biblical writers tell us). With such aid, the prophet-
poet, whether literate or not, can rise to heights of art beyond
mortal capacity; but on the other hand, if he lacks poetic art he will
not be capable of representing, in the words of his language, what
the Inner Voice is saying.

The Bible is a book marvellous beyond all others. We should
expect a book with such inner complexity to have either a very
knotted surface or to possess the obviously worked-over and studied splendor of literary epic, a "Virgilian" quality. Yet, though the
Bible contains passages of great beauty in the conventional literary
sense, much of it seems to be rough, casual and plain. Eighteenth-
century critics used to sneer at its "crudity," and many persons still
do.

We find then that in the literary culture of the Hebrews the craft
aspects of poetry were developed to an extraordinary degree, so
much so that great complexity could be disguised as simple plain-
speaking. When we say this we in no way call into question the
doctrine of Divine inspiration, even to the letter. We say rather
that there must have been an art in the inspired writer which was
capable of representing the Divine utterance. We can see an analogy of this, in the realm of visual art, in what the Bible tells us about
the ornamentation of the tabernacle and the Temple. The finest
craft of the age was employed, and where necessary the craftsmen

were imported from other countries—from Phoenicia, for example. But the symbols remained Divine, "ordained."

The poetic devices of the Bible have a long history. Its rhetorical tradition has roots in Mesopotamian, Egyptian and Ugaritic literatures. Some of these literatures are nobly spiritual in content, suggesting that multinominalist monotheism (the multiplication of the names of God) which many have believed to lie at the deep roots of ancient polytheism. Some represent polytheism in its most decadent form, gross and even revolting. But rhetoric, like architecture and metalworking, is an art and a science; it retains its integrity whether it is used to good or evil ends. There is also a connection with Greece here, for, as Cyrus Gordon has shown,[7] the literature of Ugarit provides a link between Hebrew and Greek literatures. It is impossible that the elaborate rhetoric of the Bible could have developed over a short period of time, and the study of ancient texts shows that it did not.

We return to the peculiarly formal character of Greek rhetorical terms. They show a link between poetic and mathematical thought. It is very unlikely that these terms, as such, are of pre-Greek origin. They bear all the marks of Greek mathematical formalism and the body of terms builds up from rhetorician to rhetorician, indicating a developing science. But the imagery itself is used, with full mastery of rhetorical device, long before the science of rhetoric exists, so that here too we have ancient ancestors. What seems likely is that the Greeks learned from the older civilizations that there is a certain link between rhetorical and mathematical manipulations, which is most clearly seen in the operations of the memory. And magic must also have played a part. We inevitably note the geometrical nature of the magical diagram and the mechanical formalism of the spell or conjuration, which so resembles the advertising slogan and other misuses of rhetorical skill (note how the idea of *coercion* attaches itself to conscious rhetorical art). The Greeks reformulated this link in their own fashion. They applied geometrical concepts to verbal figure just as they did in reorganizing the parts of musical structure in the theories of Pythagoras, Aristoxenus and many others. For some Greek musical terms are also terms of rhetoric and they show the same logical and geometrical pattern of thought. Such operations on the level of poetic craft, operations which would have been protected, at the beginning, by a tradition of bardic secrecy, did not much interest the general public. And philosophers did not regard them as very significant. Thus the tradition grew in the shadows, and by the time philosophers did take an interest in formal rhetoric the technical vocabulary was well set. In our culture, which underrates poetic art, we see this more clearly in the visual arts and music. These developed a rich repertoire of techniques from the Dark Ages on, many of scientific import. We cannot begin to list the contributions of painters and sculptors to geometry and anatomy, of composers of music to acoustics and the logic of forms. For many centuries, however, philosophers scorned such knowledge as the mere know-how of the craftsmen.

Now at this point the reader may well be asking himself what this has to do with Swedenborg, whose name has not come up often in this chapter so far. The fact is that much of what Swedenborg took for granted as part of the "form-knowledge" of the educated man is now scorned, forgotten or considered the preserve of scholars specializing in the esoteric. Furthermore, he made, in his doctrine of correspondences, an enormous contribution to this knowledge, one which remains almost unknown. Some of the necessary background must at least be sketched in. Without this we cannot begin to understand his approach to the language of the Bible, which is intimately linked with his doctrine of correspondences at all levels, even that of geometry and logic.

Our sources of knowledge of Hebrew formal rhetoric are late and indirect. Apart from Cabalistic sources, which *may* be most valuable but are undatable and suspect because of their syncretistic nature, we have only a few documents. One of these is Rabbi Nehemiah's *Mishna ha-Middot*, a treatise on geometry dating from ca. 150 AD, and apparently prefatory to a now-lost book on the proportions of the Tabernacle.[8]

What R. Nehemiah's treatise embodies is a mode of thought which would have seemed, in Greek terms, "archaic." His practical mathematics (actually, it is part of the traditional mathematics of Israel and the Bible) indicates something which is fully developed in his culture, even though his treatise is brief and cryptic. For example, his formula for discovering the area of the circle, which I shall not outline here, is the same as that found in the Greek geometers, in Archimedes and the Euclidean tradition. It would be a merely frivolous skepticism which would assume he had re-worked Greek geometry

He defines the quadrilateral and trilateral in terms of struc-tures, a building and a tent respectively, and the circle is described by reference to the "molten sea" ("brim to brim") in the temple of Jerusalem (I *Kings*: VII, 23)—

> The circle has three aspects: the circumference, the thread and the roof. Which is the circumference? That is the rope surrounding the circle; for it is written: *And a rope of thirty cubits encompassed it round about*. And the thread? That is the straight-line from brim to brim; for it is written: *from brim to brim*. And the roof itself is the area.

The temple, the sanctuary-tent and their sacred furnishings are canons of form here, like the standard measures and weights now preserved in state buildings or scientific academies. This is really as sensible as theorem-and-proof methods, when these latter are interpreted as giving the status of *self*-existent entities to logically coherent objects. Egyptian, Mesopotamian and Phoenician mathe-maticians (it is difficult to separate Phoenician and Hebrew mate-rial culture), whose achievements in architecture and city-planning attest to their mathematical skill, knew that geometry (the very word confirms it) had developed from earth-measurement. To refer a geometrical figure to the form of a temple is to give it a kind of canonical authenticity, since a temple should have "perfect form." It is also to make it a symbol of *use* (see Appendix B), a template which is drawn from an existing object and which may be function-ally generalized and applied to other purposes. But if there were no buildings or marked off garden plots or streets or city squares there would be no such thing as a geometrical square.

In a more general sense we may think of this as a mimetic theory of geometry and, more generally, of all mathematics.[9] We may compare geometrical figure to mimetic musical figure—for example, to certain ancient forms of song (the Lapp *joijk* is one

such) in which the melodic line imitates the outline of a range or
mountains or the movements of an animal.[10] The ancient temple
was itself a geometrical symbol of a universal kind, as many
studies have demonstrated. Geometry is a simplification of patterns, particularly of outline shapes and movements. But the concept of mimetic movement can be carried much farther than this,
and even to the extent that it begins to supply an answer to the
conundrum of "correspondences," which we discussed earlier with
particular reference to a passage from Swedenborg's *The Worship
and Love of God*.

In other words, a general kind of mimetic geometry—of the
abstract representation of natural and mental movements and
shapes—lies behind both Greek formal rhetoric and whatever aspect of ancient Hebrew mathematics is preserved in the treatise of
R. Nehemiah. Though this is a technique, not a theory, it obviously
rests upon a theory, a theory of universal analogy. The technique is
as old as primitive pictorial abstraction and song (as in the Lapp
joijk above) but here it is codified and abstract. Again, a theory is
obviously referred to.[11]

Analogy is the heart of the Swedenborgian system and it is
presented in a new way. In the earlier quotation from *The Worship
and Love of God* we find what might crudely be described as
"stacked paradises," each on its own level. The elevator, so to
speak, which takes us from each level to the next, is a kind of
transmuting logic machine. On the "ground floor" it takes the form:
*Light reveals the quality of an object, but the quality of the object
appears according to the state of the light, wherefore the object is not
always such as it appears*. In its movement from floor to floor the
elements of this statement change within its abstractly definable
form: "light" becomes "intelligence" which becomes "wisdom"; "reveals" becomes "discovers" which becomes "manifests"; "quality"
becomes "truth" which becomes "goodness." Everything changes
except the phrase "according to the state of..." This phrase is the
constant of these three small logical systems. It is the factor which
determines the "vertical distance" between the paradises, and it is
responsible also for the fact that they are different one from another and can thus be stacked or presented in a pseudo-vertical ar-

rangement. In other words, each "paradise" is different from the two others because it is a different *state*.

Between each of these planes of being there is an unbridgeable gap. The concept "light" cannot change gradually into the concept "intelligence": they are related as similes, as when we say light is *like* intelligence, or vice versa. No logical manipulation or extension of the described physical properties of light will turn it into intelligence, and the same is true of the other components of the sentence just quoted, which, in transformations akin to those of simile or metaphor, give us the statement: *Intelligence discovers the truth of a thing, but the truth of a thing appears according to the state of the intelligence, wherefore that is not always true which is supposed to be true.*

The reader will have noticed that we have returned by a circuitous route to the question, "How does a logic turn into a rhetoric?" We can say that in the example quoted above the process of logical/ rhetorical interchange is at least demonstrated, if not quite explained. Swedenborg's "stacked paradises" do have something like the structure of a poem, in the sense that we have a relationship between planes or levels which is based on analogy, the relationship between "light" and "intelligence" being that of the two parts of a simile or metaphor ("intelligence is like light" or "intelligence is light"). Simile and metaphor properly belong to rhetoric. However, the statement, *Light reveals the quality of its object, but the quality of the object appears according to the state of the light, wherefore the object is not always such as it appears*, is a logical statement. It may also be related to purely quantitative statements. For example, we might have some such statement as "A measuring-rod measures the length of an object, but the measured length of the object depends upon the accuracy of the measuring-rod, therefore the measurement is not always as accurate as it appears." It is true that the statement about light involves entities too complex to be considered quantitatively, since "the state of the light" may perhaps be measured by modern instruments but there is no accepted way of measuring the "quality" of an object. We are in the realm of ordinary discourse there, which commonly deals with entities and processes too complex to be analyzed, but there is a direct link with "hard" quantitative statement and the logic of measurable things. What we have here are logical statements ranked one above the other, like so many wave forms, and the process which links them into a cohesive structure is one of dynamic analogy.

Our question also seems to be related to the manner in which the quantitative is transformed into the qualitative.

It is one of the depressing facts about the thought of the "West" that the distinction between the quantitative and the qualitative has almost been banished from our logic. René Thom, in his fascinating and (at least to me) very difficult *Stabilité Structurelle et Morphogenèse*,[12] discusses this problem, beginning with the account of a physicist who repeated to him, "not without vehemence," the statement of the English physicist, Rutherford, "Qualitative is nothing but poor quantitative." And he goes on to say that, first of all, it is impossible to form a satisfactory picture of nature if we reject the qualitative, and second, that topology and differential analysis now make it possible to develop a form of rigorous qualitative thought, which is what his book proceeds to do. But it appears that the full meaning of Thom's arguments is only accessible to masters of the most subtle reaches of modern mathematics, and indeed, as the controversy surrounding them indicates, not even to all of these. On the level of formal logic as it is taught in university textbooks, the concept of the qualitative seems to have disappeared, even to the point of what looks like censorship. To give an example, one may consult a small library of books on what is called, with a remarkable degree of falsification, "Boolean logic," without once encountering the fact that the distinction between quantitative and qualitative was very important to George Boole. One feels that he would look with deep dismay upon those modern electronics courses in which busy phalanxes of apprentice computer technicians wire up "Boolean circuits."

Clear definitions of the way quantity changes into quality are found in our day (or the day before yesterday) chiefly among the Marxists. This is a pity; but the West has only itself to blame for committing itself to what the Marxists call "vulgar materialism" with idealist appendages, a system which is at once cruder and, surprisingly, less traditional than "dialectical materialism." Eli de

Gortari explains it this way, in his *Introducción a la Lógica Dialéctica*—

> The processes of the universe are subject to continual aggregation and subtraction, in respect to the magnitude of each one of their qualities. Nevertheless, this change does not constitute dissipation or absolute generation, since the variation between one process and another is relative, while quantity is maintained at a constant level within the womb of the totality of the universe. For that matter, the same quality may manifest itself in different quantities, as much from one process to another as in the course of a single process. In such a case, quality remains indifferent to variation in quantity and is invariant. Nevertheless, this invariance is not sustained in the case of every quantitative change, either in the sense of growth or that of diminution. That is to say, the permanence of a quality only exists within certain limits of its quantitative variation and is relative to these. Consequently, when quantity increases or decreases to the point where it reaches one of these limits, there is a change in quality. Thus, on being transposed to its corresponding limit, a determined quality disappears, and, in its place, the process acquires a distinct (new) quality. In other words, quantitative variation is transformed into qualitative change.[13]

The catastrophe theory of René Thom[14] now makes it possible to determine, with a considerable degree of precision, such change-points and limits. For example, it can be used in modelling one of the most obvious cases where a change of quantity brings about a change of quality—the change of a liquid to a gas when its temperature is increased to the boiling point. Such phase transitions are discontinuous; even today, for all our knowledge of the water molecule, we are not exactly sure what happens when water changes into steam. When the temperature of the liquid is graphed against the flow of heat energy there is an abrupt threshold which cannot be accounted for by a mathematics based on the physics of continuous change, but which is accounted for by catastrophe theory.

No doubt the theory has been overextended and overestimated by some, perhaps even by Thom itself. Yet if his theory only modelled a few examples of transitions from quantitative to qualitative change it would still be an important breakthrough, since more effective models could be developed from it. If it is a generally useful model of such transitions it is bound to change our conception of the relationship between logic and mathematics, since it was the very lack of such a model which made the application of dialectical logic to natural processes seem something of a philosophical fantasy or a self-serving fiction of the Marxists. Such a conceptual change will slowly change our world-view.

Parts of Thom's argument have an extraordinary fluidity, a slipperiness of reference, which reminds us of Neoplatonic philosophy at what used to be considered its worst. There is one paragraph[15] where Thom skates with amazing speed from the dynamic qualities of the ellipse and the hyperbola to Chinese yin-yang theory to the reason why men are hairier than women to the geometrodynamic representation of sexual desire in dreams. He is perhaps amusing himself at our expense, but it is still true that such transitions, which appear airily nonsensical, are justifiable by his mathematical method. It does no good to say the relationships are accidental. Thom is demanding that we redefine what we mean by "accidental" and "contingent." The entire structure of our science rests upon unexamined ideas of what qualities are essential, what contingent in an object. For example, we proceed on the assumption that the inertial mass of an object is more important than its color, that the botanical classification of a plant (its formal relationship with other plants) is more important than its ecological relationship with an animal species, that the bone-structure of a bird is more important than its song. Perhaps we are right, but how do we know? In such a solemn and almost liturgical context of received ideas, Thom's statement that "the genetic patrimony of the snapdragon contains a virtual bee" seems maddeningly frivolous.[16]

Thom's method finds no direct echo in that of Swedenborg—they have different approaches to the questions of stability and change. Nevertheless, one wonders if a consideration of the way a logic turns into a rhetoric may not provide an abstract model which would throw some light on both. I will not go into the details—they would be tedious—but when we represent logical and rhetorical functions on a graph we can see that one changes into the other in the manner of a "catastrophe" (as Thom uses the word). The relationship between the two is a conundrum of poetic theory, but it has, I believe, a wider significance. It could throw great light on ancient symbolic systems in general, perhaps also on important psychological questions.[17]

We have covered a lot of ground in the chapter so far and this is inevitable where far-ranging theories are under discussion. So let me sum up what has been said to this point, since this will show that we have indeed been heading towards a goal.

i)   There is an intimate connection between logic and rhetoric in the Swedenborgian theory of correspondences, as expressed in the philosophical works (the theological ones will develop and refine this idea, with more precise distinctions of terms).

ii) Swedenborg's logic, in that it may be extended into a doctrine of matter and even a form of mechanics, has great versatility. It may engender forms of mythological thought when the elements of the logic are seen in terms of concrete images. There are indications that this earlier form of dialectical thought is very old, perhaps as old as any known human culture.

iii) We are therefore faced with the problem of how a logic, which deals with abstract terms and relationships, can engender such forms of image-making as we find in myths and poems—in short, of how a logic can engender a rhetoric (and vice versa).

iv) A hint of how this may have occurred in ancient times is afforded by a Jewish treatise on geometry. We then find that in *more* ancient times the abstraction of shapes and movements formed the basis of both mathematical thought and rhetoric. These took on mature form in the great civilizations of Egypt, Mesopotamia and Canaan. The symbolism of temple proportions shows this early system in full development. The maturity of literary expressions of these forms made possible the writing of Divinely-inspired Scripture, by producing a suitable symbolic vessel.

v)   A further examination of Swedenborg's logic shows how the translation of logical into rhetorical terms may be achieved in a

purely formal way. This shows us that the "intimate connection" referred to in i) is not illusory. It also shows us that the
process we have traced in ancient symbolism has a modern
rational and formal analogue, or can have, if certain modern
techniques are detached from their materialist axiomatic or
philosophical bases and interpreted in a Christian context (as
modern philosophy, for example, makes materialist use of the
discoveries of Christian thinkers).

It would be entirely erroneous to assume that all the processes
of rhetorical transformation may be explained as simple variants of
logical transformation. Deeply beautiful imagery may not be created in this way. It is enough for present purposes to indicate that the
element of logic is to be found in all rhetorical transformations,
either as a mere thread of prose meaning (which may be no more
than a pretext or even misleading) or in the full form of logical
manipulation (of the attributes of the image, for example). A certain kind of poetry—Shakespeare's comedies are full of it—is a
form of free logical play. This carry over of logical into rhetorical
functions is enough to indicate that there is a varying link between
the two.[18]

There is a matter we have not cleared up. Logic has its laws; we
may express the terms of a logical statement in algebraical notation and if we do not come up with good algebra we say the logic is
faulty. Rhetorical manipulations could also in theory be reduced to
algebra, provided the imagery were simple and banal. Algebraical
treatment of the simplest image in a real poem would require many
pages of notation, and in the end we should be no wiser than before.

Yet in the arts of the machine and the arts of abstract form
(music and certain kinds of nonrepresentational visual art) we find
a truly dialectical form of logical rhetoric. A superb statement and
example of this kind of logical rhetoric may be found in the theories
and practice of Sergei Eisenstein. Some consider him the greatest
filmmaker ever; he also had much of great value to say about
poetry. In his article, *A Dialectical Approach to Film Form*,[19] he
beautifully develops the statement, "The logic of organic form vs.
the logic of rational form yields, in collision, the dialectic of the art-

form." (Collision is the wrong word, belonging to the strenuous language of early Bolshevism.) An art completely dominated by ideas of logical coherence would of course be utterly dead and academic. Yet such an art could not even exist unless the rhetorical image and the logical statement were truly related in some way. It is in the area of freedom where their respective tensions meet that the best art, including poetic art, is created.[20]

This may perhaps help us better to understand the doctrine of correspondence presented in Swedenborg's scientific and poetic works. Read with simple naivete, or with the willed naivete of the critic who founds his attack on a misreading, it appears that he is confusing relationships among poetic images with those among real things. It was bad enough, it would seem, when he confused thoughts with things, the thoughts being simply logical—but, after all, some quite respectable philosophers have done this. To confuse poetic images with things seems bad poetics as well as bad logic.

In order to dispel such an idea, we move to his *The Five Senses*. There we discover that this theory is based upon a mature and well-developed theory of language and of signs, containing ideas which would not be fully developed until our time. I shall extract from this extraordinary work only a few ideas necessary to illustrate the present discussion.[21]

Long before it becomes a theory of the relationships between ideas, Swedenborgian correspondence is a theory of mechanical interaction. The example used is that of the "harmony or correspondence" between the muscles of the forehead, which affect the upper lid of the eye, and those which control the movements of the mouth and lips in speech, song and chewing. Harmony here is a functional interconnection, and, though the example is anatomical, we could just as well refer to the relationship of the parts of a machine or the elements of an ecosystem. Correspondence is a relationship, a harmony which makes it possible for the parts of a complex to work together as one.

The relationship between "correspondence" and "harmony" is more than a pretty turn of phrase. Musical harmony itself is an example of correspondence on the level of wave functions, which Swedenborg depicts in an almost modern form, though pictorially rather than mathematically (here, once again, the required mathematical forms had not yet been developed). In harmonious sound, waves of various frequencies ("celerities" in his terminology) interact in a system of mutual cancellations and reinforcements to produce a harmonious complex; and thus correspondence in the natural world becomes, in its most abstract form, a theory of wave-functions in general.

The question then arises of whether there is natural harmony in speech. This is not unrelated to another question, which had obsessed more than one philosopher and theologian before his day, of whether there is a "natural language," of Divine origin or not. (Some thought Hebrew might be this natural language). Swedenborg says there is not such a harmony, or such a language. Language, though it contains elements, apart from ideas implicit in words, which might be considered correspondential or natural (sounds which are, for example, mimetic either of natural phenomena or of nonverbal emotional vocalizations) is in general consideration an artificial code based on convention and culture. Even the mimetic sounds have been displaced by convention and culture. In our language (my example, not Swedenborg's), the word "love," once pronounced as a rich harmony of musical consonants and long vowels (something like "loove") has become the flat "luv." There is the often-told story of the person just learning English who, when he was asked to identify the most beautifully sounding word in English, answered "cellar-door," which is indeed a beautiful word, fit to be applied to an imaginary kingdom of orange-trees, spices and gold—Selador. Banal ideas are often expressed in beautiful sounds, exalted and sublime ones in flat or ugly sounds. This is the result of a largely random process of linguistic change.

There thus exists, between words and ideas, not a preestablished but a co-established harmony. There are correspondences among ideas, and these are intellectual correspondences; there are correspondences among nonverbal sounds and these are natural and sensuous correspondences. Language stands between the intellectual and the natural-sensuous, and it does so as a system of signs. When we are moved by statements in a language, we are moved by the ideas it carries, including the ideas which involve or represent emotions.

The language of poetry and oratory can of course move us, not only by the ideas it contains, but by the way the language is used, including the order of ideas, the relationships between images and ideas, harmony of language and the other elements which rhetorical art is concerned with. These are (and here Swedenborg returns to Aristotle by an unexpected path) "imitations of nature"; but they imitate nature in correspondences which are artificial or "made by art." Here we have an apparent paradox which traditional Aristotelian poetics never grappled with. Language is *made natural* by art. In itself it is only a dry rattle of conventional signs more or less logically arranged. It becomes natural, it incorporates natural harmonies, only when it becomes artificial, since only by artifice may it be mimetic or harmonic. It is also true that it becomes more natural, in this same sense, under the stress of emotion. Thus we may say that rhymed and metered verse written with high art stressed by emotion is more natural than casual prose. For we have two meanings of "natural" here. In the context of speech patterns, casual prose is more natural in that it resembles everyday speech low in emotional content. We call such speech "natural" because we do not put much effort into it. It is not that everyday speech is without rhythm, but the rhythm is loose and manifests itself over long stretches. However, the great and small rhythms and harmonies of nonhuman nature or human nature are "natural" in the other sense. By this definition, speech itself is not natural and can imitate the rhythms of nature only in the context of art or when stressed by emotion. The connection between these two ideas is that both art and emotion impose rhythm from above the linguistic structure, making it less natural in the first sense and more natural in the second.

We then ask in what way *ideas* are related "naturally." Swedenborg says that an idea in the natural mind is a change of state in the "internal sensory" and that there is no intrinsic reason why ideas should be linked there in any particular series. That they are so linked is the result of two composite factors. These are "usage" and "culture," including the usage and culture which arise from Divinely-inspired religion, and the purely sensual linkages which result from the connections between ideas and sensations. Another idea, here, to outrage secular humanists. Man is not innately reasonable, and his thoughts are not innately coherent. Unless he "learns Divine culture," unless he becomes a citizen of Heaven by adoption and "naturalization" as willingly as he would become a citizen of France or Mexico, he remains—except for his absorption of what "Divine culture" still survives in the secular culture he was born into as an infant—an incoherent entity. We may then ask how logical thinking develops in such a way that it *seems* "natural." For it is a fact (my comment, though firmly based on Swedenborg) that patterns of logical thinking are universal. The thought-processes of a member of some primitive culture may appear at first to be absolutely impenetrable, but once we understand the premises on which they are based, we find a logic very similar to our own. Sometimes we do not even have to do that. The mathematical concepts of any exotic culture may easily be understood with a little analysis, and many proverbs of tribal peoples, forms of encapsulated logic, make immediate sense. Yet it may take us years to learn the language of such a people, and many of its idea-groups cannot be translated into English until they are broken down into their logical components, then reconstructed in terms of the English language. And the translation which we come up with is usually bad English at that. Yet, though logical thinking is universal, it is no more natural than speech. It must be learned.

Swedenborg has some astonishing responses to this puzzle, and he sets them down in a series of cryptic statements which, if expanded, would make a medium-sized book. In summary—but even here we may see a relationship with forms of modern structuralism based on the opposition of "diachronic" and "synchronic"—this is what he says.

Logical analysis operates through various series of consequences, which in the end result in conclusions. The conclusions then initiate new chains of consequences. These lead to new conclusions, which in turn generate new chains of consequences. *Ad infinitum*, new conclusions and new series of consequences are developed. We see a curious time switch at work. The string of consequences in a logical argument is successive, but they are encapsulated in the conclusion, which sums them all up, as simultaneous. This is strictly analogous to the order of the universe in which, for example, the elements of a process of growth or development enter into the comparatively static structure of the mature plant or animal, becoming fixed forms. Mathematical reasoning proceeds in the same way.

What we should note is the interplay of simultaneous and successive. Successive consequences are present in conclusions simultaneously. But the simultaneities of conclusions generate new chains of successive consequences.

Sequences and simultaneities of this kind fit easily on a Cartesian graph, in which the y-axis or vertical represents the simultaneous, while the x-axis or horizontal represents the successive. Nor can we fail to note that the vertical axis relates to the positions above and below, and the horizontal axis to, as the name itself indicates, the *horizon* positions of the four orientation points—east, south, west and north, or before, to the right, behind and to the left. These, with above and below, are the six Aristotelian dimensions. Without such "primitive" concepts geometry could not have developed.

To expand this idea, we note that in an earlier part of the *Five Senses* (No. 472) Swedenborg has described simultaneity as superior to successivity. As "superior" and "inferior" are respectively above and below, we have to deal here with a vertical axis.

In other words, we seem to be returning to the cardinal direction diagram referred to in our discussion of the *Principia*, but here in a logical form. "Above" and "below" represent the axis of the simultaneous, of conclusions, or more, accurately, of accumulated and ordered consequences seen as conclusions. The directions, "before," "to the right," "behind," and "to the left"—that is, ideal East, South, West and North—represent the horizontal axis or the plane, depending on whether we have a 2-d or 3-d graph, of the successive and thus of serial consequences. But we may define "serial consequences" more accurately as sequential conclusions, that is to say, as strings of conclusions seen as consequences.

We may begin to see now why the world of correspondences found in the scientific and poetic works is geocentric in apparent form. Though Swedenborg knew perfectly well that the earth revolves around the sun, the world of correspondences is the world as perceived by the senses, with sun, moon and stars above, the earth beneath the feet and observation bounded by the horizon. This is because our every perception and logical thought, that is, from our sensual perceptions (including the sense of balance) to our most complex forms of logical thinking, is formed by our basic sense of the physical world. We are "here" and everything else is "out there." We can neither stand nor move unless we establish the right relationship between our vertical and our horizontal. What is in front of us is at once more immediate and more knowable, thus less dangerous, than what is beside us or behind us, unless we have familiarized ourselves with the latter pair by first seeing them "in front." Thus logic turns out to be a form of orientation, "orient" equalling "East." The Swedenborgian concept of the structure of man's mind therefore relates even back to the *Principia*, with its ideal "whirling spheres" possessing analogues of poles, equator and ecliptic band. The geocentric viewpoint, with its earthbound Euclidean space, is not false as a lie is false. It is a portion cut out from universal time and space and the principles which govern its formation are, so to speak, "foci" of universal time and space, found in most various forms, even in the mind and the more subtle aspects of matter. But it *is* "cut out"; and all of nature and thought is an intricate web of "gaps," of "discrete degrees." In the last analysis, it seems, logic is deeply rooted in our sensual natures, our makeup as human animals. Indeed—the thought is almost shocking—logical thought seems to resemble the navigational skills of animals.[22]

This would seem to contradict what was said before, that man must learn how to think logically. It would seem to make logic "natural." The contradiction is only apparent. Logical thinking has a physical basis and in that sense is innate. But this innate structure does not manifest itself until we learn to use it consciously, and in this sense it is not so much innate as latent. It is therefore an "innate latency." And this innate latency is characteristic of all the mental powers, with their associated modes of thought, which man calls forth as he progresses in rationality. Natural man is not innately rational. Of himself, he is only a range of possibilities in a unique animal form. In one sense he resembles no other animal; in another he resembles all other animals. Animals other than man are born into the order of their lives; they are bound by instinct. Man, an ordered chaos of latencies, rather resembles the entire cosmos. He is a microcosmos.

The above is a major theme in the latter half of Part One of *The Worship and Love of God*. There the infant Adam, born from the Tree of Wisdom, is brought to awareness by a soul infused by God, which instructs him in a virtually external manner, and also by "spiritual essences." These latter are playful presences depicted in rococo colors—rose and gold. Yet though the surface of this poem is as ingratiating as anything we might find in the French poetry of the time, the philosophy beneath it is difficult. In any case, much of this philosophy lies beyond the limits set for this book, since it is very close to theology. All we need are the points I have made above.

Since the subject-matter of this chapter is complex enough, a further summing-up would appear to be in order. We saw in an earlier summation that Swedenborg had found a certain link between logical and rhetorical processes which pointed to a useful interpretation of the symbolisms of ancient cultures. Following on that summary we have found—

i) That language, in which all logical and rhetorical thought-processes must be expressed, is an artificial code, a system of signs.

ii) That language forms true images of the world by codifying images and things. It does so in terms of natural correspondences of two kinds. These are the correspondences among sensations *within* the body (such as the sense of balance or sensations of muscular activity), and the correspondences among natural events *outside* the body, as observed and sensed. The *synthesis* between perceptions of internal bodily sensation and the complex of sensations occasioned by living in and observing nature gives the human an ordered and interacting set of notions of time and space, of quality and quantity. These notions serve to generate and order intellectual concepts, enabling him to *work on* nature, which he must do in order to survive. In this fashion his rationality develops further. There is a certain analogy here with the Marxist idea that the mind of man is formed by labor, but this was first of all a Hegelian idea, from *The Philosophy of Right*.

iii) These processes do not occur "naturally," since the human being has no innate tendency to do any of these things, only the innate ability to do them, if this ability is called upon. But it can only be called upon in a context of usage and culture, which is ultimately of Divine origin. The simplest and most rudimentary sense of "Divine usage and culture" appears as man's sense of a *mental verticality*, of some mind above his own mind. "Divine usage and culture" begins with the sense of an order above the natural. It seems strange to call it "usage and culture," yet that is what it is, because the nature of this superior order can only be communicated by instruction, as a way of feeling, thinking and acting. It is from instruction that we learn that some ideas are high, or exalted, and others low or debased. Eventually these notions become as much a part of us as those of the culture into which we were born.

iv) The sense of mental verticality and horizontality forms the cardinal diagram on which man maps data from the senses, as well as his own ideas. This cardinal diagram, projected onto the world, grows ever richer in content and representational power. When it is related to the progress of the seasons, the movements of heavenly bodies and so on, it produces humanity's first coherent world-picture.

v) The human world-picture always was and always will be symbolic. It is expressed in the artificial code of language. Language is made up of symbols of ideas and things. Language is constructed of analogies and its relationship to the world outside the mind is a great analogy. The mind can only represent itself to itself in terms of analogy. Sequences of logic can only be related by analogy and since there is no sequence of logic which can exist entirely by itself, it follows that logic cannot exist without analogy.

vi) It is not surprising, then, that the oldest forms of ordered thought we know should be systems of ranked analogies.

I am painfully aware that the above touches in a very superficial manner on some profound questions. This cannot be helped in an introductory survey such as this. Yet the reader may be less offended by my superficiality than by the rational coldness with which, as it appears, Swedenborg discusses matters which many have thought of as deep mysteries. Some will perhaps not be mollified and may even be further offended by the suggestion that much which seems mysterious need not be so, and that, in the end, Swedenborg is not waging war against the sense of wonder, but against the night-fogs and chimerical shadows of a materialism (sometimes in religious disguise) which delights in false mysteries. But in this battle, which is long, a certain cool and sustainable courage is required, the coolness of the military officer who carefully surveys the enemy's lines for points of advantage, checks the range of his own guns and sets down a plan of attack. Christianity cannot conquer materialism until it has asserted sovereign right over the world of matter.

There is no doubt that Swedenborg's vision of the human mind is at this stage in his career a singularly formal one. It is geometrical and, so far as the techniques of the time permit, it is algebraical. It is also, in a general sense, "structuralist," though in a philosophical context which has nothing to do with twentieth-century structuralism. For, according to Eli de Gortari, "As we may easily see, it is possible to formulate very many different algebraical structures, and each of them can serve for diverse applications in mathematics itself, or for that matter in physics, chemistry, biology, linguistics, anthropology, ethnology and other scientific disciplines. In fact, the so-called structuralist method consists simply in the application of one or many algebraical structures to a given scientific domain."[23]

This procedure is particularly apparent in Swedenborg's theories of logic, rhetoric (his theory of mental correspondences at this time is really a theory of rhetoric) and language. Perhaps this does not offend the tender-minded as much as it would have a few decades ago. We have all had to cope, more or less, with the revolution of thought initiated by the French structuralists and their heirs, which has irreversibly changed our notions of both mythology and poetics.

I have hardly touched upon the deeper implications of his theory. He exposed, with a boldness which his age would have found intolerable had it understood him, a certain automatism in logic, rhetoric and language. He did so by relating them to geometrical and mechanical processes characteristic of the inanimate world. It would seem then that he virtually denies the intellectual freedom of man. This is not so. Man is free insofar as he is spiritual, as he attends to the will of God for him, in the end as he accepts the "heavenly citizenship" (my term) which validates his humanity by lifting him above the level of the animal in human shape. Most surprisingly, and in a manner all but the most hardened materialists must find terrifying, Swedenborg in effect describes the human animal as an incoherent, ineffectual and unrealized form. Nothing in the makeup of its mind dictates that its thoughts should be coherent or rational, or that its languages should make sense. These qualities can be provided only by usage and culture, and coherent patterns of usage and culture come, ultimately, from God. The human animal, unlike others, is not born into the order of its being. It is only a structure of possibility, which is its freedom. Inasmuch as it realizes its innate possibilities, that is, does what God willed at the creation, it becomes truly human. Inasmuch as it does not, its mind degenerates more and more into incoherence, which is to say that it decays in the formal sense, melts into monstrosity. It does not become animal. When we call evil behavior "bestial" we tell ourselves a curiously comforting lie. The truly evil man is not an animal but a formless horror. This is, to be sure, a coolly rational vision of the Fall of Man, of sin and of hell. Hell-fire is not here; but the vision is frightening enough. The forms of usage and culture, which come from heaven, are, however, present to some extent in even the most vicious societies, since no society can exist without them. In his hypocritical conformity with these, the human monster, or the human who is nearly a monster, presents a factitious image of coherence and rationality which masks his inner decay.

ENDNOTES

1 Swedenborg, *The Worship and Love of God*, p. 109.

2 I hope the reader familiar with poetic theory will forgive my attempt to condense a very large body of thought into three barren words: "supposedly arbitrary inventions." A satisfactory analysis of the notions implicit in these words would take us into areas of great complexity, and of confusion as well, not only in literary criticism but in philosophy. I am confident that we shall find very few if any literary theorists of reputation who would accept the idea that classifications of rhetorical figure, whether the Greek-based ones or those more modern, refer to a mental geometry as real as, if more difficult than, the geometry used by painters or the science of tonal relations used by musical composers. Not since the seventeenth century, at any rate. Indeed, the structuralists from the 1960s on, who claimed to be reviving what was useful in a discipline they characterized as a chaotic sort of *bricolage*, simply refused to recognize that the old rhetorical terms had the simplest and clearest of geometrical meanings. There was no chaotic or homemade quality at all, but rather an implicit philosophy and psychology which they could not accept.

3 One must simply keep on insisting that the phenomenon is a real one and must be either accepted as a given or explained, no matter how it offends the contemporary mind-set. A complex structure of intelligible number-relationships, a mathematical language, runs through most of the canonical books of the Old Testament and the Gospels and Apocalypse in the New. To approach the Bible as if it were an ordinary literary text, "sublime" or not, must lead to confusion.

4 Cabalistic studies, both of the Jewish and Christian schools, are most marred by such excess, though one may find flashes of the most beautiful rationality if one is patient. On the other hand, even a finely rational and profound book like Schaya's *The Universal Meaning of the Kabbalah* refers to the "science of letters and numbers" as giving "cognitive and *operative* access" (italics mine) to "eternal archetypes or divine aspects" (p. 150). The shadow of the magus darkens many books in this tradition.

I know of no easily obtained study of medieval symbolic number. Most Christian scholars treat it with an embarrassment I cannot comprehend, particularly when we so admire the physical expression of medieval mathematics in the great churches of Europe and the orthodox East. Yet here too there is numerological excess, in the habit of treating theological *lists*, such as the "seven deadly sins," as if they were real mathematical entities (Lull is also guilty of this). Byzantine mathematical symbolism, closer to the Greek tradition, seems to have had a more refined rationality than that of the West, an idea of which may be obtained by following up the references in a fine book by Gervase Mathew, *Byzantine Esthetics*. An English response to the beauty of this tradition may be found in the somewhat uneven but frequently splendid Arthurian poems of Charles Williams.

5 See also Panin (bibliography).

6 The conscious use of symbolic proportions in temple architecture is apparent in the bare text of much of *Ezekiel* and the first three chapters of the book contain a complex "vorticist" cosmology in which the "Divine in a whirlwind" engenders the cardinal-point universe. We may see this without taking any subtextual meanings into account and the linkages with the overt meanings of other biblical passages are

very many. On the level of bare text there is nothing here that a learned and intellectually gifted person of the time could not have understood. Nonetheless, Jewish and Christian writers (dogmatic literalists excepted) have always believed that great depths of meaning lie beneath the bare text. It is also clear, again from the bare text, that we have seriously underrated the intellectual culture of Israel, presumably out of impatience with its "archaic" style.

7 Gordon *passim.*

8 Midnick (ed.), pp. 522–539. I have not referred to the writings of Philo of Alexandria—deep and beautiful in the selections I have read—because I understand it is impossible to determine whether he is "Platonising" or setting out something in the then-familiar Platonic terminology which is much older than Plato. Indeed, I admit to being quite at sea when it comes to the phrases "Platonic influence" or "Neoplatonism," because so few scholars seem to consider what non-Greek influences may have played on Plato himself. How much of "Platonism" was a stream which actually ran into the works of Plato, emerging thence as "Platonic"? Such questions become even more important when we consider the Hellenistic works which purport to contain the wisdom of ancient Egypt, such as the literature attributed to Hermes Trismegistus. Budge (*Gods...* II, p. 414) believes this literature preserves some really Egyptian material, among many misunderstandings.

9 The Greeks themselves seem tacitly to have recognized that their greatest contribution to mathematics lay in the complete formalization of geometry. Greek number theory reached its highest development in the various branches of Pythagoreanism, but it was generally accepted that Pythagorean number theory was a codification of something more ancient.

10 When I began to work on this book I intended to include a chapter on "musical correspondences," as they relate to Swedenborgian "harmonic correspondences." The cardinal-directional and astronomical symbolisms of traditional Asian and ancient near Eastern musics are particularly relevant. The distinguished musicologist, Marius Schneider (see bibliography) finds a tradition of musical imagery which he relates to a very ancient "primitive Divine tradition" preserved in the "megalithic" tradition.

Unfortunately, we know very little about ancient Near Eastern music, and the interpretation of the data is dogged by controversy at every step. Schneider's book, which contains the most remarkable insights throughout, is as a whole too speculative to be cited as an authority. A discussion of his study would be unsatisfactory without an account of the divergent views of experts in ancient music, and the result would be a section of intolerable length, much of it irrelevant to the present topic and comprehensible only by specialists.

As an example of Schneider's beautiful insights I quote the following, which comes after a discussion of the relationship between spiral form and the shape of the hourglass drum.

> The inversion of values represented by this drum and the spiral movement which develops from it are two essential features of the dynamism of the mystical life. The mystical identification of thesis and antithesis constitute the base, the form and the polarity of prayer (psychologically and verbally), while the movement of the spiral represents the evolution of its rhythm. To enter into the mystical spiral is suddenly to see united that which before appeared to be separate (in different parallel planes) and even contrary or irreconcilable. (pp. 190–191)

11 The modern word "theory" reflects very poorly the reality we are looking at, though if the idea were presented in modern terms that is how it would appear. The word "system" is not much better. We have to deal with something which was, at one

time, simply thought of as "knowledge," as if there were no other kinds of knowledges, theories and systems.

In Egypt the organizing principles of the "system" are not set out as axioms or theories. They are embodied in the attributes of the god Thoth, "he who reckons in heaven, the counter of the stars, the enumerator of the earth and of what is therein, and the measurer of the earth (Budge, *Gods...* I, p. 400). His goddess-consort, Maat, "the feminine counterpart of the god" (same, p. 416) is "the personification of physical and moral law, and order and truth" (same, p. 417). Laws of mathematical order are thus particular expressions of the attributes of these two gods. It does not follow that the Egyptians did not think in a rational manner.

12 Thom, pp. 4–6.

13 de Gortari, *Introducción a la Lógica Dialéctica*, pp. 59–60.

14 Woodcock and Davis summarize the conflict raging around Thom's ideas in their useful little book, *Catastrophe Theory*. For a negative critique of catastrophe theory, see "Catastrophe Theory: The Emperor Has No Clothes" (Gini Bari Kolata in *Science*, 15th April, 1977, p. 287). The author objects to overconfident use of the theory to solve complex problems in sociology, biology and other disciplines. Thom's purely mathematical arguments are not called into question. A holistic theory of evolution related to some of Thom's ideas may be found in Rupert Sheldrake's *A New Science of Life*, Blond and Briggs Ltd., London 1981.

15 Thom, pp. 96–97.

16 Thom, p. 247. In a later chapter of this book we shall see that Swedenborg's doctrine of the evolution of life-forms is related to this idea of Thom's, though he looks, so to speak, from the other side of the mirror.

17 If there had been space here, we could have taken a look at the theory of image-making found in Baltasar Gracián's *Agudeza...* and his extraordinary feat of logical model-making in *El Criticón*. To Gracián the poetic image was essentially a form of highly ingenious logical play; but on the other hand his idea of logic was a very poetic one. The interplay of logic and rhetoric is nowhere else, to my knowledge, examined in such detail. It is almost as if we were confronting a complete cosmology, built out of logic and rhetoric. Gracián was a master of formal rhetoric and his theory is highly relevant in the present context.

18 An intermediate form, which Gracián sums up for all time, is a subversive rhetorical manipulation of the very laws of logic. The rhetorical image may be reduced to a complex logical statement, but the logical statement in its abstract form turns out to be formally coherent but playful, banal or otherwise "blank-faced." It only makes sense if it is related to some "great logical image," which is not stated. Gracián's *El Criticón* is subversive in the sense that it presents a world ruled by Fortune (chance or probability)—see Part II, *Crisi* VI. Logical statements are only the colored lights on the great merry-go-round of the Wheel of Fortune. They are themselves "figures of speech."

19 Eisenstein in *Film Form*, pp. 45–63. Eisenstein retains much of the pre-revolutionary poetic culture of Russia, with its Hegelian, symbolist and abstractionist influences. This affects his overtly Marxist esthetic. He refers slightly to the use, in the symbolist theatre, of "correspondences" of the type discussed in Chapter One of this part, based in this case on notions of synesthesia. At the same time he argues that, for formal reasons, these are very effective in cinema, leading to a heightened realism (*Film Form*, p. 187). He refers (quoting another) to "the Swedish theosophist, Swedenborg" in an ambiguously dismissive manner (*Film Sense*, p. 138). He attacks what he assumes to be Swedenborg's color theory (it is not). Then he offers his own rational explanation of the emotional effects of color. This happens to be closer to Swedenborg's own view, but only by accident, since Swedenborg's

ideas of color are, within the eighteenth-century context of knowledge, scientifically accurate. What is interesting is that he brings early nineteenth-century ideas of correspondence and the associated Swedenborg-image into the debate. This is most unusual among theoreticians of film.

20 See also Eisenstein's *The Cinematogaphic Principle and the Ideogram*, in *Film Form*, pp. 28–44.

21 The following ideas are drawn almost entirely from paragraphs 380, 607–609, 629–641, and 684 of this work. *The Five Senses* was not written for publication but is a collection of notes for his work, *The Animal Kingdom*.

22 The British zoologist, R. Robin Baker, has conducted a series of experiments designed to test the unconscious sense of direction in human subjects. The results were published in his book, *Human Navigation and the Sixth Sense*. His conclusion is that human beings possess innately (though repressed when they are literate, urbanized and "modern") the same location-finding abilities as other animals. His experiments, conducted with the help of British schoolchildren, indicate that these abilities exist. His interpretation of the strength of their presence and the associated physiological factors may be open to argument. I have not read an independent evaluation of his experimental methods.

23 de Gortari, *Elementos de Lógica Matemática*, p. 61.

3

Moses and Orpheus

In 1745 Swedenborg wrote a short work—it should rather be described as a manuscript for his own use—called, in translation, *The History of Creation as Given by Moses*.[1] His theology was still in all important respects that of an orthodox Lutheran.[2] His interpretation of the creation story is "creationist," though not precisely "literalist" in the ahistorical reading favored by many, if not all, modern "fundamentalists." (I apologize for the awkward proliferation of quotation marks; it is my feeble protest against the bellicose vagueness of these words.) I shall discuss some aspects of this treatise in more detail later, when we can see more clearly the implications of his claim that the *Genesis* account had ancient antecedents; but I begin with a summary of it, after quoting *Genesis* I: 1–19. I shall use the translation of the New English Bible, in which some aspects of the text emerge more clearly than in the familiar King James version.

> In the beginning of creation, when God made heaven and earth, the earth was without form and void, with darkness over the face of the abyss, and a mighty wind that swept over the surface of the waters. God said, "Let there be light," and there was light; and God saw that the light was good, and he separated light from darkness. He called the light day, and the darkness night. So evening came, and morning came, the first day.

God said, "Let there be a vault between the waters, to separate water from water." So God made the vault, and separated the water under the vault from the water above it, and so it was; and God called the vault heaven. Evening came, and morning came, a second day.

God said, "Let the waters under heaven be gathered into one place, so that dry land may appear"; and so it was. God called the dry land earth, and the gathering of the waters he called seas; and God saw that it was good. Then God said, "Let the earth produce fresh growth, let there be on the earth plants bearing seed, fruit-trees bearing fruit each with seed according to its kind." So it was; the earth yielded fresh growth, plants bearing seed according to their kind and trees bearing fruit each with seed according to its kind; and God saw that it was good. Evening came, and morning came, a third day.

God said, "Let there be lights in the vault of heaven to separate day from night, and let them serve as signs both for festivals and for seasons and years. Let them also shine in the vault of heaven to give light on earth." So it was; God made the two great lights, the greater to govern the day and the lesser to govern the night; and with them he made the stars. God put these lights in the vault of heaven to give light on earth, to govern day and night, and to separate light from darkness; and God saw that it was good. Evening came, and morning came, a fourth day.

We are so familiar with the text that it slides very easily over the surface of the mind. Yet it is clear that it is densely composed, containing many subtleties and formal conundrums. For one thing, we note that God does not name the things He creates until after there has been a process of (binary) separation. Thus light must be separated from darkness before they can be named, respectively, "day" and "night." Water must be separated from water before there can be a heaven and the waste of waters below it. This waste of waters seems to stretch through all of space, since it has not yet been "gathered into one place," which gathering is necessary if an earth is to appear. Also, light is separated from darkness two times, the first before sun, stars and earth are created, the second after.

There are also puzzles and paradoxes, which would have been as apparent to an ancient mind as to our own. How, for example, can there be evening and morning before sun and earth are created? There must be a reference here to non-measurable cycles of cosmic time, since everybody knew then as now that without sun and earth time cannot be measured.

Finally, the reference to the "mighty wind," which may also be translated as "the spirit of God hovering...," may be found in Greek cosmogonic myth and some of the speculations of the pre-Socratics.[3]

How does Swedenborg interpret this intricate and obviously philosophical account of the creation of the universe?

His interpretation of the statement, *And the earth was waste and void* (he is using translations by Schmidius and Castello) is that the earth, as first created by God, was "an unordered mass, called by the Ancients, Chaos." He does not mean that it was objectively such (since God cannot create a disorderly thing) but that it could only be represented in this fashion at the time *Genesis* was written. Similarly, he holds that the spirit of God which "moved upon the faces of the waters" was a form of ether or atmosphere. It is not the Holy Spirit of Christian theology which is referred to here but the "breath of God," the vital spirit which God breathed into the nostrils of Adam, so that he might live. The ancients, Swedenborg believes, thought of all atmospheres, airs and breaths as essentially the same. He was probably right; so far as we know, the concept of a separate ether was introduced in Greek times.

It is said that light was created before the sun and moon because only atmospheres, in this broad definition of them, make light visible. At this stage, however, the earth is not a solid body but a fluid substance which does not rotate in the manner of heavenly bodies. There is no difference between day and night but only a light generally diffused through the quasidiaphanous atmospheres which make up the earth. When the earth becomes solid enough to rotate and to block out sunlight, we have an alternation of light and darkness.

This process occurs over great stretches of time, as men count time. Each day of creation is a world-age. Here Swedenborg quotes *Psalm 90*, to the effect that (his paraphrase) "with God, who spake these words by Moses, a thousand years, that is, an exceeding great space of time, is only as a single day."

The appearance of dry land from the waters he interprets as the formation of the earth's solid crust on a surface which is, formally, aqueous, that is to say, fluid in some way. The elements in this crust are not earths as we know them, because such can only be formed by the decay of organic matter. Swedenborg describes the elementary particles of the first crust as "mere seeds." We learn from *The Worship and Love of God*[4] that these are particles which contain within them what will become the principles of mineral forms, then vegetable and animal life. They are what we should now call atoms and molecules, in the sense that Swedenborg has of them. This is to say that they are "quiesced" ether particles, taking on the particle-forms of the material substances we know. As first forms, generative of hard matter, they are called "seeds." Eventually the earth brings forth grass and "the herb yielding seeds" and other plants.

Readers of the *Genesis* creation account have always been puzzled by the fact that the sun and moon are mentioned only after vegetable life has been created. Swedenborg, quoting the Castellio translation, says that the key to the meaning of this is found in the description of the *purpose* of sun and moon and stars: "Let there be luminaries in the expanse of the heaven to govern the day and the night and to separate the light and the darkness." The sun, moon and stars, he says, would not be visible as such until the present atmospheric regime had been established. Nor would there be recognizable seasons and times until there were natural cycles ("autumn" and "winter"). The implication seems pretty clearly to be—though he does not say so in as many words—that without natural cycles of birth, growth and decay, the passage of time would be a functionless concept.

This is a very rational reading of the *Genesis* account, which would at least make it greatly superior to creation accounts of similar age. There are modern interpretations of the evolution of the earth to which it could be related, as an ancient naked-eye version which could be accommodated without violation to truths at a deeper level. Among these we have theories that the crust of the early earth was particularly rich in minerals and other substances which could give birth to or nourish early plant forms.

However, it would be something of a falsification to cite them in detail, since Swedenborg could neither know nor anticipate modern biochemistry. He restricts himself to the bare supposition that such mineral forms must have existed, and he does so because, in his view, the *Genesis* account demands them. There is no question of his fighting a rear-guard action to protect the Scriptures against the assaults of modern science. Modern science does not yet exist.

We are entitled to ask if Swedenborg is not wresting the statements of Scripture to suit his own proto-modern theory. Both seem to fit together very well; but Swedenborg is an intellectual with well-developed argumentative powers, and it is possible we are being misled by logical ingenuity. Furthermore, the *Genesis* account follows, we may say, a naked-eye logic of cause-and-effect, and it is in the nature of such statements that we may read into them philosophical subtleties never intended by the author, statements which do not actually violate the rough-and-ready sturdiness of the text. For example, a Haida artist could construct the most intricate geometrical art-forms without knowing a thing about what we call "geometry." All depends on whether or not a person of Moses' time or before it could have had ideas such as the above. Could he have known that the earth goes around the sun, that plants developed from mineral forms and that the earth was once a collection of gases or atmospheres?

We can only conjecture from the available texts. It is unlikely that such a man could have known that the earth goes around the sun; but it is likely that he knew the earth was either in some way a child of the sun or dependent upon it. He could have known that plant and mineral forms had a common ancestry, without understanding their relationship in a biochemical sense: many mineral forms look plantlike. He could have known that matter was, in some sense, a fluid before it was a solid, because the properties of fluids are more subtle, hence nobler or more spirit-like, than the properties of solids. All these ideas may be found in pre-Socratic philosophy and also in Egyptian. We now have a myriad of texts from ancient Egypt, translated into European languages. These texts evince a high level of philosophical thought clothed in the imagery of the senses. We do not need to be Egyptologists to recognize that the Egyptian priests, no matter how corrupted their theological and ritual beliefs and practices may have become over millennia, deserved their ancient reputation as philosophers. If many modern scholars have obscured this it is due to various forms of prejudice (including racial) and the ideological conflicts which bedevil the study of the ancient Near East.

We wish to consider the similarities among Egyptian, Phoenician and Greek natural philosophies, and their relation to the cosmological aspect of the biblical creation story. It is probably best to concentrate on the doctrines taught at Heliopolis, the biblical On. E.A. Wallis Budge tells us[5] that Heliopolis, close to what is now Cairo, was "a very convenient halting-place for travellers passing from Arabia and Syria into Egypt and *vice versa*. It is then most probable that the doctrine of Ra as taught by the priests of Heliopolis was a mixture of Egyptian and Western Asiatic doctrines..." Indeed, Pliny says that Heliopolis was founded by "Arabs," but this was a vague term in his day.

The Hebrews had a particular relationship to On. Joseph married the daughter of Potiphar the priest of On (*Genesis* XLI: 45), when he became the chief official of the Pharaoh. The Hebrews of Moses' time were particularly associated with Heliopolis because the two "treasure cities" they built for Pharaoh, Pithom and Raamses (*Exodus* I: 11), were close to that center. The landward flight of Moses after he killed the guard of an Egyptian labor-gang, which followed the land route into Midian, indicates that he also had come from this general area, which we would in any case expect because of the concentration of Hebrews there. If Moses had been educated in the "wisdom of the Egyptians" (*Acts* 7:22), it is a fair guess that this was at some school for nobles in or near Heliopolis. His name itself is an Egyptian one. As Budge tells us, there is a tradition that Plato studied at Heliopolis. Solon and Thales are also said to have visited there. Yet perhaps something more than a tradition is involved since Strabo (88 BC–AD 25), a sober and widely learned historian and geographer, visited Heliopolis and was shown the very quarters in which Plato had stayed and studied, along with the great mathematician and astronomer, Eudoxus. Plato's studies in Egypt are confirmed in two biographies of him, one by Olympiodorus and one by an anonymous author. Such evidence gives weight to the conclusion of Cheik Anta Diop that the resemblances of Plato's cosmology in the *Timaeus* to the philosophy taught at Heliopolis are in no way accidental.[6]

Much of the above was familiar to classical and biblical scholars of Swedenborg's day. They could not read Egyptian texts, of course, but they had the Bible and the classical writers. They knew, for example, that Proclus had said, in his history of mathematics, that the first forms of Greek geometry had come from Egypt, via Thebes, and that the science of number came from the Phoenicians, who had developed it to manage the complexities of their foreign trade. Swedenborg goes much farther than this, since he believes that Moses had learned in Egypt a cosmology at least roughly similar to his own. May we regard this as a rational claim? Can we point to something more concrete than is implied in my earlier statements in such forms as "Moses could have known…"?

In *The Gods of Egypt*, Budge tells us much about the god Ra, "father of the gods" and the chief god worshipped at Heliopolis. Ra is often referred to as a "sun-god" but this is certainly too narrow a description. The sun as a physical luminary was worshipped as Aten. Ra is the lord of heaven and earth, creator of earth, man and the watery abyss. He is indeed in one hymn hailed as the "disk" of the sun but it is said later in the same hymn that "thou doest give light unto the course of the Disk." He must therefore rather be the light which animates the sun, and this is indicated in other hymns, as when it is said "thou makest thy creations in thy Great Disk" and "thou hidest thy body in that which is within thee." It is also said that "thou art the Soul on high and thy bodies are hidden" (the sun is certainly not hidden); and Ra is also called "the god of motion, the god of light." Thus Ra is a god of light and motion before he is a god of the physical sun, an order of attributes which is reflected in the *Genesis* account, where God creates light before He creates the sun and stars. This could be read as the survival of some ancient Egyptian monotheistic tradition. But *Genesis* could also be reproving Egyptian imagery; light is a *created* thing.

Ra is said to have emerged from "the thick darkness which enveloped the watery abyss of Nu" and this reminds us of the cosmogony of Sanchuniathon, as recorded by Philo Byblius, in which "the sun, and the moon, and the lesser and the greater stars" shone forth from the chaos-substance of Mut. We might expect such a connection anyway, since Sanchuniathon tells us that his cosmogony came from an Egyptian source, the god Thoth or some human bearing his name: "All these things are found written in the Cosmogony of Taaut...," he says.

We commonly think of the Egyptians as possessing a naive naked-eye notion of the relationship between the earth and the sun. Their earth is a flat disk, or perhaps a section of a hemisphere, floating on the ocean stream. The sun revolves around it and when it passes under the earth it is night. Some hymns to Aten may be interpreted in this way and it is not impossible that this was one of the accepted opinions in Egypt. But the Heliopolitan hymns to Ra point to a much more sophisticated doctrine.

Thus the worshipper of Ra, in addressing him, says "...thou dost in one little moment pass over the spaces which would need millions and millions of years (for men to pass over)..." How can we reconcile this with the naive image just mentioned or more naive images of temple art—so naive, indeed, that they can only be read as symbolic—that the sky was a rectangular iron ceiling supported by a pillar at each corner, or was the body of a goddess bowed backward in an elevated horizontal position, her hands and feet resting upon the earth? The brief answer is that we cannot. If the sun in one little moment can travel a space it would take men millions and millions of years to pass over, it must be very far from the earth and travelling with unimaginable speed. It must then be immense in size, since otherwise we could not see it. The earth would be, in comparison, a mere speck of dust. Yet all ancient theories which assumed the sun revolved around the earth held it to be a comparatively small body. Common sense, without any idea of celestial mechanics or of gravitation, rebels at the idea of a huge, distant and rapidly moving body as being tied to an infinitesimal one. It could still be true that the Egyptians who framed and accepted this hymn believed the sun revolved around the earth but they could only have done so through the mediation of a theory much more elaborate than the one we attribute to them.

Then we also know that the Egyptians believed that the *Tuat*, commonly called "underworld" by us, was not actually situated under our world "but away beyond the earth, probably in the sky."[7] It is here where Ra goes when he is not visible in the sky.[8] One way or another, and ignoring symbolic interpretations of this in favor of a physical one, this means that the sun when it is invisible is still in some part of the sky. We can at least speculate that this literal interpretation is correct on its level, and that therefore the sun, between its sinking on the western horizon and rising on the eastern, is still "travelling through sky," which means that the earth is an object "floating in sky" and therefore, possibly, a sphere or other rounded shape. If the sun *is* revolving around the earth, then the Egyptian concept is nonetheless as sophisticated as the most advanced pre-Socratic cosmology. True, we only have words such as "pass over," which cannot be given a mechanical interpretation; yet if the sun does *not* revolve around the earth then it is moving, at least, in a complicated manner.

Also, the sun-god made the earth, since Ra says, "I have made the heavens and the earth, I have knit together the mountains, I have created all that is above them, I have made the water..." Can we imagine the creator of a body as its hapless slave, doomed to revolve around it to eternity? And does not the idea that a sun-god, who is at the deeper level a god of light and motion, created the world have *necessary* implications which are in no way naive?

Finally, we note that Ra is particularly associated with the geometry of the circle and what is called "the double circle." We have—"thou makest thy creations as Governor of thy Circle"; "thou art he who protecteth thy hidden spirits and they have form in thee...thou art he who gathereth together thy gods when thou goes into thy hidden Circle"; "thou goes in and comest out and thou comest out and goest in to thy hidden Circle"; "thou art indeed the bodies of the double Circle"; "thou art the maker of the Circles, thou makest bodies to come into being by thine own creative vigour"; "thou art the Soul that speaketh with the gods who are in their Circles."

Egyptian cosmology must therefore have been more sophisticated than we have imagined it to be. Its guiding principles wait to be discovered by Egyptologists working together with mathematicians and specialists in the exact sciences. For others, it is a great temptation, when they have sensed the potential richness of this field of research, to develop the most fantastic and unfounded theories.[9] It makes no sense at all to imagine an Egyptian form of modern science. It does make sense to imagine something conceptually similar to pre-Socratic philosophy among the Greeks and to the creation story of *Genesis*. This would have been worked out with all the wealth of knowledge available to a very old and settled civilization and couched in the symbolic language of a well-developed if corrupt polytheistic theology, which itself existed in a monophysite or monotheistic version for the elite. No doubt such an endeavour will be undertaken as old prejudices, which are as ridiculous as they are odious, fade away.[10]

To refer specifically to the implications of the *Genesis* account, the Bible itself informs us that the Egyptians were perfectly capable of understanding and accepting monotheistic ideas. The story of Joseph (which I need not retell) indicates as much. Now, as Europeans became aware of the religious beliefs of peoples in other parts of the world, a result of the age of exploration and imperial conquest, it became obvious that forms of monotheism could be found all over the world, sometimes in explicit form, sometimes hidden as elite cults within popular polytheistic systems. These were then interpreted as decadent remnants of the "Church of Noah," a monotheistic system spread over the world by Noah's descendants after the great flood. But the early explorers and missionaries were puzzled—and their puzzlement has continued, in secularist disguise, into present-day anthropology—by the curious vagueness and ineffectuality of this surviving monotheism. The omnipotent God was far removed behind a succession of images of other gods, as if behind so many semitransparent screens. Or he took no interest in men. Or he was too exalted to be approached in prayer. Or he was merely an entity of philosophy, a philosophy which, among many tribal peoples, took the form of a high wisdom preserved by an upper class or by elders. This knowledge was sometimes communicated by fraternities into which one was initiated;

but these must *not* be confused with such secret societies as Free-masonry because (except in the case of groups of witches and occultist criminals) they were not really secret. They were actually, since we are using modern analogies, more like institutes of higher learning. But the Supreme Entity they referred to (again using modern terminology) was usually more like a "principle" or a "force" than like a "person." Only in Africa did there seem to be a God like that of the Old Testament, one who could listen and talk to men, though often the African Supreme God was protected and hidden behind a kind of palace guard of lesser gods or spirits. Sometimes the African God could be a principle or force which could take on human form (this is the same duality we find in Egyptian religion); also, certain cults, whose beliefs we find somewhat reflected in American neo-African cults such as voodoo, regarded this principle or force as amoral and manipulable by "adepts."

Finally—and this was a real blow—the decipherment of ancient texts revealed that this state of things extended far into the past. No pure monotheism could be found. It was as if there had never been such a thing as the "Church of Noah."

It becomes clear now that the problem had been misstated. Those who looked for evidences of the Church of Noah were looking for a monotheism of Jewish, Christian or Islamic type. This would never be found. We may learn why it would not and could not be found from the First Mosaic commandment (*Exodus* XX: 3), "Thou shalt have no other gods before me." The new religion of Israel was *credal* monotheism, a conscious rejection of polytheism and a religious reform. Polytheism could not have been rejected until it had come into existence, had thoroughly entrenched itself and had been recognized as a scandal. There is hardly such a thing as credal polytheism and earlier forms of monotheism would not have been credal either. The early division of the powers of God, without which He cannot be imagined or even addressed in prayer, would not have been accompanied by any fear of polytheism because polytheism was not yet a recognizable system. The Israelites themselves had to give God various names (such as Adonai and Shaddai) and both medieval Christians and Muslims had to define the "dignities" of God (Goodness, Mercy, Wisdom and other divine attributes). There can be no coherent theology unless such analytical distinctions are made.

One fact is clear from the ancient texts, so clear as to be obvious even to a nonspecialist. It is particularly clear in the literature of Egypt. There is a constant tendency towards a multiplication, even a crazy proliferation, of gods. Yet there are also continual attempts to correct this drift into crude polytheism by demonstrations that this or that god "contains" or has "generated" all the others.[11] Such reforms are often frustrated by the rival claims of particular gods: Osiris, Ra, Ammon, the sun god Aten and many others. From time to time, also, we shall find weak syncretistic compromises—"all the gods are God" (*neter*, a word of unknown origin)—but this is such a non-statement as "All are an Allness." There can be no philosophy or theology without an identifiable first principle and identifiable derivative ones. If each god is, without differentiation, God, then there is no differentiation in any idea we may have of God—goodness, mercy and wisdom are exactly the same and we can form no idea of Him.

Further complications arise because God or the gods are at once described in terms related illustratively to visible and natural things (storm, dawn, rain...) and identified with them in a philosophical fashion. For example, the part of divine thought which created the storm is thought of as different from the part which created the sun and man. Furthermore, events of nature are often violent, many animals have dirty and noisome habits, decay and death must somehow be accounted for. Some of the gods, therefore, having degenerated into natural or philosophical principles, must also be violent and have dirty or noisome habits. Then, too, there are religious wars; the adherents of one cult are defeated by the adherents of another, and the defeated god becomes the symbol of all that is evil and wretched. The system becomes as morally equivocal as logic, science and history are. Since the temple scholars, or the wise old men of the tribe, are custodians of all higher learning, theology actually *becomes* logic, science and history.

In the end, those who read learned accounts of Egyptian religion, trying to make sense out of them, have to make up their own minds. There is no consensus. We have four major positions to choose from.

i) Egyptian religion was a collection of ancient animistic and polytheistic beliefs with no principle of order;

ii) Egyptian religion was a polytheism, but since all men and gods, in Egyptian belief, had a certain element or essence in common, they could melt into each other and combine their behaviors in various ways. A certain appearance of oneness comes out of this, yet it is not really monotheism but monophysitism, the sharing of a single nature.

iii) The true core of Egyptian religion was a high *philosophy* centered on an idea of the One or the Absolute, with a polytheistic religion for the uninitiated.

iv) Egyptian religion is marked from beginning to end by a dual tendency, towards monotheism and towards polytheism; sometimes the monotheistic tendency approaches the nobility of Old Testament thought at its best.

For my part, I find the first position unreasonable. It is not true of other African religions. The second and third ideas are really related. The third idea (see note 11) comes from Greek and Roman sources, passes through Renaissance occultism and settles into a kind of sacrosanct immobility in the Masonic tradition. It links with the second in this sense, that if the "single nature" referred to in argument ii) is thought of in philosophical terms (as it must have been in such a well-developed civilization) it approaches an idea of the One or the Absolute not unrelated to concepts found in Greek philosophy. Yet, while it is reasonable to think that certain schools of Egyptian thought held such a philosophy, we have many expressions of Egyptian belief which speak of devotion to a God Who reminds us much more of the God of the Old Testament than the philosophical One or Absolute of the Greeks.[12] There are also, of course, relationships with the Father-God of the old African tradition.

Accordingly, it seems reasonable to me to accept the fourth position. I think that one can accept the existence of beliefs like those in ii) and iii) as possible philosophical extensions of it. As to the first position, it again seems to me unreasonable, not only because it would make Egyptian religion less well-organized than, say, West African, but because of the rigidity of Egyptian religious terminology and pictorial representation, which of itself indicates that the ideas were ordered in some way.

This is, I repeat, a choice. The interested reader will no doubt make his own. The study of Egyptian religion is an academic battleground.

Swedenborg's position, in his philosophical writings, is somewhere between the third and the fourth, tending towards the fourth. The common educated opinion of his time varies between the first and the third.

We may learn much more about the religious history of the pre-Israelite churches from Swedenborg's theological works. In the works we are concerned with here, his idea of pre-Greek and particularly Egyptian religion comes from the Greek authors themselves, who more or less recognize the dialectical "pre-Platonic" nature of the latter. In this respect Swedenborg resembles Hegel, who forms a generalized picture of the main outlines of Egyptian thought by examination of Greek authors, though in a more thorough fashion than Swedenborg. Hegel is only slightly assisted by the rudimentary Egyptology of his time, and actually has little more data to work upon than his predecessors.

Swedenborg's approach is narrowly and selectively rational. He does not follow the common practice of his time, that of scatter-gun comparison of biblical and mythological images, but focuses on a distinct ideology, the Orphic cosmogony. He does not identify it as such in the *Principia*, perhaps to avoid entering into literary and philosophical controversy, but the system he refers to is undoubtedly Orphic. In this respect he seems to align himself to a certain degree with Renaissance Neoplatonic interpretations of Greek myth and with eighteenth-century survivals of this tradition, but in a cautious and minimal fashion, without reference to Greek ideas of Egyptian mysteries, occult traditions and so forth. [13] He has arrived at this position by way of geometry and mechanics. He is interested in ancient natural philosophy and cosmogony, not magic.

We do not know if Orpheus was a mythical figure or an historical reformer turned into a demigod by his later followers. Most Greek writers and the learned scholar, Jane Harrison, thought him to have been a real man.[14] I will follow this line because it seems to me that Orphism, like Pythagoreanism, has all the qualities of a philosophical cult based upon ancient images, that it was invented by an intellectual or intellectuals. It is hard to imagine how it could have been at any time a religion of ordinary people, who have always preferred concrete imagery.

Swedenborg's discussion arises out of his consideration of the sun enclosed in its self-generated vortex. Unless the sun were surrounded by such a vortex, which set limits to the solar space, there could be no such solar space at all: there is no space without limits. Only the sun is to be found in this space, no non-solar matter.

Yet there must be something here which will later give birth to the planets, since reason tells us, he says in the *Principia*, "...that the planets must derive their origin from causes in time and in place; that causes are latent in first principles; in short that the earths in our system must have originated successively." These causes must have existed in the active solar space. The life-giving power of the sun is apparent to the senses, and is accompanied by a form-making power. Solar heat, as an expression of creative Providence, which determines the lives of things, must also determine their forms, because these are expressions of the life. Since ancient man had the same powers of reason that we have he could therefore have arrived at the idea of a generative solar chaos. The italics in the following quotation are mine. I wish to stress that he is referring to intuitive reasoning, not the logic based on experiment of his own *Principia*.

> Therefore the ancient philosophers, *from the use of reason alone,* maintained that there was a kind of universal condition both of the sun and planets, in which there was simultaneously everything which could

conduce to the perfection of the world-system. That is to say that both Tartarus and the sun, day and night, soft bodies and hard, were latent, in a word, all the seeds and elements of the things that were subsequently produced. And if this universal condition were in the vortex, it follows that it could be only near the sun. Let us first consider these opinions of the ancient philosophers, before we proceed to the immediate subject of our chapter. All, with the exception of Aristotle, seem to have favored the conjecture, that, primevally, there was only an unformed, composite, confused mass, in which there was as yet no differentiation; that from this mass all things afterwards went forth as an infant from the womb. From this conception they afterwards deduced the origin of things. *They supposed that there was a state of conflict among these elements, not unlike that in fermentation, for they knew that nature by a kind of combat and collision tended to a state of equilibrium.* On the cessation of discord, heavy bodies passed to their place, and light bodies to theirs; bodies without motion and bodies with motion sought respectively their proper positions; and thus *from reason guided by only a very few phenomena*, they concluded that when the strife of nature was over, a harmonious world-system arose out of chaos. These philosophers, therefore, were shrewd enough to guess the preexistence of a chaotic condition; *although they were ignorant of the series by which the various things were brought into existence.* The philosopher naturally embraces the opinion which seems to him to be the most agreeable to reason, the most resembling visible nature, and which presents the least difficulties; for he is anxious, of course, that in future ages his system should not fall to pieces, in consequence of inherent contrarieties. *The mind, therefore, naturally chooses the least difficult path, which it pursues like a traveller in the dark, who gropes his way in the direction in which he meets with fewest obstacles; and so follows the path, although he does not see it; he touches the various objects that come in his way, though he knows nothing of what he is touching, and arrives at the end of his journey, though he cannot tell how.* In the same way, the ancient philosophers were led to surmise the existence of a chaotic state common to the sun and the planets; *although in what manner it existed, of what kind it was, and by what means it came to be such, they were entirely ignorant.* This at least we may assume from ancient philosophy—a conclusion highly agreeable to reason—that primevally there was a *universal chaotic condition both of the sun and planets*; on the other hand, any other hypothesis is less conformable to the facts. Epicurus maintained that the whole universe arose from a chaotic state; not only the earth, but the planets, the sun, and all the stars; that is to say, the whole world-system. Hence Aristophanes observes:

> "Chaos and night
> Black Erebus, and squalid Tartarus,
> Were first of all; earth, air, nor heaven was yet.
> But in unmeasured gulfs of Erebus,
> The black-winged Night first lays a windy egg,
> Whence in the circling hours sprang wished-for LOVE,
> The golden feathers glitt'ring on his back,
> Resembling the tempestuous vortices;
> He through the wild domain of Tartarus
> Mingled with chaos' darkly winged form,
> Begot our race and brought us forth to light.
> Th'immortal kind, ere LOVE confounded all things,
> Had no existence yet; but soon as they
> Were mingled, heaven with earth arose, and earth
> And all the gods' imperishable race."[15]

This is followed by a long quotation from Ovid's *Metamorphoses*, Book I, Fable II, which describes how the four elements were separated from chaos, a passage of remarkable beauty and power which always reminded commentators, before it became a scholarly *gaffe* to draw attention to such things, of the Book of Genesis.[16] As William Golding says in the "Epistle" accompanying his 1567 translation of the *Metamorphoses*—

> What man is he but would suppose the author of this booke
> The first foundation of his woorke from Moyses wryghtings tooke?

—which is not Swedenborg's position (he believes in a parallel tradition) but is certainly better than ignoring the problem. Swedenborg goes on—

> It was the general opinion of ancient philosophers that Night and Tartarus originated from chaos; that from Night sprang the Earth, the Ocean, the Heaven or the ether, and also Love; so that Night and

Tartarus were first-born and twins; that from these arose everything else of which the world consists. The ancients held also that, from the same chaos, the gods and goddesses derived their origin; hence they believed that their origin was not from eternity, but in time, and coeval with that of the earth; especially as some god or other presided over each element, and, indeed, over everything of which they had any general conception. The God who separated the various things out of the chaotic mass they denominated Love. Ovid, however, says that he was ignorant which of the gods it was that performed this office; for he observes:

"The Power divine
Or kindlier Nature bade their contest cease"

And again:

When thus whoever of the Gods it was
Disposed the severed mass, and severing ranged
Its elements,—first, lest our Earth should lie
From end to end one flat and level tract,
Into the fashion of a mighty globe
He orbed her form"

Aristophanes likewise observes:

Th'immortal kind, ere LOVE confounded all things,
Had no existence yet; but soon as they
Were mingled, heaven with ocean rose, and earth
And all the gods' imperishable race."

The Mosaic philosophy in some measure coincides with the ancient philosophy of the Egyptians, and with this of the Greeks and Romans; for Moses also believes that there was a chaos, since he relates that "The earth was unformed and void, and darkness was on the face of the abyss; [and the Spirit of God moved upon the face of the waters;]" he makes mention, therefore, of a chaos, darkness, an abyss, and also of a Spirit. Some have, consequently, held the opinion that the chaos of Moses was the same as the chaos of the ancients; that the darkness he mentions was the same as their night, which arose from chaos; that his abyss was the same as the Tartarus or ocean of the ancients; that the "Spirit upon the waters" was the same as the Intelligence and Love of their theory. Moses, having narrated the origin of the earth from chaos, begins with light; and afterwards places the greater and lesser luminaries in the heavens, such as the sun, moon and stars. Having stated these facts, he says that, "The heavens and the earth were finished, with the whole host of them." He also refers to certain gods and sons of gods who disported with the daughters of men; and also to other details, to which we find resemblances in ancient philosophy. It is said in the eighth chapter of Proverbs that God set the world (or sphere) on the face of the abyss; and many other things which authors have shown who have written on chaos.[17]

The central image of the above complex is that of the cosmic egg, the egg laid, Aristophanes says, by "black-winged Night." This is the primary image of the Orphic cosmogony, here related by Swedenborg to the sun enclosed in its vortex. The aforementioned Jane Harrison, a highly regarded scholar of the beginning of the twentieth century, says, of the same passage from Aristophanes' *The Birds* which Swedenborg quotes, "This is pure Orphism."[18]

There are the best reasons in the world for taking seriously the statement of Proclus (see footnote 13), that "All theology among the Greeks is sprung from the mystical doctrine of Orpheus." True, the myths and iconographies of the Greek gods have very complex and ancient roots, some of them going back to Indo-European cultures well outside the Near East and Mediterranean. Proclus, though, is writing of theology, of discussions, in philosophical terms, of the nature of God and the gods. And here we can find nothing older in Greece than the Orphic tradition. In identifying this as the thread to be followed, Swedenborg chose wisely.[19] We can now identify a clear line of proto-Greek and Indo-European culture running back through the Greek "Dark Ages" to earlier Mycenean and Minoan times, and there we find ourselves, at least in the Minoan case, in a sophisticated culture in full intellectual contact with Egypt and the Levant. The Greek culture we know came into being in the 8th and 7th centuries BC as a result of stimuli from Asia Minor and the Levant, quickly taking on a character of its own. The Greeks adopted in particular the Phoenician alphabet, which is phonetic, and this in itself must have been a major determinant of what we think of as the "Greek miracle." The art of writing was no longer a difficult and cumbersome if ideologically rich representation of *meanings*; it was a mere code, easy to learn, of the sounds of speech. A vast area of traditional learning is "blocked out," will never reach the Greek mind; but at the same time the Greeks are protected from the huge and oppressive knowledge-bureaucracies of the older societies, in which knowledge is codified in such a fashion that it can never be accessible to the ordinary person.[20]

In *The Art of Greece: its Origins in the Mediterranean and Near East*, the Turkish scholar Ekrem Akurgal demonstrates the complete dependence of early Greek high culture on that of its Near Eastern neighbors. He points out, for example, the debt owed by the *Theogony* of Hesiod to the mythology of the Hurrians and Hittites. He tells us that the so-called "archaic smile" of early Greek sculpture came from Syria, and that such fantastic figures as "griffins, sphinxes, centaurs, sirens, chimaeras and images of Pegasos and the Gorgon" came from older Near Eastern arts, as did styles of clothing and hairdressing, musical instruments and ornamental designs. The first canons of artistic form, what Akurgal calls the "guiding codes" of Greek art, also came from the Near East. And he says that "...from the mysterious wisdom of Near Eastern priests and from the millenial lore of the Orient, philosophy and the exact sciences developed in the sixth century BC in the Ionian territory of Anatolia."[21]

Nevertheless, the reworking of the inherited tradition was in many cases almost complete. We can see the Hurrian-Hittite elements in Hesiod clearly enough, if we look for them, but they are thoroughly transmuted and it would be foolish to talk of the *Theogony* as a "neo-Hittite" poem. If we attack those who feel they can praise Greek mathematics and science only by besmirching the achievements of Egyptian mathematics and science, which the Greeks themselves held in high regard, we attack the racism and ahistorical blindness of this point of view, not the achievements of Greek culture, whose glory, if no longer that of a miracle, remains.

What we are interested in here is something which is not completely transmuted, in which the line of transmission from more ancient times may be seen clearly.

I am not brave enough to tackle the question of where Orpheus and his cult came from. Herodotus tells us that the Orphic rites were Egyptian and Pythagorean. He says they were the same or almost the same as the rites of the wine-god Dionysus (note Swedenborg's reference to fermentation as a cosmogonic symbol). Apollodorus says that Orpheus "invented the mysteries of Dionysus." Yet Orpheus was a Thracian. To further complicate things, he is said to have been buried in Lesbos. His cult has distinct Cretan affinities, yet Diodorus tells us, again, that he studied in Egypt. What is certain, though, is that the Orphic cosmogony is closely related to cosmogonies the Greeks themselves attributed to Phoenicia, Syria and Egypt. Since Crete had close cultural connections, at various times, with both Egypt and the Levant, this evidence does not necessarily contradict the confusing biographical data. It is possible that if we knew much more (we probably never shall know enough) a synthesis of these apparently conflicting statements would be possible. In the meantime, though, the Phoenician and Syrian affinities must be our best guide.

What we want to look at is the Orphic idea of the creation of the cosmos, since this and this only is relevant to Swedenborg's argument. And, as Harrison says, "The cardinal essential doctrine is the world-egg from which sprang the first articulate god, source and creator of all, Eros." This egg is Chaos, in which the primal elements are intermingled in Orphic belief. The very universe has the shape of an egg, according to Achilles Tatius.[22]

The Orphic cosmogony is, as stated above, clearly related to a set of cosmogonic beliefs which Greek authors attributed to the Phoenicians and Syrians.[23] And I hope the reader will excuse the "catalogue" nature of the paragraph which follows. It is made up of fragments culled from authors who are themselves only known to us in fragments, namely from passing quotations in works on other subjects.

Mochos (ca. AD 500, but basing himself on older material of Phoenician origin) describes the Phoenician cosmogony as beginning with Fire and Air. They engender a son, 'Olam (Greek Chronos), who "makes love to himself" (an Egyptian idea), and thus engenders Chusorus, who in turn engenders the cosmic egg. This egg is the sky (Greek Uranus) but on cracking open it becomes a binary—sky and earth—and from the cracked open egg emerge the winds. Eudemos (fourth century BC) has 'Olam or Chronos giving birth to Desire and Darkness: these in turn engender Fire and Breath, who become the parents of the cosmic egg. Eudemos identifies this cosmogony as "Phoenician" but he also gives us a specifically Orphic one, in which the first entity is Chronos, who engenders Fire, Air and the Void, from which the cosmic egg is born. Athenagoras (fourth century AD but probably using sources of the sixth century BC) has Water as the first entity; from Water comes Mud, which is female, and their child is Chronos/Heracles—a composite god possessing the body of a dragon and two heads, one that of a lion and the other that of a god. Chronos/Heracles lays the cosmic egg, which splits in two to form heaven and earth. The theory of Athenagoras, I might add, is particularly close to the creation-account in the Akkadian creation epic, *Enuma Elish*, in which "Sweet Water" and "Salt Water" engender silt (see Thorkild Jacobsen in the collection of essays tendentiously titled *Before Philosophy*).

The above is bound to seem a bit of a jumble. This can not be avoided, because the meaning of the symbols had been lost by the time these accounts were set down. A complete system has dwindled into a few bizarre images. At least two things are clear, though.

First of all, this particular story of creation must have been given an iconographic representation, such as we find in temple art. The image of the two-headed dragon is the sort of thing we should find in a frieze or sculpture. Second (apart from the adaptations to Greek myth, which must have come later), we have both Egyptian and biblical resonances here. Olam's making love to himself is unmistakably reminiscent of an Egyptian story about Ra, in which he engenders worlds by masturbation, a repellent symbol of an intellectually subtle idea, which reminds us of the ambiguity of "ancient wisdom" as it has come down to us. However, we also have the separation of heaven and earth in the cracking of the cosmic egg, reminiscent of the vault which separates the waters above from the waters below in the *Genesis* account; the winds moving between the heaven-vault and the earth remind us of the Spirit of God moving on the face of the waters; the marriage between Water and Mud reminds us of the earth-mound emerging from the primeval waters in Egyptian, Mesopotamian and *Genesis* accounts; "Desire" and "Darkness" remind us of the form-making intent of the God of *Genesis* hovering over the dark primeval waters. We are not, on the basis of this evidence, justified in saying that the Orphic and Phoenician cosmogonies, which are to all intents and purposes the same, are derived from the Bible. They may well be more ancient, relating to some "Bible before the Bible," so to speak. We can, though, say that there is a clear relationship.

We can also say that this system was highly philosophical, at least in its origins. The folk imagination does not invent cosmogonies which begin with "Desire" and "Darkness." What we have, in the marriage of Water and Mud, of Fire and Air (or Breath), and their origin in the marriage of Desire and Darkness is a symbolic form of four-element theory, of the kind associated with Empedocles.

The most detailed account of the Phoenician cosmogony—and it is still nothing more than a wretched summary—is found in Philo of Byblius, a Phoenician of Hellenistic culture who lived in the first century AD. His *Phoenician History* was preserved in part by the early Christian writer, Eusebius. Philo transcribed or paraphrased the writings of a Phoenician priest or poet, Sanchuniathon (sometimes spelled "Sanchoniathon"), who lived, it seems, sometime between 1300 and 900 BC. I will attempt to clarify this problem of dates later.

Everything began, Sanchnuniathon says, in what we may describe as a two-part void. We have "dark air" or a chaos of activity symbolized by dark and stormy air, and, opposed to it, a "turbid chaos." Both were unbounded and without limit and "for many ages" remained so. After this very long period of time the dark wind became "enamoured of its own first principles," and in this inward-turning or self-conjoining act, which Sanchuniathon calls "Desire," there took place the first formation of the creative principles of things. "Desire" had no consciousness of itself—and here it becomes clear that we are dealing with an early form of materialism—but from the union of the dark wind with itself was generated a certain elementary form of life which resembled a slime or the putrescent form of a fluid secretion. All the seeds of creation and the universe itself sprang from this mixed watery/solid substance. Sanchuniathon calls this slime *Mot*, a Phoenician god identified with the heat of the summer, death and sterility. We note the dualism of thought, a chaos which is both generative (wet) and sterile (dry).

Among the first entities to appear in this viscous sea were "animals without sensation." We learn nothing of these creatures or things; but from them, in time, "intelligent animals" were produced. These were called "Watchers of the Heavens"[24] and were egg-shaped. Then there shone forth from Mot the sun, the moon and the stars. The air carried their light, and thus sea and land were warmed, and winds, clouds and tempests of rain were produced. The heat of the sun produced the circulation of elements, which were separated, carried out of their places and met in the air. From their collisions there came lightning and thunderbolts. These aroused the "intelligent animals" and they began, male and female, to move about in the sea and on the land.

It is not difficult to see that the cosmogony of Sanchuniathon, which he directly attributes to Taaut (Egyptian Thoth), was rationalist in the materialist mode, and ancestral to many of the speculations of the pre-Socratic Greek philosophers. Sanchuniathon, or his source of mixed Egyptian/Phoenician culture, does not believe in the gods. This is clear in the next section of the text, where Sanchuniathon says scornfully that men began to worship the very fruits of the earth on which they fed, thus creating the gods out of "their own weakness and timidity of soul." But behind the skepticism of Sanchuniathon (and/or some priest of Taaut) lies a sacred text, a theistic account of creation which he is attempting to debunk. And this may be related without difficulty to the traditional cosmologies of Egypt and Phoenicia. That the text is ancient can

hardly be questioned. The Phoenician god Mot was not known to us
until the discovery of the Ugaritic texts in 1929. In addition, Sanchuniathon relates his cosmogony to an Egyptian source, but Philo
of Byblos draws no attention to the most obvious Egyptian connection and was probably unaware of it. For Mot must be related to
Mut, the wife of Ammon or Amen-Ra: her name, Budge tells us,
means "Mother"; and he adds that "in all her attributes we see that
she was regarded as the great 'world mother' who conceived and
brought forth whatever existed."[25] In Egyptian myth she is said to
have been self-produced, and this is not really in contradiction with
Sanchuniathon, who has her, him or it as the end-product of a
process which began with the self-fertilization of the "dark wind," a
process which, as a whole, is certainly self-production. She is, says
Budge, another form of Nut, "the great primeval water abyss from
which all things sprang."[26]

As I have implied more than once (e.g. in reference to Marxism),
the enemies of Christianity sometimes turn out, unwittingly, to be
her best friends. Thus I take pleasure in quoting Porphyry's *Against
the Christians* (third century AD).

> The truest history of the Semitic peoples is contained in that (of)
> Sanchuniathon of Beirut because his most closely agrees with the
> topology and onomastics of the region. Furthermore he used as raw
> material the records of Hierobalus, the priest of Ieuo (pronounced "Yeh-
> woh"—NN)), and dedicated his book to Adibalos, the king of Beirut,
> since it had been approved by the king and his scholars. These men
> lived before the Trojan War, almost about the time Moses did, as the
> Phoenician king-lists show. Sanchuniathon, who fell in love with the
> subject, collected and wrote his work from the records of the local cities
> in Phoenicia and from the temple registers. It is further said that he
> lived during the reign of Semiramis, the Assyrian queen whom the
> chroniclers tell us flourished either before the time of the Trojan War or
> else was its contemporary.[27]

In his own introduction to his summary of Sanchuniathon, Philo
Byblius says—

> ...Sanchuniathon, who happened upon the writings of the Ammoni-
> ans, composed secretly in their temples (and naturally not known to all

men), set to work to master them. Having done that, he was able to write, and, most importantly, to put away the received myths and their attendant allegories. However, the priests, who came later, wishing to restore the mythic character, swathed the *History* in silence and obscurity, whereupon the mystic sense arose, even among the Greeks, it not having touched them previously.

Philo is thus attributing the origin of the "mystic sense" among the Greeks to the influence of Phoenician and Egyptian priests, and probably, though his wording is vague, to priests of the cult of Ammon. Porphyry is saying that he received his raw material from a priest of Ieuo or "Yeh-woh." But since Sanchuniathon says that his cosmogony came from Thoth, this must mean that the priest of Ieuo was in possession of Egyptian texts.

Of course, we must approach such late commentators as Porphyry and Philo with caution. At the same time we have no grounds to reject them, particularly when their data square with facts we know and they did not. On the evidence, Ieuo is pretty obviously "Yahweh," the Hebrew Jehovah.[28] Unless the God of the Hebrews had been adopted into the Phoenician pantheon at this time (which is remotely possible, considering the syncretistic nature of Phoenician religion), the teachings of Taaut were perhaps transmitted to Sanchuniathon by a priest of Israel.

Summing up, we have seen that Swedenborg at this time in his life interprets the *Genesis* creation in terms of what is now called the "Day-Age" theory. This is based on the statement in Psalm 90, verse 4, that "a thousand years in thy sight are but as yesterday when it is past." So Swedenborg's position, when he thinks of the development of the cosmos in temporal terms, can resemble modern theories of Divinely-directed evolution, though he will also insist that the notion of instantaneous creation is closer to the non-temporal reality.

He believes firmly in the verbal Divine inspiration of the *Genesis* account. Yet he must still find a contemporary philosophical basis for it. God does not communicate with men in words they cannot understand and their understanding is formed in large part by their sense of how the material world works. The *Genesis* account arose in a world dominated by Egyptian ideas of the cosmos; indeed it was set down by a man educated in "all the wisdom of the Egyptians." Although the early eighteenth-century idea of Egyptian thought is spotty at best and in many respects plain wrong, he is able to form an idea of the philosophical basis of Egyptian symbolism which will in many respects resemble that of Hegel roughly a hundred years later. In particular he concentrates on a certain Egyptian tradition which, he assumes, was ancestral on one hand to the physical cosmologies of the Orphics and pre-Socratics, and on the other to that of the "Mosaic philosophy."

A remarkable series of conclusions may be drawn from the above and we shall consider them in the next chapter. They involve some speculation but not of a rash kind. They fit in with established chronologies, and with opinions on the nature of the Egyptian gods which, if not universally accepted, are held by many respected scholars. They throw a new light on parts of the Bible. In doing so, they reveal the rationality of Swedenborg's belief that the way back to the sources of the Mosaic cosmology may be traced through a cosmogony which he found in the poets, but which we now call "Orphic."

ENDNOTES

1 Alfred Acton included this in his translation of *The Word Explained*, but it is also available separately.

2 At about this time he was warned in a dream not to discontinue attending church and taking communion (Sigstedt, p. 203). After his illumination he attended church from time to time, particularly the Swedish church in London (ibid., p. 381), though he found the implicit tritheism of the sermons deeply disturbing. At his time of death he received communion according to the Lutheran rite (ibid., pp. 431–433).

3 Of course, I am not suggesting at all that the *Genesis* account was influenced by the pre-Socratics. It is much older than that. I am not a biblical scholar so I do not comment on textual matters, but comparative studies of mythology emphatically show that much of the account, as story, is as old as anything in human culture.

4 Swedenborg, *The Worship and Love of God*, pp. 24–25.

5 Quotations and materials in this section come from Budge, *The Gods of the Egyptians* I, pp. 322–358 and II, pp. 68–84. Apart from quotations, any paraphrase of Budge's conclusions is specifically attributed to him. References to other sections of the book are individually noted.

6 Diop, *Civilisation or Barbarism*, p. 345.

7 Budge, *Gods...*I, p. 173.

8 Same, I, p. 203.

9 An amusing if fascinating collection of such theories is found in Peter Tompkins, *Secrets of the Great Pyramid*. Its appearance in the bibliography does not mean

I subscribe to any of these, but Tompkins' book is the most complete collection of notions about the Great Pyramid, good or bad.

10 An example of such may be found in Otto Neugebauer, one of the finest minds of the older school to devote himself to ancient astronomy. Unfortunately, he simply loses control of himself when he is discussing Egypt. After pointing out that the Egyptian calendar was carried into our culture by Hellenistic astronomers and was used as late as 1543 AD by Copernicus, he triumphantly announces the reason for this. It is that the usefulness of the Egyptian calendar is due to its simplicity, and that "the simplicity of the Egyptian calendar is a sign of its primitivity; it is the remainder of primitive crudeness..." (p. 196). Furthermore, it has no astronomical basis (p. 197) and "is in all respects the result of practical needs alone." Not only does he inexplicably dismiss the testimony of Greek authors on the astronomical origins of the Egyptian calendar; he takes simplicity and practicality as indicators of primitive crudity, when it is normal to take them as indicators of the science of civilized peoples. In an article on the Egyptian decans he says that they are based on "a cylinder projection of the celestial sphere with the equator as circle of contact" (p. 207). (Could Anaximander's strange cylindrical earth have arisen from a misreading of this?) He further tells us that the decans survived in some form in the Hellenistic world and in India, also "forming an important element in the iconography of the late Middle Ages and the Renaissance." However, it is clear that after the decline of Egyptian civilisation the geometry of the decan system, which he has reconstructed from Egyptian texts of the Middle and New Kingdom, had been lost. Once again he describes the Egyptian system as "crude," but if this is so we may wonder at the greater crudity of the Greek, Indian and European astronomers who had forgotten, and could not reconstruct, the original mode of projection. This had to await, note, a skilled modern mathematician like Neugebauer himself. Finally, he shows how the Great Pyramid was oriented "with remarkable accuracy" (pp. 211–213), but we are not surprised to learn that this remarkable accuracy was due, once again, to the *primitive* nature of Egyptian procedures. All this is both sad and ridiculous. I do not presume to peer into Neugebauer's mind. But it *looks* as if his regard for factual truth and mathematical accuracy has led him to conclusions which show that Egyptian astronomy and mathematics were on a high level and were locally developed, while his prejudices have dictated a belief that no "negro" or "mulatto" civilisation could possibly have made such discoveries. The result is completely irrational.

11 Budge, *Gods...*, passim. Cheik Anta Diop, in *The African Origin of Civilisation* (pp. 6–7), argues convincingly that Egyptian monotheism began with the worship of the Sudanese Amon (Dogon form *Amma*), who had a dialectical male/female form (p. 112).

In a book written when the decipherment of Egyptian texts had hardly begun, Sir J. Gardner Wilkinson said—

> The division of God into his attributes was in this manner. As soon as he was thought to have any reference to his works, or to man, he ceased to be quiescent; he became an agent; and he was no longer the One, but distinguishable and divisible, according to his supposed character, his actions and his influence on the world. He was then the Creator, the Divine Goodness (or the abstract idea of Good), Wisdom, Power, and the like; and as we speak of Him as the Almighty, the Merciful, the Everlasting, so the Egyptians gave to each of his various attributes a particular name. But they did more; they separated them; and to the uninitiated they became distinct gods. As one of these, the Deity was Amun; probably, the divine mind in operation, the bringer to light of the secrets

of its *hidden* will; and he had a complete human form, because man was the intellectual animal, and the principal design of the divine will in the creation. (*The Ancient Egyptians* I, p. 327).

This idea seems to be put together from various Greek sources, such as the Neoplatonists. The manner in which the thought is formulated is not an Egyptian one. From the texts we have it appears that the Egyptian method was to show rather than to tell. They represented their philosophies in images, as if concepts such as "goodness" and "mercy" meant nothing when they were not attached to concrete entities. Yet it is surprising how well Egyptian religion yields to this interpretation.

12 See Budge, *The Book of the Dead*: Introduction, pp. lxxxii xc, also his *Egyptian Religion* throughout.

13 The Renaissance idea of the Orphic theology was derived largely from such as Iamblichus and Proclus, the latter having written, "All theology among the Greeks is sprung from the mystical doctrine of Orpheus" (Wind, p. 36). An example of the survival of this tradition into the eighteenth century may be found in the text and notes of Mark Akenside's poem, *The Pleasure of Imagination* (1743). The tradition reemerges in full glory among the Romantic poets. The Orphic "world-egg" image also occurs in Thomas Burnet's *Telluris Theoria Sacra* (1681).

14 Harrison, p. xi.

15 Swedenborg, *Principia* II, pp. 174–176. The Victorian translation of Aristophanes is by C.A. Wheelwright and is provided by the translators. Discussing its merits or seeking to find a better version would take us too far afield.

16 Ovid was often treated with troubled respect and even a kind of veneration by Christian commentators up to the Renaissance, at which time the Christian and biblical interpretation of Ovid began to fade. Only the amorality of his *Art of Love* (which he fully repented of in his *Tristia*) prevented his elevation to the full rank of "pagan sage." This interpretation was to some extent revived during the nineteenth century, as illustrated in the notes of Henry Riley for the literal-prose Bohn Library translation of 1851, where he frankly says that Ovid's account of the Creation is of biblical origin. The philosophical content of the *Metamorphoses* is now seriously undervalued, as we might expect (see Otis, p. 394).

17 Swedenborg, *Principia* II, pp. 177–178. The translations are by King (Ovid) and Wheelwright (Aristophanes).

18 Harrison, *Prolegomena to the Study of Greek Religion*, p. 625.

19 If I adhere to Harrison's statement that the Orphic rites were "a blend of Egyptian and primitive Pelasgian (p. 459), I have made a choice of interpretations. Eliade (*Le Shamanisme*, p. 351 et seq.) finds many elements of ancient shamanism in the Orpheus myth, if not in the Orphic theology.

20 As I understand it, we cannot as yet determine in a scientific fashion the extent to which the Phoenician and Hebrew alphabets, which represented sounds and numbers, embodied symbolic systems. If the *Cabala* could be entirely trusted, then the treatise, *Sepher Yetzirah*, and the commentaries upon it, would indicate that the sounds of the Hebrew alphabet became as it were vocal hieroglyphics, each sound representing a category or class of symbolic meanings. Furthermore, each of these sounds would be associated with a symbolic number. But the *Cabala* contains so many elements from non-Hebrew religions, from the oldest documents to the medieval *Zohar*, that its witness appears very equivocal.

21 Akurgal, p. 223.

22 Harrison, p. 628.

23 The following accounts are paraphrased from Doria and Lenowitz (eds.) in *Origins*. The translations, in a 1960-ish beat jargon sprinkled with street obscenities, are annoying to read; but I must refer to this book because it is the most complete collection of a nonspecialist kind I have encountered and it includes much which is not available elsewhere.

24 The "Watchers of the Heavens" appear in the *Book of Enoch*. This is a text discovered in Ethiopia in 1773. Scholars say it dates from not long before the Christian era but do not explain its archaic world-picture, which seems to date from a much earlier time. There the "Watchers" are a generation of men of earliest times, who "polluted themselves with women" and engendered giants. They seem to be related to the angels who had intercourse with the daughters of men in *Genesis* VI: 1–4. Less familiar relationships also open up. In the *Greater Holy Assembly* of the *Cabala* the eyes of Macroprosopus, the Supreme Tri-Unity (Mather, *The Kabbala Unveiled*, p. 125, also Schaya, refs. *Arikh-Anpin*) are compared to the eyes of "the whales and fishes of the sea, which have no coverings for their eyes, nor eyebrows above their eyes, who sleep not, and require not a protection for the eye." Other elements of Sanchuniathon's account may be related to the *Cabala* but, as pointed out more than once herein, problems of dating make interpretation impossible.

25 Budge, *Gods...* II, p. 28.

26 The New Church scholar, C.Th. Odhner, discusses the figure of Mut in his *Correspondences of Egypt* (p. 86). There he relates her to "that first passive, receptive and reactive element in which and out of which all lower forms have been conceived and created." Some of Odhner's statements appear to be fantastic because he is writing for a New Church readership and need not explain the background of his ideas. He also has a tendency to confuse ancient natural philosophy with theology. Yet his book contains some remarkable formal insights. These would emerge more clearly if his arguments were reworked and more carefully substantiated, using the terms of Egyptian texts as well as the Christian terminology of Swedenborg.

27 Doria and Lenowitz (eds.), *Origins*, pp. 137–138, as also the quotation from Philo Byblius, which follows.

28 The name *Yah* appears as part of the name of a minor Ugaritic mythological figure, *Yah-El*, which is the same as Hebrew *Yo-El* or *Joel* (Gordon, pp. 24 and 61). There was no Canaanite god named *Yahweh* to my knowledge.

4

The Cosmic Egg

ncient texts cannot be interpreted unless we know when they were written. The dating of texts is a dull subject, but unless it is carefully considered we wander in the dark. It is really necessary that we try to date Sanchuniathon as well as we can. People who like puzzles will, I hope, enjoy the first pages of this chapter. But there is no harm in skipping, if the reader is simply content to accept my conclusions as made.

We have seen that the Orphic cosmogony may be traced at least as far back as the time of Sanchuniathon. Porphyry assumes that Sanchuniathon wrote when an Adibalos ruled in Beirut. This would have been, he says, before the Trojan War and at about the time of Moses and the Assyrian queen, Semiramis. There must have been a strong Egyptian influence in Phoenicia at the time—this would explain the presence of the "Ammonians" in Philo Byblius[1]—and there already existed an established cult of Ieuo, presumably "Yahweh." Now, this dating does not make sense at all. There could have been no established cult of Yahweh in Canaan at the time of Moses, and, though Egyptian cultural influences were then present in Phoenicia, as always, it was politically independent at the time.[2]

We do know there was, *at a much later time*, a king of Byblos named Abibaal, a name which, with the change of a consonant, would become Adibaal. Beirut and Byblos were only 28 miles apart, so the difference in town-names is not crucial, considering the vagueness of Porphyry's sources. We hear of Abibaal because an inscription has been found, carved on a statue of the Pharaoh Sosenq or Shishak: "Abibaal, king of Byblos, and the Egyptian overlord of Byblos have offered this to the goddess (Baalat) of Byblos and the god (Baal) of Byblos."[3] This can be dated to the last half of the tenth century, since the reign of Sosenq the First, or Shishak, was from about 945 to 912 BC, with the authorities differing by ten years or so. Abibaal was a king of Byblos, though not necessarily Beirut (we do not know), at a time of Egyptian overlordship. The name "Abibaal" is not "Adibaal" but the change of a consonant is not bad, considering the length of time this tradition was preserved.

We come now to the date of Semiramis. The inaccurate Greek version of Assyrian history, which was all Porphyry and early Christian chroniclers had to go on, recorded two Semiramises. The first was the wife of Ninus, a mythical king of Assyria. Ninus and Semiramis are said to have conquered the known world from Libya to the borders of India in very ancient times. It is this Semiramis that St. Augustine refers to (*City of God*, Bk. XVIII, Ch. 2) when he says that she was a contemporary of Abraham. He then attempts to date her in relation to the Great Flood of the Bible and to flood-stories in Greek history. He quotes (Ch. 8) St. Jerome and the Christian historian Eusebius as believing that the "flood of Ogyges" occurred during the reign of Phoroneus, "second king of the Greeks," but he also refers to other writers who placed it three hundred years earlier. Finally, Augustine has ten "Siconian kings" (ten thirty-year generations of them, totalling three hundred years) between the time of Semiramis and that of Phoroneus, which would mean that the "other writers" he refers to would date Semiramis to the time of the Ogygian flood. The chronologists of the early church usually assumed that the exodus of the Hebrews from Egypt, with the drowning of the Egyptian cavalry in the rising waters of the Red Sea, took place at about the time of either "the flood of Ogyges" or "the flood of Deucalion," two deluge-stories in the Greek tradition.

By the way, the reader need not worry if he has trouble figuring out the above. There is nothing to figure out. The chronology is a mess. Nothing fits together.

We now have two faulty reconstructions of ancient history, one holding that Semiramis lived at about the time of the flood of Ogyges, another holding that the "flood of Ogyges" occurred during the time of Moses. Though I do not know which historian Porphyry was using as a source (and it does not matter since they were all wrong), this explains why he could believe that Semiramis lived at the time of Moses. He has collated two errors to arrive at a third.

The Trojan War was commonly dated by the Greeks at about 1184 BC, while the modern date for the Exodus from Egypt, thus for the time of Moses, is in the area around 1290 BC. The Exodus date, thanks to the clarity of the biblical account (the confusion arises when attempts are made to relate biblical history to those of other peoples), would then be close to that accepted in the time of Porphyry, as before the Trojan War (see the quotation from him in the last chapter). There is no point in quibbling about a century here or there when the whole is so imprecise.

However, there was another Semiramis, a historical ruler of Assyria who had taken on, in the Greek mind, some of the attributes of the mythical one. Herodotus tells us that (this) Semiramis lived some five generations before an occupation of Nineveh by the Medians. We now know that this would have taken place either in 653 or 612 BC.[4] If we take a generation as about thirty years, its usual meaning, Semiramis would have lived about 150 years before 653 or 612 BC, thus about 803 or 762 BC. Once again, Herodotus surprises us by his accuracy! An Assyrian stele indicates that a Semiramis was regent for about five years on behalf of her young son, Adadnirari III, who formally began to rule when his father died in 810 BC.[5] Thus her rule plausibly extended from 810 to 805 BC, close to 803 BC and less than half a century from 762 BC.

It turns out then that the dates of Porphyry fall into two roughly-defined groups. The first is about the time of Moses, before the Trojan War and during the reign of the mythical Semiramis, a period which covers roughly a century between 1290 and 1184 BC. The second, if we assume that "Adibalos of Beirut" was really Abibaal of Byblos (this is only a reasonable guess) falls somewhere in between the last quarter of the tenth (1000–900) to the end of the ninth (900–800) century BC, and includes the reign of the or a real Semiramis. Again, we have a loosely-defined period of about a century. It is therefore reasonable to assume that Porphyry and his sources, working on the tradition that Sanchuniathon had lived in the time of Semiramis, had tried to work him into "universal history" by proceeding on the belief that Semiramis had lived during the time of Moses.

Perhaps the key to the mystery is that the name "Semiramis" is a Greek version of Assyrian Shammurat, which means "dove," the bird of Ishtar, Lady of War and Queen of Love. The Semiramis I have called "mythical" was probably the goddess Ishtar herself. This was the final opinion of the great Assyriologist, Francois Lenormant (see note 5).

By dating Sanchuniathon so early, though, Porphyry had made the figure of Hierobalus incomprehensible. In the story of Porphyry he is a priest, probably of Jehovah, who bears a mixed Greek-Phoenician name and is apparently depicted as passing along secret Egyptian religious writings to a Phoenician. He could not have lived during the time of Moses, when the Hebrews had not yet conquered what would become Israel and Judah. Such a figure, however, would be typical of the period following the reign of Solomon (whose dates are 961–922 BC), a time of Hebrew/Canaanite syncretism of the type continually denounced by the prophets. Furthermore, the cosmology of Sanchuniathon seems to belong to a period of syncretism and religious doubt, more like the ninth than the thirteenth century BC. As to the incongruously part-Greek name, "Hierobalos," this would have been a translation, by some chronicler, of a Semitic original.

It then appears, though the case could not be said to be proven until we have discovered the text of Sanchuniathon himself, that a reasonable if uncertain interpretation of what evidence we have is that Sanchuniathon wrote sometime between 945 and 800 BC. This period is close to the time when the developing Greek civilisation we know (not, that is, the earlier cultures of Mycenean type) was being strongly influenced from Phoenicia and other Near Eastern regions. It is now assumed, for example, that Greek adoption of the Phoenician alphabet took place in the first half of the eighth century BC. The earliest Greek cosmogonies may thus be traced back to Phoenicia in a historical sense, as many Greeks said they were. We can easily see that these Greek/Phoenician resemblances are not fortuitous or due to the folk-survival of myth-patterns.

Sanchuniathon's cosmogony is of mixed Egyptian and Phoenician origin, and it is attributed to the "Ammonians" or followers of Amen-Ra. There must have been in the traditions of the Ammonians something to interest a priest of "Yeh-woh," if he was the one who collected the materials which Sanchuniathon used. We know nothing of his motives, of course. He could have been a syncretist, attempting to prove that all gods are the same. He could have been an atheist or agnostic, attempting to prove that all stories of gods are fables. He could have been an orthodox Hebrew controversialist, attempting to prove that, as opposed to Jehovah, the Egyptian and Phoenician gods were only embodied natural forces and dimly remembered national heroes. He could have been simply a man who liked to collect manuscripts. It is even possible that he was not a priest of Yahweh and that Ieuo was some other god of the same name, but this would be purely conjectural because we know of no such god.

Amen was a very ancient god in Egypt, but his worship took on a new character after the heresy of Akhnaton or Amenhotep IV. Akhnaton is sometimes thought of as "the father of monotheism" but this assumption is quite false, since monotheism was as old in Egypt as the culture itself.[6] Akhnaton worshipped Aten, the visible disc of the sun, and it soon became clear that he would tolerate no other cult. Budge calls his religion "something like a glorified materialism."[7]

It could be argued, though, that the attack on polytheism implicit in the Aten cult, even though it may have arisen out of a materialist bias, made it clear to the priests that some form of overt monotheism was now necessary. For in the cult of Amen, revived after the Akhnaton heresy was destroyed, we find a form of *credal* monotheism, a monotheism which consciously declares itself to be such and somewhat equivocally asserts itself against polytheism by declaring Amen the source of all divine substance. With the beginning of the XIXth dynasty which began in roughly 1305–1290 BC with the accession of Rameses I, who had taken over after the restorationist Horemheb, we find Amen described as the One God. By the time of the XXth or XXIst dynasty, thus some time roughly between 1200 and 1050 BC (the authorities do not agree on precise dates), Amen-Ra is "the chief of all the gods...the father of the gods and the creator of men and women...the lord of intelligence...the Only One." He is also a universal god: "...though makest the color of the skin of one race to be different from that of another, but however many may be the varieties of mankind, it is thou that makest them to live." By the time of the XXIst dynasty (beginning in the 1060s BC), Amen-Ra is "the first divine matter which gave birth unto subsequent divine matter...the Only One who hath made every thing...whose vicar is the divine Disc."[8]

We must speak only of a "form" of credal monotheism. Many Egyptian gods were already called the "One" or the "Only," as if to say they were all forms of the One God. This is a form of monotheism which admits a polytheist interpretation. But Amen-Ra is beginning to dominate all the others. Even then, his hymns are composed with what appears to be a conscious ambiguity. In one sense he is the chief of the gods, head of a pantheon in which all the other gods have distinct personalities, functions and honored positions. In another sense these gods exist only as attributes of Amen-Ra, and if we read them in this sense the hymns to Amen-Ra may remind us of the Psalms of the Bible. It appears that the "Ammonians" were too politically astute to offend the devotees of the other gods and the reform stops halfway, in a system of dual meaning.

In the naming of Amen-Ra as "the first divine matter which gave birth unto subsequent divine matter" we have what appears to be an early philosophical idea of substance. In the same hymn, which is of the XXIst dynasty, the attributes of Amen Ra are related to other clearly philosophical ideas of evolution, transformation, duality and inner (as opposed to outer) form. His "evolutions are manifold": he is "the god Baiti who created the divine transformations," "the terrible one of the double divine face" and "the divine form who dwelleth in the forms of all the gods." Such terms remind us of the First Cause of Greek philosophy; they also remind us of the natural philosophy (not the theology) of Swedenborg. They may be and probably are very old and I am not suggesting that they were invented as attributes of the newly dominant cult of Amen-Ra, only that they now appear in the context, if I may repeat myself, of a quasicredal monotheism.[9]

That there were "Ammonians" in or near Phoenicia is beyond dispute. The worship of Amen-Ra extended as far as Syria, "at several places which were called Diospolis."[10] The meaning of this, in the present context, is that a basic assumption of Swedenborg (and many others) has been vindicated.

The study of Egyptian divine philosophy, with all its implications for the history of religion, is a fascinating one in itself, but to carry it much farther would take us beyond our purpose in this chapter. The intention was, first of all, to demonstrate the rationality of the statement that Moses was "learned in the wisdom of the Egyptians," as earlier Christian writers said and Swedenborg believed. This wisdom was such that it could support a truly philosophical monotheism. The god of Moses was not Amen-Ra and the religion of *Genesis* is a radical break with all preceding religions. But it had to occur in an intellectual framework. The "I Am" which Moses hears from the burning bush is, if certainly not the beginning of philosophy and theology, the beginning of the philosophy and theology we know, and such a monotheism could not have been received if there had not been some precedent. It is of Amen that the Egyptian hymns say, "Thou art unknown, and no tongue hath power to declare thy similitude: only thou thyself canst do this."[11] This is as much as to say that only God can say what He is, but that when He does so no mortal mind can understand the statement. Thus, if God says "I am such and-such," the "such-and-such" cannot be understood, and one hears only the "I Am..." No matter how pictorial or poetic the form, this is true "Divine philosophy."

The question of "Egyptian wisdom" and its nature cannot, of course, be discussed in a few paragraphs. It is one of those matters of debate which have intrigued and puzzled us from Greek times.

From the Renaissance on, many believed that this wisdom lay buried in the hieroglyphs, which constituted in some fashion "a philosophy in pictures." They were supported in this by the emblem-manuals of such as the Alexandrian writer, Horapollo Niliacus, whose *Hieroglyphica* was found on the Greek island of Andros in 1419.[12] Swedenborg himself believed something like this, though his statements are very generalized. He does not follow the wild guesses of writers like Athanasius Kircher and Giordano Bruno. He says only that Egyptian writing was based on a system of "correspondences," and could be interpreted by following a system similar to that used in biblical exegesis of a symbolic kind.[13] There is a difference, though. Those with the common idea of Egyptian wisdom believed the hieroglyphic system was a secret *code*, thus leaving unanswered the question of how it was used as an everyday system of writing. Swedenborg believed it embodied a hierarchy of ideas, in which the everyday meaning was as real as the second-level one. And, as we have seen, he believed its structure was based on a transformational logic in pictures.

Now that we can read hieroglyphics, it is commonly believed that the idea that they embody a philosophy even in their formal structure is nothing more than a piece of Greek fantasizing, complicated by Renaissance and Baroque mystagogues. I must confess that I do not understand this position, and this on grounds which have nothing to do with whether or not I can read hieroglyphics (I cannot). The fact that Athanasius Kircher's attempt to read hieroglyphics resulted in nonsense is quite beside the point. The case rests on the nature of a developed picture-writing. If I represent *any abstract, philosophical or theological idea whatsoever* in a picture-language, using the objects of everyday life, I am "writing in correspondences" in the most general sense of this word. This is because the expression of an abstract idea by a picture of an object is based on the assumption that object and idea correspond. (This exalted science has its banal side; if it did not, it would not be a science.) If it can be shown that the sign-language I use is systematic, that is to say, based upon some ordered idea of the relationship between ideas and material objects, then my sign-language is in "systematic correspondences." This is certainly the case in Egypt, where the imagery of the hieroglyphic system is reproduced in the poetry of the temple and the appurtenances of the gods. If the sign language corresponds in some way to the symbolism of the Bible, and many translated Egyptian texts do so in the most obvious way, then to that extent my sign-language is in "biblical correspondences" (I avoid here the distinctions, made in the theological works, among correspondences, representations and significatives). If the system uses the same symbols as the temple art it must (unless we assume the Egyptians had no sense of the sacred) have a strong philosophical and theological content. It is as simple as that. What remains is to determine *how* systematic hieroglyphs were.

The basic structure of a Swedenborgian system of correspondential imagery is that of the vertical analogies discussed in our consideration of *A Hieroglyphic Key*. It is important to remind ourselves that in the example we considered it was not merely said that light "is like" intelligence. A complete statement was made about light and, "in the plane above it," a complete statement was made about intelligence. Isolated entities (if such can be realistically imagined, which I doubt) cannot be in correspondence one with the other. Only systems can be. A statement is a system of words; a completed action is a system of causes and effects; the little ecology of an insect species is a system of biological exchange.

There is an image known to every reader of books about Egypt, or to every visitor to Egypt who has been accosted by clamorous vendors of identical carvings of scarab beetles in various sizes. It was known also to the ancient Greeks. It probably impresses itself easily on the imagination and memory because of its seeming absurdity and triviality. This is the comparison to the sun of the little ball of dung in which scarab beetles lay their eggs. These insects place them, to great number, in masses of dung, which they push about with their legs until they are ball-shaped. They then roll them to holes, which they have previously dug. In these holes the eggs are hatched by the heat of the sun, the larvae feeding upon the covering of dung which protected them. As Budge tells us, "The mind of the primitive Egyptian associated the ball of the beetle containing potential germs of life with the ball of the sun, which seems to be rolled across the sky daily, and which was the source of all life."[14]

It would be meaningless to say merely that the scarab beetle is like the sun. It is the reproductive cycle of the scarab which resembles the path and the generative power of the sun. Two actions, completely within the range of the desired comparison, are vertically related, the lesser symbolizing the greater. Furthermore, it is the real sun which hatches the life in the (corrupt) model sun made by the scarab. This is formal correspondence as a logical and rhetorical concept. The application can be simple or complex.

When Swedenborg says in the philosophical works that the symbolism of Scripture is related to that of the Egyptians, it is to this form of thought he refers. The statement seemed rash in his day, when the hieroglyphs could not be read. Now it is a truism, both of Old Testament scholarship and the more generalized study of ancient literatures, that the Old Testament shares a common image-base with the literature of Egypt, and with those of Mesopotamia and other ancient cultures as well.[15] It is naively or dishonestly evasive to assume that we are dealing with a mere network of customary associations. We are dealing with a body of knowledge: a science and a philosophy; and with an organized system of expression: a logic and a rhetoric. The very banality and everyday unpleasantness of the scarab-beetle image shows that we are *not* dealing with a mere reflex of awe before the unknown.

In *The History of Creation as Given by Moses* and in the *Principia* Swedenborg assumes that the ancients possessed some archaic form of his own physical theory. He is thus easily convinced that the "world-egg" which he discovers in the Latin and Greek poets, an Orphic concept of Phoenician/Egyptian ancestry, can be interpreted as the image of a physical world-system something like his own. He is particularly struck by the fact that Ovid, in Fable II of Book I of the *Metamorphoses*, describes the world as a vast globe, an idea commonly said to date from Parmenides or Pythagoras. This naturally brings us again to the question of the real age of the belief that the earth is a sphere in space.

It must be said, first of all, that there are two ideas here. The surviving fragments of the most ancient overtly natural-philosophical cosmologies do not make it possible to separate them definitively. The pre-Socratic Greeks describe the physical earth in various ways, as a hemisphere in space with a separate and invisible counter-earth (Pythagoras), as a flat disc in a vortex (Diogenes of Apollonia), as simply flat (Heraclitus and Xenophanes) and as a cylinder or short column (Anaximander).[17] But the world-system or cosmos as a whole has the *ideal* shape of a sphere or a vortex. The surviving fragments give us no idea of the mathematical and mechanical principles by which the pre-Socratic philosophers related their variously-shaped earths to this ideal sphere or vortex. In some cases, they must have been well worked out, premises granted.[18] We find a reflection of the cosmic egg in this ideal world-system, not in the mere shapes of heavenly bodies and the earth. Sun, stars, moon and earth are often described in the most bizarre terms, and it is in this very bizarre nature of the description that we may see a strong dependence on abstract and philosophical/geometrical patterns of thought. They do not correspond to common sense perception. Descriptions of the earth as a hemisphere with a matching but separate hemisphere as a counter-earth, or as a free-floating cylinder, are such oddities as only philosophers are capable of.

It is possible that as a physical image the cosmic egg refers to the earth as the yolk in the middle of the egg. The earth would then be floating in some kind of universal fluid, with the top half of the egg representing the sky vault and the bottom half the space under the earth. But the earth is not the egg, since the sky, with its luminaries, is also included. In other words, the egg is a symbol of the universe. If this is so, we still have no way of knowing whether the symbol was understood in a physical sense or as a schematic diagram representing nature "as the gods see it." It is even possible that it was commented upon in a complex fashion which included both these interpretations.

Swedenborg would have been in error had he assumed that the ancient Egyptians or Moses himself had a physical theory of the

origin of the earth *closely* similar to that of his *Principia*. But this is
not what he says. The position taken in the *Principia* is a modest
and defensible one. This is that the cosmic egg cosmogony he finds
in Aristophanes and others, which we have seen to be Orphic and
Phoenician in origin, is historically related to the cosmologies of
Egypt at the time. The ancients, he believed, had arrived at this
symbolic cosmogony by a process of naive (but not stupid) reasoning from comparisons of naked-eye phenomena, not by experiment
and formal logic. This position is still defensible, because the Orphic cosmogony can be traced to an Egyptian/Phoenician cosmogony of the time of Sanchuniathon. And the purely cosmogonic
argument of Sanchuniathon, which is found at the beginning of his
Phoenician History, before he goes into stories of early Phoenician
kings and heroes, is related in the most obvious way to older
Egyptian cosmogonies, particularly those associated with the cult
of Amen-Ra.

We turn now to Swedenborg's theory of the creation of animals
and men, a remarkable development of cosmic-egg theory. Initially,
he appears to have three theories. The first, based upon the literal
meaning of the *Genesis* account, is that man was directly moulded
by God from dust, in a quasi-manual fashion. He cites this view in
The History of Creation without going into it further. It is clear that
he considers direct creation from dust as a symbolic notion, not one
to be taken literally. He does not dismiss it; he says there is no way
of being sure about such things, which in any case do not affect
basic questions of faith, but he does not favor it. The second theory
is found in the *Principia*. It is an early form of directed-evolution
theory, which is as much as to say a form of creation theory, in
which man develops from a more rudimentary entity by, in effect,
responding to environment. This theory speaks of the evolution of
the creation, and of the body of man which is its crown, towards
higher and more complex states of equilibrium. The third theory he
sets out as a speculative fiction in his poem, *The Worship and Love
of God*. This theory holds that the seeds of all animals, including
man, were produced by a kind of transmutation of substances in
the seeds of plants. Yet there is a further complication in *The
Worship and Love of God*. The poem itself is quasi-mythical in style

and is intended to represent, rather in the manner of a historical novel, the thought of some ancient and unidentified culture. It is in the copious notes that Swedenborg provides us with a philosophical interpretation of the imagery of the poem. Here we may find, as I shall show later on in this chapter, a reconciliation of the second and third theories.

Swedenborg's theory of the development of life-forms is difficult for us to grasp, and that for the very reason that it *is* a theory of forms; of forms, that is, and of their dynamic interrelationships in the functions of structures, or in "uses." (As, for example, in the Egyptian analogy between what the sun does and what a scarab beetle does). Genetic relationships, those of ancestry, are secondary.

The difficulty is complicated by the fact—obvious, of course—that Swedenborg knows nothing of genetics as we understand the word. What strikes him most of all is the interdependence of animal and plant species. He cannot imagine the snapdragon as existing without the bee, and *vice versa*. (The example is not his, but is my adaptation of an image of René Thom's referred to earlier.) The relationship is so important to him that he imagines the species of the vegetable kingdom as producing the animal species which depend upon them.

Therefore, as in the case of his theory of inorganic forms, his theory and the preferred ideas of modern biology rest upon opposite axiomatic bases. We may or may not contend that he has anticipated some modern notions of the development of what we now call "ecospheres." Yet his theory as a whole makes no sense unless we believe that the world was Divinely created in the order of time; and this is not what we mean by evolution.

Now this statement may appear too radical. Can we not say that accurate images of the world will be the same whether they assume a creative God or not? Regrettably, the answer must be in the negative. They will or should coincide on the simple observational or mensural level, but not on the level of basic law. To refer to an obvious example, if the universe was created and is sustained by God then its energy ultimately comes from outside the system. The laws of conservation of energy, still true, are no longer *basic*. They are laws of appearances or of fully realized (i.e. not primary) matter.

The Swedenborgian doctrine of the creation of plants, animals and man, then, is not only a scientific theory. Like the *Principia*, it rests upon the idea that creation was from the Eternity and Infinity of God, which have nothing to do with endless time or boundless space. The Divine Eternity and Infinity acted *into* time and space, which were themselves created. It follows that we can form no true idea of the organic creation if we take time and space as absolutes.

We could say that the Swedenborgian theory combines creationism and evolutionism, but the statement would really be meaningless. According to this model of the universe the biblical fundamentalists and the evolutionists would be equally in error. Both assume a time and space continuum which exists independently of the things within it. This is philosophically untenable: it is as if the space of the life sciences were still Newtonian. Instead we have an idea something like the following, which I introduce with a statement which must appear at once platitudinous and maddeningly ambiguous—*The world is as developed as the most developed thing within it.*

Vegetable growth is a process in time. If a maize plant is created so rapidly that it appears, at once, in complete ear-bearing form, its parts nevertheless have cause and effect relationships. The root draws nourishment from the earth, the stalk bears the leaves and the whole plant the ear of corn. Cause and effect can neither be reversed nor abolished. The leaves cannot bear the stalk, nor the full ear the leaves. Nor, in the world of time, can the effect appear simultaneously with the cause. Any creation in time must *take* time, even if the process is very rapid.

Nevertheless, somewhere between the world of time and space and the World of the Divine Intent there must be the world of cause and effect out of time. In the mind of an omniscient and omnipotent being cause and effect are simultaneously conceived, because such a being immediately sees the effect which will follow the cause or understands the cause which will produce the desired effect. In the mind of such a being creation is (*as we should see it*) instantaneous. And this is the deeper reality. If we think of creation as instantaneous we are not merely performing a mental act of philosophical abstraction; rather, we are closer to the truth. The world of consecutive cause and effect, of time and space, is less real (in the sense of "less perfect") than the thought in the mind of the Divine Being. The world of causes and effects out of time can only be thought of as "structure," particularly a structure of functional interrelationships. Here it is not the first event in time which is primary, but the central component which determines the nature of the structure, a structure, in this case, of mutually supportive "uses."

Yet—and this is an important philosophical argument of the *Principia*—the world of cause and effect out of time has itself three parts. The concepts of cause and effect which exist in the Divine Mind are forever beyond our knowing, as are the "levels of descent" between the Divine Mind and the first natural point. But they engender a tertiary cause-and effect world which is protomaterial, the world or plane which causes time and space themselves. As we have seen in our discussion of the primary point, we may visualize it, very broadly and simply, as a plane of realized logic, while recognizing that when we do so we imagine a symbol, since the world of logic itself is a symbolic world.

We therefore take a dual view. In time and space the creation took a considerable length of time. Organic material must die into the earth over many generations of organisms before the more developed plants can grow, and much more time must pass before the world is ready to support animals and man. The first natural form, the first element of creation, is time-space itself. We can never count back to the beginning of time and space; it would be like counting back through fractions of a number, or through infinitesimals, with the hope of reaching zero. The quasi-infinity of time/space will confront us everywhere, in the small as in the large.

To put it another way, our common idea of time is dual. We think of time as a sequence of causes and effects *and* we think of it as a measurement system based on the movements of objects (e.g. the earth) in space. These are related but not the same. As to the scientific notion of time, this is inseparable from the idea of space. And when we search, in time, for a beginning of time, we encounter the same problem as when we search, in space, for a beginning of space. We cannot find some point beyond the stars or at the center of a particular single particle where space begins. The age of the universe is a problem like that of the (measurable) size of the universe—innately insoluble. So is the absolute age of any part of the universe, since even a fossil plant is inextricably linked with the whole.

If, however, we postulate a world in which causes and effects are simultaneous, then the creation appears to be instantaneous. It appears to spring into being the moment time/space is created. For the infoldings of time and space create all physical entities, beginning with the "first element." And, "as seen from the primary point," the process is seemingly instantaneous, because time and space at once involve and generate all that follows, including material bodies, which are durations of times and extensions of spaces. Yet, throughout all this, it must be remembered that the word "instantaneous" is really inadequate, because it is a time-notion. Indeed, in everyday intuitional thought, it seems to be very difficult to separate logic-time and matter-time.

Swedenborg's theory may look something like a precursor of Darwinian evolution, but it is not. For in *The Origin of Species* (chapter Six, section heading *Organs of Extreme Perfection*) Charles Darwin says, in discussing the human eye: "If it could be demonstrated that any complex organ existed, which could not possibly have been formed by numerous successive slight modifications, my theory would absolutely break down. But I can find no such case." From the Swedenborgian point of view, to say that a structure may be seen as "formed by numerous successive slight modifications" is another way of saying that it is coherent, that it may be analyzed as a complex developing from a simple. Darwin is saying that his argument rests upon the coherence of nature, its analyzability. This is, however, a mere inversion of the theistic argument from design. If the eye were not a coherent and analyzable structure we could not imagine more primitive forms of it; yet neither could we imagine that it had been created by a reasoning entity.

Swedenborg's general argument in *The Worship and Love of God*, which he published in 1745,[20] is that vegetable and animal species were created and divinely developed in tandem. A vegetable species depends upon animals to transport its seeds and assist it in other ways, even to pollination; an animal species depends upon one or several vegetable species for its food and other needs. As we should say in modern terms, there can be no individual or individual species outside of a complete ecology, and a creature which is not at home in an ecology, whether we consider it "superior" or not, cannot survive. The genetic patrimony of the snapdragon, to repeat the earlier quotation from Thom, contains a virtual bee. Thus the whole–part dilemma presents itself in biology as it did in logic and mathematics. Conventional creationism and conventional evolutionism fail to be logically satisfactory not so much because they cannot solve this dilemma (it is insoluble) but because they fail to recognize it. To believers in a God, God cannot create an individual entity (the part) without creating an entire environment (the whole); he cannot because the concept is nonsensical. Unreasonable omnipotence is not a divine but a demonic quality, yet not even that, because an unreasonable being cannot be omnipotent. Similarly, the individual entity cannot evolve unless its entire environment evolves in tandem with it. If by chance it develops a faculty or organ which is not able to work harmoniously within and on the environment then the faculty or organ is excrescent and either useless or redundant, a drawback in the postulated struggle for survival. No multiplication of "maybes" or face-saving hypotheses or postponing an answer to the science of the future can work around this problem—because it is really one of logic, not science— unless we can show that the entire environment mutates at once.

The Worship and Love of God is a philosophical poem (in Latin), not a work of science or even of natural philosophy in the narrow eighteenth-century sense. It presents organic nature—plants, animals and man—as a structure of uses and forms, which come together in the relationships of correspondence. The poem takes the form of a creation narrative loosely tied to the *Genesis* account, and it ends with the marriage of Adam and Eve, about two-thirds of the way through the projected work. For Swedenborg only published the first two parts in 1745; the third part was not completed and only some manuscript pages of it survive.

The central panel of the First Part is the birth of Adam from an egg nourished in a fruit of the Tree of Life. This image is so striking and bizarre that it has dominated all discussion of *The Worship and Love of God*. As it is preceded by descriptions of the births of other animal forms from less noble trees, shrubs and grasses, it has been assumed that Swedenborg is here advancing an extremely novel (some might say absurd) *theory*, thinly disguised in imagery. This is an unfortunate misunderstanding, which might have been corrected by a little more knowledge of the poetic style of the time in which it was written, or rather of the period just before it was written. Swedenborg's poetic style is old-fashioned in the playful exuberance of its logic-based imagery, reminding us of the transition period between baroque and rococo.

The notes to the poem, if they had been read with due care, might also have corrected this false impression. They indicate (I cannot quite say "make clear," because the argument is a very complicated one) that the narrative line of the poem infolds a variety of cause-and-effect lines with two great sequences dominating. The first of these sequences is a structure out of time, the structure of interweaving use-relations or function-relations between plant and animal, beginning with the simplest plants and animals and culminating in man. The second is a sequence of causes and effects in time, and this more or less follows the order of creation in the *Genesis* account. When the two sequences are combined, along with lesser sequences dependent upon them, they create the "fable-time" of the poem. In this imaginary time-sequence the creation of man, the culmination of the timebound cause-and effect sequence, coincides with the completion of the function structure, where we find man in symbiotic relationship with the "Tree of Life," actually a "Tree of Wisdom," and, through this tree, with the whole material creation.

The structure is, we now see, that of symbolic myth. *The Worship and Love of God* was therefore an enormously ambitious enterprise. I do not think it is unjust to say that Swedenborg's purely poetic gifts were not up to the task. Poetry is an art which insists on total commitment and which demands, in addition, certain temperamental qualities. Swedenborg fully understands the technical and scientific (i.e. "rhetorical") aspects of poetry. He invents beautiful formal structures. But he is somewhat weak and derivative in his imagery and we soon become aware that poetry is only a pastime for him. His comments on English poetry in his letters (no quotations are needed) are as perfunctory as those of any young man gifted in science rather than the arts. He shows, for example, an embarrassing fondness for the empty courtliness of such poets as William Strode, one of whose poems he turns into Latin.

The result of all this is very strange. *The Worship and Love of God* contains ideas of great beauty and its structure suggests new poetic architectures. Yet he cannot resist analyzing his own imagery. The work becomes less a poem than a very innovative rhetorical system with examples. We compare this approach with the precise detail of his scientific observations and come to the conclusion, obvious after all, that Swedenborg was more a scientist and a philosopher than he was a poet. The poem is indeed beautiful, but as science and philosophy. Rational ideas are cloaked—one almost said "draped"—in such imagery as might occur to a cultivated man with a good classical and biblical education, a sense of poetic decorum, and a deeply harmonious and inventive mind.

The above, I know, appears somewhat dismissive. It is not intended to be. However, others (and I in another place) have been so moved by the philosophical beauty of this work that they have overestimated its purely poetic qualities. A cool realism demands that they be taken into account. The reader need only bear in mind that the *text* of this book is to be read as "scientific poetry," like Sir John Davies's *Orchestra* or the works of such Renaissance Neoplatonists as Lefèvre de la Boderie, that is, as harmoniously illustrated *Idea*. His theory is touched upon in the notes, as also in some other works—the *Principia*, *On the Infinite* and *The History of Creation as Given by Moses*. Indeed, the theological works also show us a philosopher and scientist, rather than a poet.

Swedenborg's properly scientific theory here is never advanced with the confidence of the theories of the *Principia*. One may not build a biology on geometry and logic. Yet it is a most interesting theory, particularly for its time, and it demands close attention.

In essence it postulates that the "seeds" or "eggs" of animal forms were produced in plants, plants of a peculiar order which existed in early times but have perished, though their modified descendants survive. They are not identified, except for one—the "strawberry tree" or *Arbutus Unedo*, a reference which nobody has been able to explain. Swedenborg cannot be very specific in defining his "seeds" or "eggs" because nothing was known in his time of the structure of animal and plant cells. They have as much in common with the monads of Leibniz or the "seminal reasons" of Augustine as they do with familiar seeds and eggs. The forms which develop from these seeds or eggs should be described as "proto-animal" rather than animal, since their instinctive behaviors have not yet been developed. These behaviors or "more interior principles" develop over the life-spans of several successive generations, thus, in the case of species of reptiles and worms, "after the life of the (first) reptile or worm had ceased."[21]

The eggs produced by the primal plants in question contain fluids which will later become the blood and other vital fluids of the animals which emerge from the eggs. Just as in the *Principia*, everything begins in fluid forms. It is the force of generative fluid form which generates both the bodies and the behaviors of animals, including the physical form of man.

If we were to reconstruct this theory in modern terms we should have to say that the primary transformation-set with which he is concerned is something like an albumen (protein) cycle. He refers very often to egg-like substances and forms. He says, for example, that "...it is a common opinion, that everything is produced from an egg; even the viviparous creatures of the animal kingdom, first in the ovaries, next within the chorion and amnion, which, with their liquid, resemble the shell with the white in the egg. The seeds of vegetables also represent the same thing, being covered with little coats and encompassed within with a juice resembling that of animals."[22]

The basis of the theory is set out in a note of great philosophical depth, and also of some difficulty. I will quote it and attempt to set out the main arguments as well as I can.

> The vegetables themselves, in imitation of their great mother (the earth—NN), were primitively, as it were, mere seminaries and ovaries, but which produced not only after their own kind, but also after a kind different from themselves, for one thing lay so folded up in another, that the other did not come forth until all things which might serve for the exercises and necessities of its life were ready. From the series itself of productions, it may be manifest whence came the souls of brutes, which are said to have been ingenerated in the seeds of the vegetable kingdom ("said," that is, in the poem—NN); for as the seeds of vegetables arose from the conjunction of the active powers of nature with the inert powers of the earth, through the medium of the radiation of the sun of the world, so these seeds, which are animated, arose from that form or spiritual essence, which is spiritual and living, infused into the forms or active powers of nature, through the medium of the radiation of the Sun of Life; wherefore these lives went forth in the same subordinate series as those powers of nature themselves which constitute the atmospheres, consequently in the same as the seeds of vegetables themselves, from which they were finally hatched. And since that life from its fountain breathes nothing but uses, and nature is nothing but an effect for the sake of uses, it is evidence that it was so foreseen and provided, that uses themselves as effects might unfold themselves. He is totally blind and in the grossest darkness who does not discover what is Divine in these things.[23]

The first and most important thing to note, because all the argument springs from it, is that we have here a structure of *uses*, created by the Divine Mind. Nature, which includes time and space and everything we imagine or perceive as occurring in time and space "is nothing but an effect for the sake of uses." To quote a useful architectural platitude, "Form follows function."

In a structure of organic entities, uses are the interrelationships which preserve the unity and equilibrium of the whole, the biosphere. They include such things as the food and reproductive cycles in which plants and animals cooperate. Bees, in taking away nectar from flowers, transfer pollen to other flowers; birds eat berries and drop the seeds in their dung, which enables the seeds to germinate; plants are nourished by the decaying bodies of animals. And in such a system, of course, the busy scarab beetle is very much at home.

Swedenborg is imagining an early form of life which is neither vegetable nor animal. It is a rudimentary form which will in time give birth to both. Its seeds are animated, like the rudimentary forms postulated by Sanchuniathon, the pre-Socratics and others. What animates them is the Divine intent to create the forms of uses which will develop from them. We may say that they contain all subsequent forms "in real potential." From this first rudimentary form, or class of rudimentary forms, emerge two more rudimentary forms or classes of elementaries. The first is that of the "seeds of vegetables," animated by a conjunction "of the active powers of nature with the inert powers of the earth, through the medium of the radiation of the sun of the world." The second form is that of the seeds of animals, which are more directly informed by "use-structures," which the Sun of Life (a manifestation of God) has infused into the active powers of nature. It should be noted, though, that the forms of plants also represent what we might call "infused use-structures." The difference between plants and animals is that the primal seeds of the former develop out of use-structures already implicit in the forces of nature, while those of the latter embody an additional or superior set of use-structures infused into nature. The active powers of nature themselves, as embodied in plants, represent use-structures already (in logic-time, not conventional time) infused into nature. This in effect makes vegetable-forms closer to mineral ones than are animal forms.

Nonetheless, difficulties remain. Swedenborg, who as a trained observer can describe vividly what is before him, is not at home in imaginative fiction, despite his literary culture. A gifted and experienced imaginative writer will manage his tone the way a good actor manages the inflections of his voice. Because this tone includes manipulations of grammar, syntax and the connotations of words, much of it will come out in good translation. The effect is that the reader is nudged towards a certain Point 0, or Observer Position, appropriate to the *basic* interpretation of a particular scene. Thus, for example, he will be able to determine whether a character in a novel is really seeing something, consciously using his visual imagination or hallucinating. Swedenborg is not an experienced creator of fictions; furthermore, as a scientist, he has a professional distrust of the free imagination, which in science can lead one into plausible falsities.

To avoid a purely literary analysis which is not appropriate here I shall simply restate what other analyses of this puzzling unfinished work have found. There are ambiguities of tone which cannot be completely resolved. The poem takes the form of a communication from the past, of an imaginary ancient theory, while Swedenborg's notes provide a contemporary interpretation consonant with his own philosophy. Its central image, as we have seen, is that of a novel form of plant-animal correspondence, in which the "seeds" of various animal species, including man, are produced in plants. However, despite the notes, we do not quite know how to interpret this image. Is it a symbol of truly poetic kind, in which a deep reality is contained within the symbol? Is it supposed to represent an archaic speculation, a mere guess at scientific truth, clothed in appealing imagery? Or is it presented as a correct theory, which we find bizarre only because it is new to us? We are not helped—indeed, we are further confused—by the fact that on the purely formal side the argument has the refined complexity and rational beauty we expect from its author. His notes do not answer such questions. It appears that Swedenborg thought they were adequately dealt with in the body of the poem.

Such conundrums are presented by many "scientific" poems, not only this one. There is a confusion between the "as if" of poetic imagery and the "we might illustrate the argument in the following pictorial manner" of popular simplification of philosophical and scientific ideas.

This means that any full interpretation of this poem must include much that is tentative and partial.

It seems, at least to me, that Swedenborg has encountered a question which could not even be intelligently phrased, much less answered, until the modern discovery of DNA. He recognizes, as we shall see, that there are chemical affinities between the living substances of plants and animals. He also understands, as well as possible in his time, that animal and plant species are closely connected and mutually dependent in what we now call "ecologies." He also knows from Ovid and other Greek and Roman writers that the "ancients" believed that plant and animal forms could change into each other. Such relationships suggest to him the image of animals being born from plants. His reasoning seems to be somewhat as follows—

Immature animal forms are more delicate and easily-harmed than vegetable ones; they also take longer to develop and are particularly vulnerable as they do so. They must be protected. He therefore imagines that they were first protected and nourished in the seeds of plants, emerging to propagate and multiply in the usual way of reproduction. He supports this by the common belief of his time, founded on naked-eye observation, that animal-forms could be produced inside the seeds of plants. Tiny insects had actually been found in seeds and it was assumed they must have originated there. We now know that they would have arisen from tiny eggs deposited there by burrowing insects, but the naked eye cannot, or cannot easily, see these eggs or the holes of ingress. Swedenborg further believes that in this process vegetable substances were somehow transmuted into animal ones.[24]

In this aspect of his theory he is, of course, in error. Close reasoning from bad data has led to a bizarre conclusion. Yet, in his determination to leave no problem unexamined, he has at least faced an important issue. As I understand the nonspecialist literature, Darwinian evolution and its modern adaptations have still not solved the problem of how an animal is protected during the period in which it is developing a new faculty or organ. An organism in this state must inevitably be vulnerable and unstable, not stronger but weaker than its well-adapted neighbors. Even if we

assume that, by some marvel of mutation, the new faculty or organ
appears immediately in fully-functioning condition, where will be
the instinctive knowledge of how to use it? We must imagine some
equivalent of a learning stage, even in animals governed by instinct, and a learning animal is, again, a weak and vulnerable
animal. It seems that a basic logical issue is being evaded here. It is
certainly true that nature continually denies our simplistic logic.
Nevertheless, until hard and incontrovertible data is discovered,
logic is all we have. A statement like "it simply happened that way"
is not acceptable. Nothing is proved by arguments drawn from
changes in the wing-colors of moths, to adapt to this or that surface
on which the moths alight, since we are talking about changes in
fundamental behavior and deep structure. No matter how useful
they will prove to be in the future, new and "improved" organs are,
at the moment of appearance, crippling or at least disabling defor-
mities.

Some, of course, may object to my use of the word "logic." What
could be more illogical, they might say, than the alternative, the
doctrine of Divine creation? The answer must be that, premises
granted, the doctrine of Divine creation is entirely logical. What
they mean is that they find the premises incredible. But the word
"incredible," when applied to basic premises, is a word of emotion,
not reason.

Swedenborg's theory is a series of strict logical consequences
flowing from the dual principle of cascading or growing perfections
in conceptual time (successiveness) and of the correspondent ladder of perfections considered in static or quasi-spatial terms (simultaneity). The mineral kingdom must engender the vegetable
kingdom, and the vegetable the animal. The entire theory and its
form of presentation are governed by one idea. It is true that the
process of world-creation by a Divine Mind cannot, by very definition, be understood by finite and mortal man. We must *attempt* to
do so by dual thinking: first in cause-and-effect time in which
sequentiality is considered, but not the durations of times; and
then in structural or quasi-spatial time in which the rational and
analyzable qualities of a form are assumed to be vertically superior
to or internal to its material expression. In uninformed human

thought, neither way is fully satisfactory and each excludes the other.

To understand this theory better, it is useful to break it into two other parts, a morphological part and a part relating to substance. First we have the idea of a formal connection and a functional relationship between plants and animals. Very many animal parts resemble plant parts in shape and operation: the reproductive parts, for example; and we also have the mutual interdependence of plants and animals which is so obvious in nature. These connections and interrelationships were really all he needed to exemplify the philosophical aspects of the system, along with the assumption that this order was created by God.

Yet Swedenborg had been struck as early as 1721, when he published *On the Principles of Chemistry*, by the similarities between the substances found in plants and animals. This went to confirm the second part of his theory, that plant seeds could have given birth to or sheltered animal forms, or their antecedents. He pays much attention, in part XIV of this work, to oils, the albumen of eggs and what he calls "urinous salts." The chemical methods of his time were very crude, and only a historian of chemistry thoroughly familiar with the laboratory methods of the time could give modern names to some of the terms he uses, which often include substances we consider to be chemically unrelated. He is struck by the presence of oils in seeds and of "urinous salts" in both plant and animal substances, and also by the relationships between blood and egg albumen. The relationships he discovers are certainly real. We know that uric acid is closely related to vegetable compounds, such as caffeine in the coffee bean, theophylline found in tea, and theobromine, which is found in the cocoa bean. We understand the relationship between vegetable oils and animal fats and the protein base of animal and plant life. We know that the class of albumins includes serum-albumins, which are found in milk, animal lymph and blood serum but also in certain seeds, and includes in addition such vegetable albumins as leucosin (wheat, rye and barley) and legumelin (peas, beans and lentils). Facts such as these may now be found in any encyclopedia by people like me, but in Swedenborg's day they were on the cutting edge.

In *The History of Creation* Swedenborg says that the question of whether man was formed "immediately from the earth, and thus without passing through his periods from infancy to manhood," or "mediately from an egg" is not a question of religious faith. For the latter statement also has his being formed from the dust of the earth, though mediately or less directly. In the latter interpretation, which he clearly favors, the process would have taken place over "an entire space of time or a lapse of many years."[25] The process would necessarily have involved some transformational event in the vegetable egg "whereby the essences that were to pass into his blood might be rectified." In modern language this means some form of transformation of vegetable substance into a corresponding animal substance, a "mutation of genes," as we might now say. It might seem fantastically tendentious for me to refer to genes in this context, since Swedenborg knew nothing of genes and his biological ideas are, by modern standards, extremely primitive. But close philosophical reasoning can work wonders on unpromising material, provided this material is merely crude rather than wrong. It is a fact that Swedenborg's theory of the development of organic life, like his theory of the microcosmos, is nothing else but an eighteenth-century ancestor—an extraordinarily well-developed one—of the "theory of information" so important in modern genetic theory. Nor is he alone in this, since similar anticipations of information theory may be found in Leibniz.[26] Once again, we are not removing him from the context of his time.

Recent genetic technology has confirmed a part of his genetic theory, if not the whole. Genetic engineers are now (terrifyingly) inserting human genes into plants, thus "turning the plants into miniature factories that can produce large quantities of useful human protein."[27] They have grown tobacco plants which produce antibodies and potatoes which make serum albumin, a human blood protein. Apparently the process was not difficult even in the earlier stages; human DNA was shot into leaves by what was called a "gene gun." We know, furthermore, that on the primitive level of living creatures there is a mutual exchange of DNA, called "horizontal gene transfer." It seems probable that there have been in the past exchanges of genes among bacteria and the cell forms of animals, plants, fungi and protozoa (included in the omnibus category, *eukaryotes*). We also know of the existence of ancient microbes having properties of both bacteria and *eukaryotes*. In addition, we know that plant cells, as complicated in their way as human cells, assemble human proteins in their proper configuration, and do so more effectively than bacteria, which must be carefully tended.

In another form of transfer, the gene gun is not used. Immune cells, which produce an antibody, are inserted into a bacterium commonly found in soil. The bacterium then passes the gene into fragments of tobacco leaf. Since plants may be cloned from a single cell, it has proved possible to grow entire tobacco plants from these fragments. When these plants are crossed sexually, they produce human antibodies.

Whether a related process could occur in nature, under unique but imaginable conditions, I do not know. It appears that plant cells, like animal ones, reject alien genes. The molecular biologist who developed the bacterium method, Andrew Hiatt, solved the rejection problem by attaching mouse-protein to the genes of human antibodies. These protected the antibodies from attack by plant enzymes, guiding the antibody "to a cell membrane where the assembly of the antibody is completed and is then secreted."[28]

Of course, this in no way demonstrates the validity of Swedenborg's theory as a whole. What it shows is that under carefully controlled laboratory conditions plants may harbor animal genes. That is why I say it confirms "part of his genetic theory."

Another theory, remarkably (if considered out of context) like the Marxist notion of "evolution by reflection, is found in the first chapter of the *Principia*. He says—

> To begin, then, with man in his state of integrity and complete perfection. In such a man we may conceive that there was such a complete contiguity throughout the parts of his system, that every motion proceeding with a free course from his grosser parts or principles could arrive, through an uninterrupted connection, at his most subtle substance or active principle, there being nothing in the way which could cause the least obstruction. Such a man may be compared

to the world itself, in which all things are contiguous from the sun to the lowest part of our atmosphere. Thus the motions about the sun, or rays, proceed with an uninterrupted course, and *almost instantaneously, by means of contiguity* (my emphasis—NN), through the more subtle or the grosser elements, through ether to the air, till they reach the eye and act upon it, by virtue of such connection, as if they were present; for *contiguity occasions the appearance of presence* (my emphasis—NN). When, therefore, the most subtle active principle of man, by the providence of God, clothed itself with a body, and added, by degrees, parts upon parts, all the motions in the most subtle elements which were present would necessarily move or affect that extremely impressionable and tender substance, and would gradually imprint themselves and their own mechanism upon it. So also would the motions in the grosser elements, such as the air; for this, always moving and undulating around it, and perpetually acting upon the same substance, would also form to itself something similar, and, by its continual motion, cause itself, as in the case of the other elements, to be received within. The same would occur in regard to whatever was fluent in the air with a more unequal motion, for the atmosphere is always stored with the effluvia of plants etc.; this, therefore, by its continual contact, would form its own mechanism in the sense of smell. In a word, during the growth of the very tender parts possessing motion and life, every motion that was perpetually present must necessarily have left indications of itself, and must consequently have naturally formed its own mechanism, so as afterwards to be received more interiorly, but in the same manner as in the yet tender substances.[29]

This is the Adam of literal *Genesis*, even though he is not moulded from dust. He is a perfect microcosm, and he can sense all the harmonic motions of nature, as Swedenborg goes on to say in a part I have not quoted. Notions of geometrical and mechanical order are not strange to Adam. His natural reasoning powers work in concert with his exquisitely healthy perception of the order implicit in natural processes, as reflected in the response of his senses. He may therefore draw correct logical conclusions—obviously simple ones at first—without effort. He does not know celestial mechanics and calculus, of course, but his natural response to harmonic motion is such that he senses the main elements of cosmic movement in his own being. He is to the entire world of experience what the boy Mozart was to music—an intuitive seizer of significant form.

We have here "man," not "a man." Nevertheless, it is an individual Adam who is referred to here because we have earlier: "No man seems to have been able to arrive at true philosophy, since the age of that first of mortals who is said to have been in a state of the most perfect integrity, that is to say, who was formed and made according to all the art, similitude and scheme of the world, before the existence of vice."[30]

It is said, in the longer quotation above, "When, therefore, the most subtle active principle of man, by the providence of God, clothed itself with a body, and added, by degrees, parts upon parts, all the motions in the most subtle elements which were present would necessarily move or affect that extremely impressionable and tender substance, and would gradually imprint themselves and their own mechanism upon it."

What does he mean by "added, by degrees, parts upon parts"?

In the philosophy of the *Principia*, instantaneous creation in time, given an *already existing cosmos*, is seen as contrary to natural order and the Divine order on which it depends. Material sequences of causes and effects must now take place in time and space. If the laws of time and space were violated in the natural world there would be a rent or tear, so to speak, in its internal structure. A complex temporal event, which occurred in all respects instantaneously, that is to say, in which all causes within the complex happened at the same time as their effects, would violate the entire natural fabric. That the Divine Being may act in a miraculous fashion in the world he has created is beyond dispute, but if He violated the laws of that world, then His own dignity would be impugned by that act, as if He had made a faulty creation through which He could not act without altering it. Of course we cannot fully understand the laws of time and space—this would be to understand the natural expression of the Divine Providence— and therefore it may well appear that a miracle defies the laws of time and space. Yet we cannot think that God tinkers with His creation or that He has to suspend its laws to act directly through it.

The statement referred to says that the internal part of man, his "most subtle active principle" or soul, was created first. The parts of the body were added one by one—and here we must not think of some cloudy entity budding a leg here, a rib there, but of an organism which grows in complexity from something like a cell, while remaining, throughout its development, cohesive and viable.

These developing parts of the developing body are formed by external stimuli, received by the whole organism in a manner consonant with its own nature. Man is a recipient form, comparatively passive. The laws of mechanics in the physical world which surrounds the developing organism form his body; they determine the pressure and weight of organs and dictate posture. The air forms the lungs and the apparatus whereby the body absorbs the elements of the air; the sense of smell is developed by "what is there to be smelled"; light forms the eye and so on. This is, in modern language, a system of growth (or evolution) by feedback.

It cannot be said that Swedenborg developed an entirely isolable theory of the origin of living forms or animated matter. He approaches the problem from two viewpoints—the genetic and morphological—without entirely reconciling the two. By an "isolable theory" I simply mean something which can be considered on its own and summed up in a series of neat (or apparently neat) propositions. We may do this with Darwin and with a number of modern evolutionists who acknowledge Darwin—sometimes with more piety than truth—as a direct intellectual ancestor.

Swedenborg's central concept is that of *tremulation*, which runs throughout matter and is manifested in animated matter as *sensation*. Animals and in their way, plants translate natural vibrations (those of light, for example) into forms of fixed experience, of information, we might say. These take the form of *memory*, which has its inanimate analogy in such forms as chemical change in response to stimuli or the tendency of material objects to take on new forms in response to stress. There develops from this a definition of the highest animal, man, as possessing the most inclusive sensory apparatus linked with the most comprehensive memory, a memory capable, finally, of containing abstract ideas.

Obviously, then, an isolable theory of evolution is not *possible* in this context of thought. Swedenborg's idea of human evolution involves his entire system, beginning with the Active and Passive of the primary point. It would then be a radical falsification to speak of progression towards organic complexity as occurring through chance mutations of the physical parts of living bodies. What is evolving, first of all, is a *mind*, the base-form of which may be found in a formulaic pattern, that of stimulus and response to stimulus, which runs throughout nature.

It is not that inanimate nature "thinks." It is rather that it possesses the mechanical qualities which will later become the corporal basis of thought. And this is, as we have seen, because logic and mechanics are intimately interrelated.

If we read the following passage from *The Worship and Love of God* in a sufficiently generalizing and abstract spirit we shall see that it describes a flux of information through the senses, which the soul infills with meaning. The now-meaningful images enter the memory, and there they take on an ordered structure described as "harmonious." This word is, as we have seen, of very wide resonance in Swedenborg. His entire theory is one of natural harmonies. If we generalize this we can see that all evolutionary development arises from a structured response to stimuli. Unstructured or chance response can lead only to degeneration. The structured response is a harmonious one, and it is in the nature of a harmonious structure that it should possess a capacity to evolve to an optimal form. The form then becomes fixed within certain limits of variation, the range of which is determined by the deep roots of the form. We may see simple man-made analogies to this in the development of verse-forms like the sonnet, of musical forms like the symphony and of utensil-forms such as the pot. We may see further that there is no reason intrinsic in the theory why the physical traces of such a form of evolution should not take forms similar to those found in the fossil record; but the traces would have to be interpreted in a theistic context.

Hence it is as clear as light that life has ordained nature to be a consort with itself; but since they are thus entwined, we must unfold the manner by which one inflows into the other, or what is the order, and what are laws according to order: for the Founder of laws and of rights never acts in any case but from the wisest order. That one inflows into the other, is plainly declared by existence itself, from which we ought to judge concerning subsistence; for as we exist so also we subsist. But although this is evident from the generation of all things, and especially from our own, it behooves me in order to place the truth in its own light to unravel a little the web, just now woven, from its ultimate threads. The soul has received the images themselves which are the forms of nature and of her light, entering in by the way of the eye, and having breathed her life into them, has conducted them into the chambers of the memory, and has suitably assigned to each its abode there; and at the same time has forbidden them to rush into our Olympus or sacristy (the inmost dwelling of the soul—NN), without our permission or order. These she has afterwards arranged so harmoniously, according to the genius and nature of each, when called forth, that at length she constructed from them, as from members, a kind of society or body. Hence we intelligences and wisdoms were born in that form of beauty which thou beholdest; what therefore we derive from nature, and what from life, thou clearly distinguishest with thine eyes. Our soul herself seems indeed to have produced this effect, and on that account we acknowledge and venerate her as a pious mother; nevertheless, she herself does not live from herself, being only a power which lives and acts from another. The life itself, as her soul, inflows into her from the fountain of all things that live, or of all lives, and thus through her into us, her offspring; therefore we are heavenly in our origin, and therefore we are called wisdoms. It was that life, which, by the instrumentality of our soul, went to meet the lights and shades, or forms of nature, and when she had converted them into ideas, through the little cells of the memory, arranged them into classes and tribes, according to genera and species; it was the same life which afterwards called them forth into thy Helicon, whence we derive our birth. Such now was order; and such the influx of life into nature; according to the same we exist, as I said, and according to the same we subsist, or live and act. From this it is now clear, that nature durst not at all, without command or summons, introduce herself into the chambers of our life, but that the

Supreme and His Love, according to the intuition of ends, that is, according to His own decision, adopted nature and adapted her forms altogether to those uses which He intended. This therefore is the order from which all our laws and decrees of nature flow, and from which comes our fate; all these things are derivative veins from that one single Fountain. Supreme things, therefore, or things superior in order, inflow into inferior things, and these into ultimate things, but not *vice versa*; hence inferior things derive their powers and perfections, or hence flow all the abilities and powers of inferior things. When this order is established, then there is nothing so complicated and abstruse which is not explained and unfolded, for it is Light itself which sees, and Living Force itself which acts.[31]

Swedenborg was correct, as I have implied earlier, in assuming that the idea he had developed was, in general philosophical outlines, a very ancient one, particularly in the form he had given it in the *Principia*. Sanchuniathon has his egg-shaped seeds of life, the "Watchers of the Heavens," the ancestral forms of intelligent life. He tells us that they were not "awakened" until the air began to carry light, until the warming of land and sea produced winds, clouds and rain, and until thunders and lightnings were produced. The noise of the thunder "woke up" the seeds of life and they began to move about.

We do not know how the knowledge-elite of Sanchuniathon's Phoenician/Egyptian culture interpreted the inner meaning of the myth referred to above. For one thing, the account in Philo Byblius is a degenerate sketch of a complete philosophical myth. Yet we can see on the face of it that the myth says that the birth of intelligence, volition and physical movement in the "seeds of life" was the result of the moulding pressures of external natural forces. The story may be interpreted in both a theistic and a materialist context, and this shows, no matter how naive we may think it to be, that we are dealing with an autonomous form of natural philosophy, though in pictorial form.

It is also as obvious as anything can be that the ideas found in the cosmogony of Sanchuniathon may be traced back to the Egypt of an earlier period, at least to the time of Moses. It is, as the early commentary itself says, "Ammonian." Sanchuniathon himself, or

Philo's representation of him, says that he is setting out the cosmogony of Taaut, Egyptian Thoth, the god of literary and scientific wisdom. There is not an image or idea in his creation-myth which may not be found, in more sophisticated and elaborate form, in Egyptian myth of the time of Moses and earlier. It would be very tempting to demonstrate this quite conclusively from what we now know—but it would falsify the nature of Swedenborg's thought at this time to go further. He knew nothing more of Egyptian religion than could be found in the Greek writers. He could not move beyond the opinion of Grotius, who wrote in his *De Veritate Religionis Christianae* (1627), a work which Swedenborg, as we know from his notebooks, had carefully read and annotated, copying down this very passage—

> We have also the testimonies of many people alien to the Jewish religion, which show that the most ancient traditions among all nations are in agreement with the writings of Moses. What he wrote concerning the origin of the world, is almost the same as what is given in the most ancient histories of the Phoenicians as collected by Philo Byblius, and is in partial agreement with traditions among the Hindoos and Egyptians.[32]

We do not know if Swedenborg had read the account of Sanchuniathon. I suspect he had not, because he refers to it nowhere else, though it would have given much support to his theory. His idea of the origin of life relates most closely to that of Leibniz, part of whose *Theodicea* he quotes in his notebooks.[33] The essence of Leibniz's argument is that "the generation of an animal is nothing else than a transformation and augmentation" and that animals spring from "animalcules or living seminules" of "a lower genus." Somewhat similar ideas are held by other authors whom Swedenborg quotes in his notes. They may be traced back to Augustine's "seminal reasons," and thence into Greek philosophy and its antecedents. These connections, however, are philosophical ones, and rather vague at that. In its specificity, Swedenborg's theory is entirely his own, and his searching out of an ancient antecedent for it is also his own.

We may now sum up as follows.

The dating of Sanchuniathon, if I am correct, shows us that the Egyptian/Phoenician version of a philosophy clearly ancestral to the Orphic was known in Phoenicia, and probably also in Israel, at about the time of the first kings. The Greek account of Sanchuniathon's cosmogony relates it to the cult of Egyptian Ammon and to doctrines attributed to the Egyptian wisdom-god, Thoth. The essence of this doctrine is therefore much older than the time of Sanchuniathon and could be linked with Ammon cults at about the time of Moses. If my argument is wrong and the other date we have for Sanchuniathon, which would place him close to the time of Moses, is correct, the link with Ammon-cults in the time of Moses would be even more direct, though historically puzzling. Swedenborg's assumption is therefore rational and sustainable, the more remarkably so because, while he notes the existence of the Sanchuniathon account as preserved by Philo Byblius, he does not take it into account as part of a line of ideological transmission.

His own analysis of the dialectical nature of Egyptian thought, part of his *Hieroglyphic Key*, is also rational and sustainable. His belief that the Egyptians had some kind of cosmic-egg symbolism *very* similar to his own seems rash, but there is certainly a degree of similarity to be found. His doctrine of animal/man creation, based on the symbiosis of animal and plant forms, is also ancient in a general sense, though to all appearances not in the specific form he gives it.

Swedenborg is therefore correct in assuming that certain aspects of his physical and evolutionary theory extend back to the time of Moses and form part of the intellectual climate in which the *Genesis* account was written. His description of the nature of this historical connection, which we find scattered through many of his works, is as accurate as any eighteenth-century account could be. Finally, his theories on the genesis of plant and animal forms are of great philosophical interest, though the scientific knowledge of his time did not allow him to develop them into a full theory of the development of organic forms.

ENDNOTES

1 In Book II of Herodotus the Ammonians are described as a distinct people, of mixed Egyptian and Ethiopian origin, and worshippers of Ammon; but we are only concerned with the latter characteristic.

2 Harden, pp. 50–51.

3 Harden, p. 121. I have followed Harden, an authority in the field, in identifying the Libyan pharaoh Sosenq with Shishak of the Bible.

4 Ghirshman, pp. 98 and 112.

5 Akurgal, pp. 50–51. This stele is discussed in an old book by the Orientalist, Zenaide Ragozin, *Assyria* (Unwin, London, 1891, p. 202). Ragozin quotes (p. 201) a private letter from Francois Lenormant, in which he retracts a former opinion and concludes that the mythical Semiramis was really the goddess Ishtar.

6 Budge, *Egyptian Religion* and *Tutankhamen: Amenism, Atenism and Egyptian Monotheism*, both *passim*.

7 Budge, *Gods...* II, p. 74. All attempts at a conclusive interpretation of Akhnaton's cult founder before the fact that he and his followers left no (surviving) ideological defense of their actions, but Budge's interpretation seems to make the best sense out of what we have. In *Tutankhamen...* (pp. xiv–xv) he argues as follows: "His 'Teaching' proclaimed the 'oneness' of Aten, which has been compared to the monotheism of Christian nations; but for centuries before his time the priesthoods of Heliopolis, Memphis, Hermopolis and Thebes had proclaimed this self-same oneness to be the chief attribute of their gods." Of the hymns to Aten, he says: "I cannot find in them a single expression that contains any spiritual teaching, or any exhortation to purity of life, or any word of consciousness of sin, or any evidence of belief in a resurrection and a life beyond the grave."

8 Budge: *Gods...* II, pp. 5–16.

9 We often forget that the pharaoh of the Exodus is not disturbed by the monotheism of Moses, but wishes to keep the Israelites as slaves. In his arguments with Moses he never invokes any god of a polytheistic system and his magicians, referring to Aaron's plague of lice, say, "It is the finger of God" (*Exodus* 8: 19).

10 Budge, *Gods...* II, p. 22. Jacob Bryant (see Holwell, bibliography) has an interesting discussion on the Ammonians, in which he touches on the Arachne myth, saying that weaving was invented at Arach (Erech or Warka in modern terminology) in "Babylonia." He refers to the poet Nonnus as calling Erech "Arachne" (p. 183). Nobody would take Bryant as an authority nowadays, but he says some interesting things, which might be worthy of exploration. His etymological approach leads to absurdities, but he is not the inane "Arkite" of scholarly caricature. For example we now know what Bryant merely surmised, that the Egyptians symbolized the new moon as a man seated in a boat (Budge, *Gods...*, pp. 412–413). In effect, Bryant considers the worship of Ammon, whom he identifies with the sun, as a decadent monotheism. In this, as in certain other respects, he is prescient.

11 Budge, *Gods...* II, p. 5.

12 Seznec, pp. 99–100.

13 The belief in such a connection is also found in the Cabalistic tradition. The Cabalists say that the wisdom of the pre-Mosaic patriarchs was preserved, though in a degenerate form, in Egypt, and it was there that Moses learned it. The Masonic tradition, adapting a medieval story about Hiram of Tyre, adds a Phoenician influence. See particularly Mathers, *The Kabbalah Unveiled*, pp. 5–6, with other references to Egyptian wisdom therein, also Waite, *The Holy Kabbalah* (index refs. "Egyptians"). See also *Amos* V: 26 and *Acts* VII: 43. Swedenborg did not know the *Cabala* and derived his very skimpy notion of it from Christian writers, such as Grotius.

14 Budge, *Gods...* I, p. 356. What does Budge mean by "primitive" here? The idea seems carefully worked out. The eggs of the scarab beetle thrive on the decay of the dung-ball. By analogy, we may say that the germs of life in the sun are quickened by decay of the sun. Even if this only means that the sun's fire is self-consuming, this is to have some idea of the energy-cycle. The word "primitive" seems to be a snobbish reaction to the village-square familiarity of the image, coupled with puritan distaste of a myth involving excrement.

15 Correspondential imagery may be found in many ancient cultures, of course; I concentrate on Egypt because the systematic nature of Egyptian thought makes it easier to analyze it in that setting.

16 For a creationist form of this view, see Bullinger, *The Witness of the Stars*.

17 Here I have adhered to the interpretations of J.L.E. Dreyer, in *A History of Astronomy from Thales to Kepler*, Chapters I and II, but I have not followed him in his belief that the Parmenidean earth is spherical.

18 The modern interpretation of Plato's Atlantis myth could lead to the reconstruction of some such mathematical/philosophical scheme. Harold A.T. Reiche (in Brecher/Feirtag eds., pp. 153–189) has discovered that the measurements of the mythical continent are based on a squared spiral figure. His demonstration is convincing because it involves methods of approximation consistent with ancient mathematics. It is still difficult to determine whether these proportions are Greek, Egyptian or a conflation of both. Of course, very complicated mathematical and mechanical problems would have confronted any ancient mathematician trying to formalize a three-dimensional vortex, but a squared spiral is easily dealt with.

19 Budge, *Gods...* II, pp. 75–79.

20 The following is based in general on the first section of Swedenborg's *The Worship and Love of God*, pp. 9–62. As the summary is general, I have not given specific page references, except for quotations.

21 Swedenborg, *The Worship and Love of God*, p. 41. See also p. 44, where we see that, just as in the *Principia*, Swedenborg considers the form-in-potential as being as real as, if not identical to, the fully realized form. Thus, all the "creatures" referred to may have been only what we would now describe as single cells or something even more rudimentary because "...unless what is universal be in single things and with single things or in least things as in greatest, it is not universal." In all these creatures or entities the end, which is the fully-developed species, must be regarded as existing, in true potential but different form, in the most elementary beginning. This is also expressed in the footnote on pp. 48–49 "...the ends themselves and uses are altogether different from the causes and means in their first origin."

Some of Swedenborg's ideas on the relationship between plants and animals are crudely recapitulated by Erasmus Darwin, the grandfather of Charles Darwin—and of some of his theories. In a note to his poem, *The Botanic Garden* (additional note XXXIX, quoted by Grabo (see bibliography), pp. 66–67) Darwin says: "I am acquainted with a philosopher, who contemplating this subject thinks it not impossible, that the first insects were the anthers or stigmas of flowers; which had by some means loosed themselves from their parent plant, like the male flowers of Vallisneria; and that many other insects have gradually in long process of time been formed from these; some acquiring wings, others fins, and others claws, from their ceaseless efforts to procure their food, or to secure themselves from injury. He contends, that none of these changes are more incomprehensible than the transformation of tadpoles into frogs, and caterpillars into butterflies." The mysterious philosopher is not identified. Since this is a caricature of Swedenborg's morphological view, it is impossible to tell whether this idea comes from somebody who had read Swedenborg or from Darwin's own misinterpretation of him or from some other source.

22 Ibid., p. 19.

23 Ibid., pp. 40–41.

24 It is often said that Swedenborg believed in "spontaneous generation," but in the strict sense this is not so. He believed that first-form animalcules could develop in the substances emitted by the "odours, effluvia and exhalations" of plants, or in subtle substances emitted by organic materials in decay. He always has organic matter developing from organic matter in the physical sense (the structure of uses apart) except in the primal creation.

25 Swedenborg, *The History of Creation*, pp. 6, 14–15.

26 Wiener, *Cybernetics*: see index refs. "Leibniz."

27 Sandra Blakeslee for *New York Times News Service*, Jan. 20, 1990. "Bacterial Gene-Swapping in Nature," by Robert V. Miller, *Scientific American*, January, 1988, pp. 66–71.

28 As 27.

29 Swedenborg, *Principia* I, pp. 42–43.

30 Ibid I, p. 38.

31 Swedenborg, *The Worship and Love of God*, pp. 143–147.

32 Swedenborg, *A Philosopher's Notebook*, p. 248. Sanchuniathon also has a theory, if I interpret his mythical/poetic language correctly, that animal forms were produced from plant forms, which were themselves produced in a kind of mud. Thus the source of all life is Mot, "which some call slime and others excrescence of watery secretion." This may be an organic slime, such as accumulates on rocks in water, but the phrase "excrescence of watery secretion" suggests it is earth precipitating out of water. The latter interpretation is more historically plausible because, if accepted, it would make this part of Sanchuniathon's argument a virtual doublet of an ancient Mesopotamian account, in which the primeval gods first engender forms of "silt," Lahmu and Lahamu (Frankfort et al, *Before Philosophy*, pp. 182–187). Mesopotamian influences on Phoenician religion are as well-known as Egyptian ones.

It is interesting that a modern theory has organic life developing from inorganic molecules in clay (see Cairns-Smith, *Seven Clues to the Origin of Life*, a popular summary of the author's *Genetic Takeover*.

33 Swedenborg, *A Philosopher's Notebook*, pp. 278–285.

CONCLUSION

The Logic of Correspondences

The broad rationality of Swedenborg's thought had been demonstrated, though unintentionally, by the end of the nineteenth century. Vortices were being discovered everywhere—sometimes called by that name, sometimes not. Late nineteenth-century vortices were directly physical for the most part, not the exemplars and form-generating paradigms of Swedenborg. Lord Kelvin had hypothesized "vortex-atoms," tiny whirlpools in an inert and perfect fluid which filled all of space. Maxwell had developed a theory of molecular vortices which produced the wave-motions of light, electricity and magnetism. Rankine had maintained that molecules were vortices and that the heat in bodies took vortical form, in which form it also passed from body to body. Osborne Reynolds had postulated a "granular ether," some of whose qualities remind us of the Swedenborgian ether, though superficially. The problem with most such theories was that, unlike the theory of Swedenborg, they could not explain the generation of invariable quantities of mass, of crystalline forms, and of permanent deformations of solid structures.

In spite of or perhaps because of this no credit was given to Swedenborg. When nineteenth-century physicists, particularly in

England, looked for an eighteenth-century ancestor of the "new physics," they found him in the neo-Pythagorean Boscovich, not Swedenborg. Boscovich's *Theory of Natural Philosophy* (first edition, 1758) begins with a universe of active dimensionless points in a void, governed by binary principles of attraction and repulsion. His waveforms and helix-forms may be interpreted in such fashion that they lead to vortex atoms, such as those of Lord Kelvin. Many of his mathematical and mechanical conclusions, taken one by one, may be found in Swedenborg, though their visions of deep microphysical forms and forces are not the same. We shall never know if he had read Swedenborg's *Principia* or not: the *Principia* was on the Vatican's index of forbidden books and, as a Jesuit, he could not refer to it.

The real mystery here is that nineteenth-century vorticism seems to adapt Boscovich in the direction of Swedenborg, without mentioning the latter. Since Swedenborg was so little read, the conclusion must be that this was forced upon them by the evidence.[1]

Nobody now works with the vortex-atoms of Lord Kelvin, but they are obsolete in the way of coarse early models of concepts which would later become more refined and precise, not in the way of archaic absurdities. The vortex-universe of the late nineteenth century was an ancestor, in the direct line, of the modern one. Thus Lord Kelvin held that matter was made up of the rotatory parts of a perfect, inert and incompressible fluid, which fills all of space. This fluid is a substance, since it transmits wave motion, but it is certainly not matter, as the nineteenth century thought of matter. It *generates* matter. This is much more interesting—and anticipatory—than the caricature of a "rigid-jelly ether" found in books of "How-Relativity-Changed-the-World" variety.[2] Indeed, such ideas are still with us, but the fluid is no longer called ether. The fluid is now space/time itself, thus, it would seem, a mental creation rather than a physical substance. Yet there is a philosophical ambiguity here. How can an entity which may be bent by the action of physical forces, as space/time is supposed to be in black holes (but not only there), be anything but a physical substance, no matter how abstractly conceived? It would then be a kind of "ether" in a non-

Swedenborgian sense (it would actually mix characteristics of Swedenborg's first three elements, primary, magnetic and etheric).

At the same time, of course, we must recognize that nineteenth-century vorticism was not really Swedenborgian in spirit. For, as we have seen, the Swedenborgian universe is not one of simply physical vortices but of the forms of classical geometry and mechanics as generated by vortical *functions*, which produce, in the first case, the cone and its sections. In other words, the Swedenborgian theory did explain (speculatively, of course) the formation of solid and massy objects, crystalline forms and so on. But there was, we know, a cost to pay. His theory demanded that material energy come from a superior source of energy at the generative point of the universal vortex; it also demanded that this vortex have the qualities of an intellectual structure. It was based unalterably on a religious philosophy. And, sadly, the majority trend of the thought behind the science of the nineteenth and twentieth centuries refused to accept, on *a priori* grounds, any objectively theistic form of natural philosophy. If theistic interpretations were naive enough to be easily demolished they were pilloried with glee. If they were on a higher intellectual level, they were ignored. Only a subjective religiosity was allowed, a humble request that those whose ingrained habits did not permit them to think otherwise be allowed to focus religious emotions on the marvels of the universe. A vague deism was also permitted, but its god was the "wraith" of Jack London's *The Iron Heel* (Chapter 19).

In a rewarding study on the ethics of Swedenborg,[3] W.R. Woofenden refers to a question commonly asked by those who have become aware of Swedenborg's scientific achievements. "Why," they ask, "is a man of such obviously astonishing achievement in the physical and biological sciences almost completely ignored in the annals of science? Why is he not ranked, as he apparently deserves to be, with such scientific explorers as Bacon, Galileo, Kepler, Newton and Darwin?" In answer to this, Woofenden quotes another Swedenborgian scholar, Philip H. Johnson: "The answer probably lies in the fact that he wrote the *Arcana Coelestia*."

This was certainly a major factor. On the other hand, even an agnostic science will often accept the discoveries of scientists who are, in certain respects, disreputably "mystical," provided that this "mysticism" is not overtly Christian. Newton believed that the Great Pyramid contained a unit of measure, a "sacred cubit," of Divine origin and he spent many years in studies of biblical symbolism. But Newton—a sort of Unitarian or Deist whose precise beliefs are still in dispute—was not a Christian. The Polish mathematician of the nineteenth century, Wronski, claimed that the Key of the Universe had been revealed to him. This was a formula for "the Generation of Quantities," and it appears as a symbol on the title pages of all his works, written on the pedestal of a sphinx whose head is encircled by a zodiac. Wronski was an electic of occultist inclination, not a Christian. Hegel claimed that his own work was the sum and crown of all philosophy and, by inclusion, theology. I ally myself with those who hold that Hegel was a Lutheran as he claimed to be; but the majority view is that he regarded Christianity as a mere adumbration or sketch of his own system and subtly denied the historical truth of the Gospels. This seems to me an unwarranted simplification of a position which is heretical (a neognostic revision of Lutheran "faith alone") rather than non-Christian. But few think of him as a Christian, heretical or not.

Now Newton is still held in the highest esteem; the "Wronskian" is a determinant well-known to students of differential equations, and not even the most determined opponents of Hegel deny his significance. If his Christianity were not a hidden issue, the nineteenth and twentieth centuries could well have accepted Swedenborg's scientific discoveries, while deploring or keeping silent about his "visions."

I would also suggest there was something else involved, something explicitly present in Swedenborg's science and natural philosophy.

First of all Swedenborg reconciled an opposition which many of the pioneers of our science wished to see sharply defined, that between ancients and moderns.[4] The rise of modern science and technology was inextricably connected with the rise of capitalism and factory industry. The new science accepted the patronage of "enlightened" monarchs but it was deeply antagonistic to the confining effect of ideologies associated with church and court. It was not anti-traditional only when traditional beliefs were incorrect. It was anti-traditional right or wrong. Swedenborg was a servant of the Swedish court and the son of a bishop. His writings, though he is never overtly anti-republican or even political, are full of the imagery of court ceremonial. His very style is courtly. It was the Swedish monarch, Adolf Frederick, not the advocates of the "new freedom," who protected him when the clergy ineffectually attacked his theological writings as heretical. There is simply no doubt that his revitalization of "Great Chain of Being" structure, the philosophical foundation of ideas of social hierarchy, put him squarely—so far as bourgeois and capitalist revolutionaries were concerned—in the reactionary camp.

Secondly, his philosophy was deeply incarnationist. The science of his time, as of ours, was based upon one very deeply held idea. This was that science must examine the physical world as if God did not exist. Even Christian apologists maintained that God had created the world so that it operated according to certain cyclically regular laws, like those exemplified in the mechanics of clockwork, and had left it to run on its own, only intervening in the case of the miracles recounted in the Bible. The deists reduced the role of the Divine still further and atheists and agnostics ignored it completely. There were those who objected to the "mechanical philosophy," but they were such as Henry More, the Cambridge Platonist, a figure out of the mainstream.[5]

Yet if, as Christians believe, the Incarnation took place as an event in the world of matter, it was an event of scientific as well as theological import. Of course I am not suggesting that science can effectively probe or even begin to probe the mystery of the Incarnation. I mean that a Christian's idea of the physical world—the world studied by physics, chemistry, biology and so on—must be such that it will accommodate a descent of the Divine into it. The material cosmos must be, above all, something *receptive*, and even, at some point in the continuum, incomplete. It cannot be self-contained, an enclosed cycle. The clockwork world of eighteenth-century apologetics, even the coldly magnificent expanse of the

Newtonian universe, was such that the Incarnation could not have taken place within it. This would have violated every one of its ordering principles. Such an event—though most eighteenth-century thinkers shut their eyes to such implications and those who were aware of them kept silent—would have torn the cosmos apart. Not only that, but the Resurrection, when the Lord transformed His physical body into a spiritual one, would have resulted in another disruption of the natural frame, an atomic explosion of some kind.[6]

In the Swedenborgian universe matter has no intrinsic properties at all. It does not even exist on its own. Rather, it exists (the phrase first appears in the theological writings but is applicable to the scientific ones) *as of* itself. It is also, to the despair of those who hoped to save Swedenborg by turning him into an idealist, *completely real*, and this because God has created it.

In my view, we must add these two scandals to the other one, the obvious scandal that Swedenborg claimed to have been admitted, by the Lord's special Providence, into the spiritual world. Perhaps, in some large sense, the three scandals are the same.

Swedenborg's vision of the cosmos may be summed up in one word. It is a system of *correspondences*, of universal analogy. If world-systems did not operate in a parallel manner on a multitude of levels there would be no universal order, or any order at all. Even the logic of cause and effect is referred, in the end, to the logic of analogy. And here we have another scandal—for the logicians this time. It is commonly believed that the drawing of analogies, despite the fact that scientific thought clearly rests upon a recognition of similarities among apparently diverse phenomena, is a vague and subjective activity. It is often said that when we say two things are alike we are at best classifying them, at worst merely reasoning from inadequate sensual knowledge. When we know physical causes or probabilities we need no longer rely on analogies.

Yet there is something wrong here. The universe does not consist only of one cause and effect but of a multitude of them. How do we relate sequences of causes and effects? The heat of the sun causes flowers to bloom in the spring; the application of heat in the laboratory causes chemical changes in substances. How can we arrive at any idea of heat as a causative entity unless we can compare these two events, which appear completely unrelated? How else can we develop a science of heat, include in one category all the effects of heat? It is altogether reasonable to say that, without systematic analogical thinking, man would have been unable to conceptualize sequences of causes and effects and relate them to each other.

Nevertheless, we must deal somewhat more precisely with the logician's scorn of analogical thinking, and we shall do so. It is a tedious subject but it must be dealt with—not in a finally conclusive way but in such a fashion that the reader interested in logical procedures may develop the argument on his own. First, though, let us look at a few aspects of Swedenborg's analogical thinking and relate them to what were identified in the first chapter as key ideas.

The principle which determines the development of his argument rests upon what I then called "a certain analogy" between geometrical/mechanical and logical form. Now we can be more specific. In the last analysis logic is not only *like* algebra, it *is* algebra. The relationship with geometry and mechanics follows on its own. As we saw in an earlier discussion of his *Algebra*, he holds that algebra embraces "whatever contains any likeness or proportion, let its species be what it may." This is because the equals sign is a representation of the equilibrium of forces and the equivalence of forms. Algebra deals with all those ratios which can, by various manipulations, be brought into equilibrium or equivalence. When pure quantities are dealt with, certain entities which are selected for use in the equation are brought into equality. It is thus a form of the science of analogy. That the same statement applies to logic we now know (this was an avant garde notion in Swedenborg's day) by the very fact that logic may be set out as an algebra.

I say "selected for use," yet an equation is useless unless there is a certain relationship among the attributes which are not selected. Let us say I have stated that the weight of a dead horse is exactly the same as the weight of a given quantity of cement. The quality in both entities which makes this comparison possible is the fact that both contain the same quantity, by weight, of matter in the earth's

gravitational field. But I have now defined them as material entities, and this means that they are made up of substances with
atomic and molecular structures. These structures differ in both
entities; the body of the horse is made up of organic substances, the
load of cement is made up of inorganic ones. However, there are
also known resemblances between organic and inorganic substances. On this level, the structures are not identical but are *like* each
other. And the similarities fan out in this fashion, the degrees of
mutual likeness being almost imperceptible at the outer edge of the
fan shape. Without an idea of the totality "horse" and the totality
"cement," from which totalities we have selected two equal quantities, the equation would be completely meaningless.

In other words, any exact quantitative relationship among material things, every relationship which can be reduced to an equation, carries with it a penumbra of likenesses which are more or
less close.

Abstracting the argument a little bit, we may say that every
equation is surrounded by a penumbra of analogy. This is true even
of pure numbers. In the equation 25-21=4, 4 and 25 are *alike*
because they are both squares of numbers. Also, 21 is 3 x 7 and 3
and 7 are both prime numbers. Without such likenesses, mathematics would have no structure and equations would be meaningless. These likenesses are not accidental, fugitive or illusory.
Swedenborg often calls attention to such likenesses, in passages
which have been misconstrued as vague attempts at quantitative
description.

Swedenborg believes that the universe of the large is built on
the same principle as the universe of the small and that one great
law governs the microworld and the universe of galaxies. This law
is developed from the principle just stated, with the emphasis now
placed on the equilibrium of forces and the functional equivalence
of forms. As a "great law" it can hardly be summed up in a phrase,
but we may at least put a label on it. It is a law of parallel and
interacting systems, the parallels being analogical and the forces of
interaction those of cause and effect.

Because his thinking is, in this very wide sense, algebraical,
Swedenborg erects hierarchies of structures which may most easily

be related by equilibrium and equivalence. This results in an extraordinary degree of rationality within the system, though the density of argument is such that we may sometimes lose sight of this. It is true that Swedenborg can sometimes be betrayed by the generalizing tendency of this rationality, as we saw in our discussion of the magnetic element. He is also often misled by erroneous data and, as is obvious, the rational development of an error leads to greater error.

Nevertheless, using rational means alone he does come up with scientific anticipations so extraordinary that they appear miraculous, tempting us to stop thinking about what he is saying and to drift into a mood of uncritical wonder. He really does discover structures of wave-functions, point-particles and related fields. Yet, if there are miracles here, they are only the miracles of genius. Swedenborg knows the waveforms he observes in the everyday world—water-waves, the vibrations of bodies which produce musical tones, the behavior of light-waves in prisms and water-films and the patterns iron-filings form around magnets. His anatomical studies have made him aware of the tremulations of muscles and nerves. From these he has developed a theory of tremulation and undulation, with pressure and local movement, as the four basic motion-forms of nature.

He must now explain, somehow, how wave-patterns can produce solid objects. This requires a new geometry or at least a geometry which, though its elements taken singly are classical, evolves in a nonclassical sequence. He picks up an old idea still important in his day that nature is a structure of vortices. The vortex is a form of wavelike motion which concentrates on a point, and wave-motions can only generate particles if they gather together, in some fashion, in a point. Thus the vortex becomes the norm or generative form of his system. Obviously nature cannot be made up of vortices tucked together and spinning side by side, like some animated set of bedsprings. It is rather that vortical forms engender all the others, which are to be related to vortices as Euclidean forms are to be related to the complex of point, line and plane. Though Swedenborg does not state in so many words how he relates his new geometry to that of Euclid, we can easily see that he relates the vortex to the straight-line forms of standard geometry by using the geometry of the spiral and the cone and by thinking of the straight-line forms familiar to us from Euclid as evolving from spirals and conic sections. And again, the universal diagram he develops from this is a massive structure of formal analogy.

From this new geometrical approach there emerges the idea of a point-particle at the center of an elementary of more tenuous matter. This is so close to our idea of a "field" that the use of the modern word is justified. I have not described with the necessary care and rigor the steps leading to this astounding discovery. The argument is so clear and pictorial that the development of a theorem-and-proof structure is a matter of scrupulous, patient and professional labor. Still, only a highly skilled mathematician could trace the line of argument in detail and develop a modern equivalent. What we can say, though, is that from his primary vortical form he generates shapes resembling forms discovered by modern science—atom-forms, molecule-forms, crystal forms and simple plantlike forms. He distributes these through the interior realms of nature in a schematic and idealized fashion, and he is frequently mistaken in his attribution of specific forms to specific substances.

With the vortex as his primary form, he is able to evolve a universe of discrete parts arranged in series. The largest or most generalized parts of this universe of forms are his elementaries. Swedenborg relates these to his own development of four-element formalism. In this development, the four "outer" levels correspond to our phases of matter—solid, liquid, gaseous and plasmic. He adds two more interior fields, an electromagnetic field and a field which we may think of as one of space/time functions.

As a result we have successive "planes" or "spheres" of matter, each formed by the plane or sphere conceptually above it or within it. These planes contain very different phenomena, yet Swedenborg tells us that they are all the same. Again, this puzzling statement follows from his belief that the universe is made up of waves. We know, from his early treatise, *On Tremulation*, and his later *The Five Senses*, that Swedenborg understood the behavior of sound very well. He knew that a complex sound or timbre may be created by superimposing simple sound waves one upon the other, engendering a more complicated pattern of vibrations. It is true that the simple wave illustrated in *The Five Senses*[7] resembles a triangle more than a sine wave, the sound wave we now know to be the simplest, but this is a schematic diagram, so drawn to make geometrical analysis easier. In any case, it is his wave-theory of matter which enables him to say that "all nature is the same," while his text seems to show that it is full of variety.

As a result of the geometrical and mechanical laws which Swedenborg then develops we have a universe which may be apprehended in terms of harmonic functions and cycles, point-particles and fields and more complex particles with their fields, as well as the distances and times which give them quantitative solidity.

Swedenborg had some talent as a poet, though he had neither the time nor the passionate inclination to develop it.[8] His early love of poetry, nonetheless, not only refined his style but helped him to a knowledge of rhetoric as a living science. This enabled him to extend his theories of correspondence to include a theory of language and imagery. I have not been greatly concerned with this except in the context of the *Principia*. He wishes to demonstrate that his scheme is closely related to the creation account in *Genesis*, the "Mosaic philosophy." The Mosaic philosophy is said to have in some measure coincided with the ancient philosophy of the Egyptians. In considering this philosophy, Swedenborg makes full and intelligent use of fragmentary summaries in Greek and Roman authors, and of Greek and Roman poetry themselves, particularly those which show an influence of Orphism.

In his attempt to understand the relationship between his own and more ancient philosophies he writes a short work, apparently intended only for his own use, called *A Hieroglyphic Key*. On casual reading it seems to have nothing to do with hieroglyphics. Furthermore, it appears to be of little interest, a collection of rather banal statements related by analogies, none of which is particularly striking. All this is deceptive, as we have seen (see also Appendix C).

If we are to sum up his theory of universal analogy, we must first determine what the syllogism of analogy is. Old fashioned logic is rarely taught in schools now and it is often considered to be faulty, an opinion which Swedenborg shared. But at the same time much has been lost, since modern logic has little respect for reasoning by analogy.

Here is an example: "I who talk and act am conscious; Caesar is a being who talks and acts; therefore he is conscious."

The "I who talks and acts" is a singular entity, but the *ability* to talk and act is a lesser universal, since it is characteristic of all persons who do not have some defect which renders them incapable of talking and acting. We may say that I am a single member of a small universal class of persons who talk and act. We know nothing of Caesar until we determine that he talks and acts. So we may say, while we are waiting to find this out, that he is a characterless particular: he might as well be called "John" or "Fido" or "X." There is a certain large universal quality to which we wish to relate "I who talk and act" and "Caesar," and that is the state of being conscious.

There is a hidden presupposition here. It is that the fact that I talk and act is *necessarily* linked to the fact that I am conscious. If it were not, the statement "I who talk and act am conscious" would not be of much significance. Such "tacit statements" always lie behind syllogisms of analogy. This means that this syllogism assumes an antecedent statement: "In my case, talking, acting and being conscious are necessarily related states." This is the statement of a necessary relationship between states, an assumption of correspondence between consciousness and talking and/or acting. Analogy and argument from necessity require each other.

If we defined consciousness in a different way, the above syllogism might not be absolutely true. If "Caesar" were the name of a computer, we should only agree with it if we agreed that a computer really talks and acts. Otherwise, we could only agree on some such wording as: "Humans who talk and act are conscious; the computer 'Caesar' imitates talking and acting; therefore in this respect he is like a conscious human being." I would then be saying that the computer is a model of one kind of human behavior, and my statement would also be in the realm of logical model-making or the literary simile. On the other hand, if I said: "I who talk and act am a conscious human being; Caesar talks and acts; therefore he is a conscious human being," I would seem to exclude the idea that Caesar is a computer. Yet the syllogism would still not be necessary or categorical, because I would not finally have excluded the possibility that things other than I can talk and act yet not be conscious human beings. Also, the person reading my syllogism may not know that I am assuming an antecedent: "In my case, talking, acting and being conscious are necessarily related states." Indeed, only in context, the context of my standing before him, does the person listening to me know that *I* am not a computer. For that matter, a diehard believer in artificial intelligence (if there are any left) might respond, "Well, you *are* a computer, or at least your brain is one." When we take all these qualifications into account, the syllogism diminishes into a rather lame statement of a subjective kind: "So far as I know, given my idea of consciousness, I who talk and act am conscious. Caesar talks and acts in a similar way, and therefore I assume he is conscious too."

However, there is a categorical or tautological or necessary form of this syllogism, which makes the assumption of an antecedent statement unnecessary. It is: "Only conscious human beings can talk and act; Caesar talks and acts; therefore he is a conscious human being." There is now no way Caesar can be a computer. My initial premise excludes the idea that machines can talk and act, though of course it does not deny that automata can be so constructed as to imitate thought and action. My listener still need not agree with me, but now he must question the truth of my syllogism, not its form.

I do not deny the crudity of my illustration. There are formal complexities which I have simply skipped over. And I do not pretend to be a master of the subtleties of either formal or dialectical logic. I intended to illustrate only two points—

The first is that the syllogism of analogy assumes as an antecedent some assumption of correspondence between the two points of the major premise ("I who talk and act//am conscious"). The second is that the syllogism of analogy is on a sliding scale. At one end of the scale (or perhaps in its middle) is tautology or necessity. At the other end (or stretching to either side of the central point of tautology) is an expression of personal opinion which makes sense only in the context of an argument in which the unspoken attitudes of the arguers are more or less tacitly taken into account. Yet there is always that one point, the point of tautology or necessity, at which it is "precise" in the sense that it has only one meaning. Therefore the scale slides between the necessarily or absolutely true and the contingently true. It also slides, as Hegel says,[9] between the individual entity as a general or universal idea (an exemplar) and the individual as a material and immediate object. And finally it slides (as in the earlier comparison of the dead horse and the load of cement) between the identical and the more or less alike. It takes in a world of philosophy both Platonic and Augustinian, for as Swedenborg said in something I quoted a while back, "spiritual things are exemplars," and *exemplar* in this case is pretty close to the Platonic idea as reinterpreted by Augustine.

This gives the syllogism of analogy, then, a peculiar flexibility or fluidity, which brings us back to the fluid geometry of the *Principia*. In this work the human is found in a balance between the opposites of determinism and the illusory freedom of disorder, both of which appear in his philosophy as forms of death or inertness.

The above kind of reasoning is not found in classical logic, but we must remember that Swedenborg has a radically skeptical view of classical logic as a guide to absolute truth. His reasoning is relativistic, not in the Einsteinian sense but in the sense that it deals with ratios. Classical logic found it difficult to deal with the relatively true, except as a corruption of the absolutely true; but logic has changed, for as the Roumanian logician, Moisil, has said, "there are several different logics," including a nonclassical "logic of the contingent."[10]

Perhaps it will be thought that I have been implying that Swedenborg is making all forms of logic special forms of the logic of analogy. I do not mean this. It is too reductionist. Rather, I mean something like the following. In his natural philosophy, and particularly in the *Principia*, he is everywhere concerned with problems of the relationship between the continuous and the discrete, a problem raised by the mathematics of calculus, which were then new. He had to consider such problems because the relationship between the Active and the Passive presented itself as a binary one, closely equivalent to the relationship between True and False in traditional logic. But obviously the Passive is not the False. Furthermore, a logic without a developed sense of the contingent and the possible, or which treats them only as badly formulated versions of the necessarily true or false, cannot model either the processes of thought or those of physical nature. What was needed was a logic which could model thoughts and physical processes on a sliding scale, yet could also approach quantitative precision at a particular point on the scale, since thoughts and physical processes are at the same time, depending on how we look at them, both continuous and discrete. The syllogism of analogy, because it embodies a sliding scale between the contingent and the necessary, represents the principle of continuity, *except* at the point at which the argument becomes necessarily true, where it represents the discrete.

To put it another way, the syllogism just discussed unites two different beings, "I" and "Caesar," at the point where they have something in common, the ability to talk and act. It then loops back, so to speak, to deduce, from the common faculty of talking and acting, a larger more inclusive category, that of consciousness, or the state of being conscious. In effect this loop-back takes us on to another syllogism of analogy, that of consciousness, which can take such a form as "I who am conscious can understand some natural processes; Caesar is conscious; therefore he is able to understand some natural processes." We note again a hidden presupposition, which in this case is that Caesar's consciousness is *normal* like mine, that is, that Caesar's consciousness is not deranged, that he is not, for example, in some unusual trance state in which he is aware of things but cannot form conclusions about them. Of course the truth of the syllogism is not affected by the fact that Caesar and I may have very different levels of mental ability. My understanding of nature may be that of the man in the street, while Caesar may be a physicist who has just won the Nobel Prize.

The categorical or necessary syllogism does not loop back. The statement: "Only conscious human beings can talk and act; Caesar talks and acts; therefore he is a conscious human being," is a closed statement. The very word "only" draws a circle around it. Certainly

I can add another statement to it. It might be something like: "Only beings who talk and act can utter intelligent statements from experience; Caesar utters intelligent statements from experience; therefore he can talk and act." But this statement lies side by side with the preceding one. Both statements are separate and closed, though related. They are "discrete," like points of necessity themselves. But the syllogism with which we started, the syllogism of analogy, is linked by "loop-back" with the syllogism which follows it. Here the two structures are continuous. Yet the syllogism of analogy has one point, the point of necessity, where it becomes the syllogism of necessity, and it is there part of a discrete structure. That is why it is considered inclusive. There are very good reasons for preferring the syllogism of necessity over the syllogism of analogy when we want an airtight statement. But a logic of nature cannot be built out of airtight statements. Living creatures die in an airtight environment and living thoughts die in a verbal universe made up only of airtight statements. In any system built upon rational analogy, we can find as many points of necessity as we need. Furthermore, if there is not at least one point of necessity in an analogy, it is not a good analogy. (The reader will of course understand that I am speaking here of simple and uncomplicated rational analogies, not of complex poetic figures, where the point of necessity cannot be defined so simply.)

Hegel says something interesting about the syllogism of analogy: "...the middle term of Analogy is an individual, which however is understood as equivalent to its essential universality, its genus or essential character."[11] This is another way of referring to what I called the "antecedent." Thus, when I say, "I who talk and act am conscious," I am assuming that the two attributes are necessarily connected, the first inside the second. If I said, "I who talk and act weigh 165 pounds," there would be no such necessary connection. I say the one is inside the other because the class of people who talk and act (the small universal) is included in the wider category of beings who have consciousness (the large universal). "Talking and acting" is a subset of "being conscious." We have a kind of shell structure here, which could extend very far. For example, beings which are conscious would be contained in a larger class of beings which are living organisms.

Hegel says that the individual entity is understood as equivalent to its essential universality. This is to say that the individual entity in this case is an exemplar, a type. Once again we find a link with the Platonic Idea as interpreted by St. Augustine.[12] Yet we must always keep in mind that Augustine thought of all the great insights of Greek philosophy as fading embers of ancient revealed truths and in some cases as having been derived, directly or indirectly, from Holy Scripture. Thus, for all his love of Plato and Plotinus, he is under no compulsion to follow them to the letter. He is looking for something behind them.

One of the expressions of the unity of God, according to Augustine, is that He resembles Himself, and from this come all the resemblances among earthly things. "...Likeness in creatures is the substitute for the perfect unity which belongs to God alone." Further, "...in the Augustinian doctrine likeness plays the role of intermediary between absolute unity, which is God, and pure multiplicity, which in its extreme condition would be identical with nothingness."[13] This formal relationship between unity and likeness is strictly reflected in Swedenborg's idea of algebra, that equality engenders analogy.

Some idea of universal analogy is therefore very old in Christian philosophy, and not only in the Augustinian tradition,[14] though it is most clearly found there. Without some such perception of universal analogy there would have been no symbolic interpretation of Scripture, no typology linking the Old and New Testaments, no liturgy or liturgical art, and the parables of the New Testament would have been meaningless anecdotes.

We see then that the doctrine of correspondences in Swedenborg's natural philosophy, though it is new and indeed revolutionary in its application and is built furthermore on a philosophical basis typical of the early eighteenth century, is unequivocally in the line of patristic and medieval thought or, at least, of a central tradition therein.

So Swedenborg's is not the first system to be based on universal analogy, and neither is Augustine's. Without going into the immense age and worldwide spread of such systems, we can say that it is intuitively obvious that any system which assumes an intrinsic difference between spirit and matter, yet has spirit dwelling in and informing matter, must be a system of ranked analogies. Spirit cannot act on matter—for example, a spiritual idea cannot create a material thing—unless there is a certain similarity between the spiritual idea and the material thing. At the same time spirit and matter must be different and spirit must be superior to matter and preexistent to it. Spirit is in certain ways like matter and in other ways different from it, and the differences are such that it is superior to matter and able to act upon it by its own intrinsic power. (The reader will appreciate that I am *not* speaking of "mind over matter" in the context of beliefs in telekinesis etc.). Thus the relationship is one of analogy and of ranked analogy, because one is superior to the other. But there are points of ordered contact between spirit and matter, and among these is a point of equilibrium. This is the central idea of a doctrine of correspondences very crudely expressed, and simply avoiding all the complexities a well-developed philosophy can bring to such things.

Formal categories of thought are not classified, so far as I know, in ancient Egyptian literature. Yet most logical categories may be found in practical use in this literature, whose formulaic structure, with its clear separation of themes, itself indicates a well developed practical logic. Such qualities may be apparent in a single maxim, as in the case of one found in the *Maxims of Khensu-hetep*

> When thou makest an offering unto thy God, guard thou against the things which are an abomination unto him. Behold thou his plans within thine eye, and devote thyself to the adoration of his name. He giveth souls unto millions of forms, and him that magnifieth him doth he magnify.[15]

The thoughts here are contrasted and developed in an almost mathematical way. In the first sentence, we have the positive and the negative of a devotional act, making an offering which is pleasing to God and avoiding actions which are displeasing to Him. In the second sentence we have the inner and outer aspects of devotion, seen in terms of intellectual faith and duty. The worshipper regards inwardly his vision of the Divine intent and devotes himself, in an obedient exterior or dutiful action, to the adoration of the *name* of God. The last sentence is logically complex, embodying the first two movements. God's giving of souls to millions of forms finds its reciprocal (or responsive negative) in the worshipper's magnification of (the name of) God. The worshipper who interiorly magnifies the name of God will be given external blessings of life (will be magnified). The last sentence may easily be put in the modern form of a syllogism, such as—

> The forms that God has made are magnified to the degree that they participate in God; man is a form which God has made; therefore as man participates in God he will be magnified.

There is no need to expand on the perfectly obvious, that this kind of literary construction is found throughout the Old Testament. Nor need I do more than indicate a well-known scandal of Egyptian religion, which is that the same pattern of thought which is found in this beautiful maxim is also found in statements of the grossest superstition and in the manipulative formulas of magic.[16]

I do not doubt it was this ancient form of rational thought which Swedenborg sensed behind the confusing accounts of Egyptian religion available to him in the Greek and Latin writers. It also seems that it helped him, along with the Augustinian tradition, to find the "universal mathesis" he speaks of. This is what the *Principia* is, when we read it as a canon of forms rather than as a book of speculative physics. It is indeed the latter, but before it is physics it is an extended treatise about the way we may generate all geometrical forms from a fundamental Active/Passive binary. This development is in all ways parallel to a system of dialectical logic. When, furthermore, we go carefully through this book, noting his systematic use of such terms as the Active, the Passive, the Finite, the Elementary, the Similar, the Dissimilar, the Successive, the Simultaneous and Variety, along with some other terms, we find that he is describing the relations and qualities which distinguish one mathematical and mechanical entity from another. His doctrine of harmonic correspondence shows us how to construct logical equations which embody these relations and qualities. We then find a set of morphological analogies between logical and mathematical operations, which may be extended to include very many of the forms of nature. Morphology connects with geometry and thus his scheme terminates in the forms of classical geometry and massy objects.

Swedenborg's particular endeavour, that of finding a "universal mathesis"—what we should now call a natural logic or a logic of nature—is one of the great quests of his time and a little earlier. The most obvious connection is with Leibniz, but he draws broadly from the philosophy of his period without committing himself to any individual or school, as his notebooks show. And though he develops his universal mathesis far beyond the understanding of his contemporaries, the endeavour itself is still identifiably of his time. In the nineteenth century this endeavour will seem a futile one. Positivism (though not the quasi religion of Comte) and an exclusive concentration on "hard fact" dominate most of the century, except among the Hegelians. This changes at the end of the nineteenth and beginning of the twentieth century, when forms of universal mathesis return with the logic of Boole, the natural philosophy of the Marxists, early forms of systems theory and so on.

In the end, then, Swedenborg's greatest contribution to natural philosophy turns out to be his development of a remarkably efficacious logic of nature. His successes are explained by his logic and, as I have said more than once, so are his failures. His logic is so supple that, when he does go wrong, we can see, if only in hindsight, why he did. Some times the data are bad; sometimes he generalizes too rashly; sometimes, because he has imagined things beyond the mathematical capacities of his day, he cannot work out his theories in detail. In all these cases, the system proves to be better than his applications of it. Even if this system is only crudely valid, and I believe it is much more finely tuned than that, the

Principia is one of the most revolutionary works ever written by a natural philosopher, and it is as revolutionary today as it was in the eighteenth century.

ENDNOTES

1 Isaiah Tansley discusses such affinities in his fine if inevitably outdated introduction to the 1912 *Principia*. He finds in Swedenborg such ideas as that matter is a form of electric charge in motion. He quotes Sir Oliver Lodge to the effect that "ether is not matter at all. It may be the substance or substratum or material of which matter is composed...," and he quotes a similar comment by Gustave Le Bon. He finds anticipations of Maxwell's electromagnetic theory of light. And of course of the vortex-atom and the solar-system atom. This in 1912.

Tansley has some trouble with Swedenborg's ether because he identifies it too closely with the ether-concept of the late nineteenth and early twentieth centuries. It is closer to the "fire-mist" of Laplace (p. lxii of Tansley's *Introduction* and quotation from Sir Robert Ball, p. lxiv), a form of very hot gas. But Swedenborg, who of course writes well before Laplace, gives this very hot gas a distinct structure in his phase-state system. It must therefore be called a plasma. Tansley also misses the pure formalism of Swedenborg's vorticism.

2 From time to time I draw a distinction between Swedenborgian ideas of relative form and Einsteinian relativity. In his introduction to his *Space-Time-Matter*, Hermann Weyl sets out the philosophy on which his mathematical exposition of Einsteinian relativity is based. As I understand his argument, it is a distinctively subtle combination of subjective idealism and a belief in a "cosmic wisdom" (cf. Spinoza's Nature-God) which realizes itself through human consciousness. A difficult but beautiful mathematical system is built upon this philosophy. The mathematical system is, as it should be, freestanding in the coherence of its internal logic, and Weyl's position as a mathematical physicist is unassailable. But at the end the philosophical arguments return as if they had been proved. This is not possible because they are unprovable.

In other words we have a physics based on a philosophy of the nature of human perception. It is true that uninformed sense-perception and intuition are rejected as indicators of ultimate reality. But mathematical perception, as represented by the position of an observer in a world of mathematical entities, is not so rejected, and it is interpreted in a philosophical manner. Yet there can be no *inevitably* preferred position of a mathematical observer, hence no inevitable philosophy. The point 0 of a Cartesian or other graph can represent Creator, Observer, an Observer who is also a Creator, or a point observed or created by any of these. It can represent nothingness or the source of everything. The same graph serves all philosophies.

This then is a form of natural philosophy which has sought out and constructed an appropriate mathematical form, a form which is itself clearly valid and has proved to be greatly effective as a tool of physics. But the philosophy is not proved by the mathematics. Nor is Swedenborg's philosophy proved by his mathematics. But he does not claim it is.

3 Woofenden, W.R., "Swedenborg's Concept of Love in Action" *The New Philosophy*: October/December, 1969 and January/March, 1970. The value of this study is that it considers Swedenborg's ethical philosophy without theological reference, except that proper to the domain of philosophy. The reader may thus approach the philosophy on the level of reason alone. In the case of Swedenborg, so often called a "mystic," this is a necessary procedure. In his study Woofenden points out Sweden-

borg's debt to St. Augustine. Many Swedenborgian scholars have not been aware of this and have assumed a direct influence from Neoplatonism.

4 See Jones, *Ancients and Moderns, passim*. Francis Fukuyama's recent *The End of History and the Last Man* develops this opposition in triumphalist fashion. Many years ago, however, Fackenheim (p. 222) anticipated Fukuyama's argument about "the end of history" and characterized it as "absurd."

5 More (1614–1687) believes that the experimenters of the Royal Society will rout the mechanical philosophy, which he says is "a philosophy that professeth, that matter having such a quantity of motion as it has, would contrive itself into all those phaenomena we see in nature. But this profession cannot rightly be called *the mechanical philosophy* but *the mechanical belief of credulity"* (Jones, p. 250). I have cut out More's capitalization of nouns and excessive italicization, for the sake of easier reading.

6 It was probably some sense of this which enabled alchemy to linger on till the late eighteenth century, though its irrationality on the empirical level had become apparent by medieval times. If elements could be transmuted into each other in a gradual or non-catastrophic way, then they could also be transmuted into subtle spiritual or at least quasi-spiritual substances. Or so it seemed. Most alchemical philosophy tended towards a heretical neo-Manichaeism, but there was also a Christian form, sometimes associated with the imagery of the Grail and the idea of the transubstantiation of elements in the Mass.

7 Swedenborg, *The Five Senses*, p. 235.

8 The last word on Swedenborg's purely poetic gifts can only be spoken by somebody familiar with eighteenth-century Latin verse. Perhaps he might find that I have, in the preceding chapter, somewhat underrated these. However, in later years, Swedenborg himself said, as quoted by one Christian Johansen, that *The Worship and Love of God* "...was certainly founded on truth, but somewhat of egotism had introduced itself, as he had made a playful use in it of the Latin language, on account of his having been ridiculed for the simplicity of his Latin style in later years" (Sigstedt, p. 202). Here he commits himself to the ideas embodied in the poem but more or less states that the style clothes them in a self-consciously fanciful manner. Such a procedure is legitimate, but does not produce the organic unity of the greatest poetry.

9 Stace, *The Philosophy of Hegel*, p. 258. Hegel's own discussion of analogy may be found in No. 190 of his *Science of Logic*. Hegel dislikes analogy as a cosmic principle because he believes it leads to a probabilistic universe (*Phenomenology of Mind*, p. 290), certainly one Christian point of view.

10 Moisil, *Essais sur les Logiques Non Chrysippiennes*, pp. 39 and 49. Moisil discusses a great variety of "unconventional" logics. But in referring to this valuable and fascinating book I wish only to indicate the present openness of formal logic to forms *similar* to those of Swedenborgian logic. No exact analogue of Swedenborgian logic may be found in Moisil, nor have I encountered one elsewhere. By way of a complicated analysis it would be possible to relate it to the logic of Lukasiewiz, discussed by Moisil, in which *yes*=1, *no*=2 and *perhaps*=1/2—but not very closely.

11 Hegel (trans. Wallace), *Hegel's Logic*, p. 252.

12 Augustine's theory of "likeness" is scattered through many volumes. I have relied on the summary of Etienne Gilson in *The Christian Philosophy of Saint Augustine*, pp. 187–224. In Augustine the attributes of God are real entities. They are not, as they would be in the case of a man of whom we say "he is good" or "he is wise," mere conclusions drawn from behavior, so that we really mean "he acts as if he were good" or "he acts as if he were wise." No mortal may be good or wise of himself but only as he follows the will of God, Who is good and wise in Himself. God

also contains within Himself all the necessary principles which order the human and nonhuman worlds. Augustinian ideas are "principal forms or stable and unchangeable essences of things. They are themselves not formed, and they are eternal and always in the same state because they are contained in God's intelligence. They neither come into being nor do they pass away, but everything that can or does come into being and pass away is formed in accordance with them" (Gilson, p. 199).

13 Gilson, p. 211.

14 See index references, "Analogy," in Copleston's *A History of Philosophy*, Vol II, and note particularly an illuminating discussion of the treatment of analogy by St. Thomas Aquinas (II: pp. 358–362).

15 Budge, *Egyptian Religion*, p. 29.

16 The basic logic of the Egyptian system as a generalized philosophical whole is set out by Cheik Anta Diop in *Civilisation or Barbarism*, pp. 310–313. There is simply no doubt that his interpretation is, as he says, "...rigorously faithful to the Egyptian texts; it is not a tendentious interpretation." His love of his subject leads him somewhat to underplay the unpleasant aspects of Egyptian civilisation, but the resultant slight distortion is much less than that found, for example, in most texts on MesoAmerican civilizations. The reasons for favoring his arguments are based on his knowledge and reasoning power, not on "political correctness," as some last-ditch defenders of a chimerical "white Egyptian civilisation" have stated.

APPENDICES

A
Swedenborgian Influences on Imaginative Literature

In order to substantiate somewhat more fully the statement that Swedenborg had very little real influence on nineteenth-century literature I should summarize the influences at play on a few writers commonly mentioned in discussions of literary Swedenborgianism. It becomes apparent that the Swedenborg referred to is a mere lay figure of the occultist tradition. His true thought cannot be assimilated with that of the literary figures mentioned. Consultation of good biographies and critical studies of the writers in question will show that in almost all cases they did not seriously study his writings, but relied on summaries and casual references in the works of others.

William Blake - Blake had read Swedenborg, but valued Paracelsus and Boehme more. He was also much influenced by a form of neo-Druidism which would eventually become absorbed in the complex known as "British Israel," not to mention the Cabalistic Rosicrucianism of Robert Fludd and the literature of the Levellers and Ranters. Absorbed in such a complex, any specifically Swedenborgian thought quite loses its character.

Coleridge, the Brownings and Emerson - We have evidence of some serious reading on the part of Coleridge, one of the very few who seriously examined Swedenborg's theology. He remained fascinated but completely ambivalent. I do not know enough of the poetry of E.B. Browning to comment in her case but I find no evidence of influence on Robert Browning. Emerson's understanding is superficial.

Gérard de Nerval - The influences playing upon him include those of almost all the figures of French occultism of the early nineteenth century, among which that of Swedenborg is barely discernible.

Balzac expresses great enthusiasm for Swedenborg, but the ideas he attributes to his "Buddha of the North" in *Louis Lambert* belong more to Martines de Pasqually and Wronski.

Baudelaire takes from Swedenborg not so much the idea of correspondence as the mere word; his specific notion of the image-symbol has its roots in Renaissance and Baroque symbolic thought as it comes to him through the poetic tradition. He is also influenced by Wronski, whose thought, though symbolic, is incompatible with that of Swedenborg.

I have been able to find only one nineteenth-century writer of importance in which a Swedenborgian influence is unequivocally strong. This is Coventry Patmore. His verse and thought are full of such resonances, almost all referred, as to a center, to ideas of conjugial love. He did not acknowledge this too openly, because he was a Roman Catholic and Swedenborg was on the "Index." Nevertheless, he is able to relate Swedenborgian (theological) concepts of married love to the chivalric and courtly-love tradition so deeply present in English poetry from medieval to Stuart times, and also to the image of the Virgin Mary as a form of *Sophia* or the Divine Wisdom. This image, though typical of Eastern Christianity, is also to be found in the West. By incorporating these elements in a narrative context of Victorian domesticity he achieves something truly fine, an incarnated symbolism which demands no scholarly glosses or conscious withdrawal to the proudly hermetic archaism of the ivory tower. His symbolism comes to rest in daily life, as he says in his poem, *Wind and Wave*, "after the narrow mode the mighty Heavens prefer..."

B
Marxian Labor—Value and the Doctrine of Correspondences

A specific object of a material kind, whether inorganic or organic—a road, a table, a horse—is also a representation of intellectual and spiritual qualities, a non-arbitrary symbol. This is true not only in the Writings of the illumination period but also in the philosophical writings of the period we are concerned with here. In saying this, I do not contradict an earlier statement that correspondential relationships exist between parallel sets of functions. An object is a set of functions. We must not imagine—this was never the right way of looking at things but modern science has made its inadequacy clear to everybody—that material objects are self-enclosed entities whose relationships with other entities are only external. We must not imagine, for example, that if we were to visualize a horse in a pasture, and were then to take away from our mental picture the pasture with its trees and grasses, the fence around the pasture, the road running by the pasture which links it to the farm buildings and the town beyond the farm, leaving us in the end with a horse suspended in empty space, that we should then have a true picture of a horse, or even of the corpse of a horse. For one thing, the bones and flesh of the horse have been formed by the grasses it ate in the pasture. Every object is a network of functional relationships which tie it to other objects, and this interconnectedness is found even among the smallest objects known to physics, as we are all aware.

The pre-illumination doctrine of correspondences is a remarkable development of analogical reasoning. This becomes the rationale of a theory of parallel systems which are interrelated in complex fashion. Logic itself becomes a theory of parallel systems, and is related in this fashion to geometry and mechanics.

The use of the syllogism by analogy was present in the thought of the physiocrats. They compared the exchange of values in economic systems with the exchange of nutrients in the body, for which the blood is responsible. Since this concept was treated structurally, rather than as a passing illustration, we may say that their key economic image, the basis of their system, was a true analogy. In the case of Hegel, when he says that Christianity expresses in symbols an absolute truth which is identical with his philosophy, and that the Christian religion is God's revelation of Himself, he in effect makes the entire world-system an analogical one. Only by analogy may a coherent structure of symbols parallel a coherent structure of logically-defined truths. This is a coarse simplification and to simplify a Hegelian argument is always to coarsen it. Furthermore, Hegel does not define his system as an analogical, but as a dialectical one. Yet, though I have coarsened, I do not believe I have falsified, its essential nature.

It is not surprising, then, that we should find the appearance of a strange relationship between Marxian and Swedenborgian thought. It is, except in a restrictedly formal sense, illusory. The real relationship is with the thought of Hegel and the physiocrats, whose influence on Marx and Engels is extensive and obvious. The former in turn are somewhat related to Swedenborg because they think analogically or dialectically. We can trace no direct influence by Swedenborg on Hegel or the physiocrats. Hegel was knowingly influenced by Renaissance Lullism (and Lullism is an analogical and dialectical system); Quesnay, the founder of physiocracy and a medical doctor, was influenced by the analogical thinking which pervaded pre-modern medicine.

The Marxists hold that the value of an object is determined largely by the amount and kind of labour which goes into it—and of course this raw idea is a truism of classical economics and not at all unique to the Marxists. In Marx the purely economic development of this argument is subtle and precise; but there is a philosophical form which goes much deeper, an argument of importance and intrinsic interest. This Marxist argument has been well discussed by the Soviet philosopher, Yu. K. Pletnikov.[1]

---

[1] Pletnikov, Yu. K., *Social Relations*, in *Philosophy in the USSR: Problems of Historical Materialism*, pp. 52–71.

Labour creates a world of worked or fashioned objects, each of which represents a portion of transformed matter. We may say that the laborer "puts himself" into the object he makes or transforms and that it then becomes an *objectification* or a *realization* of his subjective values. We can see this clearly in a work of fine art, but it is true of every work of man. Even if I am only turning over the earth to plant a row of onions, I put myself into every thrust of the fork into the ground and an elementary sense of fitness will govern the straightness of my row, just as a simple form of botanical knowledge will determine the depth of the holes in which I place my bulbs, their distance apart and so on. In every object possessed, used or consumed by man, there exists a real component of embodied effort, knowledge and subjective values, which we may think of as reified labour, as something abstract or seemingly abstract which has become material. And, precisely because it is reified, it can no longer be thought of as merely abstract or subjective.

It is the reified labour in the objects men make for possession, use or consumption by others which gives these objects a seeming life or value of their own, i.e. a "meaning," particularly when this matches a need on the part of the possessor, user or consumer. When, in buying a table, I call it a "table," instead of "a horizontal plane of wood fastened to four vertical pieces of wood," I recognize the intent of the woodworker to make a table and, by recognizing it as such, I affirm that he has done so. I recognize that his "idea" has entered the world of reality by saying that it is real to me, that it matches my mental idea of a table, that it can be used as such and that it has exchange or monetary value. I recognize that his thought has become a real thing and that the wood of which it is made has become the passive substratum of the idea "table." I ignore for purposes of argument the value of the wood itself, which takes us back to an earlier stage of the evolution of value. And I also ignore the complications introduced by machine and particularly by computerised production, which has the effect of socializing the realization of the idea. I mean by this that the summarized industrial skills of a society, represented in production-line organization or the program of a robot, go into the production of a generalized

mass-idea of a table. This can be thought of as a communal variation of the reification discussed by Marx, in which the "cultural
heritage" is embodied.

Thus Marx can say that "the value of commodities is the very
opposite of the coarse materiality of their substance, not an atom of
matter enters into its composition."[2]

Now this happens, though there is no question of influence, to be
very close to the pre-theological Swedenborgian doctrine of correspondences, and the relationship becomes more not less apparent
as the subtleties of Marx's theory are explored (which we cannot do
here). In this doctrine, which forms the basis of his later specifically
theological ideas of "use," things have a "use" in the familiar sense
of the word: they are useful for this or that human purpose. They
have a "use" in the scheme of Providence, a "good use," and even in
what opposes that scheme, since there are "evil uses." Also, when
man, by labour spiritual or material, acts purposefully and produces a result which is either a completed act or a worked and fashioned thing, he "performs a use," which is embodied in the act or
thing. The doctrine is not fully expressed in the philosophical
works, but is there stated in a more limited way, as in the following
quotation from *The Worship and Love of God*—

> The uses which tend to the fruition of goodnesses, are like souls, or
> ends in the soul, which from nature call forth stores to themselves,
> whereby they effigy to themselves a kind of body, by which they may
> prepare and expand themselves and their uses in order that there may
> be effects. For they are not in their uses until they are in effects;
> therefore when they are in these, they are in themselves as in their own
> forms; so that effects are only uses thus unfolded and brought forth into
> the gyre of nature. Wherefore these flowering ornaments are nothing
> but external representations of uses, which therefore charm by their
> harmonies the external senses of our body and their entrances, even for
> this use, that they may penetrate our minds by an easy passage. But
> while they penetrate my mind they appear to me as naked without
> clothing, thus most beautiful, because they sparkle from the effulgence

---

[2] Marx, K., *Capital*: vol. I, cited in Pletnikov, p. 55.

of good and the brightness of truth. Hence I already observe that the discriminations of uses alone are what sport together through so many varieties, and through so many genera and species, and that each of them performs its own gyre, and has a kind of perpetuity; since they flow from a certain first principle, through mediums to the ultimate, and from this again to their first; for I have not as yet seen a single point of the series which is not from use, by use, and for use. From this single view, while I examine all things from single things and single things in all, I discover that no knowledge of anything escapes me, but that general things, with their particulars, from their very sanctuaries, flow in into my mind; hence particular representations are to me so many mirrors of things general, and *vice versa*. But what has principally exalted the inmost sense of my delights, even almost above itself, is the consideration, that all the goodnesses and uses of the universe have reference to higher goodnesses and uses, and at length to the Supreme, in a certain order distinguished by degrees, from which they seem to me to be distant, according to the excellence of the series, in which they are by nature; for one thing is continually for the sake of another, and all things finally for the sake of One, or our GOD, the fountain of all goodnesses and uses.[3]

The speaker is Adam in the Garden. The beautiful and enthusiastic limpidity of the style, since clarity can also obscure, may blind us both to the philosophical depth of the above passage and the fact that it has a hard physical application. And to its traditional background, because it is firmly rooted in the Christian idea which we are familiar with in the form of the medieval saw, *Laborare est orare*. Even Swedenborg's use of the word "good" is etymologically traditional: the idea of the generically "good" cannot be separated from the notion, "good for some purpose," which is how "good" is defined in the languages of several tribal peoples.

The performance of useful work is, as in a cloudy mirror, a reflection of the labour of the Divine in His creation. In strict language, of course, we cannot say that God labors in creation, since the word implies the arduous overcoming of difficulties in an already existing matter: we are imagining, in human terms, the

---

[3] Swedenborg, *The Worship and Love of God*, pp. 100–102.

sequence of Divine creative and formative acts. The analogy is particularly well developed by Ramon Lull, who in his beautiful *Cent Formes*[4] and elsewhere approaches the Swedenborgian doctrine of use.

As to Marx, Pletnikov says—

> The object world that people have created, its transformed or humanized nature, is the total product of human labour. On the one hand, products of labour are the result of people's intentional activity. They are reproduced by people in accordance with their needs and therefore include in their content something subjective, something that loses its functional meaning without the subject. On the other hand, the products of labour have the same objective form of being with regard to the subject as other objects of the material world. They are capable of being physically alienated from their immediate producers and assimilated by other individuals. Thus, through alienation of the products of their labour (this alienation is, in the first place, the realisation of the division of labour between individuals) individuals become useful to each other, correlating, as it were, part of themselves with other individuals. The product of human labour functions as the material mediator between persons. It is not matter itself, but labour, including reified labour, which is present, unseen, in the transformed matter, that links people into an integral whole, transforming their life activity into the life activity of social beings.

> This is the source of social relations. Under the conditions of commodity production, however, this source is hidden, camouflaged by the seeming independence of the movement of things. The commodity production, as it emerged and developed in the history of society inevitably gave rise to commodity fetishism—the illusion that things have naturally inherent social properties. The relation of commodity producers to aggregate labour and, consequently, to each other, appears to these producers to be a kind of social relations of things themselves. The solution to the mystery of commodity fetishism and elucidation of the real genesis of social relations, of their deeper links with things (the

---

[4] Lull, R., *De les Cent Formes*, in *Arbre de Ciència*, pp. 570–590 in *Obres Essencials*, Vol. I.

products of human labour), links that, unlike their commodity—monetary forms, are not transient, is one of Marx's remarkable achievements.[5]

Perhaps the phrase "one of Marx's remarkable achievements" is not unjustified, but the achievement is, in the end, a transposition and reworking of ideas. The logical content of the Marxian formulation is Christian and Hegelian. Specifically he has adapted a Hegelian doctrine of work (in the *Philosophy of Right*, articles 189–208), which actually favors a welfare state based on private enterprise and private property (arts. 231–249) and overtly rejects communism (see throughout, but particularly art. 200). The reader will determine for himself whether this should be called "adaptation," "perversion" or something between the two.[6]

---

[5] Pletnikov, pp. 53–54.

[6] For my part I find the word "perversion" more appropriate, since Hegel's system was a Christian one. Hegel (art. 200) defines the demand for (economic) equality as a "folly of the Understanding," which projects its own abstract notion of equality and its "ought-to-be" onto a world of *implicit* dissimilarity and multiplicity. When we read his arguments in context we see that they cannot be logically inverted and thus cannot be adapted to the Marxian world-view. They are completely tied to his theory of nature. Marx knew Hegel and had fine logical capacities, so the conclusion as I see it must be that he twisted the dialectic to suit his purposes and covered over the discrepancies with strenuous revolutionary language. The same may be said of many of his other attempts to stand Hegel on his head. It could therefore be maintained that he neither adapted nor inverted the logic in these cases, but rather perverted it. So did most other Young Hegelians since, as Besancon says (p. 43) Hegel's synthesis broke down on his death (as a continuing and cohesive influence, that is, not as a philosophy).

Of course, it is *logical* perversion I speak of. Marx was a materialist, not a diabolist or magician.

C
An Example of the Active/Passive Relationship in Swedenborg's *A Hieroglyphic Key*

I refer again to an earlier quotation from *A Hieroglyphic Key*. The reason for the letter-symbols will come clear later on.

> From effects and phenomena (A_1) judgment is made concerning the world and nature, and from the world and nature (P_1) conclusion is made as to effects and phenomena.
>
> From actions and inclinations (A_2) judgment is made concerning man and the rational mind, and from man and his mind (P_2), when known, conclusion is made as to actions and inclinations.
>
> From works and the testimonies of love (A_3) judgment is made concerning God and from God (P_3) conclusion is made as to His works and the testimonies of His love.

Harmony or Analogy

> As the world stands in respect to man, so stand natural effects in respect to rational actions.
>
> As man stands in respect to God, so stand human actions in respective to Divine works.

Swedenborg does not use words carelessly, and when he says "harmony," relating it to analogy, he is referring to musical and other forms of harmonic motion as matters of ratio. In music, the ratio of the interval of the fifth (*doh* up to *sol*) to the tonic, in terms of vibrations per second, is as three is to two. In the complex entities he is dealing with in his analogies, which are universals, ratios cannot be measured quantitatively, but these universals will realize themselves eventually in quantitative particulars. In the relationship of God to man no ratio is even imaginable, but he insists there is something like ratio, perhaps an analogue of ratio. Thus he says, as we have seen—

> From the several examples that have been adduced, a certain analogy may be formed, and from the analogies an equation, which may again be reduced to its own analogies: as in the following: as the world stands in respect to man, so stand natural effects in respect to rational

actions; and so likewise in the other examples. And if the world be denoted by w, man by m, effects by e and actions by a, they may be joined together in the form of an analysis, to wit, w is to m, as e is to a. That the manner in which these terms should be associated with others (may be) multiplied, and from them an analysis (may be) formed, will come for demonstration elsewhere. These are the first rudiments of that universal mathesis of which mention was made above. There is also a continuous ratio or analogy; for example, As the world is to man so man is to God. From which analogy it follows that God passes over into the world through man; or that God has nothing in common with nature except through man; also, that the perfection of nature depends on the perfection of man; for God, the founder of nature, disposes the world no otherwise than in accordance with the quality of the medium or man whereby he communicates with the world.

When we look at the first quotation we see that certain words are repeated: "from...," "judgment is made concerning...," "and from...," and "conclusion is made as to..." These words make up the bare-bones structure of each of the sentences in the three similar statements. The variables are "effects and phenomena," "the world and nature," and similar phrases in the two following statements. The repeated words are so formal that we could well replace them with conventional signs. As to the variables, we can properly represent them by algebraical letters, since it is the general pattern of the statement we wish to discover in this instance, not its meaning. So the three phrases, "effects and phenomena," "actions and inclinations," and "works and the testimonies of love" may be denoted by the symbol x, meaning no more than that these can be seen as representing the general category of entities from which judgment is made. By applying this principle to the other variables in the three statements we eventually come up with the following formula—

From x judgment is made concerning y, and from y conclusion is made as to x.

The relationship between x and y is the relationship between active parts and passive whole. For, taking the x's and y's in each statement, effects and phenomena are included in the world as its active parts; actions and inclinations are included in man and his rational mind as their active parts; works and the testimonies of love are included in God as His active parts. I add that of course we do not realistically think of God, or, for that matter, of the world and man, as being passive in the sense of "inert." It is rather that when we think of God's works and the testimonies of His love He is passive in a conventional and grammatical sense: e.g. in the statement "God loves," "God" as the noun is the passive part and "loves" is the verb or active part.

In other words, what we have here is an Active/Passive binary logic. The typical or most representative version of the above statement is: From (an initial idea of) the Active judgment is made concerning the Passive, and from the Passive conclusion is made as to (the nature of) the Active. Thus we have a circular relationship or, more correctly, a spiral one. Our knowledge expands during the process and what we return to is not x but a *conclusion* about x.

This actually becomes a statement in Swedenborgian physics when we put it in this form: the Active seeks out and creates the Passive and the Passive bounds and reflects, and therefore defines, the Active. Perhaps I should explain this a little more. When we make a judgment about something ("judgment is made...") we examine it, without at first knowing what it is, and eventually we form an image of it in our minds, assigning it a characteristic of some kind. It is a bit like feeling out for something in the dark, grasping it and revolving it in our fingers until we can determine what kind of shape it has. We reach out, define and withdraw. In this case, the object we are feeling for exists before we start looking for it. In the case of the Primal Active, which we considered in the first chapters of Part One, we metaphorically compare it to a thinking subject, but it actually *defines itself* (as an inert instrument of creative Providence) by feeling in the dark of the uncreated void and creating the Passive. It reaches out, defines and is reflected. The purely formal relationship is meaningfully similar in both cases.

In addition to this, we have a structure which is meaningful on many levels of philosophical sophistication. It may be realized on the level of abstract logic, but it may also be realized in a picture or myth.

We then have—

As the world stands in respect to man, so stand natural effects in respect to rational actions.

As man stands in respect to God, so stand human actions in respect to Divine works.

To interpret this in a formal sense, let us return to the paragraph preceding it, with the added symbols. We then read, P standing for Passive and A for Active—

As P_1 is to P_2 so A_1 is to A_2. As P_2 is to P_3 so A_2 is to A_3.

Or $P_1/P_2 = A_1/A_2$ and $P_2/P_3 = A_2/A_3$.

In other words, ratios of passive and active are equal throughout the system. A mechanical analogy may be found in Newton's third law of motion, that action equals reaction, and in general theories of the conservation of forms and forces. This does not seem to be much of a discovery. In mechanical terms at least Swedenborg has led us to something we already knew. Yet this was just what he was trying to do. The point is that logic and mechanics (with geometry) *correspond*.

The reader may wonder if I am not putting something over on him, by giving him a brief sample from the middle of an argument. This kind of dishonesty is not uncommon, after all. But *The Hieroglyphic Key* begins with the statement ("First Example") that "As long as motion endures so long does conatus endure; for conatus is the motive force of nature. But conatus alone is a dead force." This is the generalized mechanical argument from which Swedenborg develops his theory of the primary point. I have spared the reader a discussion of the meaning of the word "conatus" and have drastically simplified Swedenborg's argument.

Why have I done this? Swedenborg has been forced by his system to separate the "impetus" of Newton—the force applied to an object to make it move—into two components: the force and the gathered or concentrated potential to exert force. The notion arises out of his attempt, in his chapter in the *Principia* on the first natural point, to redefine the Newtonian concept of inertia. He accepts this and other aspects of Newtonian mechanics as empirically correct but finds them philosophically and logically unsatisfactory. This arises out of his commitment to a doctrine of Divine creation. In this case, something is required to relate the causative effect of "inertial force" (which as a verbal phrase appears to be an oxymoron) to ideas of logical causation. Thus he chooses the word *conatus*, used in philosophy to refer to the faculty of willing or desiring (cf. *Desire* and *Love* in pre-Socratic terminology). To explore this idea would lead us into a quagmire of disputed ideas. I will simply note that there is nothing "mystical" about his starting point: it is a basic assumption of orthodox theology. And his use of the word here indicates that the logic of the *Hieroglyphic Key* is closely and rigorously based on and related to the geometry and mechanics of the *Principia*.

Swedenborg refers to the ratios above as constituting "the first rudiments of that universal mathesis of which mention was made above." Actually, it is surprising how complete these rudiments are. If we analyze the various kinds of Active and Passive referred to in this little book, and relate them to the complex entities discussed therein, we can develop, without too much trouble, a system which does not appear to be rudimentary at all. We must keep in mind, though, that the context of Active and Passive changes continually, as it must, since they are universals. To give only a few examples, a noun is passive in relationship to a verb; when we are immersed in the moving details of a system, they appear active in relationship to the passive serenity of the whole; when man contemplates the Providence of God as it operates in the world, it seems an active force, while God Himself seems "a distant noun." Yet a verb can be turned into a noun ("I take *a walk*"); the system may be seen as generating its parts; and God may be seen (in such an image as man may form of God) as actively employing His attributes.

D
Leibniz on Chinese Natural Philosophy

The approach of Leibniz to the traditional natural philosophy of China, as he understands it from missionary accounts, is in some respects not dissimilar to Swedenborg's approach to Greek natural philosophy and the Mosaic account.[1] Leibniz finds there a refined and sophisticated structure of thought. The familiar symbol of the circle enclosing the Yin-Yang diagram, which he takes to represent primal reason or the foundation of all nature (*Li*), he identifies with God as the source of active powers. *Li*, by interacting with primal matter, which is passive, produces the matter we know.

He objects to the statement of the Jesuit, Father Longobardi, that Chinese philosophy was basically materialist, and he adds—

> The Sing-Li Philosophy, Book 26, p. 8, says that the directing and procreating virtue is not found in the disposition of things and does not depend on them but is composed of and resides in the *Li* which has dominion over, governs, and produces all. Parmenides and Melissus spoke in the same way but the sense which Aristotle gives them appears different from the sense given to Parmenides by Plato. Spinoza reduces all to a single substance, of which all things are only modifications. It is not easy to explain how the Chinese understand it but I believe that nothing prevents according them a rational interpretation. With respect to that which is passive in them, all things are composed of the same prime matter, which differs only by the forms which motion gives it. Also, all things are active and possess Entelechies, Spirits and Souls only by virtue of the participation of the *Li*, i.e., the same originative Spirit (God), which gives them all their perfections. And matter itself is only a production of this same primary cause. Thus everything emanates from it as from a central point... (pp. 87–88)

Towards the end of his essay, which is in the form of a letter, Leibniz relates this philosophy to his form of binary arithmetic, with which we are familiar through its use in computer mathematics. He then relates this binary arithmetic to the trigrams of the *I*

---

[1] Leibniz, *Discourse on the Natural Theology of the Chinese* (see bibliography). Page references are to this work.

Ching, assuming that it was discovered independently by "Fohi," the legendary author of the *I Ching*.

"Not dissimilar" does not mean "the same," of course. What is relevant to our present discussion is that Leibniz finds in China a natural philosophy based on a primary pair and thereby linked with a mathematical system. And also with a logical one, since he says in his essay (later crossing out the sentence) that he had discovered that the binary arithmetic of ancient China "...further expresses the logic of dichotomies which is of the greatest use, if one always retains an exact opposition between the numbers of the division" (p. 158).

We have no evidence that Swedenborg had read the essay or letter of Leibniz, though it is quite likely that he was aware of Leibniz's opinion of Chinese philosophy. In any case there are only a few points of similarity.

i) Leibniz relates Chinese philosophy to that of Parmenides, as Swedenborg in effect relates Egyptian philosophy to that of the Orphics and pre-Socratics. The assumption in both cases is that pre-Socratic philosophy embodies an ancient form of wisdom.

ii) Leibniz believes that Chinese philosophy embodies an ancient wisdom which he traces back to the Biblical patriarchs (p. 107). Swedenborg is more discreet. He does not directly relate Egyptian wisdom to that of the pre-Mosaic patriarchs, because he has no evidence for this, but he seems to assume an indirect relationship.

iii) Leibniz believes Chinese philosophy is based on a binary logic/ arithmetic which is the basis of natural science (p. 37), and in this he shares the opinion of the Jesuit missionary, Father Joachim Bouvet. This system, he believes, survives in the *I Ching* and is the same as his own binary arithmetic. Swedenborg evolves a binary logic/geometry which he puts forward as a modern form (his own). He does not say the ancients used this system but rather that they had something like it, expressed in terms of their own culture.

I do not wish to enter into a discussion on the extent to which Leibniz and his Jesuit sources misinterpreted Chinese beliefs.[2] There is simply no doubt that the logic of the *I Ching* greatly influenced Chinese mathematics[3] though the Chinese did not use a system of binary notation. The purpose of this appendix is to demonstrate further that Swedenborg's enterprise was in the spirit of his time. Yet, despite its magnitude and daring, it is cool, rational and cautious. Though Leibniz passes as a great rationalist and Swedenborg as a visionary, we cannot fail to notice that, on this issue, Leibniz is the rasher of the two and that Swedenborg's argument is developed more consistently and with greater ratiocinative density than is that of Leibniz. It is true that the thesis of Leibniz appears only in a letter and an unfinished one at that. It would be unfair to judge it as a finished work. Thus no criticism of Leibniz is implied and I only wish to point out further evidence of the high level of rationality in Swedenborg's argument.

---

[2] Perhaps it is not even a legitimate question. I gather that traditional Chinese opinions on the nature of the *I Ching* are extremely varied and always have been. It is folly to question the knowledge of the Jesuit missionaries, some of whom were such masters of Chinese that they could write in an impeccable courtly style.

[3] See, in Midnick, excerpts from mathematical texts by Ch'in Chiu-Shao (pp. 250-258), Chou Kung (pp. 259-261) and Chu Chi-Chieh (pp. 262-265). In other words, despite its rashness of generalization, Leibniz's theory has much of value in it.

E
A Note on Gravity

In the *Hieroglyphic Key*, Swedenborg says the following—

> The force of inertia and passive force is the principle of gravity and the cause of rest in the substances of the world.

He explains this as follows—

> 1. The force of inertia is not a dead force, but it exists when a body is deprived of the force of reacting in the same ratio as it is acted upon, that is, deprived of its elastic power. Thus the impressed force is absorbed, since that body does not then give back as much as it receives. 2. Such is the nature of corpuscles of the angular form; for in such corpuscles all the least points become quiescent, that is, they enjoy no force or conatus of action,—this being due to a certain perpetual resistance and collision in their least constituents. Hence it follows that in such corpuscles there is gravity, rest, cold and the like, which are purely terrestrial predicates.[1]

This is the briefest of statements, yet it is extraordinarily pregnant. Note that gravity is related, not only to inertia, but to degrees of angularity of form and of elasticity. Swedenborg's theory of the elasticity of microparticles is, like his theory of inertia, not unrelated to relativistic notions,[2] and both go back to his elementary particle. Yet his notion of gravity is also distinctly related to the structure of Euclidean space, the very space of angular, quiescent and sense-apparent form. In the text I have had to content myself with the more general statement that gravity is a constant which develops throughout the entire system and which is based, as the above quotation makes clear, on Swedenborg's fundamental Active/Passive dualism. The very hint of such a possibility indicates the magnitude of the task with which the *Principia* confronts us.

---

[1] The two quotations are from *Psychological Tracts*, pp. 165-166.

[2] See Born, *Einstein's Theory of Relativity*, pp. 109-115. After discussing the theory of elasticity in a one-dimensional diagram (action along a line), Born says (p. 113), "*All* laws of contiguous action in theoretical physics are of this type. If, for example, we are dealing with elastic bodies that are extended in all directions, we get analogously formed terms for the other two space dimensions. Moreover, pre-

cisely similar laws hold in the theory of electric and magnetic events. Finally, the gravitational theory of Einstein has also been brought into such a form."

Of inertia he says—

Now we know of only one kind of interaction between all material bodies, namely, gravitation. Further, we know that experiment has exhibited a remarkable relationship between gravitation and inertia, which is expressed in the law of the equality of gravitational and inertial mass...Thus the two phenomena of inertia and attraction which are so different in Newton's formulation must have a common root.

This is the great discovery of Einstein which has transformed the general principle of relativity from an epistemological postulate into a law of exact science. (Born, p. 313)

See also Chapter XX of Einstein's own book for the layman, *Relativity, the Special and the General Theory*, entitled *The Equality of Inertial and Gravitational Mass as an Argument for the General Postulate of Relativity*.

BIBLIOGRAPHY

With very few exceptions, this bibliography only lists books mentioned in the text. Some, of course, are of little or disputable scholarly value but represent points of view discussed herein. Familiar literary or philosophical classics, widely available in many editions, are not listed, Hegel excepted. Paperback reprints, as more generally available, are preferred over hardcover editions.

This book was completed some years before publication and this is reflected in the dates of books in the bibliography. As general attitudes towards Swedenborg's natural philosophy have not significantly changed in the past few years I have not revised it. Some books by Marxist authors may now be more difficult to obtain.

Akurgal, Ekrem. *The Art of Greece. Its Origins in the Mediterranean and Near East.* Translated by Wayne Dynes. New York: Crown Publishers, 1968.

Arjiptsev, F.T. *La Materia Como Categoría Filosófica.* Translated by A.S. Vasquez. Mexico, D.F.: Editorial Grijalbo, 1986.

Artsimovich, A. *A Physicist's ABC on Plasma.* Translated by Oleg Glebov. Moscow: Mir Publishers, 1985.

Ault, Donald. *Visionary Physics. Blake's Response to Newton.* London: University of Chicago Press, 1974.

Baker, Gregory L. *Religion and Science. From Swedenborg to Chaotic Dynamics.* New York: Solomon Press, 1992.

Baker, R. Robin. *Human Navigation and the Sixth Sense.* New York: Simon and Schuster, 1981.

Besancon, Alain. *The Rise of the Gulag. Intellectual Origins of Leninism.* New York: Continuum, 1981.

Boas, Franz. *Primitive Art.* New York: Dover Publications, 1955.

Bollack, Jean. *Empédocle.* Paris: Les Editions de Minuit, 1965.

Bonelli, M.L. Righini and Shea, William R. *Reason, Experiment and Mysticism in the Scientific Revolution.* New York: Science History Publications, 1975.

Boole, George. *An Investigation of the Laws of Thought.* New York: Dover Publications, Inc., 1958.

Born, Max. *Einstein's Theory of Relativity.* New York: Dover Publications, Inc., 1965.

Boscovich, Roger Joseph. *A Theory of Natural Philosophy.* Translated by J.M. Child. Cambridge, Mass.: M.I.T. Press, 1966.

Boulez, Pierre. *Boulez on Music Today.* Translated by Susan Bradshaw and Richard Rodney Bennett. London: Faber and Faber, 1957.

Bouwsma, William J. *Concordia Mundi. The Career and Thought of Guillaume Postel.* Cambridge, Mass.: Harvard University Press, 1957.

Bova, Ben. *The Fourth State of Matter.* New York: St. Martin's Press, 1971.

Bové, Salvador. *El Sistema Científica Luliano. Ars Magna.* Barcelona: Tipo grafía Católica, 1908.

Brecher, Kenneth and Feirtag, Michael, eds. *Astronomy of the Ancients.* Cambridge, Mass.: M.I.T. Press, 1979.

Budge, Sir E.A. *The Egyptian Book of the Dead.* New York: Dover Publications, 1967.

——————. *Egyptian Religion.* New York: Bell Publishing Co., 1959.

——————. *The Gods of the Egyptians.* 2 vols. New York: Dover Publications Inc., 1969.

——————. *Tutankhamen. Amenism, Atenism and Egyptian Monotheism.* New York: Bell Publishing Co., n.d.

Bueno, Eramis. *Lógica Polivalente.* Havana: Editorial de Ciencias Sociales, 1976.

Bullinger, E.W. *Figures of Speech Used in the Bible.* London: Eyre and Spottiswoode, 1898.

——————. *Number in Scripture.* Grand Rapids, Mich.: Kregel Publications, 1971. (First British edition, 1894.)

——————. *The Witness of the Stars.* London: The Lamp Press, 1954.

Cairns-Smith, A.G. *Seven Clues to the Origin of Life.* Cambridge: Cambridge University Press, 1985.

Clowes, Rev., John. *A Treatise on Opposites.* Manchester: J. Gleave, 1833.

Cohen, I. Bernard. *The Birth of a New Physics.* New York: W.W. Norton, 1960.

Copleston, S.J., Frederick. *A History of Philosophy, Book One.* 3 vols. New York: Doubleday,1985.

Cornford, Francis. *Plato's Cosmology.* London: Routledge and Kegan Paul, 1937.

Cumont, Franz. *Astrology among the Greeks and Romans.* Translated by J.B. Baker. New York: Dover Publications, Inc., 1960.

de Charms, Rt. Rev. George. *Lectures on the Philosophy of Swedenborg's Principia.* Reprinted from *The New Philosophy*, Oct.–Dec. 1963 to Jan.–Mar. 1965. Bryn Athyn, Pa.: Swedenborg Scientific Association.

de Gortari, Eli. *Dialéctica de la Física.* Mexico, D.F: Universidad National Autónoma de México, 1964.

——————. *Elementos de Lógica Matemática.* Mexico, D.F.: Océano, 1984.

——————. *Introducción a la Lógica Dialéctica.* Mexico, D.F.: Editorial Grijalbo S.A., 1979.

Diaz-Bolio, José. *La Geometría de los Mayas.* Mérida, Yuc., Mexico: Documental Arqueológico, 1967.

Diop, Cheik Anta. *The African Origin of Civilisation.* Translated by Mercer Cook. Westport: Lawrence Hill Co., 1974.

——————. *Antériorité des Civilisations Nègres.* Paris: Présence Africaine, 1967.

——————. *Civilisation or Barbarism.* Translated by Yaa-Lengi Meema Ngemi. New York: Lawrence Hill Books, 1991.

Dingle, Herbert. *Swedenborg as a Physical Scientist.* London: Swedenborg Society, 1938.

Dobbs, Betty Jo Teeter. *The Foundations of Newton's Alchemy.* Cambridge: Cambridge University Press, 1975.

Dreyer, J.L.E. *A History of Astronomy from Thales to Kepler.* New York: Dover Publications, 1953.

Duhamel, M. *Eléments de Calcul Infinitésimal.* Paris: Gauthier-Villars, 1886.

Einstein, Albert. *Relativity, the Special and the General Theory; A Popular Exposition.* Translated by Robert W. Lawson. New York: Crown Publishers, 1961.

Eisenstein, Sergei. *Film Sense and Film Form.* Translated by Jay Leyda. Cleveland, Ohio: Meridian Books, 1957.

Encyclopedia of Physics. Edited by Rita G. Lerner, and George Trigg. Reading, Mass.: Addison-Wesley Publishing Co., 1981. (See footnotes for refs. to specific articles.)

Engels, Frederick. *Dialectics of Nature.* Translated by Clemens Dutt. New York: International Publishers, 1940.

Euclid. *Elements.* Translated and edited by Sir Thomas Heath. New York: Dover Publications, 1956.

Fackenheim, Emil. *The Religious Dimension in Hegel's Thought.* Boston, Mass.: Beacon Press, 1967.

Frankfort, Henry, et al. *Before Philosophy.* Harmondsworth, Middlesex: Penguin Books, 1949.

Ghirshman, R. *Iran.* Harmondsworth, Middlesex: Penguin Books, 1954.

Gillings, Richard. *Mathematics in the Time of the Pharaohs.* New York: Dover Publications Inc., 1972.

Gilson, Etienne. *The Christian Philosophy of Saint Augustine.* Translated by E.M. Lynch. New York: Vintage Books, 1960.

Girard, Raphael. *Le Popol-Vuh.* Paris: Payot, 1954.

Gleick, James. *Chaos.* New York: Penguin Books, 1988.

Gordon, Cyrus. *Ugarit and Minoan Crete.* New York: W.W. Norton, 1966.

Grabo, Carl. *A Newton Among Poets.* New York: Cooper Square Publishers, 1968.

Gracián, Baltasar. *Agudeza y Arte de Ingenio.* Buenos Aires: Espasa-Calpe, S.A., 1942.

_____ . *El Criticón.* Madrid: Espasa-Calpe, S.A., 1968.

Graves, Robert. *The White Goddess.* New York: Creative Age Press, 1948.

Griaule, Marcel. *Conversations with Ogotemmeli.* Translated by R. Butler, A. Richards and B. Hooke. London: Oxford University Press, 1965.

Guénon, René. *Le Symbolisme de la Croix.* Paris: Union Générale d'Editions, 1957.

Harden, Donald. *The Phoenicians.* London: Thames and Hudson, 1962.

Harrison, Jane. *Prolegomena to the Study of Greek Religion.* New York: Meridian Books, 1955.

Heer, Friedrich. *The Medieval World.* New York: New American Library, 1963.

Hegel, G.W. *Encyclopedia of the Philosophical Sciences.* Spanish edition, translated by E. Ovejero y Mauri. Mexico, D.F: Editorial Porrúa, 1977.

_____ . *Lectures on the History of Philosophy.* Translated by E.S. Haldane and Frances H. Simson. 3 vols. New York: Humanities Press Inc., 1955.

_____ . *Logic.* Translated by W. Wallace. In *Encyclopedia of the Philosophical Sciences.* Oxford: Clarendon Press, 1975.

_____ . *The Phenomenology of Mind.* Translated by J.B. Baillie. New York, N.Y, Harper Colophon Books, 1967.

_____ . *The Philosophy of Right.* Translated by T.M. Knox. Chicago, Mich.: Encyclopedia Britannica Inc. *Great Books* series, 1952.

_____ . *The Science of Logic.* Translated by A.V. Miller. Atlantic Highlands, N.J.: Humanities Press International Inc., 1989.

Herman, John R., and Goldberg, Richard A. *Sun, Weather and Climate.* Washington, D.C.: National Aeronautics and Space Administration, 1978.

Herrera, Juan de. *Discurso sobre la Figura Cúbica.* Madrid: Editora Nacional, 1976.

Hewson, J.B., ed. *A History of the Practice of Navigation.* Glasgow: Brown, Son and Ferguson, 1987.

Hofmann, Joseph Ehrenfried. *The History of Mathematics.* Translated by Frank Gaynor and Henrietta O. Midnick. 2 vols. New York, N.Y: Philosophical Library, 1957.

Holwell, William. *A Mythical, Etymological and Historical Dictionary.* London: C. Dilly, 1793.

Huntley, H.E. *The Divine Proportion.* New York: Dover Publications Inc., 1970.

Hurewicz, Witold. *Lectures on Ordinary Differential Equations.* New York: Dover Publications, 1990.

Huyghe, René. *Formes et Forces.* Paris: Flammarion, 1971.

Jones, Richard Foster. *Ancients and Moderns.* Berkeley: University of California Press, 1965.

Konstantinov, F.V. et al. *Philosophy in the USSR. Problems of Historical Materialism.* Translated by Sergei Syrovatkin. Moscow: Progress Publishers, 1981.

Kuznetsov, I.V. et al. *Philosophical Problems of Elementary Particle Physics.* Moscow: Progress Publishers, 1968.

Lanczos, Cornelius. *Albert Einstein and the Cosmic World Order.* New York: Interscience Publishers, 1965.

Laplace, Pierre Simon, Marquis de. *A Philosophical Essay on Probabilities.* Translated by F.W. Truscott and F.L. Emory. New York: Dover Publications, 1951.

Lautmann, Albert. *Essai sur l'Unité des Mathématiques.* Paris: Union Générale des Editions, 1977.

Lee, E.W. *Magnetism.* Harmondsworth, Middlesex: Penguin Books, 1963.

Leibniz, G.W.F. von. *Discourse on the Natural Theology of the Chinese.* Translated by Henry Rosemont, Jr., and Daniel J. Cook. Honolulu: University Press of Hawaii, 1977.

_____ . *Selections.* Edited by Philip P. Weiner; various translators. New York: Charles Scriber's Sons, 1951.

Léon-Portilla, Miguel. *Aztec Thought and Culture.* Translated by Jack Emory Davis. Norman: University of Oklahoma Press, 1963.

Lévi-Strauss, Claude. *Mythologiques.* 4 vols. Paris: Librairie Plon, 1964-1971.

Lindley, David. *The End of Physics.* New York: Basic Books, 1993.

Lull, Ramon. *Arbre de Ciència in Obres Essencials, Vol.1.* Barcelona: Editorial Selecta, 1957.

_____ . *Doctrina Pueril.* Palma de Mallorca: Obrador, 1906.

_____ . *El Libro del Ascenso y Descenso del Entendimienta*. Translated by anonymous. Madrid: Imprenta La Rafa, 1928.

Mach, Ernst. *The Science of Mechanics*. Translated by Thomas J. McCormack. La Salle, Ill.: Open Court, 1960.

Marx, Karl. *Capital, Part I*. Translated by Eden and Cedar Paul. 2 vols. London: J.M. Dent and Sons, 1930.

Mathers, S.L. MacGregor. *The Kabbalah Unveiled*. Partial translation of and commentary upon Christian Knorr von Rosenroth: *Kabbala Denudata*. London: Routledge and Kegan Paul, 1954.

Mathew, Gervase. *Byzantine Esthetics*. New York: Harper and Row, 1964.

Meliujin, Serafin T. *Dialéctica del Desarrollo en la Naturaleza Inorgánica*. Translated by Lydia Kuper de Velasco. Mexico, D.F: Editorial Grijalbo, 1963.

Mersenne, Marin. *Traité de l'Harmonie Universelle*. Paris: Guillaume Baudry, 1627.

Midnick, Henrietta O. Edited by. *The Treasury of Mathematics*. New York: Philosophical Library, 1965.

Moisil, Gr. C. *Essais sur les Logiques Non-Chrysippiennes*. Bucharest: Editions de l'Academie de la République de Roumanie, 1972.

McMullin, Ernan, ed. *The Concept of Matter in Greek and Medieval Philosophy*. Notre Dame: University of Notre Dame Press, 1965.

Nahm, Milton C. Edited by. *Selections from Early Greek Philosophy*. New York: Appleton-Century Crofts Inc., 1947.

Nathorst, A.G. *Emanuel Swedenborg as a Geologist*. Stockholm: Aftonbladets, 1908.

Nasr, Seyyed Hossein. *An Introduction to Islamic Cosmological Doctrines*. Boulder, Colo.: Shambhala, 1978.

Neugebauer, Otto. *Astronomy and History. Selected Essays*. New York: Springer-Verlag, 1983.

Nicomachus of Gerasa. *Introduction to Arithmetic*. Great Books. Translated by Martin L. D'Ooge. Chicago: Encyclopedia Britannica Inc., 1952.

Odhner, Hugo Lj. *The Human Mind, its Faculties and Degrees*. Bryn Athyn, Pa.: Swedenborg Scientific Association, 1969.

Odhner, C. Th. *The Correspondences of Egypt*. Bryn Athyn, Pa.: Academy Bookroom, 1914.

Omelyanovsky, M.E. *Dialectics in Modern Physics*. Moscow: Progress Publishers, 1979.

Otis, Brooks. *Ovid as an Epic Poet*. Cambridge: Cambridge University Press, 1966.

Ovid. *Metamorphoses*. Various translators; edited by Dr. Samuel Garth. London: J. Walker, 1818.

Panin, Ivan. *Bible Chronology*. Toronto: Armach Press, 1923.

Patai, Ralph. *The Hebrew Goddess*. New York: Discus Books, 1978.

Pauling, Linus and Hayward, Roger. *The Architecture of Molecules*. San Francisco, Calif.: W.W. Freeman and Co., 1964.

Peierls, R.E. *The Laws of Nature*. New York: Charles Scribner's Sons, 1956.

Pillot, Gilbert. *Le Code Secret de l'Odyssée*. Paris: Robert Laffont, 1969.

Podolny, R. *Something Called Nothing*. Translated by Nicholas Wein stein. Moscow: Mir Publishers, 1986.

Prier, Raymond Adolf. *Archaic Logic. Symbol and Structure in Heraclitus, Parmenides and Empedocles*. The Hague: Mouton, 1976.

Pring-Mill, Robert. *El Microcosmos Lul.lia*. Palma de Mallorca: Editorial Moll, n.d.

Raper, Henry. *The Practice of Navigation*. London: Spottiswoode and Co., 1903.

Renéville, Rolland de, ed. *Les Cahiers d'Hermès*. Paris: Editions du Vieux Colombier, 1947.

Reymond, E.A.E. *The Mythical Origin of the Egyptian Temple*. Manchester: Manchester University Press, 1969.

Rist, J.M. *Stoic Philosophy*. Cambridge University Press, 1977.

Rosnay, Joel de. *Le Macroscope. vers une Vision Globale*. Paris: Editions du Seuil, 1975.

Rucker, Rudy. *Infinity and the Mind*. New York: Bantam Books, 1982.

Russell, George E. *Hydraulics*. New York: Henry Holt and Co., 1942.

Sambursky, Shmuel. *Physics of the Stoics*. London: Hutchinson and Co., 1971.

Santillana, Giorgio de, and Dechend, Hertha von. *Hamlet's Mill*. Boston, Mass.: Gambit Inc., 1969.

_____ . *The Origins of Scientific Thought*. New York: New American Library, 1961.

Schaya, Leo. *The Universal Meaning of the Kabbalah*. Baltimore, Md.: Penguin, 1973.

Schmidt, Otto. *A Theory of Earth's Origins*. Translated by George H. Hanna. Moscow: Foreign Languages Publishing House, 1958.

Schneider, Marius. *El Origen Musical de los Animales-Simbolos en la Mitologia y la Escultura Antiguas*. Barcelona: Instituto Española de Musicologia, 1946.

Scholem, Gershom. *Kabbalah*. New York: Dorset Press, 1974.

Science. Washington D.C.: American Association for the Advancement of Science. [See notes for specific articles cited.]

Scientific American. New York: Scientific American Inc. [See notes for specific articles cited.]

Séjourné, Laurette. *Burning Water. Thought and Religion in Ancient Mexico*. New York: Grove Press, Inc., 1960.

Sigstedt, Cyriel Odhner. *The Swedenborg Epic*. New York: Bookman Associates, 1952.

Stace, W.T. *The Philosophy of Hegel*. New York: Dover Publications Inc., 1955.

Stiskin, Nahum. *The Looking-Glass God*. Tokyo: Autumn Press, 1972.

Swedenborg, Emanuel. *Algebra*. Manuscript in English anonymously translated. Uppsala: J.H. Werner, 1718.

Swedenborg, Emanuel. *Angelic Wisdom Concerning the Divine Providence*. Anonymously translated. London: Society Swedenborg, 1934.

_____ . *The Five Senses*. Translated by Enoch S. Price. Philadelphia, Pa.: Swedenborg Scientific Association, 1914.

_____ . *The History of Creation as Given by Moses* from *The Word Explained*. Translated by Alfred Acton. Bryn Athyn, Pa.: 1928-1948.

_____ . *The Infinite and the Final Cause of Creation*. London: Swedenborg Society, 1965.

_____ . *Letters and Memorials.* Translated by Alfred Acton. Bryn Athyn, Pa.: Swedenborg Scientific Association, 1955.

_____ . *Miscellaneous Observations* Translated by C.E. Strutt. London: William Newberry, 1847.

_____ . *Ontology.* Translated by Alfred Acton. Bryn Athyn, Pa.: Swedenborg Scientific Association, 1964.

_____ . *On Tremulation.* Translated by C. Th. Odhner. Boston, Mass.: Massachusetts New Church Union, 1899.

_____ . *A Philosopher's Notebook* Translated by Alfred Acton. Philadelphia, Pa.: Swedenborg Scientific Association, 1931.

_____ . *Principia.* Translated by James R. Rendell and Isaiah Tansley. London: Swedenborg Society, 1912.

_____ . *Psychological Transactions and Tracts.* Translated by Alfred Acton. Bryn Athyn, Pa.: Swedenborg Scientific Association, 1955.

_____ . *Some Specimens of a Work on the Principles of Chemistry.* Translated by C.E. Strutt. London: William Newberry, 1847.

_____ . *The Worship and Love of God.* Translated by A.H. Stroh and F. Sewall. Boston, Mass.: Massachusetts New Church Union, 1956.

Taylor, Thomas. *The Theoretic Arithmetic of the Pythagoreans.* York Beach, Maine: Samuel Weiser Inc., 1983.

The New Philosophy. Bryn Athyn, Pa.: Swedenborg Scientific Association. [See notes for specific articles.]

Thom, René. *Stabilité Structurelle et Morphogénèse.* Paris: Interéditions,1972.

Thompson, Eric. *Maya Hieroglyphic Writing.* Norman: University of Oklahoma Press, 1971.

Tompkins, Peter. *Secrets of the Great Pyramid.* New. York: Harper and Row, 1971.

Trefil, James S. *The Moment of Creation.* New York: Collier Books, 1983.

Westheim, Paul. *The Art of Ancient Mexico.* New York: Anchor Books, 1965.

Weyl, Hermann. *Space-Time-Matter.* Translated by Henry L. Brose. New York: Dover Publications Inc.,1952.

Wilkinson, Sir J.G. *The Ancient Egyptians.* New York: Bonanza Books, 1989.

Wilkinson, J.J.G. *Oannes According to Berosus.* London: James Speirs, 1888.

Wind, Edgar. *Pagan Mysteries in the Renaissance.* Harmondsworth, Middlesex: Penguin Books, 1967.

Words for the New Church IV. Authors anon. Philadelphia, Pa.: J.B. Lippincott and Co., 1879.

Yates, Frances. *The Art of Memory.* Chicago: University of Chicago Press, 1966.

_____ . *Giordano Bruno and the Hermetic Tradition.* New York: Vintage Books, 1969.

_____ . *The Rosicrucian Enlightenment.* St. Albans, U.K.: Paladin, 1975.

Yavorsky, B, and Detlaf, A. *Handbook of Physics.* Translated by Nicholas Weinstein. Moscow: Mir Publishers, 1975.

INDEX

References to Swedenborg's *Principia* are not indexed,
since they occur throughout

A

Acton, Alfred   313
Adam   243, 252, 279, 289, 334, 345, 346, 387
Akchurin, I.A.   109, 110, 117
Akurgal, Ekrem   306, 315, 353
Algebra   207
Allen, Edward   58
Amen, Ammon   298, 311, 312, 317, 321, 322, 323, 328, 350, 352, 353
Anansi   213
Anaxagoras   154
Anaximander   250, 251, 252, 314, 327
Animal Kingdom   286
Apollo   232
Apollonius   191
Arachne   213, 214, 215, 353
Archimedes   99, 191, 265
Aristophanes   303, 304, 305, 315, 328
Aristotle   xviii, 21, 26, 67, 89, 95, 101, 193, 196, 201, 202, 204, 209, 216, 237, 239, 248, 275, 277, 302
Aristoxenus   263
Arjiptsev, F.T.   181
Artsimovich, A.   181
Aten   293, 294, 298
Augustine   xviii, xxii, 4, 18, 22, 55, 56, 57, 66, 68, 79, 95, 126, 161, 198, 208, 243, 318, 336, 351, 370, 373, 374, 378

B

Bacon, Roger   201
Baker, Gregory   xxi, xxii, 58, 117
Baker, R. Robin   286
Balzac   382
Barker, J.A.   188, 216
Baron, Robert   31
Barrett, W.F.   25, 119, 120, 121
Baudelaire   227, 228, 382

Bernoulli, Daniel   71
Besancon, Alain   389
Blake, William   vii, 381
Blakeslee, Sandra   355
Boas, Franz   256
Boehme, J.   221
Bollack, Jean   115, 255
Bonelli, M.L. Righini   89
Boole, George   10, 32, 41, 42, 43, 58, 236, 268, 376
Born, Max   155, 156, 181, 398
Boscovich, Roger   8, 204, 206, 216, 358
Boulez, Pierre   256
Bouwsma, William J.   26
Bova, Ben   149, 181, 182
Brock, Erland J.   xxii, 216
Browning, Elizabeth Barrett   381
Browning, Robert   381
Bruno, Giordano   52
Bryant, Jacob   353
Budge, E.A.W.   256, 284, 285, 292, 293, 311, 313, 314, 315, 316, 321, 325, 353, 354, 379
Bullinger, E.W.   260, 261, 354

C

Cairns-Smith, A.G.   355
Caracena, Fernando   117
Carlson, John B.   149
Chalcidius   vii
Champollion, J.F.   246
Charles XI, King of Sweden   4
Charles XII, King of Sweden   5, 8
Chemistry   185, 216
Clowes, John   xxii
Cohen, I. Bernard   58
Cole, Wertha Pendleton   150
Coleridge, S.T.   381
Copernicus   21, 314
Cornford, Francis   97
Cortes, Martin   130
Croce, Benedetto   224
Croxall, Samuel   213

D

Darwin, Charles   332, 340, 347, 354, 359
Davis, Charlotte Gyllenhaal   58
de Charms, George   xxi
de Cisterney du Fay, Charles Francois   127
de Gortari, Eli   xx, 11, 13, 26, 58, 268, 281, 285, 286
de Nerval, Gérard   227, 255, 382
Descartes, René   xviii, 4, 30, 62, 183, 206, 209, 210, 237, 238
Detlaf, A.   216
Diaz-Bolio, José   249, 256
Dingle, Herbert   xxi, 118
Diogenes Laertius   115
Diogenes of Apollonia   327
Diop, Cheik Anta   115, 216, 255, 293, 313, 314, 379
Divine Providence   xviii
Dobbs, Betty Jo Teeter   89
Dreyer, J.L.E.   354
Dryden, John   217, 225
Dugdale, Bert E.   212
Duhamel, M.   98, 116
Dupleix, Scipio   31

E

Ebert, Charles H.   58
Economy of the Animal Kingdom   181
Edwards, Jonathan   89
Einstein, Albert   29, 30, 117, 118, 153, 154, 156, 164, 201, 216, 370, 398
Eisenstein, Sergei   272, 285, 286
Emerson, Ralph Waldo   381
Empedocles   115, 231, 232, 233, 234, 255, 309
Engels, Frederick   xvii, xix
Epicurus   303
Euclid   xix, 15, 17, 18, 23, 62, 95, 104, 116, 158, 182, 200, 202, 210, 265, 278, 365, 398
Evans, F.   138, 150
Eve   334

F

Fitzpatrick, Donald   xxii
Five Senses   125, 149, 273, 277, 286, 366, 378
Fresnel, Augustin   154

G

Galileo   21
Gauss, K.F.   147, 148, 149
Geminus   18, 23
Ghirshman, R.   353
Gilbert, William   127, 130
Gillings, Richard   116
Gilson, Etienne   378
Gladish, Richard R.   26
Gleick, James   90, 117
Godel, Kurt   241
Goldberg, Richard A.   149
Golding, William   303
Gordon, Cyrus   263, 284, 316
Gorgias   225, 231, 234
Grabo, Carl   354
Gracián, Baltasar   58, 285
Grassineau, James   239
Graves, Robert   237
Griaule, Marcel   213, 217
Grosseteste, Robert   201
Grotius, Hugo   351, 353
Guénon, René   255
Gutbrod, Hans   210

H

Hadley, John   130
Halley, Edmund   132, 133, 134, 150
Harden, Donald   353
Harrison, Jane   301, 305, 307, 315, 316
Hartley, Thomas   4
Hayward, Roger   185, 216
Hegel, G.W.   xviii, xix, 13, 18, 42, 44, 49, 51, 52, 53, 57, 59, 68,
     69, 86, 89, 90, 104, 191, 227, 228, 229, 231, 236, 237, 245,
     255, 259, 280, 285, 300, 313, 360, 370, 372, 376, 378, 384, 389

Henderson, Douglas   188, 216
Heraclitus   193, 232, 327
Herman, John R.   149
Herodotus   196, 248, 307, 319, 353
Herrera, Juan de   57, 216
Herschel, William   173
Hewson, J.B.   150
Hieroglyphic Key   240, 242, 245, 246, 325, 352, 367, 390, 393, 398
History of Creation as Given by Moses   326, 328, 336, 343, 355
Hofmann, Joseph Ehrenfried   26
Holwell, William   353
Huntley, H.E.   117
Hurewicz, Witold   54
Huyghe, René   212, 217

I

Ishtar   320, 353

J

Jacobs, J.A.   151
Janus   217
Jeans, James   118
Johansen, Christian   378
Johnson, Philip H.   359
Jones, R.F.   378
Jove   214, 215
Juno   216
Jupiter   216, 243

K

Kant, Immanuel   xiii, xviii, 26, 181
Kelvin (Lord), William Thomson   357, 358
Kircher, Athanasius   324
Kolata, Gini Bari   285
Kuznetsov, I.V.   117

L

Laplace, Pierre Simon   42, 43, 58, 90, 173, 181, 377
Lautman, Albert   25
Lee, E.W.   135, 136, 144, 148, 150, 151

Leibniz, G.W. von   xviii, 30, 64, 98, 101, 116, 160, 202, 206, 209, 216, 217, 238, 336, 343, 351, 355, 395, 396, 397

Lenormant, Francois   320, 353

Letters and Memorials   26

Lettvin, Jerome V.   230, 231, 237

Lévi-Strauss, Claude   231, 246

Lull, Ramon   xviii, 26, 44, 49, 50, 52, 57, 59, 64, 68, 90, 104, 199, 201, 202, 216, 229, 254, 255, 283, 384, 388

M

Maat   116

Mach, Ernst   90

Malebranche, N.   237, 238

Markov, M.A.   59

Marx, Karl   xvii, xviii, 11, 13, 18, 26, 59, 68, 73, 104, 180, 225, 268, 270, 280, 285, 311, 344, 376, 384, 386, 388, 389

Mathers, S.L. MacGregor   316, 353

Mathew, Gervase   283

Maxwell, James C.   357, 377

Meliujin, Serafin T.   89

Mersenne, Marin   239

Michison, G.J.   117

Midnick, Henrietta O.   284, 397

Miller, Robert V.   355

Minerva   214, 215

Minor Principia   111, 117

Miscellaneous Observations   3, 25, 62, 67, 95, 157

Moisil, Gr.C.   378

Morrison, J.   173

Moses   17, 96, 289, 291, 292, 304, 311, 317, 319, 320, 323, 327, 350, 351, 352, 353

Musschenbroek, Pieter Van   119, 120, 121, 133, 139, 149, 156, 157, 190

N

Nahm, Milton C.   115, 216, 255, 256

Nasr, Seyyed Hossein   199, 216

Neptune   215

Neugebauer, Otto   99, 116, 314

Newton, Isaac   xxi, 21, 25, 28, 36, 57, 58, 62, 63, 89, 98, 149, 156, 159, 183, 205, 330, 359, 360, 362, 393, 399

Newton, Norman   xv, xxii
Nicomachus   32, 57
Noah   296
Norman, Robert   130
Notes on Ontology   26, 31, 32, 55, 57

O

Odhner, C.Th.   255, 256, 316
Odhner, Dewey   58
Odhner, Hugo Lj.   216
Okeanos   196, 248
Omelyanovsky, M.E.   59, 110, 117
On the Principles of Chemistry   342
On Tremulation   20, 26, 216, 366
Orpheus   301, 305, 307, 315, 317, 326, 328, 352, 367, 396
Osiris   298
Otis, Brooks   217, 315
Ovid   213, 215, 217, 303, 304, 315, 326, 340

P

Pallas   213, 214, 215
Panin, Ivan   283
Paracelsus   49
Parmenides   96, 97, 98, 100, 101, 111, 115, 171, 232, 233, 326,
    395, 396
Pascal, Blaise   182
Patai, Ralph   116
Pauling, Linus   185, 216
Peierls, R.E.   181
Philo Byblius   294, 311, 316, 317, 350, 351, 352
Philosopher's Notebook   160, 216, 255, 355
Pillot, Gilbert   150
Plato   xviii, 4, 9, 18, 21, 22, 23, 26, 55, 56, 79, 155, 158, 185, 193,
    202, 207, 216, 224, 225, 231, 233, 234, 247, 284, 292, 354,
    361, 370, 373, 395
Pletnikov, Yu.K.   384, 388, 389
Pliny   292
Plotinus   373
Plutarch   250, 252
Podolny, R.   59, 117
Poincaré, H.   25

Pope, Alexander   225
Porphyry   311, 312, 317, 318, 319, 320
Posidonius   91
Postel, Guillaume   21, 26
Prier, Raymond Adolf   97, 115, 232, 255
Pring-Mill, Robert   216
Proclus   18, 23, 26, 293, 305, 315
Psychological Tracts   255
Pythagoras   4, 23, 100, 101, 128, 200, 215, 217, 233, 236, 240,
    246, 263, 284, 301, 307, 326

R

Ra   292, 293, 294, 295, 298, 308
Rabbi Nehemiah   264, 266
Ragozin, Zenaide   353
Rankine, W.J.N.   357
Raper, Henry   132, 137, 138, 143, 150, 151
Reiche, Harold A.T.   354
Renéville, A. Rolland de   14, 26, 255
Reynolds, Osborne   357
Richer, Jean   150
Rist, J.M.   91, 115
Rosnay, Joel de   172, 181
Rucker, Rudy   255
Russell, George E.   90
Rutherford, Ernest   268

S

Saffman, P.G.   90
Sambursky, Shmuel   vii, 94, 95, 115
Sanchuniathon   194, 196, 244, 246, 247, 294, 309, 310, 311, 312,
    316, 317, 320, 328, 338, 350, 351, 352, 355
Sandstrom, Erik   xxi
Santillana, Giorgio de   89, 97, 98, 116, 249, 255
Schaya, Leo   115, 116, 283, 316
Schmidt, Otto   181
Schneider, Marius   vii, 284
Schonberg, Arnold   254, 256
Sewall, Frank   216
Shea, William R.   89
Sheldrake, Rupert   285

Shelley, P.B. 223, 224, 225, 229
Shishak 318, 353
Sigstedt, Cyriel Odhner 25, 26, 150, 313, 378
Simplicios 94, 95, 100
Sosenq 318, 353
Spinoza 59, 68, 377, 395
Stace, W.T. 52, 59, 68, 89, 378
Stiskin, Nahum 249, 256
Stocker, Horst 210
Swedberg, Jesper 4, 5

T

Tansley, Isaiah 181, 377
Teilhard de Chardin, Pierre xvii, 64
Tethys 196, 248
Thales 149, 196, 248, 250, 251, 292
The History of Creation as Given by Moses 287
Thom, René 58, 268, 269, 270, 271, 285, 329, 333
Thompson, Eric 256
Thoth 116, 234, 285, 294, 310, 312, 351, 352
Toland, John 63
Tompkins, Peter 313
Trefil, James S. 181

U

Ulrica Eleanora, Queen of Sweden 5

V

van der Waals, Johannes D. 188
Vasa, Gustavus, King of Sweden 4
Very, F.W. 26, 57
Von Dechend, Hertha 89, 98, 116, 249, 255

W

Watkins, George D. 216
Westfall, Richard S. 89
Weyl, Hermann 118, 377
Wheeler, John Archibald 117
Wilkinson, J.G. 314
Wilkinson, J.J.G. 255
Wolff, Christian xviii, 31

Woofenden, William R. xxii, 182, 359, 377
Word Explained 313
Worship and Love of God 45, 55, 58, 59, 182, 186, 187, 216, 258, 266, 279, 283, 290, 313, 328, 333, 334, 335, 348, 354, 355, 378, 386, 387

X

Xenophanes 327

Y

Yates, Frances 26, 255
Yavorsky, B. 216

Z

Zeno 89
Zeno of Cition 95, 115
Zeno of Elea 94, 98, 115
Zeus 213